PERSUASIVE WRITING

A COLLEGE READER

PERSUASIVE WRITING
A COLLEGE READER

KARL ZENDER

LINDA MORRIS

University of California, Davis

HARCOURT BRACE JOVANOVICH, INC.

New York   San Diego   Chicago   San Francisco   Atlanta
London   Sydney   Toronto

The editors are grateful to the following for permission to reprint various quotations that appear in Gilbert Highet's essay "Kitsch" (pp. 100-107): The quotations from works by Amanda McKittrick Ros are reprinted by permission of Chatto and Windus Ltd. on behalf of the literary estate of Amanda Ros. The verses by William McGonagall are from *Poetic Gems Selected from the Works of William McGonagall* . . . and are reprinted by permission of the publisher, Gerald Duckworth & Co. The lines from Ezra Pound's "N.Y." appear in his *Collected Early Poems*, copyright © 1976 by The Trustees of the Ezra Pound Literary Property Trust, all rights reserved, and are reprinted by permission of New Directions. The excerpt from Stephen Spender's "The Funeral," from his *Collected Poems 1928-1953*, is reprinted by courtesy of the publisher, Random House, Inc.

The lyric from "One of These Things" (p. 143) is copyright © 1970 by Jonico Music, Inc.; music by Joseph Raposo and lyric by Bruce Hart; used by permission; all rights reserved.

ISBN: 0-15-598300-8

Library of Congress Catalog Card Number: 80-85465

Printed in the United States of America

Persuasive Writing: A College Reader has three purposes, one innovative and two traditional: The traditional purposes are to illustrate the characteristics of the various rhetorical modes and to provide student writers with examples of good writing to read and imitate; the innovative purpose is to demonstrate the importance of *persuasion* to the writing process.

We take the term *persuasion* to apply to any writing in which writers seek to convince their readers that their subjects are significant and interesting and worthy of serious consideration. Viewed in this manner, persuasive writing has a broad range indeed. It can move us to action or can simply have us look at an object or idea in a new way. As the essays in this book show, persuasive writing can be exuberant or restrained, ornate or simple, fanciful or matter-of-fact, humorous or somber. In all its varieties, though, its defining characteristics are an alertness to the needs of the audience and a willingness to serve those needs. Studying persuasive writing, we believe, can help students recognize the importance of developing a mature sense of audience in their own work.

The organization and content of *Persuasive Writing* reflect its threefold purpose. The book contains an opening chapter on the writing process, eight chapters of essays illustrating the various rhetorical modes, and a final chapter of readings for further analysis. Both the opening chapter and the introductions to the succeeding chapters are aimed at helping students learn how to write effective persuasive essays. In the opening chapter, we suggest that the need to persuade is central if we are to write well, and we outline a practical step-by-step procedure students can use to gain command of the writing process. In the introductions to the chapters that follow, we discuss and illustrate the characteristics of the different rhetorical modes. Here too, we emphasize the persuasive aspect of writing, showing how it manifests itself in each of the different modes.

The eight middle chapters of *Persuasive Writing* are arranged in a logical progression, beginning with description and narration, continuing through the expository modes (definition, classification, comparison and contrast, process analysis, and cause and effect), and culminating in argumentation. The chapters are all self-contained so that instructors can use them in any order or omit some of them entirely if they wish. Within each chapter, the selections are arranged in order of increasing rhetorical complexity; readers interested in studying the modes in their "pure" forms should therefore begin each chapter with the initial selection.

The apparatus accompanying each selection is of three sorts: a biographical headnote, a set of questions for discussion, and a set of suggested activities. The questions for discussion focus on style and content and on the interaction between the two; the suggested activities combine essay topics and ideas for class discussion with small, informal research projects. In the final chapter ("Readings for Further Analysis"), we have omitted all apparatus except the biographical headnotes in order that students may have the opportunity to apply their analytic skills without assistance. Also, we have frequently included two selections by the same author, in the hope that comparing these pairs of essays will allow students to trace stylistic continuities and will help them to see how a writer's subject matter influences his or her choice of rhetorical mode.

In selecting the readings, we have been guided by the definition of persuasion discussed earlier. In addition, we have been guided by two other main criteria: richness of style and content, and appropriateness to the rhetorical mode being illustrated. We have tried to strike a balance between writers like Orwell, Woolf, and Swift, whose writings have long withstood the test of classroom use, and exciting contemporary writers like McPhee, Hoagland, Kingston, and Abbey. Most of the readings are of average length, though a few are quite brief and one or two are somewhat longer than the current fashion in composition texts would seem to dictate. However, even the longest selection—James Baldwin's "Notes of a Native Son"—can easily be read in a single sitting. Almost all the selections are either complete, independent essays or whole chapters from books. In only one instance (Calvin Trillin's "Low and Slow, Mean and Clean") have we made any substantial internal elisions.

We are grateful for the helpful suggestions and comments given us by Max Byrd, Kimberly Davis, Elin Diamond, Carl Diehl, Don Jordan, Marean Jordan, Cathy Gallagher, Jon Sands, Patricia Tollefson, Stephen Tollefson, Robert Torrance, and Paige Wickland. We also wish to thank Susan Eno, Matthew Milan, Jr., Roberta C. Vellvé, Jerry Lighter, and Christine Pearson, of the staff of Harcourt Brace Jovanovich, for their insightful comments and their work in producing the book. For typing and other assistance, we wish to thank Janet Humble, Aida La Caro, and, especially, Evelyn Kasmire, without whose labors no deadline would ever have been met. Finally, we wish to thank Lynn, Matthew, and Jacob Zender and Kate Morris for their forbearance during a long, hard summer of writing.

KARL ZENDER

LINDA MORRIS

contents

3

narration 41

4

definition 77

5

classification   109

comparison and contrast   143

7

process analysis   181

cause and effect   211

9

argumentation   249

10

readings for further analysis   281

PERSUASIVE WRITING
A COLLEGE READER

the writing process

Writers all write differently. The French novelist Marcel Proust was so easily distracted by noise that he had to write in a cork-lined room. Samuel Johnson, the English poet and essayist, could write effectively only when he was so close to a deadline that the printer was practically standing at his door. Another French writer, the poet Guillaume Apollinaire, claimed to be inspired to write by the smell of rotten cucumbers. So how can teachers of English tell anyone how to write? Well, the truth is that we can't, at least not at a very fine level of detail. We can't tell you whether you need to outline or not, whether you'll write best in bits and pieces or in one steady flow, whether you should revise as you go along or after you're done. Only you can answer these questions for yourself.

When can we do, then? Basically, two things: we can give you some practical advice that will be useful regardless of the particular way you write, and we can provide you with examples of good writing to read and imitate. Doing these two things is the purpose of this book. The examples of good writing—quite interesting ones, we think—make up the bulk of the following eight chapters. The advice comes in two places: in the introductions to the chapters of readings, and in this opening chapter. In the chapter introductions, we will give you information about the different *rhetorical modes.* In this opening chapter, we will offer suggestions about the *process* of writing. Central to the writing process is the idea of purpose. So let's begin there.

Purpose

We write for many reasons. We write to explain things and to express ourselves, and many of us write as well to experience the sheer delight that comes from making something beautiful out of words. Underlying all these reasons for writing, though, is a basic desire to persuade. Whenever we write, we're trying to convince someone to look with favor on what we have to say. Even if our readers are only imagined—like the hypothetical readers of a private diary—they are nevertheless present in our mind, and we write to gain their approval. To use Robert Grave's memorable image, every time we put pen to paper, someone peers over our shoulder.

In a very real sense, then, learning how to write well is the same as learning how to persuade. This doesn't mean that it's the same as learning how to lie, or to soft-soap a teacher, or to sling bull. No reader was ever persuaded for very long into believing something that a writer didn't believe himself. But on the other hand, blunt, unadorned expressions of opinion aren't very persuasive either. When we cheer or boo, we express our true feelings, but we don't persuade the people who are rooting for the other team to agree with us. Persuasion means moderating between our feelings and ideas and the needs of our audience. It means presenting our beliefs in a manner that will convince a fair-minded reader that they are reasonable ones to hold. Persuasion, in short, means dressing to advantage what we truly feel and think.

How does one learn to write persuasively? For most people, doing so takes a lot of practice and some tough, fair criticism. A place where you're likely to receive both of these is the course in which you're using this book. But whenever you're writing, whether for a course or not, you can help yourself improve by keeping the idea of persuasion in the forefront of your mind. In the pages that follow we will suggest some practical ways of doing this at each stage of the writing process.

Topic and thesis

When the Greeks first looked at composing as a process, they divided it into three stages: invention, arrangement, and delivery. Today, scholars prefer to call the first stage "prewriting," but the change in name hasn't changed the nature of the stage or its importance. Prewriting is the crucial work that takes place *before* you begin to write, and it consists basically of two activities: finding your topic, and deciding what your thesis will be.

These two terms—topic and thesis—are so often confused that we ought to take a moment to distinguish between them. Simply stated, the *thesis* is the persuasive point of an essay, the one central, unifying statement around which the essay is organized. The *topic,* by contrast, is simply the specific subject of the essay. For example, say you were asked to write an essay on current energy resources. Since this subject is obviously far too large to cover in an essay, you might decide to narrow it down to a comparison of the economic advantages of three alternatives to fossil fuels. This is your topic. Why isn't it your thesis? Because it doesn't express a point of view. To transform it into a thesis, you would need to *interpret* and *evaluate* the three alternatives. If you did so, you might come up with a thesis like this one: "Although nuclear and solar power can both help to lessen our dependence on fossil fuels, neither is as economical as wind power."

The thesis, then, is a step further along in the writing process than the topic. It is an interpretation and evaluation *of* the topic. As such, it is crucially important to both the reader and the writer. From the reader's point of view, the value of a controlling thesis lies in its ability to foreshadow the essay's development and limit its scope. For example, the thesis that we formulated in the last paragraph would tell attentive readers that the tone of our essay was going to be fairly serious and that the argument would probably be developed through comparison and contrast. At the same time, the readers would learn that they could set aside other aspects of the subject as a whole—geothermal energy, say, or hydroelectric power—since these weren't going to be considered in the essay.

For a writer, having a clear thesis serves much the same function as it does for a reader. A good working thesis helps you decide exactly what information needs to be included in your essay and allows you to ignore information pertinent to the subject at large but irrelevant to your particular topic. It helps you to organize your material by suggesting which mode of development you should use, and it reminds you of the tone you'll need to maintain in the body of your essay. Given all these advantages, then, it should be clear that formulating a clear working thesis before you begin to write is a crucial step in gaining command of the writing process. Now let's look at how to do this.

Generating a thesis

After reading a well-written essay that has a clearly stated thesis, beginning writers often despair of ever producing anything similar. For something to read so effortlessly, the thesis must surely have come to the writer in a blinding moment of insight. But it probably didn't. Theses rarely appear full-blown in writers' minds, but instead grow and develop as they explore their topics. The exact form that this exploration takes varies from person to person and situation to situation. But we can recommend four steps to follow while you're learning your own particular way of getting from topic to thesis:

1. List a lot of initial observations about the subject.

2. Narrow the subject to a topic that interests you.

3. State your own attitude toward the topic in a single sentence (your tentative thesis).

4. Expand your tentative thesis to include possible objections or opposing points of view.

In order to illustrate the use of these steps, let's suppose you've been asked to write an essay on the subject of propaganda for your composition class. You've been discussing the language of political propaganda in class, but your instructor has asked you to consider other forms of propaganda, choose one form, and explore its impact on contemporary American society. The mode by which you're to develop your essay has been left to your own judgment, and you're not expected to do any library research.

So what should you do first? Well, why not start with what you know? Even though the assignment asks you to explore forms of propaganda other than political ones, those are the ones you've been discussing, so you may as well start with them. Write down the word "politics," and then try listing related ideas: the aims of political propaganda, the means of its dissemination, its effect on American society. Nothing of any use? Then maybe you should turn to the dictionary to see if it mentions other forms of propaganda. It tells you that propaganda is the systematic dissemination of doctrines of belief. No help there either. But you also happen to notice that when the word "propaganda" is spelled with a capital "P," it refers to the agency of the Roman Catholic Church responsible for preaching Christian doctrine in non-Christian countries. So you write down the word "religion." You look at it a while. You write it down again. You look at it. You doodle. You get up and go to the bathroom. You come back and sit down, you look at the word again, and you decide that there's no hope of your writing a paper on religious propaganda, and perhaps no hope of your writing anything. Ever again.

The process we're describing here is agonizingly familiar to all writers. When you experience it, the important thing is to wait out the uncertainty rather than settle on a topic you can't or don't want to handle simply in order to be doing something. For our present purposes, though, let's foreshorten the agony by assuming that you went back to the word "politics," noticed that one of the main ways political propaganda is disseminated is through television commercials, and realized that advertising itself can be thought of as a form of propaganda. Moreover, it's something you're interested in and know a good deal about.

So now you've reached the second stage in the process of developing a thesis: you've reduced your large subject to a potential topic, "advertising as a form of propaganda." But you're not home free, because merely identifying advertising as a form of propaganda doesn't suggest your own attitude. It doesn't *interpret* and *evaluate,* the key functions of a thesis statement. To formulate such a statement, you need yet more material. So it's back once more to the first step, as you begin listing kinds of advertising you consider to be propagandistic: election ads, army recruitment ads, public service ads, ads promoting the "American way of life." Maybe you jot down notes on particular ads as well. And maybe upon reflection you decide that ads for products also have an underlying propagandistic purpose, in that they're trying to encourage us to be active consumers.

At this point in the process of generating a thesis, your own attitude toward your topic can begin to emerge. If you happen to enjoy a number of commercials and think that our economic well-being depends on a certain amount of forced consumption, you might want to write an essay in praise of advertising. But let's assume that you're disconcerted by the thought that commercial advertising works in devious ways to encourage us to buy things we don't really want. With this thought in mind, you formulate the following tentative thesis: "Product advertising is a subtle and dangerous form of propaganda."

Now you need to step back and assess the usefulness of your thesis as a controlling idea for an essay. In particular you need to ask yourself whether your thesis is sufficiently complex to hold the interest of your audience. One way of doing this is to consider objections to your thesis, even to adopt an opposing point of view for a moment. If you have difficulty in doing this—if there don't seem to be any feasible objections—then your thesis is probably too simple. Why? Because in order for your essay to persuade someone, there has to be someone for it to persuade. If everyone agrees with your thesis, as you can assume they must if there aren't any feasible objections to it, then you're preaching to the already converted.

In the case of our example, though, we saw a counterperspective in our judgment that there was something entertaining and perhaps even economically beneficial about advertising. So a point of view opposed to the tentative thesis does exist. Now that you've discovered this viewpoint, what are you to do with it? Most of all, *don't ignore it.* One of the worst mistakes beginning writers make is trying to bludgeon their readers into agreement by only presenting evidence in favor of their own position. Instead of ignoring the contradictory point of view, you should *incorporate it into your own thesis.* By doing this, you convince your readers that you hold a reasonable, moderate point of view toward your topic, and you create a thesis of sufficient complexity to entice them to read further.

So let's take our own advice and incorporate the opposing point of view into the tentative thesis we've been working with. Here's what we get: "Although product advertising can be entertaining and beneficial to our economy, basically it's a subtle and dangerous form of propaganda." Finally, then, we have a working thesis. It's complex, interesting, and shows promise of leading to a good essay. But note that we're still in the prewriting stage of the writing process. Still to come are what the Greeks called "arrangement" and "delivery," and what we'll call—in a three-part division—*organizing, writing,* and *revising.* So it may seem that we've taken a long time to come a short way. Really, though, much of the hard work is done. By taking the time to develop a clear working thesis, we've put ourselves in a position to perform the remaining steps of the writing process in a purposeful and efficient way. Trying to save time in the prewriting stage is penny-wise and pound-foolish. Spend some time now, and you'll save a lot more of it later.

Organizing the essay

But you're still not quite ready to write. What you have at present is a working thesis (still subject to revision), a few bits and pieces of information, and some ideas. Before actually beginning to write, you need to increase your store of information and ideas and arrange it coherently in relation to your thesis. There are three specific suggestions we can make to help you with this phase of the process:

1. Analyze the key terms in your thesis.

2. Use the key terms to help you develop additional arguments and examples.

3. Use the thesis as a guide to the organization of the essay.

Following the first of these suggestions should help you come to an intimate awareness of the implications of your thesis. Consider, for example, our working thesis about advertising and propaganda. Here the key terms are "product advertising," "entertaining," "beneficial," "economy," "subtle," "dangerous," and "propaganda." How you should approach each of these depends on what sort of term it is and how it functions in the thesis. As it happens, our key terms consist of three nouns and noun phrases ("product advertising," "economy," and "propaganda") and four adjectives ("entertaining," "beneficial," "subtle," and "dangerous"). Let's look at these two groupings and see what emerges.

Any time you see nouns and noun phrases in your thesis, you should ask if they need to be defined. The first two of ours are clear enough to be understood without definition, though you will probably want to use examples to show your readers exactly what you mean by "product advertising." In the case of "propaganda," though, a definition is needed. Recall that the dictionary said propaganda is a *systematic* attempt to disseminate a doctrine. Since advertising doesn't systematically try to convince us to consume more, you'll need to extend the definition to include indirect, unintentional forms of propaganda. Note too that you should frame your extended definition in your own words. Although it was useful to consult a dictionary when you were first thinking about your topic, it's rarely wise to quote a dictionary definition directly in your essay. Words are just too complex and have too many shades of meaning for a dictionary definition to convey exactly what you have in mind.

Now let's turn to the four adjectives. In a sense, these are the heart of your thesis, since they're what give it its evaluative dimension. The basic need here, then, is to be as clear in your own mind as you possibly can about the implications of the terms you're using. You say that ads are beneficial. Whom do they benefit and in what ways? In what way is advertising subtle? What is dangerous about it? Is it dangerous only to individuals or to society as well? Is it more dangerous to some groups than to others? Clearly, the questioning could continue for some time. But here let's say you happen to remember recent objections to ads for high-sugar cereals on children's television programs. It occurs to you that children are especially susceptible to advertising, so under "dangerous" you write "children," and you note down the example of the high-sugar cereal as well. If you have a little brother who goes out of control a month before Christmas because of TV-generated excitement, you note *him* down too.

As you analyze the key terms, then, you already find yourself developing additional examples and arguments. Continue the process, moving through the terms one by one and using them as headings under which to list what you discover. At the same time, look for interconnections that may lead you to want to modify your thesis. For example, say you've reached the point where you're listing the dangers of advertising. Back when we first framed the thesis, we assumed that forced stimulation of the economy was beneficial. But doesn't forced stimulation lead to inflation? And isn't inflation dangerous? On the other hand, though, could our society survive in its present form if it had a steady-state economy? You're not sure, so you don't modify your thesis. But you do decide to bear in mind that a benefit from one point of view can be a liability from another.

By using the key terms as headings, you've provided yourself with a ready-made organization for the examples and arguments you've been developing. Once you're done accumulating them, you need to turn to organizing the essay itself. What we said at the beginning of this chapter still goes: only you can decide whether to outline your essay before writing it. Some people (but probably only a few) use full formal outlines, complete with Roman numerals, Arabic numerals, and the like. Others make do with a tentative, sketchy outline of the major divisions of the argument. It's your choice.

Whether you use an extensive outline or not, it's helpful to look at the structure of your thesis to see if it implies a structure for the essay as a whole. If we do this with our hypothetical thesis, we notice a sharp contrast between the subordinate "Although . . ." clause and the main clause. This suggests that a contrastive structure might be appropriate for the essay as a whole; it also implies a tone you could use. Perhaps you might start with the positive aspects of advertising, and a light, half-humorous tone. Then you could become more solemn in tone when you shift from the benefits to the dangers. Perhaps, you think, those innocent children watching TV could be the bridge between the two. You imagine the scene, and as you do, you begin to jot down words, phrases, even a sentence or two.

Writing

So now you *are* writing. And here we fully enter the portals of the mystery. How you write—whether with rotten cucumbers in plentiful supply or in the nearest cork-lined room—is your affair. We can, however, offer some simple suggestions to help you out along the way.

The first and simplest suggestion is that you waste some paper. Every teacher of composition has seen students' drafts so crowded onto the page that the writers themselves couldn't figure out what they had written. On the first draft, it's best to leave ample margins—top, bottom, and sides—and double- or even triple-space between lines. If you're writing by hand rather than typing, write on every other line. Think of your first draft as working copy on which you will want to make changes, and leave yourself plenty of room in which to make them.

The second suggestion is that you not start writing at the beginning of the essay if you don't want to. Some writers need to write a clear, exact opening before doing anything else, but many find themselves paralyzed if they try to write the introduction before they've written the body of the essay (and thus learned exactly what it is they're introducing). Related to this suggestion is another one: look at the *last* paragraph of your first draft to see if it can be transformed into the *first* paragraph of your second draft. Surprisingly often, it can. The reason is simple. Although writing is an act of communication, it's also an act of exploration. Sometimes, no matter how much prewriting and organizing we do, we don't know our exact attitude toward our topic until we've written all the way through it. Only when we're at the end of the essay do we finally discover what we really think. If this happens to you, bring your true opinion up to the front of the next draft and see if your essay isn't strengthened as a result.

The third suggestion comes from Ernest Hemingway, who said that a writer should always write a little of the way up the next hill before taking a break. The meaning of Hemingway's metaphor is that you shouldn't interrupt your writing exactly at the end of a major phase of your argument. Doing so can make it hard to get started again. If you instead write two or three sentences of the next paragraph before stopping, then the next stage of the argument can be working in the back of your mind while you're away from your desk, and you'll find it easier to come back and pick up the pencil again.

The fourth and final suggestion is that you outline your first draft after you finish writing it. This suggestion isn't as frivolous as it may sound. Once you've finished a draft, you need to see whether or not it holds together coherently, and the easiest way of doing this is by outlining. Here you might consider developing what is called a *thesis-topic outline.* To do this, simply list your thesis sentence at the top of a sheet of paper, and then under it write the topic sentences of each paragraph of the body of the essay, in the order in which they occur.

Once you have your thesis-topic outline, test each topic sentence against the thesis. Do they in fact all support your thesis, and if so, how? If one or another of them doesn't, you have three options open to you: (1) you can rewrite the offending topic sentence (and the accompanying paragraph); (2) you can rewrite the thesis statement to accommodate the topic that's presently out of line; or (3) you can throw out the offending topic sentence and its accompanying paragraph. Whichever of these options you choose—and even if you don't choose any of them—you've now begun revising your essay. So it's time to turn to the last stage of the writing process.

Revising the rough draft

The most important single piece of advice we can give you about revising your writing is to do it. Once you've worked your way through to a clear thesis and argument and written them down in essay form, you may be tempted to think that you're done. You have, after all, decided on your beliefs about a topic, refined them, and set them down on paper. But remember that truly persuasive writing doesn't just present ideas; it dresses them to advantage. If you take the time to proofread, to cut wordy constructions, and to smooth out tortuous syntax, your readers will sense your care and concern, and they will be inclined to give your argument a favorable hearing as a result.

The areas you should first concentrate on in your revision are those in which you happen to have particular problems. Is spelling something of a mystery to you? Then read through your draft once looking for nothing but misspelled words. (If this doesn't work, then look for them while reading through the draft *backwards*.) In the same way, concentrate on other matters that you know to be of particular concern. You may even want to develop a checklist of the sorts of problems that recur in your writing, in order to help you be especially on guard against them.

In addition to paying attention to your own idiosyncracies as a writer, try doing four other things that can help improve your draft. All of them have the goal of making your writing as clear and economical as possible. They can be stated in the form of four simple rules.

1. Substitute active constructions for passive ones whenever possible. In an active construction, the subject of the sentence *performs* the action indicated by the verb ("John hit the ball"). In a passive construction, the subject *receives* the verb's action ("The ball was hit by John"). One reason for preferring the active voice over the passive is that it's more economical. As the examples show, an active construction uses fewer words than does a passive one of equivalent meaning.

A more important reason for preferring the active voice, though, is its greater clarity. The passive voice creates a muddy impression in the reader's mind when it is used, as it often is, to present an action without saying who performed it. Consider some examples: "the budget was exceeded"; "the village was bombed"; "it has been decided that certain students may no longer attend this university." *Who* exceeded the budget? *Who* bombed the village? *Who* kicked the students out of school? We don't know, and we can't find out. But if the authors of the sentences had used the active voice, we would surely be able to answer these questions. When you revise your rough draft, then, look at each passive construction and ask whether it is causing a loss in clarity by needlessly omitting the agent of the action. If it is, rewrite the sentence in the active voice. (Be sure, too, that you identify yourself as the agent when appropriate. Don't say "it is thought" when you mean "I think.")

2. Avoid using forms of "to be" as main verbs whenever possible. Verbs give energy to writing. In the basic subject-verb-object sentence pattern ("John hit the ball"), the verb tells what happens. It states the action performed *by* the subject *on* the object, and it gives the sentence its sense of thrust and forward movement. But in the "to be" pattern of subject-verb-adjective ("John is handsome"), the verb doesn't carry an action from the subject to an object. Instead, it helps define the subject by linking it to a word or phrase specifying one or more of its attributes. Whereas the subject-verb-object pattern is linear and progressive, the "to be" pattern is circular, moving from the subject to the verb and back to the subject. Herein lies its danger. Because of its circularity, the "to be" pattern can give prose an eddying quality and make it seem to lack energy.

There will, of course, be many times when you need to use "to be" as a main verb. John may be handsome and you may need to say so. But you can help ensure that your prose will have vigor if, as you revise, you test every sentence that has a form of "to be" as a main verb to see if it should be rewritten. Be especially watchful for the needless sort of "to be" construction that begins "there is" or "it is." The statement "it is certain that the volunteer army deserves higher pay" means the same thing as "the volunteer army certainly deserves higher pay" but uses a needless three extra words. "There is" and "it is" are almost always deadwood and should be pruned away.

One other piece of advice about "to be" constructions: when you're clearing them out, *look for the true verb elsewhere in the sentence.* Often, as in our sample sentence about the volunteer army, the true verb ("deserves") will already be a verb in form, but will be tucked away in a relative clause. At other times, the true verb will be concealed inside a participle, gerund, or noun. "Fantasizing is something all people do" hides the verb inside "fantasizing." "America's production of geothermal power is minute" hides it inside "production." Revise these sentences, and they become "All people fantasize" and "America produces little geothermal power."

3. Cut out clutter. In an attempt to sound impressive, people sometimes use five words where one or two would do. It doesn't work. A wordy style just bores readers, so try to use as few words as you can while still being clear. A good way of doing this is by keeping an eye on your prepositional phrases. When you're revising, take a minute to circle every preposition on a page or two of your rough draft. If you find you're using more than four per sentence, chances are your style is wordy. Look, for example, at how the prepositional phrases in the following sentence diffuse its meaning and blunt its impact: "Attempts *by* the politicians *in* the state legislature to deceive the people *of* the state *of* California *by* vote-switching will not be tolerated." Cutting some of these prepositional phrases and revising others into single-word modifiers greatly increase the effectiveness of the sentence: "Californians will not tolerate deceptive vote-switching by state legislators." By reducing the number of prepositional phrases from five to one, we've turned a muddy twenty-three-word sentence into a clear nine-word one.

4. Vary the length and type of your sentences. This final guideline for revision is a way to guard against boring your readers. Because most of us like the sound of our own voices, whatever we write usually grips our attention. But readers aren't as enamored of our prose as we are, and nothing will put them to sleep faster than monotonous repetition. You can keep this from happening in your writing if you make a conscious effort to vary your sentences. But it's not enough merely to change sentence length and type randomly; you need to do so in relation to the rhythm of your paragraphs. If you don't feel you have a fully developed sense of prose rhythm, then work to improve it. As you read the essays in the following chapters of this book, note sentence patterns that you find especially pleasing, and then try to imitate them in your own writing. By doing this, you'll acquire a repertoire of prose rhythms that you can draw on in forming your own distinctive style.

Now your essay is done. You've written it, revised it, submitted it, and you have a week or so to yourself before the next one is due. Are there any further pieces of advice we can give you here? We have just one, and it's less a piece of advice than an observation: once people learn how hard writing is, it gets easier for them. This sounds grim, but it really isn't. All it means is that there aren't any shortcuts. In the long run, waiting for inspiration to strike or stewing over whether your readers will notice that fuzzy patch on the second page is harder work than is the approach to writing we've outlined here. We hope you'll give this approach a try. If you do, we think you'll soon find yourself increasing your command of the writing process.

description

If someone asks you to describe something, you probably don't stop to wonder what the term means before you begin. This is so because describing is something we all spend much of our time doing. It's one of the main ways we have of shaping and communicating our experiences. Yet like many of the other important activities of our lives, it's more complex than it at first appears to be.

The complexity of description lies in the fact that it contains both *objective* and *subjective* elements. On the one hand, description is closely tied to the external, physical world. Unlike most other kinds of writing, which are primarily concerned with ideas, description is rooted in the senses. How something looks, tastes, feels, sounds—this is what we try to convey when we write description, and to do so we need to be as true to the facts of the matter as possible. Is the apple red, or is it a mottled reddish-green, with the red tending to be dominant on the parts farthest from the stem? Is the book jacket uniformly brown, or are there places where the paper has been worn white through use? The more closely we observe the *objective* characteristics of whatever we're describing, the better chance we have of conveying an accurate, vivid picture of it to our audience.

But on the other hand, description is more than just a matter of how things look. It's a matter of how they look *to* someone. There are a few types of writing—scientific reports, legal briefs, instruction manuals—where we need to communicate sense impressions in a way that divorces them from our reactions

13

to them. But in most writing, we must pay attention both to the object we're describing and to our *subjective* response to it. Rather than merely report our observations, we need to ask ourselves what feelings the object evokes in us, and then choose descriptive details that will convey those feelings.

This need to pay attention to our subjective responses becomes especially important when we move from *simple* to *extended* description. Unlike simple description, which deals with small, static objects like apples and book jackets, extended description deals either with something too large to take in at a single glance (Huxtable's "Houston") or with something dynamic (Angell's "On the Ball"). In this sort of writing, the stance of the observer is all-important. No one can hope to describe all the physical sensations aroused by something as complex as a city or a baseball game—at least not without running the risk of boring readers to death. Instead, writers of extended description must ask themselves what the experience has meant to them, and must then present only those details that can best help to convey this meaning. Though their aim, like that of writers of simple description, should be to convey an accurate picture, it cannot be to convey the *whole* picture, for this is too complex to be contained within any one description. It is the truth of one person's experience, of one point of view chosen from among many possibilities, that is the primary concern of the writer of extended description.

The following paragraph from Elizabeth Drew's book on Senator John Culver illustrates how a writer combines objective and subjective elements in an extended description:

> Culver's office is rather ordinarily furnished with large brown leather chairs and sofa and a green carpet. There are photographs of his family around—the Culvers have four children—and on his desk is a very large ear of corn encased in Lucite. "Harold Hughes gave that to me," Culver remarks. "We explain that it must have been a drought year." Over the mantel is a painting of a Victorian building that Culver himself restored in McGregor, Iowa—a small town on the Mississippi River, in the northeast corner of the state. Culver maintains a home there, in addition to one in Washington. On the mantel are a drawing of a showboat on the Mississippi River; a framed poem, "Song of the Great River," which was written in 1973 by Paul Engle, the former head of the University of Iowa's International Writing Program, for the tricentennial celebration, arranged by Culver and held in McGregor, of the discovery of the upper Mississippi by Marquette and Joliet. There is also a framed saying:

> Until you've been in politics
> you've never really been alive
> it's rough and sometimes it's
> dirty and it's always hard
> work and tedious details
> But, it's the only sport
> for grownups—all other
> games are for kids.
>   —HEINLEIN

And there are on the mantel busts of John F. Kennedy and Robert F. Kennedy, and a collection of miniature pigs that Culver has gathered in the course of his travels around the world. On the walls are rice-paper drawings he bought during a trip to China last year.[1]

At first glance, this paragraph may seem entirely objective—as indeed it is, if by this we mean only that all the details it contains are true. Yet notice how Drew selects just those details that will create a warm, friendly, positive impression not only of the office but of the senator himself. He is a family man (the photographs), proud of the state he represents (the ear of corn, the painting and the drawing, the poem), loyal to his party (the busts of the two Kennedys), and proud of his profession (the framed saying). By the details she chooses to present, Drew makes clear her admiration for Senator Culver. Presumably, a writer who is hostile toward Culver would choose different details to present, ones that would create a colder and less inviting impression.

But even if the hostile writer used the same details as Drew does, he still could create a different impression. Say he wanted to create a view of Culver as a yokel, a rube senator from a farm state. What might he have done with the unsophisticated enthusiasm of the quotation from Heinlein? the ear of corn in Lucite? the miniature pigs? A writer conveys his evaluation of what he describes not only by *selecting* details but by *arranging* and *emphasizing* them. Take the miniature pigs out of the context of the busts of the two Kennedys and the trip to China, combine them with the ear of corn, and put the combination in a prominent place in the paragraph (near the beginning or the end), and you will create a vast change in their effect.

Selection, arrangement, and emphasis, then, are basic concerns of the writer of description. In addition, there are two specific guidelines that such writers generally follow:

1. Show, don't tell.

2. Choose a clear pattern of organization.

The first of these guidelines is a caution against too much abstraction. When we write description we usually need to draw conclusions from our sense experiences, so we may be tempted to bypass the experiences and go directly to the conclusions themselves. But consider the difference between saying "John Culver has a good sense of humor" and retelling his little joke about the ear of corn. Retelling the joke is surely the more vivid way of writing. It is also the more convincing way, for if Drew had simply said that Culver has a good sense of humor she would have been forcing us to accept her statement on faith, something we might well be reluctant to do. A word of caution, though: just showing whatever randomly comes to mind isn't any better than telling. The details you show your readers have to be the ones (and only the ones) that will guide them to the conclusion you want them to reach.

[1] Elizabeth Drew, *Senator* (New York: Simon & Schuster, 1978), pp. 37-38.

The second guideline is a fairly easy one to follow. If you're describing a visual experience (by far the most frequent subject for a descriptive essay), you can almost always follow a *spatial* order of presentation. But which spatial order should you follow? The answer to this question will be at least partly determined by the nature of the thing you're describing. If you're describing a house, for example, you might choose to move from outside to inside, or from upstairs to downstairs. Other orders frequently used are from side to side, from back to front, from near to far, and from small to large.

Just because a description has a clear-cut spatial order, though, doesn't mean that you should plod relentlessly through it. In some ways, being a writer of description is like being a movie director. If you can imagine what a movie would be like if there were never any changes in scene or in camera position, then you should be able to see how important it is to vary your pace and your point of view when writing extended description. As you read the essays in this chapter, look at how their authors handle these matters. Ask yourself why they give a good many details at some points and few or none at others. Note how they summarize from time to time, and how they occasionally shift their angle of observation. Look at the ways they make us aware of their presence as observers at some points and efface themselves at others. If you incorporate what you learn from studying these essays into your own extended descriptions, chances are you'll be a stronger writer as a result.

The Death
of a Moth

ANNIE DILLARD

Annie Dillard was born in Pittsburgh, Pennsylvania, in 1945 and
lived for ten years in Virginia, the setting for "The Death of a
Moth" and her Pulitzer Prize-winning *Pilgrim at Tinker Creek*
(1974). She is the author of two other books, *Tickets for a
Prayer Wheel* (1974) and *Holy the Firm* (1977), and is a contrib-
uting editor to *Harper's*. The selection reprinted here demonstrates both Dillard's interest in the metaphysical aspects of the
natural world and her ability to use vivid, concrete images to
evoke strong responses in her readers.

I live alone with two cats, who sleep on my legs. There is a yellow one, and a
black one whose name is Small. In the morning I joke to the black one, Do you
remember last night? Do you remember? I throw them both out before breakfast,
so I can eat.

There is a spider, too, in the bathroom, of uncertain lineage, bulbous at the
abdomen and drab, whose six-inch mess of web works, works somehow, works
miraculously, to keep her alive and me amazed. The web is in a corner behind
the toilet, connecting tile wall to tile wall. The house is new, the bathroom
immaculate, save for the spider, her web, and the sixteen or so corpses she's tossed
to the floor.

The corpses appear to be mostly sow bugs, those little armadillo creatures who live to travel flat out in houses, and die round. In addition to sow-bug husks, hollow and sipped empty of color, there are what seem to be two or three wingless moth bodies, one new flake of earwig, and three spider carcasses crinkled and clenched.

I wonder on what fool's errand an earwig, or a moth, or a sow bug, would visit that clean corner of the house behind the toilet; I have not noticed any blind parades of sow bugs blundering into corners. Yet they do hazard there, at a rate of more than one a week, and the spider thrives. Yesterday she was working on the earwig, mouth on gut; today he's on the floor. It must take a certain genius to throw things away from there, to find a straight line through that sticky tangle to the floor.

Today the earwig shines darkly, and gleams, what there is of him: a dorsal curve of thorax and abdomen, and a smooth pair of pincers by which I knew his name. Next week, if the other bodies are any indication, he'll be shrunk and gray, webbed to the floor with dust. The sow bugs beside him are curled and empty, fragile, a breath away from brittle fluff. The spiders lie on their sides, translucent and ragged, their legs drying in knots. The moths stagger against each other, headless, in a confusion of arcing strips of chitin like peeling varnish, like a jumble of buttresses for cathedral vaults, like nothing resembling moths, so that I would hesitate to call them moths, except that I have had some experience with the figure Moth reduced to a nub.

Two summers ago I was camped alone in the Blue Ridge Mountains of Virginia. I had hauled myself and gear up there to read, among other things, *The Day on Fire*, by James Ullman, a novel about Rimbaud that had made me want to be a writer when I was sixteen; I was hoping it would do it again. So I read every day sitting under a tree by my tent, while warblers sang in the leaves overhead and bristle worms trailed their inches over the twiggy dirt at my feet; and I read every night by candlelight, while barred owls called in the forest and pale moths seeking mates massed round my head in the clearing, where my light made a ring.

Moths kept flying into the candle. They would hiss and recoil, reeling upside down in the shadows among my cooking pans. Or they would singe their wings and fall, and their hot wings, as if melted, would stick to the first thing they touched — a pan, a lid, a spoon — so that the snagged moths could struggle only in tiny arcs, unable to flutter free. These I could release by a quick flip with a stick; in the morning I would find my cooking stuff decorated with torn flecks of moth wings, ghostly triangles of shiny dust here and there on the aluminum. So I read, and boiled water, and replenished candles, and read on.

One night a moth flew into the candle, was caught, burnt dry, and held. I must have been staring at the candle, or maybe I looked up when a shadow crossed my page; at any rate, I saw it all. A golden female moth, a biggish one with a two-inch wingspread, flapped into the fire, dropped abdomen into the wet wax, stuck, flamed, and frazzled in a second. Her moving wings ignited like tissue paper, like angels' wings, enlarging the circle of light in the clearing and creating out of the darkness the sudden blue sleeves of my sweater, the green leaves of jewelweed by my side, the ragged red trunk of a pine; at once the light contracted again and the moth's wings vanished in a fine, foul smoke. At the same time, her six legs clawed, curled, blackened, and ceased, disappearing utterly. And her head jerked in spasms, making a spattering noise; her antennae crisped and burnt away and her heaving mouthparts cracked like pistol fire. When it was all over, her head was, so far as I could determine, gone, gone the long way of her wings and legs. Her head was a hole lost to time. All that was left was the flowing horn shell of her abdomen and thorax — a fraying, partially collapsed gold tube jammed upright in the candle's round pool.

And then this moth-essence, this spectacular skeleton, began to act as a wick. She kept burning. The wax rose in the moth's body from her soaking abdomen to her thorax to the shattered hole where her head should have been, and widened into flame, a saffron-yellow flame that robed her to the ground like an immolating monk. That candle had two wicks, two winding flames of identical light, side by side. The moth's head was fire. She burned for two hours, until I blew her out.

She burned for two hours without changing, without swaying or kneeling — only glowing within, like a building fire glimpsed through silhouetted walls, like a hollow saint, like a flame-faced virgin gone to God, while I read by her light, kindled, while Rimbaud in Paris burnt out his brain in a thousand poems, while night pooled wetly at my feet.

So. That is why I think those hollow shreds on the bathroom floor are moths. I believe I know what moths look like, in any state.

I have three candles here on the table which I disentangle from the plants and light when visitors come. The cats avoid them, although Small's tail caught fire once; I rubbed it out before she noticed. I don't mind living alone. I like eating alone and reading. I don't mind sleeping alone. The only time I mind being alone is when something is funny; then, when I am laughing at something funny, I wish someone were around. Sometimes I think it is pretty funny that I sleep alone.

Questions for Discussion

1. At first glance, this essay may seem disjointed. Is it? How does Dillard connect the opening and closing sections to the central description of the death of the moth?

2. Arthur Rimbaud was a nineteenth-century French poet. While still a teenager, he developed a theory that he could increase his creativity by using drugs and experimenting with homosexuality. He stopped writing poetry before he was twenty and died at the age of thirty-seven. How is this information useful in understanding Dillard's essay? What connection does she draw between Rimbaud and the moth?

3. Although Dillard uses many comparisons in describing the death of the moth, she rarely uses them to help us visualize the physical situation. What does she use them for? How effective is her use of them?

4. Dillard speaks of the sudden flare of light from the burning moth as "creating out of the darkness the sudden blue sleeves of [her] sweater." What is unusual about her point of view here? Is it consistent with her point of view in the rest of the essay?

5. Dillard speaks of sow bugs that "travel flat out in houses, and die round." What play on words is she using here? What other examples of word play can you find in her essay? How effective are they?

6. How would you describe Dillard's attitude toward the death of the moth? Is she detached? cruel? scientific? How does your own attitude toward the death of insects compare to hers?

Suggested Activities

1. Draw up a list of the comparisons Dillard uses in describing the death of the moth, then make up another list of comparisons she could have used but didn't. What would be the effect of substituting your set of comparisons for hers?

2. Write an essay describing the death of something small. Try to convey your attitude toward the death without stating it directly.

3. Write an extended description of a spider's web. Find a real web, look closely at it, and be as particular as you can in describing it.

Low and Slow,
Mean and Clean

CALVIN TRILLIN

Calvin Trillin (b. 1935), a frequent contributor to *The New Yorker*, is the author of several books, including *U.S. Journal* (1970) and *Alice, Let's Eat* (1978). "Low and Slow, Mean and Clean," reprinted here, focuses on a relatively new California custom, lowriding. Trillin creates a fascinating picture of the lowriders' cars, with their hydraulic lifters, automatic door openers, chandeliers, and crushed velvet seat covers.

In California, it is common for a young Mexican-American to lower his car to within a few inches of the ground, make it as beautiful as he knows how both inside and out, and drive it down the street very, very slowly. The custom is called lowriding. The car a lowrider drives — almost always a sedan produced by the General Motors Corporation — is also called a lowrider, or a ride. If it has been altered with conspicuous success — a multicolored lacquer paint job, say, and metal-spoke wheels, and skimpy tires that seem to belong on a Datsun rather than a 1967 Chevrolet Impala, and a welded-chain steering wheel no bigger around than a 45-r.p.m. record — it is called a clean ride, or a bad ride. "Low and slow," lowriders sometimes say. "Mean and clean." A car can be lowered by cutting some of the coils from the springs or simply by melting the springs with a blow-torch. In the past several years, more and more lowriders have installed hydraulic lifts — the sort of hydraulic lifts used to raise and lower the tailgates of trucks —

LOW AND SLOW, MEAN AND CLEAN   By Calvin Trillin, from *The New Yorker*, July 10, 1978. Excerpt reprinted by permission; © 1978 The New Yorker Magazine, Inc.

so that a car that seems to be only two or three inches off the ground can be raised to eight or ten inches in order to go over a bump or past a policeman. (Some policemen enforce the California law against having any part of a car's chassis below the lowest point of the wheel rim; a few policemen even apply the law against driving a car in "unsafe condition" to cars that have tiny steering wheels or small tires or, for that matter, hydraulic lifts that can raise a car as it goes past a policeman.) Cars that are lifted, or "juiced," with hydraulics ordinarily have separate systems for the front and back—each run off two or three huge batteries—so that a lowrider can make the front of his car rear up like a horse. When lowriders are travelling in a caravan—which is the way a lot of lowriders prefer to travel—they can move the fronts and backs of their cars up and down in a motion reminiscent of a huge dragon in a Chinese parade. At night, they can switch off their headlights and suddenly drop the fronts of their cars completely to the pavement—screeching along on a "scrape plate" that has been welded to the frame, and throwing off sparks to either side. By carefully timing the jolts of electricity to his front-end hydraulics, a lowrider can actually bounce the front wheels of his car completely off the ground, so that it moves down the street slowly—very, very slowly—like a great hopping rabbit. Not a Volkswagen Rabbit; a rabbit.

Lowriders like to cruise. On weekend nights, a section of Whittier Boulevard that runs through the sprawling Mexican section of Los Angeles—East L.A.—is so jammed with lowriders that they drive slowly as a matter of necessity as well as style. In San Jose—which has a few dozen lowrider car clubs and a magazine called *Low Rider* and a reputation as the Lowrider Capital of Northern California—the gathering place has been the intersection of Story and King. Three shopping centers built on land that was pastureland not long ago have produced there what a deputy chief of police estimates to be "around a hundred acres of parking lot." Last year, so many lowriders began spending their Saturday nights around Story and King that the local merchants—the California shopping-center sort of local merchants, like the manager of the Shakey's Pizza Parlor and the man who ran the Jack in the Box outlet and the proprietor of the Winchell's Donut House franchise—demanded that the city do something about the crowds and the litter and the occasional rowdiness.

Lowriders still gather on Saturday nights, though, at the parking lot of one shopping center—in front of the Disco East, which has reason to be hospitable, having directed its business toward lowriders so completely that the prize given to the hottest disco dancers on a Saturday night is likely to be something like a set of wire wheels. The parking lot is still dotted with large trash barrels that were installed some time ago in an effort by the car clubs at self-policing; one of the barrels, painted gold and blue, bears the club logo of the Sophisticated Ladies. On the horizon, where one freeway passes under another, three massive bridges to nowhere—a freeway interchange that was abandoned when the freeway money gave out—loom against the sky like architectural remnants left by a race of giants. Some lowriders sit in their cars listening to tapes at full volume on stereo tape decks. Some stand outside their cars, in the cacophony of clashing disco songs, talking and drinking and flirting and watching cars go by. Some of them circle the parking lot in their bad rides — very, very slowly. . . .

In the past few years, lowrider car clubs have begun to sponsor "lowrider happenings" — car shows at which trophies are awarded for the best interior and the finest paint job and the highest hop off the ground. In a contest, hopping is done at a dead stop. In order to lighten the front-end load, the driver sometimes stands outside the car, impassively flicking the hydraulic switches at the end of a cable, while the judges, armed with yardsticks, scamper around under the front wheels. A 1964 Chevrolet Impala is considered the best hopper. The world hopping record is two feet off the ground.

Members of a car club ordinarily drive to a happening in caravan — each car glistening from a new wax job, each car displaying in its rear window the plaque of, say, the First Impressions or New Style or First Illusions or Brown Sensations. The interior of a lowrider show car — the seats and the insides of the doors and the ceiling and even the dashboard — is likely to be upholstered in crushed velvet. The inside of the trunk is sometimes covered with crushed velvet — crushed velvet enclosing the spare tire and framing the mirror that reflects a trunk display of a polished chrome jack or perhaps a single rose. At the Fresno Lowrider Happening #2, sponsored by Thee Individuals at the Fresno fairgrounds recently, at least one car had crushed velvet lining the hood. Another contender had — in addition to a gold crushed-velvet interior that included a swivel seat for the driver and two recessed bottleholders containing champagne — a printed sign on the front seat that said "Starlight, starbright. Look up inside. Look at my chandelier light." Anyone who looked up did indeed see — in the middle of the ceiling, where some cars have a light to switch on for reading a map — a cut-glass chandelier. It was not the only chandelier at the show.

At a lowrider happening, a lot of people stroll around inspecting the cars, and a large crowd always gathers for the hopping contest. The activity always spills over to adjoining streets and parking lots. In front of the fairgrounds in Fresno, a steady line of cars moved down the street, undulating and hopping and scraping. The curb was lined with spectators. . . . A lot of them were wearing car-club T-shirts, some of which were monogrammed with the owner's name and car — "Tony, '72 Monte Carlo" or "Raul, '67 Impala." In one of the parking lots, a dozen or so members of the Midnighters de East Bay stood shining their cars and drinking beer. They were approached slowly by a 1972 Malibu Classic with a paint job that could turn heads even at a lowrider happening — a hand-painted lacquer finish in ten or twelve colors, with a sort of celestial scene on the roof. A plaque in the rear window identified the Malibu Classic as belonging to a member of Lowriders Unlimited. The Malibu Classic stopped next to the Midnighters de East Bay, who gathered around to inspect its interior — blue and gold crushed velvet, with a television set built into the dashboard. The driver and his passenger stared straight ahead, with blank expressions. The front of the car began to move up and down, then the rear. "Lifted all around," one of the Midnighters de East Bay said. Then the driver reached over to another switch that was almost buried in the velvet of the door — reaching casually, like a rich lady reaching for the switch to raise the window of her Cadillac. The trunk of the Malibu Classic — hinged on the side instead of below the rear window — began to open slowly, revealing a Tru-Spoke wire-wheel spare tire, and crushed velvet covering even the hydraulic lifts and their extra batteries. The trunk slowly opened and closed several times. The Midnighters de East Bay looked impressed. The front of the car moved up and down a few more times, then the back. Then the front took a few hops off the ground. Then the driver, still without having changed expression or uttered a word, lifted both ends of his car to their full heights and drove away, at about five miles an hour.

Questions for Discussion

1. Trillin uses the phrase "very, very slowly" three times in his essay: at the beginning and end of the first paragraph, and at the end of the third one. What is the effect of this phrase? Why do you think he places it where he does?

2. Near the end of his essay, Trillin says that the owner of the Malibu Classic reached for the trunk control "like a rich lady reaching for the switch to raise the window of her Cadillac." What is the effect of this comparison? What motive does it suggest may lie behind the custom of building lowriders?

3. Discuss Trillin's use of the language of lowriding in this essay. Does he keep his own language separate from that of the lowriders, or does he mingle the two? Why?

4. What are some examples of humor in this essay? What does Trillin's use of it reveal about his attitude toward his subject?

5. Compare Trillin's use of specific detail to Dillard's in "The Death of a Moth." Who do you think uses details more effectively? Why?

6. How does "Low and Slow, Mean and Clean" make you feel about the custom of lowriding? Does it make the custom seem silly, or does it lend a kind of dignity to it? What details in the essay give support to your point of view?

Suggested Activities

1. The next time you take a walk of any distance, note every example you see of popular art (the kind of art people make for themselves). What conclusions can you draw about the human need to make beautiful things?

2. Write an extended description of your favorite car. Try to suggest the reasons for your fondness without stating them directly.

3. Write an argumentative essay defending lowriding, cruising, or some other contemporary custom.

Houston: Deep in the
Heart of Nowhere

ADA LOUISE HUXTABLE

Ada Louise Huxtable, the first winner of the Pulitzer Prize for
distinguished criticism, is an influential critic of modern architecture and a leader in the campaign to save architectural landmarks. Her books include *Four Walking Tours of Modern Architecture in New York City* (1961), *Classic New York* (1964), and
Will They Ever Finish Bruckner Boulevard? (1970). "Houston:
Deep in the Heart of Nowhere," reprinted here from *Kicked a
Building Lately?* (1976), demonstrates how a skillful writer can
use description to express a point of view.

This is a car's-eye view of Houston — but is there any other? It is a short report
on a fast trip to the city that has supplanted Los Angeles in current intellectual
mythology as the city of the future. You'd better believe. Houston is the place
that scholars flock to for the purpose of seeing what modern civilization has
wrought. Correctly perceived and publicized as freeway city, mobile city, space
city, strip city, and speculator city, it is being dissected by architects and urban
historians as a case study in new forms and functions. It even requires a new
definition of urbanity. Houston is *the* city of the second half of the twentieth
century.

But what strikes the visitor accustomed to cities shaped by rivers, mountains, and distinguishing topography, by local identity and historical and cultural conditioning, is that this is instant city, and it is nowhere city.

Houston is totally without the normal rationales of geography and evolutionary social growth that have traditionally created urban centers and culture. From the time that the Allen brothers came here from New York in 1836 and bought the featureless land at the junction of two bayous (they could not get the site they really wanted), this city has been an act of real estate, rather than an act of God or man. Houston has been willed on the flat, uniform prairie not by some planned ideal, but by the expediency of land investment economics, first, and later by oil and petrochemical prosperity.

This is not meant to be an unfavorable judgment. It is simply an effort to convey the extraordinary character of this city — to suggest its unique importance, interest, and impact. Its affluence and eccentricities have been popularly celebrated. It is known to be devoutly conservative, passionately devoted to free enterprise and non-governmental interference. It is famous, or notorious, for the fact that, alone among the country's major cities, it has no zoning — no regulations on what anyone builds, anywhere — and the debate rages over whether this makes it better or worse than other cities. (It's a draw, with pluses and minuses that have a lot to do with special local conditions.)

Now the fifth largest city in the country, Houston has had its most phenomenal expansion since the Second World War. At last count, it covered over 500 square miles and had a population of 1.4 million, with a half million more in surrounding Harris County. A thousand new people move in every week. This record-setting growth has leapfrogged over open country without natural boundaries, without land use restrictions, moving on before anything is finished, for a kind of development as open-ended as the prairie. It has jumped across smaller, fully incorporated cities within the vast city limits. The municipality can legally annex 10 percent of its urban area in outlying land or communities every year, and the land grab has been continuous and relentless.

Houston is a study in paradoxes. There are pines and palm trees, skyscrapers and sprawl; Tudor townhouses stop abruptly as cows and prairie take over. It deals in incredible extremes of wealth and culture. In spite of its size, one can find no real center, no focus. "Downtown" boasts a concentration of suave towers, but they are already challenged by other, newer commercial centers of increasing magnitude that form equally important nodes on the freeway network that ties everything together. Nor are these new office and shopping complexes located to serve existing communities in the conventional sense. They are created in a vacuum, and people come by automobile, driving right into their parking garages. They rise from expressway ribbons and seas of cars.

Houston is all process and no plan. Gertrude Stein said of Oakland that there was no there, there. One might say of Houston that one never gets there. It feels as if one is always on the way, always arriving, always looking for the place where everything comes together. And yet as a city, a twentieth-century city, it works remarkably well. If one excepts horrendous morning and evening traffic jams as all of Houston moves to and from home and work, it is a lesson in how a mobile society functions, the values it endorses, and what kind of world it makes.

Houston is different from the time one rises in the morning to have the dark suddenly dispelled by a crimson aureole on a horizon that seems to stretch full circle, and a sun that appears to rise below eye level. (New Yorkers are accustomed to seeing only fractured bits and pieces of sky.) From a hotel of sophisticated excellence that might be Claridge's-on-the-prairie, furnished with an owner-oilman's private collection of redundant boiserie and Sevres, one drives past fountains of detergent blue.

Due north on Main Street is "downtown," a roughly 20-block cluster of commercial towers begun in the 1920s and thirties and doubled in size and numbers in the 1960s and seventies, sleek symbols of prosperity and power. They are paradigms of the corporate style. The names they bear are Tenneco, Shell Plaza, Pennzoil Place, Humble, and Houston Natural Gas, and their architects have national reputations.

In another paradox, in this country of open spaces, the towers are increasingly connected by tunnels underground. Houston's environment is strikingly "internalized" because of the area's extremes of heat and humidity. It is the indoors one seeks for large parts of the year, and that fact has profoundly affected how the city builds and lives.

The enclosed shopping center is Houston's equivalent of the traditional town plaza — a clear trend across the country. The Post Oak Galleria, a $20-million product of Houston developer Gerald Hines and architects Hellmuth, Obata and Kassabaum, with Neuhaus and Taylor, is characteristically large and opulent. A 420,000-square-foot, 600-foot long, three-level, covered shopping mall, it is part of a 33-acre commercial, office, and hotel complex off the West Loop Freeway, at the city's western edge.

The Galleria is the place to see and be seen: it is meeting place, promenade, and social center. It also offers restaurants, baubles from Tiffany and Nieman-Marcus, a galaxy of specialty shops equivalent to Madison Avenue, and an ice-skating rink comparable to Rockefeller Center's, all under a chandelier-hung glass roof. One can look up from the ice-skating to see joggers circling the oblong glass dome. The Galleria is now slated for an expansion larger than the original.

These enterprises do not require outdoor settings; they are magnets that can be placed anywhere. In fact, one seeks orientation by the freeways and their man-made landmarks (Southwest Freeway and Sharpstown, West Loop and Post Oak Tower) rather than by reference to organic patterns of growth. Climate, endless open topography, speculator economics and spectator consumerism, and, of course, the car have determined Houston's free-wheeling, vacuum-packed life and environment.

For spectator sports, one goes to the Astrodome to the southwest, which has created its own environment — the Astrodomain [sic] of assiduously cultivated amusements and motels. Popular and commercial culture are well served in Houston. There is also high, or middle, culture, for which the "brutalist" forms of the Alley Theater by New York architect Ulrich Franzen, and the neutral packaging of Jones Hall for the performing arts, by the Houston firm of Caudill, Rowlett, Scott, have been created. They stand in the shadow of the downtown oil industry giants that have provided their funding.

Farther south on Main are the Fine Arts Museum, with its handsome extension by Mies van der Rohe, and the Contemporary Arts Association building, a sharp-edged, metal trapezoid by Gunnar Birkets. They cling together among odd vacant lots in a state of decaying or becoming, next to a psychoanalytic center.

Because the city has no zoning, these surreal juxtapositions prevail. A hamburger stand closes the formal vista of Philip Johnson's delicate, Miesian arcade at St. Thomas University. Transitional areas, such as Westheimer, not only mirror the city's untrammeled development in ten-year sections, but are freely altered as old houses are turned into new shops and restaurants, unhampered by zoning taboos. (Conventionally zoned cities simply rezone their deteriorating older residential neighborhoods to save their tax base and facilitate the same economic destiny. The process just takes a little longer.)

Houston's web of freeways is the consummate example of the twentieth-century phenomenon known as the commercial strip. The route of passage attracts sales, services, and schlock in continuous road-oriented structures — gas stations, drive-ins, and displays meant to catch the eye and fancy at 60 miles an hour. There are fixed and mobile signs, and signs larger than buildings ("buildingboards," according to students of the Pop environment). Style, extracted as symbols, becomes a kind of sign in itself, evoking images from Rapunzel to Monticello. There are miles of fluttering metallic pennants (used cars), a giant lobster with six shooters, cowboy hat, and scarf (seafood), a turning, life-size plaster bull (American International Charolais Association), and a revolving neon piano. The strip is full of intuitive wit, invention, and crass, but also real creativity — a breathtaking affront to normal sensibility that is never a bore.

Directly behind the freeways, one short turn takes the driver from the strip into pine- and live oak-alleyed streets of comfortable and elegant residential communities (including the elite and affluent River Oaks). They have maintained their environmental purity by deed restrictions passed on from one generation of buyers to another.

Beyond these enclaves, anything goes. Residential development is a spin-the-wheel happening that hops, skips, and jumps outward, each project seemingly dropped from the sky — but always on the freeway. The southwest section, which was prairie before the 1950s, is now the American Dream incarnate. There is a continuing rivalry of you-name-it styles that favor French and Anglo-Saxon labels and details. If you live in Westminster, authentic-looking London street signs on high iron fences frame views of the flat Texas plains. You know you're home when you get to La Cour du Roi or Robin Hood Dell.

Because Houston is an urban invention, this kind of highly salable make-believe supplies instant history and architecture; it is an anchor to time and place where neither is defined. All of those values that accrue throughout centuries of civilization — identity, intimacy, scale, complexity, style — are simply created out of whole cloth, or whole prairie, with unabashed commercial eclecticism. How else to establish a sense of place or community, to indicate differences where none exist?

Houston is a continuous series of such cultural shocks. Its private patronage, on which the city depends for its public actions, has a cosmic range. There is the superb, *echt*-Houston eccentricity of Judge Roy Hofheinz's personal quarters in the Astrodome, done in a kind of Astrobaroque of throne chairs, gold phones, and temple dogs, with a pick-a-religion, fake stone chapel (good for bullfighters or politicians who want to meditate), shooting gallery, and presidential suite, tucked into the periphery of the stadium, complete with views of the Astros and Oilers. At the other end of the esthetic scale there is the Rothko Chapel, where the blood-dark paintings of the artist's pre-suicide days have been brought together by Dominique de Menil — a place of overwhelming, icy death. One welcomes the Texas sunshine.

Houston is not totally without planned features. It has large and handsome parks and the landscaped corridor of the Buffalo Bayou that are the result of philanthropic forethought. There are universities and a vast medical center.

But no one seems to feel the need for the public vision that older cities have of a hierarchy of places and buildings, an organized concept of function and form. Houston has a downtown singularly without amenities. The fact that money and population are flowing there from the rest of the country is considered cause for celebration, not for concern with the city's quality. This city bets on a different and brutal kind of distinction — of power, motion, and sheer energy. Its values are material fulfillment, mobility, and mass entertainment. Its returns are measured on its commercial investments. These contemporary ideals have little to do with the deeper or subtler aspects of the mind or spirit, or even with the more complex, human pleasure potential of a hedonistic culture.

When we build a new city, such as Houston, it is quite natural that we build in this image, using all of our hardware to serve its uses and desires. We create new values and new dimensions in time and space. The expanded, mobile city deals in distance and discontinuity; it "explodes" community. It substitutes fantasy for history. Houston is devoted to moon shots, not moon-viewing. The result is a significant, instructive, and disquieting city form.

What Houston possesses to an exceptional degree is an extraordinary, unlimited vitality. One wishes that it had a larger conceptual reach, that social and cultural and human patterns were as well understood as dollar dynamism. But this kind of vitality is the distinguishing mark of a great city in any age. And Houston today is the American present and future. It is an exciting and disturbing place.

Questions for Discussion

1. How do the size and sprawl of Houston influence the way Huxtable describes it? How does she give a sense of order and development to her impressions?

2. Huxtable's style combines jazzy, informal images ("residential development is a spin-the-wheel-happening . . .") with scholarly phrases and knowledgeable references to high art and culture. How effective is the combination? What do you or don't you like about it?

3. Huxtable's thesis comes at the end of her first paragraph, when she says, "Houston is *the* city of the second half of the twentieth century." How effectively does she support this thesis?

4. In speaking of one section of Houston, Huxtable says, "You know you're home when you get to La Cour du Roi or Robin Hood Dell." What irony is there in this statement? How does it relate to Huxtable's view of Houston as "nowhere city"?

5. At the end of her essay, Huxtable says that Houston is "an exciting and disturbing place." In her view, what makes it exciting? What makes it disturbing?

6. On the basis of Huxtable's description, would you like to live in Houston? Why or why not?

Suggested Activities

1. Huxtable says that Houston is "an act of real estate, rather than an act of God or man." Compare your home town with those of several of your friends. Which of these categories do the different towns fall into? Why?

2. Write an essay analyzing a distinctive geographical feature of your home town and showing how the feature helped to give the town its special character.

3. Write a descriptive essay in which you record observations you make as you move about. Some possible topics: a walk through a supermarket, art gallery, or museum; a drive from home to school; a ride on the subway.

On the Ball

ROGER ANGELL

Roger Angell (b. 1920), a native of New York City and a graduate of Harvard, has been a sportswriter and editor for *The New
Yorker* since 1956. His writings include a book of short stories
(*The Stone Arbor,* 1960), a collection of humorous essays (*A
Day in the Life of Roger Angell,* 1969), and two books of essays
about baseball (*The Summer Game,* 1972; *Five Seasons,* 1977).
"On the Ball," which is taken from *Five Seasons,* is an
extended description of a baseball. Seasoned fans are sure to
find Angell's description fresh and invigorating, and even casual
observers of baseball will be pleasantly surprised to discover
how much life he imparts to this inanimate object.

It weighs just over five ounces and measures between 2.86 and 2.94 inches in
diameter. It is made of a composition-cork nucleus encased in two thin layers of
rubber, one black and one red, surrounded by 121 yards of tightly wrapped blue-
gray wool yarn, 45 yards of white wool yarn, 53 more yards of blue-gray wool
yarn, 150 yards of fine cotton yarn, a coat of rubber cement, and a cowhide (formerly horsehide) exterior, which is held together with 216 slightly raised red
cotton stitches. Printed certifications, endorsements, and outdoor advertising
spherically attest to its authenticity. Like most institutions, it is considered inferior in its present form to its ancient archetypes, and in this case the complaint
is probably justified; on occasion in recent years it has actually been known to
come apart under the demands of its brief but rigorous active career. Baseballs are

ON THE BALL   From *Five Seasons,* copyright © 1972, 1973, 1974, 1975, 1976, 1977 by Roger Angell.
Reprinted by permission of Simon & Schuster, a Division of Gulf & Western Corporation.

assembled and handstitched in Taiwan (before this year the work was done in Haiti, and before 1973 in Chicopee, Massachusetts), and contemporary pitchers claim that there is a tangible variation in the size and feel of the balls that now come into play in a single game; a true peewee is treasured by hurlers, and its departure from the premises, by fair means or foul, is secretly mourned. But never mind: any baseball is beautiful. No other small package comes as close to the ideal in design and utility. It is a perfect object for a man's hand. Pick it up and it instantly suggests its purpose; it is meant to be thrown a considerable distance — thrown hard and with precision. Its feel and heft are the beginning of the sport's critical dimensions; if it were a fraction of an inch larger or smaller, a few centigrams heavier or lighter, the game of baseball would be utterly different. Hold a baseball in your hand. As it happens, this one is not brand-new. Here, just to one side of the curved surgical welt of stitches, there is a pale-green grass smudge darkening on one edge almost to black — the mark of an old infield play, a tough grounder now lost in memory. Feel the ball, turn it over in your hand; hold it across the seam or the other way, with the seam just to the side of your middle finger. Speculation stirs. You want to get outdoors and throw this spare and sensual object to somebody or, at the very least, watch somebody else throw it. The game has begun.

Thinking about the ball and its attributes seems to refresh our appreciation of this game. A couple of years ago, I began to wonder why it was that pitchers, taken as a group, seemed to be so much livelier and more garrulous than hitters. I considered the possibility of some obscure physiological linkage (the discobologlottal syndrome) and the more obvious occupational discrepancies (pitchers have a lot more spare time than other players), but then it came to me that a pitcher is the only man in baseball who can properly look on the ball as being his instrument, his accomplice. He is the only player who is granted the privilege of making offensive plans, and once the game begins he is (in concert with his catcher) the only man on the field who knows what is meant to happen next. Everything in baseball begins with the pitch, and every other part of the game — hitting, fielding, and throwing — is reflexive and defensive. (The hitters on a ball team are referred to as the "offense," but almost three quarters of the time this is an absolute misnomer.) The batter tapping the dirt off his spikes and now stepping into the box looks sour and glum, and who can blame him, for the ball has somehow been granted in perpetuity to the wrong people. It is already an object of suspicion and hatred, and the reflex that allows him occasionally to deflect that tiny onrushing dot with his bat, and sometimes even to relaunch it violently in the opposite direction, is such a miraculous response of eye and body as to remain virtually inexplicable, even to him. There are a few dugout flannelmouths (Ted Williams, Harry Walker, Pete Rose) who can talk convincingly about the art of hitting, but, like most arts, it does not in the end seem communicable. Pitching is different. It is a craft ("the crafty portsider . . .") and is thus within reach.

The smiling pitcher begins not only with the advantage of holding his fate in his own hands, or hand, but with the knowledge that every advantage of physics and psychology seems to be on his side. A great number of surprising and unpleasant things can be done to the ball as it is delivered from the grasp of a two-hundred-pound optimist, and the first of these is simply to transform it into a projectile. Most pitchers seem hesitant to say so, but if you press them a little they will admit that the prime ingredient in their intense personal struggle with the batter is probably fear. A few pitchers in the majors have thrived without a real fastball — junk men like Eddie Lopat and Mike Cuellar, superior control artists like Bobby Shantz and Randy Jones, knuckleballers like Hoyt Wilhelm and Charlie Hough — but almost everyone else has had to hump up and throw at least an occasional no-nonsense hard one, which crosses the plate at eighty-five miles per hour, or better, and thus causes the hitter to — well, to *think* a little. The fastball sets up all the other pitches in the hurler's repertoire — the curve, the slider, the sinker, and so on — but its other purpose is to intimidate. Great fastballers like Bob Gibson, Jim Bunning, Sandy Koufax, and Nolan Ryan have always run up high strikeout figures because their money pitch was almost untouchable, but their deeper measures of success — twenty-victory seasons and low earned-run averages — were due to the fact that none of the hitters they faced, not even the best of them, was immune to the thought of what a 90-mph missile could do to a man if it struck him. They had been ever so slightly distracted, and distraction is bad for hitting. The intention of the pitcher has almost nothing to do with this; very few pitches are delivered with intent to maim. The bad dream, however, will not go away. Walter Johnson, the greatest fireballer of them all, had almost absolute control, but he is said to have worried constantly about what might happen if one of his pitches got away from him. Good hitters know all this and resolutely don't think about it (a good hitter is a man who can keep his back foot firmly planted in the box even while the rest of him is pulling back or bailing out on an inside fastball), but even these icy customers are less settled in their minds than they would like to be, just because the man out there on the mound is hiding that cannon behind his hip. Hitters, of course, do not call this fear. The word is "respect."

It should not be inferred, of course, that major-league pitchers are wholly averse to hitting batters, or *almost* hitting batters. A fastball up around the Adam's apple not only is a first-class distracter, as noted, but also discourages a hitter from habitually leaning forward in order to put more of his bat on a dipping curve or a slider over the outer rim of the plate. The truth of the matter is that pitchers and batters are engaged in a permanent private duel over their property rights to the plate, and a tough, proud hurler who senses that the man now in the batter's box has recently had the better of things will often respond in the most direct manner possible, with a hummer to the ribs. Allie Reynolds, Sal Maglie, Don Drysdale, Early Wynn, and Bob Gibson were cold-eyed lawmen of this stripe, and the practice has by no means vanished, in spite of strictures and deplorings from the high chambers of baseball. Early this year, Lynn McGlothen, of the Cards, routinely plunked the Mets' Del Unser, who had lately been feasting on his pitches, and then violated the ancient protocol in these matters by admitting intent. Dock Ellis, now a Yankee but then a Pirate, decided early in the 1974 season that the Cincinnati Reds had somehow established dominance over his club, and he determined to set things right in his own way. (This incident is described at length in a lively new baseball book, *Dock Ellis in the Country of Baseball*, by Donald Hall.) The first Cincinnati batter of the game was Pete Rose, and the first pitch from Ellis was at his head—"not actually to *hit* him," Ellis said later, but as a "*message* to let him know that he was going to be hit." He then hit Rose in the side. The next pitch hit the next Red batter, Joe Morgan, in the kidney. The third batter was Dan Driessen, who took Ellis's second pitch in the back. With the bases loaded, Dock now threw four pitches at Tony Perez (one behind his back), but missed with all of them, walking in a run. He then missed Johnny Bench (and the plate) twice, whereupon Pirate manager Danny Murtaugh came out to the mound, stared at Ellis with silent surmise, and beckoned for a new pitcher.

Hitters can accept this sort of fugue, even if they don't exactly enjoy it, but what they do admittedly detest is a young and scatter-armed smoke-thrower, the true wild man. One famous aborigine was Steve Dalkowski, an Oriole farmhand of the late nineteen fifties and early sixties who set records for strikeouts and jumpy batters wherever he played. In one typical stay with a Class D league, he threw 121 strikeouts and gave up 129 walks and 39 wild pitches, all in the span of 62 innings. Dalkowski never made it to the majors, but, being a legend, he is secure for the ages. "Once I saw him work a game in the Appalachian League," a gravel-voiced retired coach said to me not long ago, "and nothing was hit *forward* for seven innings—not even a foul ball." An attempt was once made to clock Dalkowski on a recording device, but his eventual mark of 93.5 mph was discounted, since he threw for forty minutes before steering a pitch into the machine's recording zone.

Better-known names in these annals of anxiety are Rex Barney, a briefly flaring Brooklyn nova of the nineteen forties, who once threw a no-hit game but eventually walked and wild-pitched his way out of baseball; Ryne Duren, the extremely fast and extremely nearsighted reliever for the Yankees and other American League clubs in the fifties and sixties, whose traditional initial warm-up pitch on his being summoned to the mound was a twelve-foot-high fastball to the foul screen; and a pair of rookies named Sandy Koufax and Bob Feller. Koufax, to be sure, eventually became a superb control artist, but it took him seven years before he got his great stuff entirely together, and there were times when it seemed certain that he would be known only as another Rex Barney. Sandy recalls that when he first brought his boyish assortment of fiery sailers and bouncing rockets to spring-training camp he had difficulty getting in any mound work, because whenever he picked up his glove all the available catchers would suddenly remember pressing appointments in some distant part of the compound. Feller had almost a career-long struggle with *his* control, and four times managed to lead his league simultaneously in walks and in strikeouts. His first appearance against another major-league club came in an exhibition game against the Cardinals in the summer of 1936, when he was seventeen years old; he entered the game in the fourth inning, and eventually struck out eight batters in three innings, but when his searing fastball missed the plate it had the batters jumping around in the box like roasting popcorn. Frank Frisch, the St. Louis player-manager, carefully observed Feller's first three or four deliveries and then walked down to the end of the dugout, picked up a pencil, and removed himself from the Cardinal lineup.

The chronically depressed outlook of major-league batters was pushed to the edge of paranoia in the nineteen fifties by the sudden and utterly unexpected arrival of the slider, or the Pitcher's Friend. The slider is an easy pitch to throw and a hard one to hit. It is delivered with the same motion as the fastball, but with the pitcher's wrist rotated approximately ninety degrees (to the right for a right-hander, to the left for a southpaw), which has the effect of placing the delivering forefinger and middle finger slightly off center on the ball. The positions of hand, wrist, and arm are almost identical with those that produce a good spiral forward pass with a football. The result is an apparent three-quarter-speed fastball that suddenly changes its mind and direction. It doesn't break much — in its early days it was slightingly known as the "nickel curve" — but a couple of inches of lateral movement at the plateward end of the ball's brief sixty-foot-six-inch journey can make for an epidemic of pop-ups, foul balls, and harmless grounders. "Epidemic" is not an exaggeration. The slider was the prime agent responsible for the sickening and decline of major-league batting averages in the two decades after the Second World War, which culminated in a combined average of .237 for the two leagues in 1968. A subsequent crash program of immunization and prevention by the authorities produced from the laboratory a smaller strike zone and a lowering of the pitcher's mound by five inches, but the hitters, while saved from extermination, have never regained their state of rosy-cheeked, pre-slider good health.

For me, the true mystery of the slider is not its flight path but the circumstances of its discovery. Professional baseball got under way in the eighteen-seventies, and during all the ensuing summers uncounted thousands of young would-be Mathewsons and Seavers spent their afternoons flinging the ball in every conceivable fashion as they searched for magic fadeaways and flutter balls that would take them to Cooperstown. Why did eighty years pass before anybody noticed that a slight cocking of the wrist would be sufficient to usher in the pitchers' Golden Age? Where were Tom Swift and Frank Merriwell? What happened to American Know-How? This is almost a national disgrace. The mystery is deepened by the fact that — to my knowledge, at least — no particular pitcher or pitching coach is given credit for the discovery and propagation of the slider. Bob Lemon, who may be the first man to have pitched his way into the Hall of Fame with a slider, says he learned the pitch from Mel Harder, who was an elder mound statesman with the Indians when Lemon came up to that club, in 1946. I have also heard some old-timers say that George Blaeholder was throwing a pretty fair slider for the St. Louis Browns way back in the nineteen-twenties. But none of these worthies ever claimed to be the Johnny Appleseed of the pitch. The thing seemed to generate itself — a weed in the bullpen which overran the field.

The slider has made baseball more difficult for the fan as well as for the batter. Since its action is late and minimal, and since its delivery does not require the easily recognizable arm-snap by the pitcher that heralds the true curve, the slider can be spotted only by an attentive spectator seated very close to home plate. A curve thrown by famous old pretzel-benders like Tommy Bridges and Sal Maglie really used to *curve;* you could see the thing break even if you were way out in the top deck of Section 31. Most fans, however, do not admit the loss. The contemporary bleacher critic, having watched a doll-size distant slugger swing mightily and tap the ball down to second on four bounces, smiles and enters the out in his scorecard. "Slider," he announces, and everybody nods wisely in agreement.

The mystery of the knuckleball is ancient and honored. Its practitioners cheerfully admit that they do not understand why the pitch behaves the way it does; nor do they know, or care much, which particular lepidopteran path it will follow on its way past the batter's infuriated swipe. They merely prop the ball on their fingertips (not, in actual fact, on the knuckles) and launch it more or less in the fashion of a paper airplane, and then, most of the time, finish the delivery with a faceward motion of the glove, thus hiding a grin. Now science has confirmed the phenomenon. Writing in *The American Journal of Physics,* Eric Sawyer and Robert G. Watts, of Tulane University, recently reported that wind-tunnel tests showed that a slowly spinning baseball is subject to forces capable of making it swerve a foot or more between the pitcher's mound and the plate. The secret, they say, appears to be the raised seams of the ball, which cause a "roughness pattern" and an uneven flow of air, resulting in a "nonsymmetric lateral force distribution and . . . a net force in one direction or another."

Like many other backyard baseball stars, I have taught myself to throw a knuckleball that moves with so little rotation that one can almost pick out the signature of Charles S. Feeney in midair; the pitch, however, has shown disappointingly few symptoms of last-minute fluttering and has so far proved to be wonderfully catchable or hittable, mostly by my wife. Now, at last, I understand the problem. In their researches, Sawyer and Watts learned that an entirely spinless knuckler is *not* subject to varying forces, and thus does not dive or veer. The ideal knuckler, they say, completes about a quarter of a revolution on its way to the plate. The speed of the pitch, moreover, is not critical, because "the magnitude of the lateral force increases approximately as the square of the velocity," which means that the total lateral movement is "independent of the speed of the pitch."

All this has been perfectly understood (if less politely defined) by any catcher who has been the battery mate of a star knuckleballer, and has thus spent six or seven innings groveling in the dirt in imitation of a bulldog cornering a nest of field mice. Modern catchers have the assistance of outsized gloves (which lately have begun to approach the diameter of tea trays), and so enjoy a considerable advantage over some of their ancient predecessors in capturing the knuckler. In the middle nineteen-forties, the receivers for the Washington Senators had to deal with a pitching staff that included *four* knuckleball specialists—Dutch Leonard, Johnny Niggeling, Mickey Haefner, and Roger Wolff. Among the ill-equipped Washington catchers who tried to fend off almost daily midafternoon clouds of deranged butterflies were Rick Ferrell and Jake Early. Early eventually was called up to serve in the armed forces—perhaps the most willing inductee of his day.

The spitball was once again officially outlawed from baseball in 1974, and maybe this time the prohibition will work. This was the third, and by far the most severe, edict directed at the unsanitary and extremely effective delivery, for it permits an umpire to call an instantaneous ball on any pitch that even looks like a spitter as it crosses the plate. No evidence is required; no appeal by the pitcher to higher powers is permissible. A subsequent spitball or imitation thereof results in the expulsion of the pitcher from the premises, *instanter*, and an ensuing fine. Harsh measures indeed, but surely sufficient, we may suppose, to keep this repellent and unfair practice out of baseball's shining mansion forever. Surely, and yet . . . Professional pitchers have an abiding fondness for any downbreaking delivery, legal or illegal, that will get the job done, and nothing, they tell me, does the job more effectively or more entertainingly than a dollop of saliva or slippery-elm juice, or a little bitty dab of lubricating jelly, applied to the pitching fingers. The ball, which is sent off half wet and half dry, like a dilatory schoolboy, hurries innocently toward the gate and its grim-faced guardians, and at the last second darts under the turnstile. Pitchers, moreover, have before them the inspiring recent example of Gaylord Perry, whose rumored but unverified Faginesque machinations with K-Y Jelly won him a Cy Young Award in 1972 and led inevitably to the demand for harsher methods of law enforcement. Rumor has similarly indicted other highly successful performers, like Don Drysdale, Whitey Ford, and Bill Singer. Preacher Roe, upon retiring from the Dodgers, in 1954, after an extended useful tenure on the mound at Ebbets Field, published a splendidly unrepentant confession, in which he gave away a number of trade secrets. His favorite undryer, as I recall, was a full pack of Juicy Fruit gum, and he loaded up by straightening the bill of his cap between pitches and passing his fingers momentarily in front of his face—now also illegal, alas.

It may be perceived that my sympathies, which lately seemed to lie so rightly on the side of the poor overmatched hitters, have unaccountably swung the other way. I admit this indefensible lapse simply because I find the spitter so enjoyable for its deviousness and skulking disrespect. I don't suppose we should again make it a fully legal pitch (it was first placed outside the pale in 1920), but I would enjoy a return to the era when the spitter was treated simply as a misdemeanor and we could all laugh ourselves silly at the sight of a large, outraged umpire suddenly calling in a suspected wetback for inspection (and the pitcher, of course, *rolling* the ball to him across the grass) and then glaring impotently out at the innocent ("Who—*me?*") perpetrator on the mound. Baseball is a hard, rules-dominated game, and it should have more room in it for a little cheerful cheating.

All these speculations, and we have not yet taken the ball out of the hands of its first friend, the pitcher. And yet there is always something more. We might suddenly realize, for instance, that baseball is the only team sport in which the scoring is not done with the ball. In hockey, football, soccer, basketball, lacrosse, and the rest of them, the ball or its equivalent actually scores or is responsible for the points that determine the winner. In baseball, the score is made by the base runner — by the man down there, just crossing the plate — while the ball, in most cases, is a long way off, doing something quite different. It's a strange business, this unique double life going on in front of us, and it tells us a lot about this unique game. A few years ago, there was a suddenly popular thesis put forward in some sports columns and light-heavyweight editorial pages which proposed that the immense recent popularity of professional football could be explained by the fact that the computerlike complexity of its plays, the clotted and anonymous masses of its players, and the intense violence of its action constituted a perfect Sunday parable of contemporary urban society. It is a pretty argument, and perhaps even true, especially since it is hard not to notice that so many professional football games, in spite of their noise and chaos, are deadeningly repetitious, predictable, and banal. I prefer the emotions and suggestions to be found in the other sport. I don't think anyone can watch many baseball games without becoming aware of the fact that the ball, for all its immense energy and unpredictability, very rarely escapes the control of the players. It is released again and again — pitched and caught, struck along the ground or sent high in the air — but almost always, almost instantly, it is recaptured and returned to control and safety and harmlessness. Nothing is altered, nothing has been allowed to happen. This orderliness and constraint are among the prime attractions of the sport; a handful of men, we discover, can police a great green country, forestalling unimaginable disasters. A slovenly, error-filled game can sometimes be exciting, but it never seems serious, and is thus never truly satisfying, for the metaphor of safety — of danger subdued by skill and courage — has been lost. Too much civilization, however, is deadly — in this game, a deadly bore. A deeper need is stifled. The ball looks impetuous and dangerous, but we perceive that in fact it lives in a slow, guarded world of order, vigilance, and rules. Nothing can ever happen here. And then once again the ball is pitched — sent on its quick, planned errand. The bat flashes, there is a new, louder sound, and suddenly we see the ball streaking wild through the air and then bounding along distant and untouched in the sweet green grass. We leap up, thousands of us, and shout for its joyful flight — free, set free, free at last.

Questions for Discussion

1. Angell waits until the fifth sentence of his opening paragraph before providing a reference for the pronoun with which the paragraph begins. Why do you suppose he does this? How effective do you find his strategy to be?

2. When we say an essay has mixed diction, we mean that it contains both formal and informal language. What examples of mixed diction can you find in this essay? How effective is Angell's use of it?

3. Angell compares a spitball to a "dilatory schoolboy." What other unusual comparisons does he use? What is your response to them?

4. If Angell's purpose were merely to help us visualize a baseball as a static object, he would have needed to write only the first half of his first paragraph. What more complex purpose does he have? How successful is he in accomplishing it?

5. Angell argues that fear plays a prominent role in baseball. Do you agree? Why or why not? In general, how important does fear seem to be in sports?

6. In his last paragraph, Angell mentions the theory that pro football is a "parable of contemporary urban society." What is his attitude toward this theory? What does he himself see baseball as being a parable for?

7. What is the significance of Angell's final image of the ball in flight? How is this image connected to the pleasure he finds in the game?

Suggested Activities

1. Compare your attitude toward baseball with Angell's and with those of several of your friends. How do you account for the differences you find?

2. Write an essay describing a "tool of the trade" for a trade you happen to know well.

3. Write two paragraphs, first describing something at rest and then describing it in motion. Some possibilities: a dancer, a jukebox, a merry-go-round, a fly-casting rod.

narration

When most people think of narration, they think of fiction—short stories or nov-els. But narration can be used effectively in nonfiction prose as well. Writers of all different sorts of expository essays use it frequently, for there's no more effective way of introducing a topic or illustrating a point than by telling a vivid story. For example, Harvey Cox begins his classification essay "Eastern Cults and Western Culture" (Chapter 5) with an engaging account of an encounter between a Zen Buddhist wise man and a pilgrim. Joan Didion concludes her process analysis of the Operations Center of the Los Angeles office of the Cali-fornia Department of Transportation (Chapter 7) with an equally engaging anec-dote. And in Chapter 8, both Berton Roueché and George Orwell use extended narratives as frameworks for their cause-and-effect analyses.

As the selections in this chapter show, narration can be used not only as an illustration or introduction but as a rhetorical mode in its own right. When it is, the writer's purpose is almost always to persuade. In contrast to fictional narratives, where the story exists for its own sake, nonfiction narratives usually exist to illustrate some larger point. Writers of such narratives accomplish their purpose by *reflecting* on the events they present and by *interpreting* the events' significance. For them, then—and for you when you write nonfiction narra-tives—merely telling the story well is not enough. Writers of nonfiction narra-tives do of course need to tell their stories as well as they can, but they must also find ways to give them a persuasive edge. With this need in mind, here are four suggestions you may find useful when writing narrative essays.

1. Be selective.   We've all heard (and been bored by) storytellers who ramble on, taking seemingly forever to get to their point. People often do this because they feel compelled by a desire for accuracy to include everything that hap-pened, regardless of its interest or relevance. But if you're not to bore your audience, you need to *shape* your narrative, and you do this by selecting details that are relevant to your overall interpretative purpose. You therefore need to know exactly what point you want to make before you begin to write. Knowing this, you can test each event and detail of the story by asking whether it con-tributes to your point. If it doesn't, omit it. Remember too that your aim is not to re-create reality (an impossible task) but to make your story *seem* real. By creating this appearance of reality you will be able to conduct your readers to the conclusion you wish them to reach.

2. Be vivid.   For a narrative to be an effective means of persuasion, it must engage the imagination of the reader. Simply saying that something happened won't do this; showing that it did in as vivid a way as possible will. For example, look at how Frank Conroy uses vivid details in "Savages" (reprinted in this chap-ter). He wishes to convince us that weak leadership at his boarding school led to uncontrolled behavior on the part of the students. So he shows us the boys being wild and brutal. Having decided to punish a student named Ligget, forty boys "lined up for one punch each":

> It was my turn. Ligget looked at me blankly. I picked a spot on his chin, drew back my arm, and threw as hard a punch as I could muster. Instant disappointment. I hadn't missed, there was a kind of snapping sound as my fist landed, and his head jerked back, but the whole complex of movements was too fast, somehow missing the exaggerated movie-punch finality I had anticipated. Ligget looked at the boy behind me and I stepped away.

Note how Conroy's careful choice of details makes the passage come alive: Ligget's blank look, the punch, the snapping sound, Ligget's look at the next boy in the line of forty. Note too how these details help to create an interpreta-tion of the event. In their dispassionate exactness, they stand in sharp contrast to Conroy's disappointment over having failed to achieve "movie-punch final-ity," and thus suggest how little the boys really understood the consequences of their actions.

3. Choose a point of view and stick with it.   One decision you always need to make when writing a narrative is whether to speak in the first person ("I") or in the third person ("he" or "she"). If you write in the third person, you also need to decide whether to limit your perspective to what you can see (third-person limited point of view) or to give yourself the power to look inside the minds of the people you're writing about (third-person omniscient point of view).

Which one of these possibilities you should use depends on the point you're trying to make and the effect you want to have on your audience. In the case of "Savages," for example, Conroy's decision to write in the first person is of crucial importance. If he had chosen to write in the third person, he would have created a distance between himself and the events he narrates and would thereby have made it possible for us to dismiss the savagery of the children as merely a freakish aberration. But by including himself in the action, he creates a more complex and troubling narrative, for if someone as sane and intelligent as he appears to be could participate in a senseless beating, then perhaps the potential for savagery is present in all of us.

In any case, once you decide on a point of view, be sure you stick with it. Your readers will quickly lose faith in you as a narrator if you pointlessly shift from the first to the third person or from a limited to an omniscient perspective. Be aware too of the need to distinguish between your narrator's point of view and that of the people you are writing about. A place where this distinction is especially important is in narratives about childhood. If you plan to write such a narrative, ask yourself whether you want to tell the story from the point of view of a child or from that of an adult reminiscing about childhood (Conroy's choice in "Savages"). Once you make your decision, be consistent throughout your essay.

4. Vary your pace.   When children write or tell stories, they give equal weight to each event by using an "and then . . . and then. . . ." narrative pattern. Mature writers, by contrast, realize that they must vary the pace of their narratives if they are to hold the interest of their readers. They do this by presenting some events in full detail, by summarizing others, and by alternating between paragraphs of direct reportage and paragraphs of reflection and interpretation.

The final paragraphs of John McPhee's "Pinball Philosophy" (reprinted in this chapter) show us a writer in full command of the pace of his narrative. McPhee is reporting a five-game pinball match between J. Anthony Lukas and Tom Buckley, yet he is highly selective in the details he chooses to present. He summarizes the first game in a single sentence: "Lukas—forty-eight thousand eight hundred and seventy—wins the first game." Only the fifth game, the tie-breaker, receives close attention, and even here McPhee chooses to describe only a part of the action:

> Game 5 under way. They are pummelling the machine. They are heavy on the corners but light on the flippers, and the scoreboard is reacting like a storm at sea. With three balls down, both are in the thirty-thousand range. Buckley, going unorthodox, plays his fourth ball with one foot off the floor, and raises his score to forty-five thousand points—more than he scored in winning the two previous games. He smiles. He is on his way in, flaring, with

still another ball to play. Now Lukas snaps his fourth ball into the ellipse. It moves down and around the board, hitting slingshots and flippers and rising again and again to high ground to begin additional scoring runs. It hits sunburst caps and hole kickers, swinging targets and bonus gates. Minute upon minute, it stays in play. It will not die.

Compared with some of the other narratives in this chapter—Kingston's and Conroy's painful childhood memories, or Mailer's account of man's first flight to the moon—McPhee's essay deals with a trivial subject. Yet by his skillful command of pace, he lends interest and excitement to his account of the contest. Notice how he sets the stage for his detailed account of the significant fourth ball of each player by first summarizing the way each person plays and then quickly reviewing the situation after the third ball. By lavishing such skill on his subject, McPhee reminds us of how much we appreciate *all* manifestations of human skill—even one as seemingly insignificant as a well-played game of pinball.

The Launch
of Apollo 11

NORMAN MAILER

Norman Mailer (b. 1923) is a prolific and controversial writer. His works include *The Naked and the Dead* (1948), *Advertisements for Myself* (1959), *The Armies of the Night* (1968), and, most recently, *The Executioner's Song* (1979), an account of the life and death of Gary Gilmore, the convicted Utah murderer who demanded his own execution. In the following selection from *Of a Fire on the Moon* (1970), Mailer adopts a third-person point of view to recount the final, tense moments of the launching of the Apollo rocket that landed the first men on the moon. By juxtaposing objective reportage with impressionistic images, Mailer transforms the liftoff into an event of metaphysical importance.

He had his binoculars to his eyes. A tiny part of him was like a penitent who had prayed in the wilderness for sixteen days and was now expecting a sign. Would the sign reveal much or little?

. . . all is still GO as we monitor our status for it. Two minutes 10 seconds and counting. The target for the Apollo 11 astronauts, the moon. At lift-off we'll be at a distance of 218,096 miles away. Just passed the two-minute mark in the countdown. T minus 1 minute 54 seconds and counting. Our status board indicates that the oxidizer tanks in the second and third stages now have pressurized. We continue to build up pressure in all three stages here at the last minute to prepare for lift-off. T minus 1 minute 35 seconds on the Apollo mission, the flight that will land the first man on the moon. All indications coming in to the Control Center at this time indicate we are GO. One minute 25 seconds and counting. Our status board indicates the third stage completely pressurized. Eighty-second mark has now been passed. We'll go on full internal power at the fifty-second mark in the countdown. Guidance system goes on internal at 17 seconds leading up to the ignition sequence at 8.9 seconds. We're approaching the sixty-second mark on the Apollo 11 mission. T minus 60 seconds and counting. We have passed T minus 60. Fifty-five seconds and counting. Neil Armstrong just reported back, "It's been a real smooth countdown." We have passed the fifty-second mark. Forty seconds away from the Apollo 11 lift-off. All the second-stage tanks now pressurized. Thirty-five seconds and counting. We are still GO with Apollo 11. Thirty seconds and counting. Astronauts reported, "Feels good." T minus 25 seconds. Twenty seconds and counting. T minus 15 seconds, guidance is internal, 12, 11, 10, 9, ignition sequence start, 6, 5, 4, 3, 2, 1, zero, all engines running, LIFT-OFF. We have a lift-off, 32 minutes past the hour. Lift-off on Apollo 11.

But nobody watching the launch from the Press Site ever listened to the last few words. For at 8.9 seconds before lift-off, the motors of Apollo-Saturn leaped into ignition, and two horns of orange fire burst like genies from the base of the rocket. Aquarius never had to worry again about whether the experience would be appropriate to his measure. Because of the distance, no one at the Press Site was to hear the sound of the motors until fifteen seconds after they had started. Although the rocket was restrained on its pad for nine seconds in order for the motors to multiply up to full thrust, the result was still that the rocket began to rise a full six seconds before its motors could be heard. Therefore the lift-off itself seemed to partake more of a miracle than a mechanical phenomenon, as if all of huge Saturn itself had begun silently to levitate, and was then pursued by flames.

No, it was more dramatic than that. For the flames were enormous. No one could be prepared for that. Flames flew in cataract against the cusp of the flame shield, and then sluiced along the paved ground down two opposite channels in the concrete, two underground rivers of flame which poured into the air on either side a hundred feet away, then flew a hundred feet further. Two mighty torches of flame like the wings of a yellow bird of fire flew over a field, covered a field with brilliant yellow bloomings of flame, and in the midst of it, white as a ghost, white as the white of Melville's Moby Dick, white as the shrine of the Madonna in half the churches of the world, this slim angelic mysterious ship of stages rose without sound out of its incarnation of flame and began to ascend slowly into the sky, slow as Melville's Leviathan might swim, slowly as we might swim upward in a dream looking for the air. And still no sound.

Then it came, like a crackling of wood twigs over the ridge, came with the sharp and furious bark of a million drops of oil crackling suddenly into combustion, a cacophony of barks louder and louder as Apollo-Saturn fifteen seconds ahead of its own sound cleared the lift tower to a cheer which could have been a cry of anguish from that near-audience watching, then came the earsplitting bark of a thousand machine guns firing at once, and Aquarius shook through his feet at the fury of this combat assault, and heard the thunderous murmur of Niagaras of flame roaring conceivably louder than the loudest thunders he had ever heard and the earth began to shake and would not stop, it quivered through his feet standing on the wood of the bleachers, an apocalyptic fury of sound equal to some conception of the sound of your death in the roar of a drowning hour, a nightmare of sound, and he heard himself saying, "Oh, my God! oh, my God! oh, my God! oh, my God! oh, my God! oh, my God!" . . . and the sound of the rocket beat with the true blood of fear in his ears, hot in all the intimacy of a forming of heat, as if one's ear were in the caldron of a vast burning of air, heavens of oxygen being born and consumed in this ascension of the rocket, and a poor moment of vertigo at the thought that man now had something with which to speak to God — the fire was white as a torch and long as the rocket itself, a tail of fire, a face, yes now the rocket looked like a thin and pointed witch's hat, and the flames from its base were the blazing eyes of the witch. Forked like saw teeth was the base of the flame which quivered through the lens of the binoculars. Upwards. As the rocket keened over and went up and out to sea, one could no longer watch its stage, only the flame from its base. Now it seemed to rise like a ball of fire, like a new sun mounting the sky, a flame elevating itself.

Many thousands of feet up it went through haze and the fire feathered the haze in a long trailing caress, initmate as the wake which follows the path of a fingerling in inches of water. Trailings of cloud parted like lips. Then a heavier cloud was punched through with sudden cruelty. Then two long spumes of wake, like two large fish following our first fish — one's heart took little falls at the changes. "Ahhh," the crowd went, "Ahhh," as at the most beautiful of fireworks, for the sky was alive, one instant a pond and at the next a womb of new turns: "Ahhh," went the crowd, "Ahhh!"

Now, through the public address system, came the sound of Armstrong talking to Launch Control. He was quieter than anyone else. "Inboard cutoff" he said with calm in his voice.

Far in the distance, almost out of sight, like an all-but-transparent fish suddenly breaking into head and tail, the first stage at the rear of the rocket fell off from the rest, fell off and was now like a man, like a sky diver suddenly small. A new burst of motors started up, some far-off glimpse of newborn fires which looked pale as streams of water, pale were the flames in the far distance. Then the abandoned empty stage of the booster began to fall away, a relay runner, baton just passed, who slips back, slips back. Then it began to tumble, but with the slow tender dignity of a thin slice of soap slicing and wavering, dipping and gliding on its way to the floor of the tub. Then mighty Saturn of the first stage, empty, fuel-voided, burned out, gave a puff, a whiff and was lost to sight behind a cloud. And the rocket with Apollo 11 and the last two stages of Saturn V was finally out of sight and on its way to an orbit about the earth.

Questions for Discussion

1. At the beginning of this selection, Mailer poses a question in religious terms: "Would the sign reveal much or little?" Where else in this selection do you find language with religious overtones? How appropriate is this language to Mailer's subject?

2. What is the answer to the question about the sign? What *does* it reveal?

3. How does Mailer maintain suspense in this narration?

4. What do you suppose was Mailer's purpose in including the quoted factual report from Launch Control?

5. In what ways does Mailer's sentence structure change when he reports the flight of the rocket after the liftoff? How do these changes affect the tone of the final portion of the essay?

6. Mailer chose to write this passage in the third person, referring to himself as Aquarius. Does this technique work for you as a reader? Why or why not?

Suggested Activities

1. In describing his responses to the launching, Mailer makes use of a number of similes. Make a list of the similes in this selection, and assess their effectiveness as narrative and descriptive techniques. Do they seem appropriate?

2. Focusing on a colorful object, write a paragraph using both objective and subjective description.

3. Write an essay in which you make extended use of description in narrating a visually dramatic event. Suggested topics: a fireworks display, a burning building, a severe storm, a flash flood.

Ainmosni

ROGER ANGELL

For biographical information on Roger Angell, see page 31. In
"Ainmosni," which is taken from *A Day in the Life of Roger
Angell* (1969), Angell uses his imagination and his reporter's eye
for details to create a witty account of his battle with insomnia.

Insomnia is my baby. We have been going steady for a good twenty years now,
and there is no hint that the dull baggage is ready to break off the affair. Three
or four times a week, somewhere between three and six in the morning, this
faulty thermostat inside my head clicks to "On," raising my eyelids with an
almost audible clang and releasing a fetid blast of night thoughts. Sighing, I
resume my long study of the bedroom ceiling and the uninteresting shape (a penguin? an overshoe?) that the street light, slanting through the window, casts on
the closet door, while I review various tedious stratagems for recapturing sleep. If
I am resolute, I will arise and robe myself, stumble out of the bedroom (my wife
sleeps like a Series E government bond), turn on the living-room lights, and take
down a volume from my little shelf of classical pharmacopoeia. George Eliot,
James, and Montaigne are Nembutals, slow-acting but surefire. Thoreau, a dangerous Seconal-Demerol bomb, is reserved for emergencies; thirty minutes in the
Walden beanfield sends me back to bed at a half run, fighting unconsciousness
all the way down the hall. Too often, however, I stay in bed, under the delusion
that sleep is only a minute or two away. This used to be the time for Night
Games, which once worked for me. I would invent a No-Star baseball game,
painstakingly selecting two nines made up of the least exciting ballplayers I could

AINMOSNI   From *A Day in the Life of Roger Angell* by Roger Angell. Copyright © 1969 by Roger
Angell. Originally appeared in *The New Yorker*. Reprinted by permission of Viking Penguin Inc.

remember (mostly benchwarmers with the old Phillies and Senators) and playing them against each other in the deserted stadium of my mind. Three or four innings of walks, popups, foul balls, and messed-up double plays, with long pauses for rhubarbs and the introduction of relief pitchers, would bring on catalepsy. Other nights, I would begin a solo round of golf (I am a terrible golfer) on some recalled course. After a couple of pars and a brilliantly holed birdie putt, honesty required me to begin playing my real game, and a long search for my last golf ball, horribly hooked into the cattails to the left of the sixth green, would uncover, instead, a lovely Spalding Drowz-Rite. In time, however, some perverse sporting instinct began to infect me, and my Night Games became hopelessly interesting. As dawn brightened the bedroom, a pinch-hitter would bash a line drive that hit the pitcher's rubber and rebounded crazily into a pail of water in the enemy dugout, scoring three runs and retying the game, 17–17, in the twenty-first inning; my drive off the fourteenth tee, slicing toward a patch of tamaracks, would be seized in midair by an osprey and miraculously dropped on the green, where I would begin lining up my putt just as the alarm went off. I had to close up the ballpark and throw away my clubs; I was bushed.

It was a Scottish friend of mine, a pink-cheeked poet clearly accustomed to knocking off ten hours' sleep every night, who got me into real small-hours trouble. He observed me yawning over a lunchtime Martini one day and drew forth an account of my ridiculous affliction. "I can help you, old boy," he announced. "Try palindromes."

"Palindromes?" I repeated.

"You know — backward-forward writing," he went on. "Reads the same both ways. You remember the famous ones: 'Madam, I'm Adam.' 'Able was I ere I saw Elba.' 'A man, a plan, a canal: Panama.' The Elba one is supposed to be about Napoleon. Here — I'll write it for you. You see, 'Able' backward is 'Elba,' and — "

"I know, I know," I snapped. "But what's that got to do with not sleeping? Am I supposed to repeat them over and over, or what?"

"No, that's no good. You must make up your own. Nothing to it. Begin with two-way words, and soon you'll be up to sentences. I do it whenever I can't sleep — 'sleep' is 'peels,' of course — and in ten minutes I pop right off again. Never fails. Just now, I'm working on a lovely one about Eliot, the poet. 'T. Eliot, top bard . . .' it begins, and it ends, 'drab pot toilet.' Needs a bit of work in the middle, but I'll get it one of these nights."

I was dubious, but that night, shortly after four, I began with the words. In a few minutes, I found "gulp plug" (something to do with bass fishing) and "live evil," and sailed off into the best sleep I had enjoyed in several weeks. The next night brought "straw warts" and "repaid diaper," and, in time, a long if faintly troubled snooze ("ezoons"). I was delighted. My palindromic skills improved rapidly, and soon I was no longer content with mere words. I failed to notice at first that, like all sedatives, this one had begun to weaken with protracted use; I was doubling and tripling the dose, and my intervals given over to two-way cogitation were stretching to an hour or more. One morning, after a mere twenty minutes of second shut-eye, I met my wife at the breakfast table and announced, "Editor rubs ward, draws burro tide."

"Terrific," she said unenthusiastically. "I don't get it. I mean, what does it mean?"

"Well, you see," I began, "there's this editor in Mexico who goes camping with his niece, and —"

"Listen," she said, "I think you should take a phenobarb tonight. You look terrible."

It was about six weeks later when, at five-fifteen one morning, I discovered the Japanese hiding in my pajamas. "Am a Jap," he said, bowing politely, and then added in a whisper, "Pajama." I slept no more. Two nights later, at precisely four-eleven, when "Repins pajama" suddenly yielded "Am a Jap sniper," I sprang out of bed, brewed myself a pot of strong coffee, and set to work with pencil and paper on what had begun to look like a war novel. A month later, trembling, hollow-eyed, and badly strung out on coffee and Dexamyl, I finished the epic. It turned out that the thing wasn't about a Japanese at all; it was a long telegram composed by a schizophrenic war veteran who had been wounded at Iwo Jima and was now incarcerated in some mental hospital. (This kind of surprise keeps happening when you are writing palindromes, a literary form in which the story line is controlled by the words rather than the author.) Experts have since told me that my barely intelligible pushmi-pullyu may be the longest palindrome in the English language:

> MARGE, LET DAM DOGS IN. AM ON SATIRE:
> VOW I AM CAIN. AM ON SPOT, AM A JAP
> SNIPER. RED, RAW MURDER ON G.I.! IGNORE
> DRUM. (WARDER REPINS PAJAMA TOPS.)
> NO MANIAC, MA! IWO VERITAS: NO MAN IS
> GOD.　　　　　　　　　—MAD TELEGRAM

My recovery was a protracted one, requiring a lengthy vacation at the seashore, daily exercise, warm milk on retiring, and eventually a visit to the family psychiatrist. The head-candler listened to my story ("Rot-cod . . ." I began), then wrote out a prescription for a mild sedative (I murmured, "slip pils") and swore me to total palindromic abstinence. He told me to avoid Tums, Serutan, and men named Otto. "Only right thinking can save you," he said severely. "Or rather, *left-to-right* thinking."

I tried, I really tried. For more than a year, I followed the doctor's plan faithfully, instantly dropping my gaze whenever I began to see "POTS" and "KLAW" on traffic signs facing me across the street, and plugging away at my sleepy-time books when I was reafflicted with the Big Eye. I had begun to think that mine might be a total cure when, just two weeks ago, nodding over *Walden* again, I came upon this sentence: "We are conscious of an animal in us, which awakens in proportion as our higher nature slumbers. It is reptile and sensual, and perhaps cannot be wholly expelled. . . ."

"Ah-ha!" I muttered, struck by the remarkable pertinence of this thought to my own nocturnal condition. Thoreau himself had said it; I could never quite escape. To prove the point, I repeated my exclamation, saying it backward this time.

I did not entirely give way to my reptile. Remembering my near-fatal bout with the telegram, I vowed to limit myself entirely to revising and amplifying existing palindromes — those famous chestnuts recited to me by my Scottish friend. The very next night, during a 4 A.M. rainstorm, I put my mind to "A man, a plan, a canal: Panama." Replacing de Lesseps with a female M.I.T. graduate, I achieved "A *woman*, a plan, a canal: Panamowa," which was clearly inadequate; she sounded more like a ballerina. Within a few minutes, however, a dog trotted out of the underbrush of my mind — it was a Pekinese — and suddenly redesigned the entire isthmus project: "A dog, a plan, a canal: pagoda." I went to sleep.

Napoleon led me into deeper waters. Bedwise by night light, I envisioned him as a fellow-sufferer, a veteran palindromist who must have been transfixed with joy to find the island of his first exile so brilliantly responsive to his little perversion. But what if the allies had marooned him on a *different* island in 1814? Various possibilities suggested themselves: "A dum reb was I ere I saw Bermuda," "No lava was I ere I saw Avalon," "Lana C. LaDaug was I ere I saw Guadalcanal." None would do; the Emperor's aides, overhearing him, would conclude that the old boy had fallen victim to aphasia. A night or two later, I replaced Boney on Elba and retinued him with a useful and highly diversified staff of officers and loyal friends — a Rumanian, a female camp follower, a Levantine, and a German. These accompanied the Emperor by turns during his habitual evening walks along the cliffs, each feigning awe and delight as the impromptu musing of the day fell from his lips. "Uncomfortable was I ere I saw Elba, Trofmocnu," he confessed to the first. To the female, smiling roguishly and chucking her under the chin, he murmured, "Amiable was I ere I saw Elba, Ima." The next evening, made gloomy by the rabbinical sidekick, he changed to "Vegetable was I ere I saw Elba, Tegev." He cheered up with the burly Prussian, declaiming, "Remarkable was I ere I saw Elba, Kramer!" but, finding the same man on duty the following night (the list had run out, and new duty rosters were up), he reversed himself, whining, "*Un*remarkable was I ere I saw Elba, Kramer, *nu*?"

That seemed to exhaust Elba (and me), and during the wee hours of last week I moved along inevitably to "Madam, I'm Adam." For some reason, this jingle began to infuriate me. (My new night journeys had made me irritable and suspicious; my wife seemed to be looking at me with the same anxious expression she had worn when I was fighting the Jap sniper, and one day I caught her trying to sneak a telephone call to the psychiatrist.) Adam's salutation struck me as being both rude and uninformative. At first, I attempted to make the speaker more civilized, but he resisted me: "Good day, Madam, I'm Adam Yaddoog," "Howdy, Madam, I'm Adam Y. Dwoh," "*Bonjour*, Madam, I'm Adam Roujnob." No dice. Who *was* this surly fellow? I determined to ferret out his last name, but the first famous Adam I thought of could only speak after clearing his throat ("*Htims*,

Madam, I'm Adam Smith"), and the second after falling down a flight of stairs ("*Yksnilomray!* . . . Madam, I'm Adam Yarmolinsky"). Then, at exactly six-seventeen yesterday morning, I cracked the case. I was so excited that I woke up my wife. She stared at me, blurry and incredulous, as I stalked about the bedroom describing the recent visit of a well-known congressman to Wales. He had gone there, I explained, on a fact-finding trip to study mining conditions in the ancient Welsh collieries, perhaps as necessary background to the mine-safety bills now pending in Washington. Being a highly professional politician, he boned up on the local language during the transatlantic plane trip. The next morning, briefcase and homburg in hand, he tapped on the door of a miner's cottage in Ebbw Vale, and when it was opened by a lady looking very much like Sara Allgood in "How Green Was My Valley," he smiled charmingly, bowed, and said, "*Llewopnotyalc*, Madam, I'm Adam Clayton Powell."

When I got home last night, I found a note from my wife saying that she had gone to stay with her mother for a while. Aware at last of my nearness to the brink, I called the psychiatrist, but his answering service told me that he was away on a month's vacation. I dined forlornly on hot milk and Librium and was asleep before ten . . . and awake before three. Alone in bed, trembling lightly, I restudied the penguin (or overshoe) on the wall, while my mind, still unleashed, sniffed over the old ashpiles of canals, islands, and Adams. Nothing there. Nothing, that is, until seven-twelve this morning, when the beast unearthed, just under the Panama Canal, the small but glittering prize, "Suez . . . Zeus!" I sat bolt upright, clapping my brow, and uttered a great roar of delight and despair. Here, I could see, was a beginning even more promising than the Jap sniper. Released simultaneously into the boiling politics of the Middle East and the endless affairs of Olympus, I stood, perhaps, at the doorway of the greatest palindromic adventure of all time — one that I almost surely would not survive. "No!" I whimpered, burying my throbbing head beneath the pillows. "No, no!" Half smothered in linen and sleeplessness, I heard my sirens reply. "On!" they called. "On, on!"

Questions for Discussion

1. How "realistic" do you find this essay to be? How much of the narration do you suppose is factual and how much fictional? What clues lead you to your conclusion?

2. Angell introduces humor at many points in this narration. How would you characterize his humor? Ironic? Sardonic? Exaggerated? Self-effacing? Be prepared to cite examples to support your answer.

3. Do you find the conclusion to Angell's essay effective? Why or why not?

4. What audience do you suppose Angell had in mind when he wrote "Ainmosni"? What support can you offer for your answer? What audience, if any, do you suppose would not enjoy this essay? Why wouldn't they?

5. When you first read the title of this essay, what did you think the subject would be? In retrospect, do you think the title is effective? Why or why not?

Suggested Activities

1. Collect a list of palindromes from your friends or from the library. Try to make up an anecdote comparable to one of Angell's to explain the longest palindrome you obtained.

2. When Angell hits upon "Suez . . . Zeus," he says he is "at the doorway of the greatest palindromic adventure of all time. . . ." Expand Angell's palindrome by at least two or three words, then compare your expansion with those created by other members of your class.

3. Write a short essay in which you describe games you have invented or played to help you through some difficult situations.

The Pinball
Philosophy

JOHN McPHEE

John McPhee (b. 1931), a staff writer for *The New Yorker*, has
lived most of his life in Princeton, New Jersey. The author of
fourteen books on topics as wide-ranging as Scotland, Arthur
Ashe, and birch-bark canoes, McPhee's most widely acclaimed
book, *Coming into the Country* (1977), vividly describes the
state of Alaska's recent growing pains. "The Pinball Philosophy," reprinted from McPhee's most recent book, *Giving Good
Weight* (1979), features J. Anthony Lukas, a Pulitzer Prize-winning author and self-proclaimed master pinball player. Especially noteworthy are McPhee's descriptions of a pinball
machine jumping to life at Lukas' touch and of a five-game
match between Lukas and his arch rival, Tom Buckley.

J. Anthony Lukas is a world-class pinball player who, between tilts, does some
free-lance writing. In our city, he is No. ½. That is to say, he is one of two players
who share pinball preeminence — two players whose special skills within the
sport are so multiple and varied that they defy comparative analysis. The other
star is Tom Buckley, of the *Times*. Pinball people tend to gravitate toward Lukas
or Buckley. Lukas is a Lukasite. He respects Buckley, but he sees himself as the
whole figure, the number "1." His machine is a Bally. Public pinball has been

THE PINBALL PHILOSOPHY   From *Giving Good Weight* by John McPhee. Copyright © 1975 by John
McPhee. Reprinted by permission of Farrar, Straus and Giroux, Inc. This material originally
appeared in *The New Yorker*.

illegal in New York for many decades, but private ownership is permitted, and Lukas plays, for the most part, at home.

Lukas lives in an old mansion, a city landmark, on West Seventy-sixth Street. The machine is in his living room, under a high, elegant ceiling, near an archway to rooms beyond. Bally is the Rolls-Royce of pinball, he explains as he snaps a ball into action. It rockets into the ellipse at the top of the playfield. It ricochets four times before beginning its descent. Lukas likes a four-bounce hold in the ellipse — to set things up for a long ball. There is something faintly, and perhaps consciously, nefarious about Lukas, who is an aristocratic, olive-skinned, Andalusian sort of man, with deep eyes in dark wells. As the butts of his hands pound the corners of his machine, one can imagine him cheating at polo. "It's a wrist game," he says, tremoring the Bally, helping the steel ball to bounce six times off the top thumper-bumper and, each time, go back up a slot to the ellipse — an awesome economy of fresh beginnings. "Strong wrists are really all you want to use. The term for what I am doing is 'reinforcing.'" His voice, rich and dense, pours out like cigarette smoke filtered through a New England prep school. "There are certain basics to remember," he says. "Above all, don't flail with the flipper. You *carry* the ball in the direction you want it to go. You can almost cradle the ball on the flipper. And always hit the slingshot hard. That's the slingshot there — where the rubber is stretched between bumpers. Reinforce it hard. And never — never — drift toward the free-ball gate." Lukas reinforces the machine just as the ball hits the slingshot. The rebound comes off with blurring speed, striking bumpers, causing gongs to ring and lights to flash. Under his hands, the chrome on the frame has long since worn away.

Lukas points out that one of the beauties of his Bally is that it is asymmetrical. Early pinball machines had symmetrical playfields — symmetrical thumperbumpers — but in time they became free-form, such as this one, with its field laid out not just for structure but also for surprise. Lukas works in this room — stacks of manuscript on shelves and tables. He has been working for many months on a book that will weigh five pounds. It will be called *Nightmare: The Dark Side of the Nixon Years* — a congenially chosen title, implying that there was a bright side.[1] The pinball machine is Lukas's collaborator. "When a paragraph just won't go," he says, "and I begin to say to myself, 'I can't make this work,' I get up and play the machine. I score in a high range. Then I go back to the typewriter a new man. I have beat the machine. Therefore I can beat the paragraph." He once won a Pulitzer Prize.

The steel ball rolls into the "death channel" — Lukas's term for a long alley down the left side — and drops out of sight off the low end of the playfield, finished.

"I have thought of analogies between Watergate and pinball. Everything is connected. Bumpers. Rebounds. You light lights and score. Chuck Colson is

---

[1] Lukas ultimately decided to be less congenial, and changed the title to *Nightmare: The Underside of the Nixon Years* (Viking Press, 1976).

involved in almost every aspect of the Watergate story: the dirty tricks, the cov-
erup, the laundered money—all connected. How hard you hit off the thumper-
bumper depends on how hard you hit off the slingshot depends on how well you
work the corners. In a sense, pinball is a reflection of the complexity of the subject
I am writing about. Bear in mind, I take this with considerable tongue-in-cheek."

With another ball, he ignites an aurora on the scoreboard. During the ball's
complex, prolonged descent, he continues to set forth the pinball philosophy.
"More seriously, the game does give you a sense of controlling things in a way
that in life you can't do. And there is risk in it, too. The ball flies into the ellipse,
into the playfield—full of opportunities. But there's always the death channel—
the run-out slot. There are rewards, prizes, coming off the thumper-bumper. The
ball crazily bounces from danger to opportunity and back to danger. You need
reassurance in life that in taking risks you will triumph, and pinball gives you
that reaffirmation. Life is a risky game, but you can beat it."

Unfortunately, Lukas has a sick flipper. At the low end of the playfield, two
flippers guard the run-out slot, but one waggles like a broken wing, pathetic,
unable to function, to fling the ball uphill for renewed rewards. The ball, instead,
slides by the crippled flipper and drops from view.

Lukas opens the machine. He lifts the entire playfield, which is hinged at
the back, and props it up on a steel arm, like the lid of a grand piano. Revealed
below is a neat, arresting world that includes spring-loaded hole kickers, contact
switches, target switches, slingshot assemblies, the score-motor unit, the electric
anti-cheat, three thumper-bumper relays, the top rebound relay, the key-gate
assembly ("the key gate will keep you out of the death channel"), the free-ball-
gate assembly, and—not least—the one-and-a-quarter-amp slo-blo. To one side,
something that resembles a plumb bob hangs suspended within a metal ring. If
the bob moves too far out of plumb, it touches the ring. Tilt. The game is dead.

Lukas is not an electrician. All he can do is massage the flipper's switch
assembly, which does not respond—not even with a shock. He has about had it
with this machine. One cannot collaborate with a sick flipper. The queasy truth
comes over him: no pinball, no paragraphs. So he hurries downstairs and into a
taxi, telling the driver to go to Tenth Avenue in the low Forties—a pocket of the
city known as Coin Row.

En route, Lukas reflects on his long history in the game—New York, Cambridge, Paris—and his relationships with specific machines ("they're like wives").
When he was the *Times'* man in the Congo, in the early sixties, the post was
considered a position of hardship, so he was periodically sent to Paris for rest and
rehabilitation, which he got playing pinball in a Left Bank brasserie. He had per-
fected his style as an undergraduate at Harvard, sharing a machine at the *Crimson*
with David Halberstam ("Halberstam is aggressive at everything he does, and he
was very good"). Lukas's father was a Manhattan attorney. Lukas's mother died
when he was eight. He grew up, for the most part, in a New England community—Putney, Vermont—where he went to pre-prep and prep school. Putney was

"straitlaced," "very high-minded," "a life away from the maelstrom"—potters' wheels, no pinball. Lukas craved "liberation," and developed a yearning for what he imagined as low life, and so did his schoolmate Christopher Lehmann-Haupt. Together, one weekend, they dipped as low as they knew how. They went to New York. And they went to two movies! They went to shooting galleries! They went to a flea circus! They played every coin-operated machine they could find— and they stayed up until after dawn! All this was pretty low, but not low enough, for that was the spring of 1951, and still beyond reach—out there past the fingertips of Tantalus—was pinball, the ban on which had been emphatically reinforced a few years earlier by Fiorello H. LaGuardia, who saw pinball as a gambling device corruptive of the city's youth. To Lukas, pinball symbolized all the timewasting and ne'er-do-welling that puritan Putney did not. In result, he mastered the game. He says, "It puts me in touch with a world in which I never lived. I am attracted to pinball for its seediness, its slightly disreputable reputation."

On Coin Row, Lukas knows just where he is going, and without a sidewise glance passes storefronts bearing names like The World of Pinball Amusement ("SALES—REPAIR") and Manhattan Coin Machine ("PARTS—SUPPLIES"). He heads directly for the Mike Munves Corporation, 577 Tenth Avenue, the New York pinball exchange, oldest house (1912) on the row. Inside is Ralph Hotkins, in double-breasted blazer—broker in pinball machines. The place is more warehouse than store, and around Hotkins, and upstairs above him, are rank upon rank of Gottliebs, Williamses, Ballys, Playmatics—every name in the game, including forty-year-old antique completely mechanical machines, ten balls for a nickel, the type that Mayor LaGuardia himself destroyed with an axe. Hotkins— a prosperous man, touched with humor, not hurting for girth—got his start in cigarette machines in the thirties, moved up to jukeboxes, and then, in 1945, while LaGuardia was still mayor, to game machines. He had two daughters, and he brought them up on pinball. They were in the shop almost every afternoon after school, and all day Saturday. One daughter now has a Ph.D. in English literature and the other a Ph.D. in political science. So much for the Little Flower. In this era of open massage and off-track betting, Hotkins has expected the ban to lift, but the courts, strangely, continue to uphold it.[2] Meanwhile, his customers— most of whom are technically "private"—include Wall Street brokerage houses where investors shoot free pinball under the ticker, Seventh Avenue dress houses that wish to keep their buyers amused, the Circus Circus peepshow emporium on West Forty-second Street, many salesrooms, many showrooms, and J. Anthony Lukas.

"Yes, Mr. Lukas. What can we do for you?"

Lukas greets Hotkins and then runs balls through a few selected machines. Lukas attempts to deal with Hotkins, but Hotkins wants Lukas's machine and a hundred and fifty dollars. Lukas would rather fix his flipper. He asks for George Cedeño, master technician, who makes house calls and often travels as far as Mas-

---

[2]And they did so until 1976, when pinball at last became legal.

sachusetts to fix a pinball machine. Cedeño — blue work smock, white shoes, burgundy trousers, silver hair — makes a date with Lukas.

Lukas starts for home but, crossing Forty-second Street, decides on pure whim to have a look at Circus Circus, where he has never been. Circus Circus is, after all, just four blocks away. The stroll is pleasant in the afternoon sunlight, to and through Times Square, under the marquees of pornographic movies — *Valley of the Nymphs, The Danish Sandwich, The Organ Trail*. Circus Circus ("GIRLS! GIRLS! GIRLS! LIVE EXOTIC MODELS") is close to Sixth Avenue and consists, principally, of a front room and a back room. Prices are a quarter a peep in the back room and a quarter to play (two games) in the front. The game room is dim, and Lukas, entering, sees little at first but the flashing scoreboards of five machines. Four of them — a Bally, a Williams, two Gottliebs — flash slowly, reporting inexperienced play, but the fifth, the one in the middle, is exploding with light and sound. The player causing all this is hunched over, concentrating — in his arms and his hands a choreography of talent. Lukas's eyes adjust to the light. Then he reaches for his holster. The man on the hot machine, busy keeping statistics of his practice, is Tom Buckley.

"Tom."

"Tone."

"How is the machine?"

"Better than yours, Tone. You don't realize what a lemon you have."

"I love my Bally."

"The Bally is the Corvair of pinball machines. I don't even care for the art on the back-glass. Williams and Gottlieb are the best. Bally is nowhere."

Buckley, slightly older than Lukas, has a spectacled and professorial look. He wears a double-breasted blazer, a buff turtleneck. He lives on York Avenue now. He came out of Beechhurst, Queens, and learned his pinball in the Army — in Wrightstown, New Jersey; in Kansas City. He was stationed in an office building in Kansas City, and he moved up through the pinball ranks from beginner to virtuoso on a machine in a Katz drugstore.

Lukas and Buckley begin to play. Best of five games. Five balls a game. Alternate shots. The machine is a Williams Fun-Fest, and Buckley points out that it is "classic," because it is symmetrical. Each kick-out well and thumper-bumper is a mirror of another. The slingshots are dual. On this machine, a level of forty thousand points is where the sun sets and the stars come out. Buckley, describing his own style as "guts pinball," has a first-game score of forty-four thousand three hundred and ten. While Lukas plays his fifth ball, Buckley becomes avuncular. "Careful, Tony. You might think you're in an up-post position, but if you let it slide a little you're in a down-post position and you're finished." Buckley's advice is generous indeed. Lukas — forty-eight thousand eight hundred and seventy — wins the first game.

It is Buckley's manner to lean into the machine from three feet out. His whole body, steeply inclined, tics as he reinforces. In the second game, he scores fifty thousand one hundred and sixty. Lukas's address is like a fencer's *en garde*. He stands close to the machine, with one foot projecting under it. His chin is high. Buckley tells him, "You're playing nice, average pinball, Tony." And Lukas's response is fifty-seven thousand nine hundred and fifty points. He leads Buckley, two games to none.

"I'm ashamed," Buckley confesses. And as he leans — palms pounding — into the third game, he reminds himself, "Concentration, Tom. Concentration is everything."

Lukas notes aloud that Buckley is "full of empty rhetoric." But Lukas, in Game 3, fires one ball straight into the death channel and can deliver only thirty-five thousand points. Buckley wins with forty. Perhaps Lukas feels rushed. He prefers to play a more deliberate, cogitative game. At home, between shots, in the middle of a game, he will go to the kitchen for a beer and return to study the situation. Buckley, for his part, seems anxious, and with good reason: one mistake now and it's all over. In the fourth game, Lukas lights up forty-three thousand and fifty points; but Buckley's fifth ball, just before it dies, hits forty-four thousand two hundred and sixty. Games are two all, with one to go. Buckley takes a deep breath, and says, "You're a competitor, Tony. Your flipper action is bad, but you're a real competitor."

Game 5 under way. They are pummelling the machine. They are heavy on the corners but light on the flippers, and the scoreboard is reacting like a storm at sea. With three balls down, both are in the thirty-thousand range. Buckley, going unorthodox, plays his fourth ball with one foot off the floor, and raises his score to forty-five thousand points — more than he scored in winning the two previous games. He smiles. He is on his way in, flaring, with still another ball to play. Now Lukas snaps his fourth ball into the ellipse. It moves down and around the board, hitting slingshots and flippers and rising again and again to high ground to begin additional scoring runs. It hits sunburst caps and hole kickers, swinging targets and bonus gates. Minute upon minute, it stays in play. It will not die.

When the ball finally slips between flippers and off the playfield, Lukas has registered eighty-three thousand two hundred points. And he still has one ball to go.

Buckley turns into a Lukasite. As Lukas plays his fifth ball, Buckley cheers. "Atta way! Atta way, babes!" He goes on cheering until Lukas peaks out at ninety-four thousand one hundred and seventy.

"That was superb. And there's no luck in it," Buckley says. "It's as good a score as I've seen."

Lukas takes a cool final look around Circus Circus. "Buckley has a way of tracking down the secret joys of the city," he says, and then he is gone.

Still shaking his head in wonder, Buckley starts a last, solo game. His arms move mechanically, groovedly, reinforcing. His flipper timing is offhandedly flawless. He scores a hundred thousand two hundred points. But Lukas is out of sight.

Questions for Discussion

1. What details in this essay give the game of pinball an air of respectability you might not otherwise associate with it?

2. Why do you think McPhee writes in the present tense in this essay?

3. McPhee cites examples of analogies that Lukas draws between pinball and life. Are these attempts to show similarities convincing? Can you think of analogies Lukas might have made but didn't?

4. How do you think McPhee feels about Lukas? Does he admire him, look down on him, or remain neutral? What evidence would you point to in support of your conclusion?

5. Look carefully at the passages in which McPhee describes a pinball machine in action. How vivid and complete are his descriptions? What use does he make of sensory impressions?

6. How does the fact that Buckley outscores Lukas at the end, without Lukas even knowing it, affect your attitude toward Lukas? What point does McPhee make by ending the essay the way he does?

7. The term "mock-heroic" refers to the use of a heightened, serious style to describe trivial events. What evidence is there that McPhee is taking a mock-heroic approach in his initial description of Lukas at the pinball machine?

Suggested Activities

1. Using resources in your library, write a report about J. Anthony Lukas.

2. In speaking of J. Anthony Lukas as a writer, McPhee says "the pinball machine is Lukas's collaborator." What sort of collaborator do you have? Write an essay describing the tricks or rituals you use to assist you with your writing.

3. Write an essay explaining one of the following games or sports and showing your audience what is attractive about it:

Pocket billiards	Bowling
Dungeons and Dragons	Miniature golf
Monopoly	One of the various computer games

Savages

FRANK CONROY

Frank Conroy (b. 1936) is a graduate of Haverford College. His book *Stop-Time*, published in 1967, is a highly regarded memoir of his childhood and early adolescence. In the selection from it reprinted here, Conroy recounts some of the harrowing events that took place at an experimental boarding school he attended between the ages of nine and eleven.

I was twelve when my father died. From the ages of nine to eleven I was sent to an experimental boarding school in Pennsylvania called Freemont. I wasn't home more than a few days during these years. In the summer Freemont became a camp and I stayed through.

The headmaster was a big, florid man named Teddy who drank too much. It was no secret, and even the youngest of us were expected to sympathize with his illness and like him for it — an extension of the attitude that forbade the use of last names to make everyone more human. All of us knew, in the mysterious way children pick things up, that Teddy had almost no control over the institution he'd created, and that when decisions were unavoidable his wife took over. This weakness at the top might have been the key to the wildness of the place.

Life at Freemont was a perpetual semihysterical holiday. We knew there were almost no limits in any direction. A situation of endless, dreamlike fun, but one that imposed a certain strain on us all. Classes were a farce, you didn't have to go if you didn't want to, and there were no tests. Freedom was the key word. The atmosphere was heavy with the perfume of the nineteen-thirties — spurious agrarianism, group singing of proletarian chants from all countries, sexual free-dom (I was necking at the age of nine), sentimentalism, naïveté. But above all, filtering down through the whole school, the excitement of the *new thing*, of the experiment — that peculiar floating sensation of not knowing what's going to hap-pen next.

One warm spring night we staged a revolution. All the Junior boys, thirty or forty of us, spontaneously decided not to go to bed. We ran loose on the grounds most of the night, stalked by the entire faculty. Even old Ted was out, stumbling and crashing through the woods, warding off the nuts thrown from the trees. A few legitimate captures were made by the younger men on the staff, but there was no doubt most of us could have held out indefinitely. I, for one, was confident to the point of bravado, coming out in the open three or four times just for the fun of being chased. Can there be anything as sweet for a child as victory over authority? On that warm night I touched heights I will never reach again — bait-ing a thirty-year-old man, getting him to chase me over my own ground in the darkness, hearing his hard breath behind me (ah, the *wordlessness* of the chase, no words, just action), and finally leaping clean, leaping effortlessly over the brook at exactly the right place, knowing he was too heavy, too stupid as an animal, too old, and too tired to do what I had done. Oh God, my heart burst with joy when I heard him fall, flat out, in the water. Lights flashed in my brain. The chase was over and I had won. I was untouchable. I raced across the meadow, too happy to stop running.

Hours later, hidden in a bower, I heard the beginning of the end. A capture was made right below me. Every captured boy was to join forces with the staff and hunt the boys still out. My reaction was outrage. Dirty pool! But outrage dulled by recognition — "Of course. What else did you expect? They're clever and devious. Old people, with cold, ignorant hearts." The staff's technique didn't actually work as planned, but it spread confusion and broke the lovely symmetry of us against them. The revolution was no longer simple and ran out of gas. To this day I'm proud that I was the last boy in, hours after the others. (I paid a price though — some inexplicable loss to my soul as I crept around all that time in the dark, looking for another holdout.)

We went through a fire period for a couple of weeks one winter. At two or three in the morning we'd congregate in the huge windowless coat-room and set up hundreds of birthday candles on the floor. They gave a marvelous eerie light as we sat around telling horror stories. Fire-writing became the rage — paint your initials on the wall in airplane glue and touch a flame to it. At our most dramatic we staged elaborate take-offs on religious services, complete with capes and pseudo-Latin. We were eventually discovered by our bug-eyed counselor — a homosexual, I recognize in retrospect, who had enough problems caring for thirty-five boys at the brink of puberty. As far as I know he never touched anyone.

Teddy announced a punishment that made the hair rise on the backs of our necks. After pointing out the inadequacies of the fire-escape system he decreed that each of us would be forced to immerse his left hand in a pot of boiling water for ten seconds, the sentence to be carried out two days hence. Frightened, morbidly excited, we thought about nothing else, inevitably drawn to the image of the boiling water with unhealthy fascination. We discussed the announcement almost lovingly till all hours of the night, recognizing a certain beauty in the phrasing, the formal specification of the "left hand," the precision of "immersed for ten seconds" — it had a medieval flavor that thrilled us.

But Teddy, or his wife (it was done in her kitchen), lost his nerve after the screams and tears of the first few boys. The flame was turned off under the pot and by the time my turn came it didn't hurt at all.

The only successful bit of discipline I remember was their system to get us to stop smoking. We smoked corn silk as well as cigarettes. (The preparation of corn silk was an important ritual. Hand-gathered in the field from only the best ears, it was dried in the sun, rubbed, aged, and rolled into pipe-sized pellets. We decimated Freemont's corn crop, ineptly tended in the first place, by leaving ten stripped ears rotting on the ground for every one eventually harvested. No one seemed to mind. Harvest day, in which we all participated, was a fraudulent pastoral dance of symbolic rather than economic significance.) With rare decisiveness Teddy got organized about the smoking. The parents of the only non-scholarship student in the school, a neat, well-to-do Chinese couple, removed him without warning after a visit. The faculty believed it was the sight of students lounging around the public rooms with cigarettes hanging expertly from their rosy lips, while we maintained it was the toilet-paper war. The parents had walked through the front door when things were reaching a crescendo — endless white rolls streaming down the immense curved stairway, cylindrical bombs hurtling down the stairwell from the third-floor balcony to run out anticlimactically a few feet from the floor, dangling like exhausted white tongues. The withdrawal of the only paying student was a catastrophe, and the smoking would have to stop.

Like a witch doctor, some suburban equivalent of the rainmaker, Mr. Kleinberg arrived in his mysterious black panel truck. Members of the staff were Teddy, George, or Harry, but this outsider remained Mister Kleinberg, a form of respect to which it turned out he was entitled. We greeted him with bland amusement, secure in the knowledge that no one could do anything with us. A cheerful realist with a big smile and a pat on the shoulder for every boy in reach, he was to surprise us all.

The procedure was simple. He packed us into a small, unventilated garage, unloaded more cigarettes than the average man will see in a lifetime, passed out boxes of kitchen matches, and announced that any of us still smoking after ten packs and five cigars was excluded from the new, heavily enforced ban on smoking. None of us could resist the challenge.

He sat behind his vast mound with a clipboard, checking off names as we took our first, fresh packs. Adjusting his glasses eagerly and beaming with friendliness, he distributed his fantastic treasure. The neat white cartons were ripped open, every brand was ours for the asking — Old Gold, Pall Mall (my brand), Chesterfields, Wings, Camels, Spud, Caporals, Lucky Strike (*Loose Sweaters Mean Floppy Tits*), Kools, Benson & Hedges. He urged us to try them all. "Feel free to experiment, boys, it may be your last chance," he said, exploding with benevolent laughter.

I remember sitting on the floor with my back against the wall. Bruce, my best friend, was next to me.

"We're supposed to get sick," he said.

"I know."

We lighted up a pair of fat cigars and surveyed the scene. Forty boys puffed away in every corner of the room, some of them lined up for supplies, keeping Mr. Kleinberg busy with his paperwork. The noise was deafening. Gales of nervous laughter as someone did an imitation of John Garfield, public speeches as so-and-so declared his intention to pass out rather than admit defeat, or his neighbor yelled that he'd finished his fourth pack and was still by God going strong. One had to scream through the smoke to be heard. It wasn't long before the first boys stumbled out, sick and shamefaced, to retch on the grass. There was no way to leave quietly. Every opening of the door sent great shafts of sunlight across the smoky room, the signal for a derisive roar — boos, hoots, whistles, razzberries — from those sticking it out. I felt satisfaction as an enemy of mine left early, when the crowd was at its ugliest.

The rest of us followed eventually, of course, some taking longer than others, but all poisoned. Mr. Kleinberg won and smoking ended at Freemont. With dazed admiration we watched him drive away the next day in his black truck, smiling and waving, a panetela clamped between his teeth.

A rainy day. All of us together in the big dorm except a fat boy named Ligget. I can't remember how it started, or if any one person started it. A lot of talk against Ligget, building quickly to the point where talk was not enough. When someone claimed to have heard him use the expression "nigger-lipping" (wetting the end of a cigarette), we decided to act. Ligget was intolerable. A boy was sent to find him.

I didn't know Ligget. He had no friends even though he'd been at school longer than the rest of us. There was some vagueness about his origins, probably his parents were dead and relatives cared for him. We knew he was in the habit of running away. I remember waking up one night to see three men, including a policeman, carrying him back to his bed. He fought with hysterical strength, although silently, as if he were afraid to wake the rest of us. All three had to hold him down for the hypodermic.

On this rainy day he didn't fight. He must have known what was up the moment he walked through the door, but he didn't try to run. The two boys assigned to hold his arms were unnecessary. Throughout the entire trial he stood quite still, only his eyes, deep in the pudgy face, swiveling from side to side as he followed the speakers. He didn't say anything.

The prosecutor announced that first of all the trial must be fair. He asked for a volunteer to conduct Ligget's defense. When it became clear no one wanted

the job a boy named Herbie was elected by acclamation. It seemed the perfect
choice: Herbie was colorless and dim, steady if not inspired.

"I call Sammy as a witness," said the prosecutor. There was a murmur of
approval. Sammy was something of a hero to us, as much for his experiences in
reform school as for his fabulous condition. (An undescended testicle, which we
knew nothing about. To us he had only one ball.) "The prisoner is charged with
saying 'nigger-lip.' Did you hear him say it?"

"Yes. He said it a couple of days ago. We were standing over there in front
of the window." Sammy pointed to the end of the room. "He said it about Mark
Schofield." (Schofield was a popular athletic star, a Senior, and therefore not in
the room.)

"You heard him?"

"Yes. I got mad and told him not to talk like that. I walked away. I didn't
want to hear him."

"Okay. Now it's your turn, Herbie."

Herbie asked only one question. "Are you sure he said it? Maybe he said
something else and you didn't hear him right."

"He said it, all right." Sammy looked over at Ligget. "He said it."

"Okay," said the prosecutor, "I call Earl." Our only Negro stepped forward,
a slim, good-looking youth, already vain. (A sin so precocious we couldn't even
recognize it.) He enjoyed the limelight, having grown used to it in the large,
nervous, and visit-prone family that had spoiled him so terribly. He got a package
every week, and owned a bicycle with gears, unheard of before his arrival.

"What do you know about this?" asked the prosecutor.

"What do you mean?"

"Did you ever hear him say what he said?"

"If he ever said that around me I'd kill him."

"Have you noticed anything else?"

"What?"

"I mean, well, does he avoid you or anything?"

Herbie suddenly yelled, "But he avoids everybody!" This was more than we
had expected from old Herbie. He was shouted down immediately.

"I don't pay him no mind," said Earl, lapsing uncharacteristically into the
idiom of his people.

The trial must have lasted two hours. Witness after witness came forward
to take a stand against race prejudice. There was an interruption when one of the
youngest boys, having watched silently, suddenly burst into tears.

"Look, Peabody's crying."

"What's wrong, Peabody?" someone asked gently.

Confused, overwhelmed by his emotions, Peabody could only stammer, "I'm
sorry, I'm sorry, I don't know what's the matter. . . . It's so horrible, how could
he . . ."

"What's horrible?"

"Him saying that. How could he say that? I don't understand," the boy said,
tears falling from his eyes.

"It's all right, Peabody, don't worry."

"I'm sorry, I'm sorry."

Most of the testimony was on a high moral plane. Children are swept away by morality. Only rarely did it sink to the level of life. From the boy who slept next to Ligget: "He smells."

We didn't laugh. We weren't stupid boys, nor insensitive, and we recognized the seriousness of such a statement.

"His bed smells, and his clothes, and everything he has. He's a smelly, fat slob and I won't sleep next to him. I'm going to move my bed."

Sensing impatience in the room, the prosecutor called the prisoner himself. "Do you have anything to say?"

Ligget stood stock still, his hidden eyes gleaming. He was pale.

"This is your last chance, you better take it. We'll all listen, we'll listen to your side of it." The crowd voiced its agreement, moved by an instant of homage to fair play, and false sympathy. "Okay then, don't say you didn't have a chance."

"Wait a second," said Herbie. "I want to ask him something. Did you say 'nigger-lip' to Sammy?"

It appeared for a moment that Ligget was about to speak, but he gave up the effort. Shaking his head slowly, he denied the charge.

The prosecutor stepped forward. "All those who find him guilty say aye." A roar from forty boys. "All those who find him innocent say nay." Silence. (In a certain sense the trial was a parody of Freemont's "town meetings" in which rather important questions of curriculum and school policy were debated before the students and put to a vote.)

The punishment seemed to suggest itself. We lined up for one punch apiece.

Although Ligget's beating is part of my life (past, present, and future coexist in the unconscious, says Freud), and although I've worried about it off and on for years, all I can say about it is that brutality happens easily. I learned almost nothing from beating up Ligget.

There was a tremendous, heart-swelling excitement as I waited. The line moved slowly, people were taking their time. You got only one punch and you didn't want to waste it. A ritual of getting set, measuring the distance, perhaps adjusting the angle of his jaw with an index finger—all this had to be done before you let go. A few boys had fluffed already, only grazing him. If you missed completely you got another chance.

It wasn't hurting Ligget that was important, but rather the unbelievable opportunity to throw a clean, powerful punch completely unhindered, and with none of the sloppiness of an actual fight. Ligget was simply a punching bag, albeit the best possible kind of punching bag, one in human form, with sensory equipment to measure the strength of your blows.

It was my turn. Ligget looked at me blankly. I picked a spot on his chin, drew back my arm, and threw as hard a punch as I could muster. Instant disappointment. I hadn't missed, there was a kind of snapping sound as my fist landed, and his head jerked back, but the whole complex of movements was too fast, somehow missing the exaggerated movie-punch finality I had anticipated. Ligget looked at the boy behind me and I stepped away. I think someone clapped me on the back.

"Good shot."

Little Peabody, tear-stained but sober, swung an awkward blow that almost missed, grazing Ligget's mouth and bringing a little blood. He moved away and the last few boys took their turns.

Ligget was still on his feet. His face was swollen and his small eyes were glazed, but he stood unaided. He had kept his hands deep in his pockets to prevent the reflex of defense. He drew them out and for a moment there was silence, as if everyone expected him to speak.

Perhaps it was because we felt cheated. Each boy's dreams-of-glory punch had been a shade off center, or not quite hard enough, or thrown at the wrong angle, missing perfection by a maddeningly narrow margin. The urge to try again was strong. Unconsciously we knew we'd never have another chance. This wild freedom was ours once only. And perhaps among the older boys there were some who harbored the dream of throwing one final, superman punch, the knock-out blow to end all knock-out blows. Spontaneously, the line formed again.

After three or four blows Ligget collapsed. He sank to the floor, his eyes open and a dark stain spreading in his crotch. Someone told him to get up but it became clear he couldn't understand. Eventually a boy was sent to get the nurse. He was taken to the hospital in an ambulance.

X rays revealed that Ligget's jaw was broken in four places. We learned this the day after the beating, all of us repentant, sincerely unable to understand how it had happened. When he was well enough we went to visit him in the hospital. He was friendly, and accepted our apologies. One could tell he was trying, but his voice was thin and stiff, without a person behind it, like a bad actor reading lines. He wouldn't see us alone, there had to be an adult sitting by him.

No disciplinary action was taken against us. There was talk for a while that Sammy was going to be expelled, but it came to nothing. Ligget never returned.

Questions for Discussion

1. Near the beginning of this selection, Conroy observes that "this weakness at the top might have been the key to the wildness of the place." What support does the narrative offer for this assertion? What other factors might have contributed to the brutality that Conroy describes?

2. Did it come as a surprise to you when Conroy announced that most of the testimony against Liggett was on a "high moral plane"? Why or why not?

3. Several times Conroy interrupts his story to step back and evaluate the events he records. Note when he makes these evaluations, and be prepared to discuss whether you find them appropriate and convincing.

4. Do you think that the actions reported in this selection are dated, or could the same things happen today?

5. What is Conroy's point of view in this selection? Is it effective?

6. How does Conroy vary his narrative pace in this selection? Why does he choose to emphasize some matters and to pass over others quickly?

Suggested Activities

1. Write an essay in which you examine the relationship between freedom and discipline in "Savages."

2. Compare your friends' present attitudes toward punishment with their childhood experiences of it. What conclusions can you reach about the relationship between the two?

3. Write an essay in which you recall some vivid event from your childhood, either an event that taught you something or one from which you can say, like Conroy, that you "learned nothing."

Silence

MAXINE HONG KINGSTON

Maxine Hong Kingston (b. 1940) was raised in Stockton, California, the daughter of Chinese immigrants. Her first book, *The
Woman Warrior: Memoirs of a Girlhood Among Ghosts* (1976),
won the National Book Critics Circle Award for general nonfiction. Her second, the recently published *China Men* (1980), continues her examination of the relationship between Chinese
myths and legends and her personal history. In the following
selection from *The Woman Warrior*, Kingston focuses on a painful period in her childhood when personal and cultural conflicts
caused her to retreat temporarily into silence.

Long ago in China, knot-makers tied string into buttons and frogs, and rope into
bell pulls. There was one knot so complicated that it blinded the knot-maker.
Finally an emperor outlawed this cruel knot, and the nobles could not order it
anymore. If I had lived in China, I would have been an outlaw knot-maker.

Maybe that's why my mother cut my tongue. She pushed my tongue up and
sliced the frenum. Or maybe she snipped it with a pair of nail scissors. I don't
remember her doing it, only her telling me about it, but all during childhood I
felt sorry for the baby whose mother waited with scissors or knife in hand for it
to cry — and then, when its mouth was wide open like a baby bird's, cut. The
Chinese say "a ready tongue is an evil."

I used to curl up my tongue in front of the mirror and tauten my frenum
into a white line, itself as thin as a razor blade. I saw no scars in my mouth. I

thought perhaps I had had two frena, and she had cut one. I made other children open their mouths so I could compare theirs to mine. I saw perfect pink membranes stretching into precise edges that looked easy enough to cut. Sometimes I felt very proud that my mother committed such a powerful act upon me. At other times I was terrified — the first thing my mother did when she saw me was to cut my tongue.

"Why did you do that to me, Mother?"

"I told you."

"Tell me again."

"I cut it so that you would not be tongue-tied. Your tongue would be able to move in any language. You'll be able to speak languages that are completely different from one another. You'll be able to pronounce anything. Your frenum looked too tight to do those things, so I cut it."

"But isn't 'a ready tongue an evil'?"

"Things are different in this ghost country."

"Did it hurt me? Did I cry and bleed?"

"I don't remember. Probably."

She didn't cut the other children's. When I asked cousins and other Chinese children whether their mothers had cut their tongues loose, they said, "What?"

"Why didn't you cut my brothers' and sisters' tongues?"

"They didn't need it."

"Why not? Were theirs longer than mine?"

"Why don't you quit blabbering and get to work?"

If my mother was not lying she should have cut more, scraped away the rest of the frenum skin, because I have a terrible time talking. Or she should not have cut at all, tampering with my speech. When I went to kindergarten and had to speak English for the first time, I became silent. A dumbness — a shame — still cracks my voice in two, even when I want to say "hello" casually, or ask an easy question in front of the check-out counter, or ask directions of a bus driver. I stand frozen, or I hold up the line with the complete, grammatical sentence that comes squeaking out at impossible length. "What did you say?" says the cab driver, or "Speak up," so I have to perform again, only weaker the second time. A telephone call makes my throat bleed and takes up that day's courage. It spoils my day with self-disgust when I hear my broken voice come skittering out into the open. It makes people wince to hear it. I'm getting better, though. Recently I asked the postman for special-issue stamps; I've waited since childhood for postmen to give me some of their own accord. I am making progress, a little every day.

My silence was thickest — total — during the three years that I covered my school paintings with black paint. I painted layers of black over houses and flowers and suns, and when I drew on the blackboard, I put a layer of chalk on top. I was making a stage curtain, and it was the moment before the curtain parted or rose. The teachers called my parents to school, and I saw they had been saving my pictures, curling and cracking, all alike and black. The teachers pointed to the pictures and looked serious, talked seriously too, but my parents did not understand English. ("The parents and teachers of criminals were executed," said my father.) My parents took the pictures home. I spread them out (so black and full of possibilities) and pretended the curtains were swinging open, flying up, one after another, sunlight underneath, mighty operas.

During the first silent year I spoke to no one at school, did not ask before going to the lavatory, and flunked kindergarten. My sister also said nothing for three years, silent in the playground and silent at lunch. There were other quiet Chinese girls not of our family, but most of them got over it sooner than we did. I enjoyed the silence. At first it did not occur to me I was supposed to talk or to pass kindergarten. I talked at home and to one or two of the Chinese kids in class. I made motions and even made some jokes. I drank out of a toy saucer when the water spilled out of the cup, and everybody laughed, pointing at me, so I did it some more. I didn't know that Americans don't drink out of saucers.

I liked the Negro students (Black Ghosts) best because they laughed the loudest and talked to me as if I were a daring talker too. One of the Negro girls had her mother coil braids over her ears Shanghai-style like mine; we were Shanghai twins except that she was covered with black like my paintings. Two Negro kids enrolled in Chinese school, and the teachers gave them Chinese names. Some Negro kids walked me to school and home, protecting me from the Japanese kids, who hit me and chased me and stuck gum in my ears. The Japanese kids were noisy and tough. They appeared one day in kindergarten, released from concentration camp, which was a tic-tac-toe mark, like barbed wire, on the map.

It was when I found out I had to talk that school became a misery, that the silence became a misery. I did not speak and felt bad each time that I did not speak. I read aloud in first grade, though, and heard the barest whisper with little squeaks come out of my throat. "Louder," said the teacher, who scared the voice away again. The other Chinese girls did not talk either, so I knew the silence had to do with being a Chinese girl.

Reading out loud was easier than speaking because we did not have to make up what to say, but I stopped often, and the teacher would think I'd gone quiet again. I could not understand "I." The Chinese "I" has seven strokes, intricacies. How could the American "I," assuredly wearing a hat like the Chinese, have only three strokes, the middle so straight? Was it out of politeness that this writer left off strokes the way a Chinese has to write her own name small and crooked? No, it was not politeness; "I" is a capital and "you" is lower-case. I stared at that middle line and waited so long for its black center to resolve into tight strokes and dots that I forgot to pronounce it. The other troublesome word was "here," no strong consonant to hang on to, and so flat, when "here" is two mountainous ideographs. The teacher, who had already told me every day how to read "I" and "here," put me in the low corner under the stairs again, where the noisy boys usually sat.

When my second grade class did a play, the whole class went to the auditorium except the Chinese girls. The teacher, lovely and Hawaiian, should have understood about us, but instead left us behind in the classroom. Our voices were too soft or nonexistent, and our parents never signed the permission slips anyway.

They never signed anything unnecessary. We opened the door a crack and peeked out, but closed it again quickly. One of us (not me) won every spelling bee, though.

I remember telling the Hawaiian teacher, "We Chinese can't sing 'land where our fathers died.'" She argued with me about politics, while I meant because of curses. But how can I have that memory when I couldn't talk? My mother says that we, like the ghosts, have no memories.

After American school, we picked up our cigar boxes, in which we had arranged books, brushes, and an inkbox neatly, and went to Chinese school, from 5:00 to 7:30 P.M. There we chanted together, voices rising and falling, loud and soft, some boys shouting, everybody reading together, reciting together and not alone with one voice. When we had a memorization test, the teacher let each of us come to his desk and say the lesson to him privately, while the rest of the class practiced copying or tracing. Most of the teachers were men. The boys who were so well behaved in the American school played tricks on them and talked back to them. The girls were not mute. They screamed and yelled during recess, when there were no rules; they had fistfights. Nobody was afraid of children hurting themselves or of children hurting school property. The glass doors to the red and green balconies with the gold joy symbols were left wide open so that we could run out and climb the fire escapes. We played capture-the-flag in the auditorium, where Sun Yat-sen and Chiang Kai-shek's pictures hung at the back of the stage, the Chinese flag on their left and the American flag on their right. We climbed the teak ceremonial chairs and made flying leaps off the stage. One flag head-quarters was behind the glass door and the other on stage right. Our feet drummed on the hollow stage. During recess the teachers locked themselves up in their office with the shelves of books, copybooks, inks from China. They drank tea and warmed their hands at a stove. There was no play supervision. At recess we had the school to ourselves, and also we could roam as far as we could go—downtown, Chinatown stores, home—as long as we returned before the bell rang.

At exactly 7:30 the teacher again picked up the brass bell that sat on his desk and swung it over our heads, while we charged down the stairs, our cheering magnified in the stairwell. Nobody had to line up.

Not all of the children who were silent at American school found voice at Chinese school. One new teacher said each of us had to get up and recite in front of the class, who was to listen. My sister and I had memorized the lesson per-fectly. We said it to each other at home, one chanting, one listening. The teacher called on my sister to recite first. It was the first time a teacher had called on the second-born to go first. My sister was scared. She glanced at me and looked away; I looked down at my desk. I hoped that she could do it because if she could, then I would have to. She opened her mouth and a voice came out that wasn't a whis-per, but it wasn't a proper voice either. I hoped that she would not cry, fear break-ing up her voice like twigs underfoot. She sounded as if she were trying to sing though weeping and strangling. She did not pause or stop to end the embarrass-ment. She kept going until she said the last word, and then she sat down. When it was my turn, the same voice came out, a crippled animal running on broken legs. You could hear splinters in my voice, bones rubbing jagged against one another. I was loud, though. I was glad I didn't whisper. There was one little girl who whispered.

You can't entrust your voice to the Chinese, either; they want to capture your voice for their own use. They want to fix up your tongue to speak for them. "How much less can you sell it for?" we have to say. Talk the Sales Ghosts down. Make them take a loss.

We were working at the laundry when a delivery boy came from the Rexall drugstore around the corner. He had a pale blue box of pills, but nobody was sick. Reading the label we saw that it belonged to another Chinese family, Crazy Mary's family. "Not ours," said my father. He pointed out the name to the Delivery Ghost, who took the pills back. My mother muttered for an hour, and then her anger boiled over. "That ghost! That dead ghost! How dare he come to the wrong house?" She could not concentrate on her marking and pressing. "A mistake! Huh!" I was getting angry myself. She fumed. She made her press crash and hiss. "Revenge. We've got to avenge this wrong on our future, on our health, and on our lives. Nobody's going to sicken my children and get away with it." We brothers and sisters did not look at one another. She would do something awful, something embarrassing. She'd already been hinting that during the next eclipse we slam pot lids together to scare the frog from swallowing the moon. (The word for "eclipse" is *frog-swallowing-the-moon.*) When we had not banged lids at the last eclipse and the shadow kept receding anyway, she'd said, "The villagers must be banging and clanging very loudly back home in China."

("On the other side of the world, they aren't having an eclipse, Mama. That's just a shadow the earth makes when it comes between the moon and the sun."

"You're always believing what those Ghost Teachers tell you. Look at the size of the jaws!")

"Aha!" she yelled. "You! The biggest." She was pointing at me. "You go to the drugstore."

"What do you want me to buy, Mother?" I said.

"Buy nothing. Don't bring one cent. Go and make them stop the curse."

"I don't want to go. I don't know how to do that. There are no such things as curses. They'll think I'm crazy."

"If you don't go, I'm holding you responsible for bringing a plague on this family."

"What am I supposed to do when I get there?" I said, sullen, trapped. "Do I say, 'Your delivery boy made a wrong delivery'?"

"They know he made a wrong delivery. I want you to make them rectify their crime."

I felt sick already. She'd make me swing stinky censers around the counter, at the druggist, at the customers. Throw dog blood on the druggist. I couldn't stand her plans.

"You get reparation candy," she said. "You say, 'You have tainted my house with sick medicine and must remove the curse with sweetness.' He'll understand."

"He didn't do it on purpose. And no, he won't, Mother. They don't under-stand stuff like that. I won't be able to say it right. He'll call us beggars."

"You just translate." She searched me to make sure I wasn't hiding any money. I was sneaky and bad enough to buy the candy and come back pretending it was a free gift.

"Mymotherseztagimmesomecandy," I said to the druggist. Be cute and small. No one hurts the cute and small.

"What? Speak up. Speak English," he said, big in his white druggist coat.

"Tatatagimme somecandy."

The druggist leaned way over the counter and frowned. "Some free candy," I said. "Sample candy."

"We don't give sample candy, young lady," he said.

"My mother said you have to give us candy. She said that is the way the Chinese do it."

"What?"

"That is the way the Chinese do it."

"Do what?"

"Do things." I felt the weight and immensity of things impossible to explain to the druggist.

"Can I give you some money?" he asked.

"No, we want candy."

He reached into a jar and gave me a handful of lollipops. He gave us candy all year round, year after year, every time we went into the drugstore. When different druggists or clerks waited on us, they also gave us candy. They had talked us over. They gave us Halloween candy in December, Christmas candy around Valentine's day, candy hearts at Easter, and Easter eggs at Halloween. "See?" said our mother. "They understand. You kids just aren't very brave." But I knew they did not understand. They thought we were beggars without a home who lived in back of the laundry. They felt sorry for us. I did not eat their candy. I did not go inside the drugstore or walk past it unless my parents forced me to. Whenever we had a prescription filled, the druggist put candy in the medicine bag. This is what Chinese druggists normally do, except they give raisins. My mother thought she taught the Druggist Ghosts a lesson in good manners (which is the same word as "traditions").

My mouth went permanently crooked with effort, turned down on the left side and straight on the right. How strange that the emigrant villagers are shout-ers, hollering face to face. My father asks, "Why is it I can hear Chinese from blocks away? Is it that I understand the language? Or is it they talk loud?" They turn the radio up full blast to hear the operas, which do not seem to hurt their ears. And they yell over the singers that wail over the drums, everybody talking at once, big arm gestures, spit flying. You can see the disgust on American faces looking at women like that. It isn't just the loudness. It is the way Chinese sounds, chingchong ugly, to American ears, not beautiful like Japanese sayonara words with the consonants and vowels as regular as Italian. We make guttural peasant noise and have Ton Duc Thang names you can't remember. And the

Chinese can't hear Americans at all; the language is too soft and western music unhearable. I've watched a Chinese audience laugh, visit, talk-story, and holler during a piano recital, as if the musician could not hear them. A Chinese-American, somebody's son, was playing Chopin, which has no punctuation, no cymbals, no gongs. Chinese piano music is five black keys. Normal Chinese women's voices are strong and bossy. We American-Chinese girls had to whisper to make ourselves American-feminine. Apparently we whispered even more softly than the Americans. Once a year the teachers referred my sister and me to speech therapy, but our voices would straighten out, unpredictably normal, for the therapists. Some of us gave up, shook our heads, and said nothing, not one word. Some of us could not even shake our heads. At times shaking my head no is more self-assertion than I can manage.

Questions for Discussion

1. Kingston says "my silence was thickest — total — during the three years that I covered my school paintings with black paint." What do you see as the relationship between these two phenomena? What do they tell us about Kingston's childhood?

2. How does Kingston compare her experiences in American school with her experiences in Chinese school? How do the differences between the two contribute to your understanding of Kingston's situation as an American-born Chinese?

3. At intervals in this narrative Kingston uses dialogue to enliven her story. How does the sentence structure in her passages of dialogue differ from the sentence structure in her narrative passages? What reason can you give for the differences?

4. What do you see as the thesis of this selection? Is there anything in the narrative that is irrelevant to the thesis?

5. In *The Woman Warrior*, the book from which this selection was taken, Kingston recounts a number of Chinese myths and explains the relevance they had for her when she was growing up. How does she use Chinese myths and traditions in this selection?

Suggested Activities

1. In her most recent book, *China Men*, Kingston attempts to understand the experiences of her male ancestors. If "Silence" intrigues you, read this book and make a report on it to your class.

2. Write an essay describing a distinctive aspect of the culture in which you were raised.

3. Write a narrative essay in which you recount a particularly difficult event or period from your own childhood.

In "The Santa Ana" (reprinted in this chapter), Joan Didion says "a *foehn* wind has distinct characteristics: it occurs on the leeward slope of a mountain range and, although the air begins as a cold mass, it is warmed as it comes down the mountain and appears finally as a hot dry wind." If we rephrase this statement, we can give it the classic pattern of a *formal definition:*

TERM		CLASS		DIFFERENTIA
A *foehn*	is	a wind	that	occurs on the leeward slope of a mountain range
			and is	hot and dry.

What we've created here should look familiar, since it's one of the two main patterns used by writers of dictionaries (the other is definition by synonym: "a dirigible is a lighter-than-air craft"). As you can see, a formal definition has two stages. First it assigns the unknown *term (foehn)* to a known *class* (winds). Then it provides as many *differentia* (place of occurrence, hotness, dryness) as may be needed to distinguish the unknown term from all other members of the class.

The formal definition is a precise, economical way of identifying something, and you'll undoubtedly have many occasions to use it. If you're writing about an obscure concept like *foehn,* for example, you certainly should give a brief definition of it before using it in the body of your essay. Also, if you're dealing with an abstract concept like "love" or "freedom" or "democracy," you may find either that it has more than one meaning or that it has different meanings for different groups of people. If so, it's a good idea to specify which meaning you have in mind through the use of a brief formal definition.

Being able to frame a formal definition, then, is an important skill to master. Generally, though, formal definitions occur less frequently in expository essays than do *extended* ones. This is especially true when definition is being used as a technique of persuasion. Because formal definitions need only be true and unambiguous, they usually have little persuasive intent behind them. Is the *foehn* truly a wind? Does our definition of it unambiguously distinguish it from all other winds? If the answers to these questions are "yes," then our formal definition has done all that can be expected of it.

Extended definitions, by contrast, face a third requirement. Extended definitions are essentially brief essays exploring the significance of a word or idea. Because they're so often used to persuade, it's not enough for them merely to be true and unambiguous. They must be evocative as well. At the same time that they're telling us what something is, they must convey the emotions it arouses. As an example, consider Didion's essay again. If her purpose had merely been to say that the Santa Ana is a *foehn* wind and then to tell us what a *foehn* wind is, she wouldn't have needed to write more than two sentences. But of course she has a much more ambitious aim. Not content merely to define the Santa Ana in physical terms, she wishes to suggest its human meaning as well.

How does she do this? Basically, by showing us examples of the wind's power over human emotions. When you read Didion's essay, notice how effectively she arranges these examples. That the Santa Ana causes violent crimes and traffic accidents would be difficult to prove conclusively. But we are all aware of the intimate connection between our own individual moods and the weather, so this is where Didion starts. Only after she has given us concrete examples of the wind's effect on her own life ("The baby frets. The maid sulks. I . . . cut my losses and lie down") does she then broaden her focus, first to the city as a whole, and then to her final, compelling image of the wind as a symbol for the fragility of life in Southern California.

In tracing out the personal and social effects of the wind, Didion engages in cause-and-effect analysis. Her ability to use this rhetorical pattern in defining the Santa Ana suggests that extended definition has no distinctive pattern of its own. And indeed this is so, for any of the rhetorical patterns discussed in the other chapters of this book can be used in writing extended definitions. Here are three examples.

1. Description. If you're defining something concrete, you'll probably find it useful to incorporate a description into your definition. In her essay "Apple Pie," for example, M. F. K. Fisher describes the pie as a "two-crust round baked shallow dish or pan, containing sliced apples, spices, sugar and butter (with perhaps lemon juice or brandy)." Be aware, though, that an extended definition will rarely be made up of description alone. In her essay, Fisher buttresses her description with process analysis (showing how an apple pie is made) and comparison and contrast (distinguishing between good pies and bad).

2. Comparison and contrast.   This rhetorical mode is particularly useful in framing definitions because one of the ways we know what something *is* is by knowing what it *is not*. If we were to compare "dirigible" to "hot air balloon," for example, we'd discover that our earlier definition of dirigible needs to be modified to allow us to distinguish between *steerable* lighter-than-air craft (dirigibles) and *nonsteerable* ones (hot air balloons).

A variation on comparison and contrast occurs when we replace one definition with another. This technique is used frequently in essays on literary and historical subjects. For example, Terrence Des Pres begins his book on life in the German concentration camps by suggesting that in modern literature the traditional view of the hero as a sacrificial victim has been replaced by a view of him as a survivor. Once Des Pres has brought our attention to this shift in definition, he is able to draw on literary examples of the survivor-hero to support his larger argument that "the grandeur of death [has been] lost in a world of mass murder."[1]

3. Classification.   It's frequently helpful to break broad, abstract terms down into smaller, more manageable units before defining them. If you were defining "romanticism," for example, you might divide the subject into its political, religious, social, literary, and artistic aspects. Once you've classified romanticism in this way, you can define it by discussing examples of it in each of your five categories.

Another type of classification found frequently in extended definitions takes the form of an *enumeration* or *list* of the properties of the subject. Here the purpose is not to be exhaustive in your list-making but merely to give your reader the flavor of what is being talked about. For example, in his book *On Writing Well,* William Zinsser defines "clutter" in this manner. He starts several of his paragraphs with sentences like these:

> Clutter is the laborious phrase which has pushed out the short word that means the same thing.

> Clutter is the ponderous euphemism that turns a slum into a depressed socioeconomic area, a salesman into a marketing representative, a dumb kid into an underachiever and garbage collectors into waste disposal personnel.

> Clutter is the official language used by the American corporation—in the news release and the annual report—to hide its mistakes.[2]

[1]Terrence Des Pres, *The Survivor: An Anatomy of Life in the Death Camps* (New York: Oxford Univ. Press, 1976), p. 6.

[2]William Zinsser, *On Writing Well,* 2nd ed. (New York: Harper & Row, 1980), pp. 15-16.

No one of these sentences is an adequate definition of clutter. But taken together, they persuasively suggest Zinsser's point: that a sort of mindless circumlocution is threatening to take control of our language.

And now, a final word of caution. As the essays that follow in this section show, definition can be a powerful and effective form of writing. But it should be used with discretion. The French philosopher Voltaire is supposed to have said that when people asked him to define his terms, he stopped talking to them. We've all had enough experience with the sort of bore who constantly calls for definitions to know why Voltaire felt the way he did. If we're to avoid a similar rejection when we use definition in our writing, we need to bear in mind that it is never an end in itself. Only when it adds to the clarity of our argument or to our ability to be persuasive should we include definition in our essays.

The Meaning
of "Normal"

JOSEPH WOOD KRUTCH

Joseph Wood Krutch (1893-1970), a professor of dramatic literature at Columbia University, was for twenty-six years the drama critic for *The Nation*. After his retirement and move to the Southwest, he gained fame as a naturalist with the publication of such books as *The Desert Year* (1952) and *The Voice of the Desert* (1955). He won the National Book Award for non-fiction in 1955 for *The Measure of Man*, in which he criticized contemporary orthodoxies. "The Meaning of 'Normal'" is a selection from *Human Nature and the Human Condition* (1959). In it, Krutch argues that the names we give to common concepts profoundly affect our attitudes toward them.

The words we choose to define or suggest what we believe to be important facts exert a very powerful influence upon civilization. A mere name can persuade us to approve or disapprove, as it does, for example, when we describe certain attitudes as "cynical" on the one hand or "realistic" on the other. No one wants to be "unrealistic" and no one wants to be "snarling." Therefore his attitude toward the thing described may very well depend upon which designation is current among his contemporaries; and the less critical his mind, the more influential the most commonly used vocabulary will be.

It is for this reason that, even as a mere verbal confusion, the use of "normal" to designate what ought to be called "average" is of tremendous importance and serves not only to indicate but actually to reinforce the belief that average ability, refinement, intellectuality, or even virtue is an ideal to be aimed at. Since we cannot do anything to the purpose until we think straight and since we cannot think straight without properly defined words it may be that the very first step toward an emancipation from the tyranny of "conformity" should be the attempt to substitute for "normal," as commonly used, a genuine synonym for "average."

Fortunately, such a genuine and familiar synonym does exist. That which is "average" is also properly described as "mediocre." And if we were accustomed to call the average man, not "the common man" or still less "the normal man," but "the mediocre man" we should not be so easily hypnotized into believing that mediocrity is an ideal to be aimed at.

A second step in the same direction would be to return to the word "normal" its original meaning. According to the Shorter Oxford Dictionary it derives from the Latin "norma," which has been Anglicized as "norm" and is, in turn, thus defined: "A rule or authoritative standard."

The adjective "normative" is not commonly misused — no doubt because it is not part of that "vocabulary of the average man" by which educators now set so much store. It still generally means "establishing a norm or standard." But "normal" seldom means, as it should, "corresponding to the standard by which a thing is to be judged." If it did, "a normal man" would again mean, not what the average man *is* but what, in its fullest significance, the word "man" should imply, even "what a man *ought* to be." And that is a very different thing from the "average" or "mediocre" man whom we have so perversely accustomed ourselves to regard as most worthy of admiration.

Only by defining and then attempting to reach up toward the "normal" as properly defined can a democratic society save itself from those defects which the enemies of democracy have always maintained were the necessary consequences of such a society. Until "preparation for life" rather than "familiarity with the best that has been thought and said" became the aim of education every schoolboy knew that Emerson had bid us hitch our wagons to a star. We now hitch them to a mediocrity instead.

Unless, then, normal is a useless and confusing synonym for average it should mean what the word normative suggests, namely, a *concept of what ought to be* rather than a *description of what is.*

It should mean what at times it has meant — the fullest possible realization of what the human being is capable of — the complete, not the aborted human being. It is an *entelechy*, not a mean; something excellent, not something mediocre; something rare, not common; not what the majority are, but what few, if any, actually measure up to.

Where, it will be asked, do we get this norm, upon what basis does it rest? Upon the answer to that question depends what a civilization will be like and especially in what direction it will move. At various times religion, philosophy, law, and custom have contributed to it in varying degrees. When none of these is available poetry and literature may do so. But unless we can say in one way or another, "I have some idea of what men ought to be as well as some knowledge of what they are," then civilization is lost.

Questions for Discussion

1. Midway through his first paragraph, Krutch switches from the first-person plural ("we") to the third-person singular ("he"). What purpose does the switch serve?

2. Krutch says: "A mere name can persuade us to approve or disapprove." Shakespeare's Juliet says: "What's in a name? That which we call a rose / By any other word would smell as sweet." With whom do you agree? Why? Can you think of any evidence in favor of the position opposed to yours?

3. What is your reaction to Krutch's suggestion that "mediocre" is a good synonym for "average"? Why do you like or dislike this suggestion?

4. What bothers Krutch about modern education? Do you agree or disagree with his opinion of it?

5. Krutch suggests that we have the power to control the meanings of words. Do you agree with his view? Why or why not?

6. Does looking at the meaning of a Latin source of a word seem like a valid way of deciding what the word's meaning should be? Why or why not?

Suggested Activities

1. Calculate the average number of words per sentence in this essay. Do the same for Trillin's "Low and Slow, Mean and Clean" and for another essay of your choice. On the basis of your findings, can you draw any tentative conclusions about the relationship between readability and sentence length?

2. Write an argumentative essay defending our common use of the word "normal" against Krutch's attack on it.

3. Write a series of paragraphs clarifying the definitions of some commonly confused words (one paragraph per pair of words). Draw on the following list for your examples:

affect — effect	ensure — insure
amount — number	fewer — less
between — among	imply — infer
capital — capitol	principal — principle
complement — compliment	respectfully — respectively
disinterested — uninterested	sensual — sensuous
emigrant — immigrant	stationary — stationery
eminent — imminent	ultimate — penultimate

The Santa Ana

JOAN DIDION

Joan Didion (b. 1934) is a native Californian whose three novels and two collections of essays have earned wide acclaim. After receiving a B.A. degree in English from the University of California, Berkeley, Didion became an editor for *Vogue*, then a writer for a variety of publications, including *The National Review*, *The Saturday Evening Post*, *Harper's*, and *New West*. In the following selection from *Slouching Towards Bethlehem* (1968), her first collection of essays, Didion captures the tensions of life in Los Angeles by focusing on the hot, dry wind that sometimes blows there.

There is something uneasy in the Los Angeles air this afternoon, some unnatural stillness, some tension. What it means is that tonight a Santa Ana will begin to blow, a hot wind from the northeast whining down through the Cajon and San Gorgonio Passes, blowing up sandstorms out along Route 66, drying the hills and the nerves to the flash point. For a few days now we will see smoke back in the canyons, and hear sirens in the night. I have neither heard nor read that a Santa Ana is due, but I know it, and almost everyone I have seen today knows it too. We know it because we feel it. The baby frets. The maid sulks. I rekindle a waning argument with the telephone company, then cut my losses and lie down, given over to whatever it is in the air. To live with the Santa Ana is to accept, consciously or unconsciously, a deeply mechanistic view of human behavior.

I recall being told, when I first moved to Los Angeles and was living on an isolated beach, that the Indians would throw themselves into the sea when the bad wind blew. I could see why. The Pacific turned ominously glossy during a Santa Ana period, and one woke in the night troubled not only by the peacocks screaming in the olive trees but by the eerie absence of surf. The heat was surreal. The sky had a yellow cast, the kind of light sometimes called "earthquake weather." My only neighbor would not come out of her house for days, and there were no lights at night, and her husband roamed the place with a machete. One day he would tell me that he had heard a trespasser, the next a rattlesnake.

"On nights like that," Raymond Chandler once wrote about the Santa Ana, "every booze party ends in a fight. Meek little wives feel the edge of the carving knife and study their husbands' necks. Anything can happen." That was the kind of wind it was. I did not know then that there was any basis for the effect it had on all of us, but it turns out to be another of those cases in which science bears out folk wisdom. The Santa Ana, which is named for one of the canyons it rushes through, is a *foehn* wind, like the *foehn* of Austria and Switzerland and the *hamsin* of Israel. There are a number of persistent malevolent winds, perhaps the best known of which are the mistral of France and the Mediterranean sirocco, but a *foehn* wind has distinct characteristics: it occurs on the leeward slope of a mountain range and, although the air begins as a cold mass, it is warmed as it comes down the mountain and appears finally as a hot dry wind. Whenever and wherever a *foehn* blows, doctors hear about headaches and nausea and allergies, about "nervousness," about "depression." In Los Angeles some teachers do not attempt to conduct formal classes during a Santa Ana, because the children become unmanageable. In Switzerland the suicide rate goes up during the *foehn*, and in the courts of some Swiss cantons the wind is considered a mitigating circumstance for crime. Surgeons are said to watch the wind, because blood does not clot normally during a *foehn*. A few years ago an Israeli physicist discovered that not only during such winds, but for the ten or twelve hours which precede them, the air carries an unusually high ratio of positive to negative ions. No one seems to know exactly why that should be; some talk about friction and others suggest solar disturbances. In any case the positive ions are there, and what an excess of positive ions does, in the simplest terms, is make people unhappy. One cannot get much more mechanistic than that.

Easterners commonly complain that there is no "weather" at all in Southern California, that the days and the seasons slip by relentlessly, numbingly bland. That is quite misleading. In fact the climate is characterized by infrequent but violent extremes: two periods of torrential subtropical rains which continue for weeks and wash out the hills and send subdivisions sliding toward the sea; about twenty scattered days a year of the Santa Ana, which, with its incendiary dryness, invariably means fire. At the first prediction of a Santa Ana, the Forest Service flies men and equipment from northern California into the southern forests, and the Los Angeles Fire Department cancels its ordinary non-firefighting routines. The Santa Ana caused Malibu to burn the way it did in 1956, and Bel Air in 1961, and Santa Barbara in 1964. In the winter of 1966-67 eleven men were killed fighting a Santa Ana fire that spread through the San Gabriel Mountains.

Just to watch the front-page news out of Los Angeles during a Santa Ana is to get very close to what it is about the place. The longest single Santa Ana period in recent years was in 1957, and it lasted not the usual three or four days but fourteen days, from November 21 until December 4. On the first day 25,000 acres of the San Gabriel Mountains were burning, with gusts reaching 100 miles an hour. In town, the wind reached Force 12, or hurricane force, on the Beaufort Scale; oil derricks were toppled and people ordered off the downtown streets to avoid injury from flying objects. On November 22 the fire in the San Gabriels was out of control. On November 24 six people were killed in automobile accidents, and by the end of the week the Los Angeles *Times* was keeping a box score of traffic deaths. On November 26 a prominent Pasadena attorney, depressed about money, shot and killed his wife, their two sons, and himself. On November 27 a South Gate divorcée, twenty-two, was murdered and thrown from a moving car. On November 30 the San Gabriel fire was still out of control, and the wind in town was blowing eighty miles an hour. On the first day of December four people died violently, and on the third the wind began to break.

It is hard for people who have not lived in Los Angeles to realize how radically the Santa Ana figures in the local imagination. The city burning is Los Angeles's deepest image of itself: Nathanael West perceived that, in *The Day of the Locust;* and at the time of the 1965 Watts riots what struck the imagination most indelibly were the fires. For days one could drive the Harbor Freeway and see the city on fire, just as we had always known it would be in the end. Los Angeles weather is the weather of catastrophe, of apocalypse, and, just as the reliably long and bitter winters of New England determine the way life is lived there, so the violence and the unpredictability of the Santa Ana affect the entire quality of life in Los Angeles, accentuate its impermanence, its unreliability. The wind shows us how close to the edge we are.

Questions for Discussion

1. At the end of her first paragraph, Didion says, "To live with the Santa Ana is to accept, consciously or unconsciously, a deeply mechanistic view of human behavior." How well does her essay support this assertion? Does it convince you?

2. This essay abounds in concrete examples. Which ones seem particularly effective to you? Why?

3. In her discussion of the fourteen-day Santa Ana period in 1957, Didion cites a number of examples of people dying. What conclusion are we being invited to reach? What further information would you need to have before you could decide whether or not the number of deaths during this period is statistically significant?

4. At one point, Didion says that Easterners complain of the absence of weather in Southern California. Later she says that Los Angeles has a "weather of catastrophe, of apocalypse." Is the word "weather" being defined in the same way in these two places in the essay? Why or why not?

5. In her last sentence, Didion says, "The wind shows us how close to the edge we are." What edge is she talking about here? Can you suggest more than one pertinent meaning for the word?

6. Didion says that "The city burning is Los Angeles's deepest image of itself." What besides the Santa Ana would make this an appropriate self-image for Los Angeles?

Suggested Activities

1. Compare your attitudes toward weather with those of someone from another part of the country. How do your childhood memories of weather compare? What differences are there in the kinds of weather you find thrilling? frightening?

2. Write a narrative essay about the most extreme weather situation you've ever been in.

3. Write an extended definition of one of the following terms: spring fever, heat wave, humidity, Indian summer. Try not only to define the term but also to evoke the emotions associated with it.

Pornoviolence

TOM WOLFE

Tom Wolfe (b. 1931), the recipient of a Ph.D. in American Studies from Yale University, began his career in journalism as a
reporter for *The Washington Post*. A regular contributor to *New
York* and *Esquire*, Wolfe is one of the originators of "new journalism," a style of reporting characterized by extended dia-
logues, highly imagistic language, and subjective narration. His
books include *The Kandy-Kolored Tangerine-Flake Streamline
Baby* (1965), *The Electric Kool-Aid Acid Test* (1968), and
Mauve Gloves & Madmen, Clutter & Vine (1976). In the essay
from *Mauve Gloves & Madmen* reprinted here, Wolfe coins a
new word, "pornoviolence," to describe a disturbing recent
phenomenon.

"*Keeps His Mom-in-Law in Chains*, meet *Kills Son and Feeds Corpse to Pigs.*"

"Pleased to meet you."

"*Teenager Twists Off Corpse's Head* . . . *to Get Gold Teeth*, meet *Strangles
Girl Friend, Then Chops Her to Pieces.*"

"How you doing?"

"*Nurse's Aide Sees Fingers Chopped Off in Meat Grinder*, meet *I Left My
Babies in the Deep Freeze.*"

"It's a pleasure."

It's a pleasure! No doubt about that! In all these years of journalism I have
covered more conventions than I care to remember. Podiatrists, theosophists,
Professional Budget Finance dentists, oyster farmers, mathematicians, truckers,

dry cleaners, stamp collectors, Esperantists, nudists, and newspaper editors — I have seen them all, together, in vast assemblies, sloughing through the wall-to-wall of a thousand hotel lobbies (the nudists excepted) in their shimmering gray-metal suits and pajama-stripe shirts with white Plasti-Coat name cards on their chests, and I have sat through their speeches and seminars (the nudists included) and attentively endured ear baths such as you wouldn't believe. And yet none has ever been quite like the convention of the stringers for *The National Enquirer.*

The Enquirer is a weekly newspaper that is probably known by sight to millions more than know it by name. No one who ever came face-to-face with *The Enquirer* on a newsstand in its wildest days is likely to have forgotten the sight: a tabloid with great inky shocks of type all over the front page saying something on the order of *Gouges Out Wife's Eyes to Make Her Ugly, Dad Hurls Hot Grease in Daughter's Face, Wife Commits Suicide After 2 Years of Poisoning Fails to Kill Husband . . .*

The stories themselves were supplied largely by stringers, i.e., correspondents, from all over the country, the world, for that matter, mostly copy editors and reporters on local newspapers. Every so often they would come upon a story, usually via the police beat, that was so grotesque the local sheet would discard it or run it in a highly glossed form rather than offend or perplex its readers. The stringers would preserve them for *The Enquirer*, which always rewarded them well and respectfully.

One year *The Enquirer* convened and feted them at a hotel in Manhattan. This convention was a success in every way. The only awkward moment was at the outset when the stringers all pulled in. None of them knew each other. Their hosts got around the problem by introducing them by the stories they had supplied. The introductions went like this:

"Harry, I want you to meet Frank here. Frank did that story, you remember that story, *Midget Murderer Throws Girl Off Cliff after She Refuses to Dance with Him.*"

"Pleased to meet you. That was some story."

"And Harry did the one about *I Spent Three Days Trapped at Bottom of Forty-Foot-Deep Mine Shaft and Was Saved by a Swarm of Flies.*"

"Likewise, I'm sure."

And *Midget Murderer Throws Girl Off Cliff* shakes hands with *I Spent Three Days Trapped at Bottom of Forty-Foot-Deep Mine Shaft*, and *Buries Her Baby Alive* shakes hands with *Boy, Twelve, Strangles Two-Year-Old Girl*, and *Kills Son and Feeds Corpse to Pigs* shakes hands with *He Strangles Old Woman and Smears Corpse with Syrup, Ketchup, and Oatmeal . . .* and . . .

. . . There was a great deal of esprit about the whole thing. These men were, in fact, the avant-garde of a new genre that since then has become institutionalized throughout the nation without anyone knowing its proper name. I speak of the new pornography, the pornography of violence.

Pornography comes from the Greek word "*porne*," meaning harlot, and pornography is literally the depiction of the acts of harlots. In the new pornography, the theme is not sex. The new pornography depicts practitioners acting out another, murkier drive: people staving teeth in, ripping guts open, blowing brains out, and getting even with all those bastards . . .

The success of *The Enquirer* prompted many imitators to enter the field, *Midnight, The Star Chronicle, The National Insider, Inside News, The National Close-up, The National Tattler, The National Examiner.* A truly competitive free press evolved, and soon a reader could go to the newspaper of his choice for *Kill the Retarded! (Won't You Join My Movement?)* and *Unfaithful Wife? Burn Her Bed!, Harem Master's Mistress Chops Him with Machete, Babe Bites off Boy's Tongue,* and *Cuts Buddy's Face to Pieces for Stealing His Business and Fiancée.*

And yet the last time I surveyed the Violence press, I noticed a curious thing. These pioneering journals seem to have pulled back. They seem to be regressing to what is by now the Redi-Mix staple of literate Americans, mere sex. *Ecstasy and Me (by Hedy Lamarr),* says *The National Enquirer. I Run a Sex Art Gallery,* says *The National Insider.* What has happened, I think, is something that has happened to avant-gardes in many fields, from William Morris and the Craftsmen to the Bauhaus group. Namely, their discoveries have been preempted by the Establishment and so thoroughly dissolved into the mainstream they no longer look original.

Robert Harrison, the former publisher of *Confidential,* and later publisher of the aforementioned *Inside News,* was perhaps the first person to see it coming. I was interviewing Harrison early in January 1964 for a story in *Esquire* about six weeks after the assassination of President Kennedy, and we were in a cab in the West Fifties in Manhattan, at a stoplight, by a newsstand, and Harrison suddenly pointed at the newsstand and said, "Look at that. They're doing the same thing *The Enquirer* does."

There on the stand was a row of slick-paper, magazine-size publications, known in the trade as one-shots, with titles like *Four Days That Shook the World, Death of a President, An American Tragedy,* or just *John Fitzgerald Kennedy (1921–1963).* "You want to know why people buy those things?" said Harrison. "People buy those things to see a man get his head blown off."

And, of course, he was right. Only now the publishers were in many cases the pillars of the American press. Invariably, these "special coverages" of the assassination bore introductions piously commemorating the fallen President, exhorting the American people to strength and unity in a time of crisis, urging greater vigilance and safeguards for the new President, and even raising the nice metaphysical question of collective guilt in "an age of violence."

In the years since then, of course, there has been an incessant replay, with every recoverable clinical detail, of those less than five seconds in which a man got his head blown off. And throughout this deluge of words, pictures, and film frames, I have been intrigued with one thing: The point of view, the vantage point, is almost never that of the victim, riding in the Presidential Lincoln Continental. What you get is . . . the view from Oswald's rifle. You can step right up here and look point-blank right through the very hairline cross in Lee Harvey Oswald's Optics Ordinance four-power Japanese telescope sight and watch, frame by frame by frame by frame, as that man there's head comes apart. Just a little History there before your very eyes.

The television networks have schooled us in the view from Oswald's rifle and made it seem a normal pastime. The TV viewpoint is nearly always that of the man who is going to strike. The last time I watched *Gunsmoke*, which was not known as a very violent Western in TV terms, the action went like this: The Wellington agents and the stagecoach driver pull guns on the badlands gang leader's daughter and Kitty, the heart-of-gold saloonkeeper, and kidnap them. Then the badlands gang shoots two Wellington agents. Then they tie up five more and talk about shooting them. Then they desist because they might not be able to get a hotel room in the next town if the word got around. Then one badlands gang gunslinger attempts to rape Kitty while the gang leader's younger daughter looks on. Then Kitty resists, so he slugs her one in the jaw. Then the gang leader slugs him. Then the gang leader slugs Kitty. Then Kitty throws hot stew in a gang member's face and hits him over the back of the head with a revolver. Then he knocks her down with a rock. Then the gang sticks up a bank. Here comes the marshal, Matt Dillon. He shoots a gang member and breaks it up. Then the gang leader shoots the guy who was guarding his daughter and the woman. Then the marshal shoots the gang leader. The final exploding bullet signals The End.

It is not the accumulated slayings and bone crushings that make this pornoviolence, however. What makes it pornoviolence is that in almost every case the camera angle, therefore the viewer, is with the gun, the fist, the rock. The pornography of violence has no point of view in the old sense that novels do. You do not live the action through the hero's eyes. You live with the aggressor, whoever he may be. One moment you are the hero. The next you are the villain. No matter whose side you may be on consciously, you are in fact with the muscle, and it is you who disintegrate all comers, villains, lawmen, women, anybody. On the rare occasions in which the gun is emptied into the camera—i.e., into your face—the effect is so startling that the pornography of violence all but loses its fantasy charm. There are not nearly so many masochists as sadists among those little devils whispering into one's ears.

In fact, sex—"sadomasochism"—is only a part of the pornography of violence. Violence is much more wrapped up, simply, with status. Violence is the simple, ultimate solution for problems of status competition, just as gambling is the simple, ultimate solution for economic competition. The old pornography was the fantasy of easy sexual delights in a world where sex was kept unavailable. The new pornography is the fantasy of easy triumph in a world where status competition has become so complicated and frustrating.

Already the old pornography is losing its kick because of overexposure. In the late thirties, Nathanael West published his last and best-regarded novel, *The Day of the Locust*, and it was a terrible flop commercially, and his publisher said if he ever published another book about Hollywood it would "have to be *My Thirty-nine Ways of Making Love by Hedy Lamarr*." He thought he was saying something that was funny because it was beyond the realm of possibility. Less than thirty years later, however, Hedy Lamarr's *Ecstasy and Me* was published. Whether she mentions thirty-nine ways, I'm not sure, but she gets off to a flying start: "The men in my life have ranged from a classic case history of impotence, to a whip-brandishing sadist who enjoyed sex only after he tied my arms behind me with the sash of his robe. There was another man who took his pleasure with a girl in my own bed, while he thought I was asleep in it."

Yet she was too late. The book very nearly sank without a trace. The sin itself is wearing out. Pornography cannot exist without certified taboo to violate. And today Lust, like the rest of the Seven Deadly Sins—Pride, Sloth, Envy, Greed, Anger, and Gluttony—is becoming a rather minor vice. The Seven Deadly Sins, after all, are only sins against the self. Theologically, the idea of Lust—well, the idea is that if you seduce some poor girl from Akron, it is not a sin because you are ruining her, but because you are wasting your time and your energies and damaging your own spirit. This goes back to the old work ethic, when the idea was to keep every able-bodied man's shoulder to the wheel. In an age of riches for all, the ethic becomes more nearly: Let him do anything he pleases, as long as he doesn't get in my way. And if he does get in my way, or even if he doesn't ... well ... we have *new* fantasies for that. *Put hair on the walls.*

"Hair on the walls" is the invisible subtitle of Truman Capote's book *In Cold Blood*. The book is neither a who-done-it nor a will-they-be-caught, since the answer to both questions are known from the outset. It does ask why-did-they-do-it, but the answer is soon as clear as it is going to be. Instead, the book's suspense is based largely on a totally new idea in detective stories: the promise of gory details, and the withholding of them until the end. Early in the game one of the two murderers, Dick, starts promising to put "plenty of hair on them-those walls" with a shotgun. So read on, gentle readers, and on and on; you are led up to the moment before the crime on page 60—yet the specifics, what happened, the gory details, are kept out of sight, in grisly dangle, until page 244.

But Dick and Perry, Capote's killers, are only a couple of Low Rent bums. With James Bond the new pornography reached a dead center, the bureaucratic middle class. The appeal of Bond has been explained as the appeal of the lone man who can solve enormously complicated, even world problems through his own bravery and initiative. But Bond is not a lone man at all, of course. He is not the Lone Ranger. He is much easier to identify than that. He is a salaried functionary in a bureaucracy. He is a sport, but a believable one; not a millionaire, but a bureaucrat on an expense account. He is not even a high-level bureaucrat. He is an operative. This point is carefully and repeatedly made by having his superiors dress him down for violations of standard operating procedure. Bond, like the Lone Ranger, solves problems with guns and fists. When it is over, however, the Lone Ranger leaves a silver bullet. Bond, like the rest of us, fills out a report in triplicate.

Marshall McLuhan says we are in a period in which it will become harder and harder to stimulate lust through words and pictures—i.e., the old pornography. In the latest round of pornographic movies the producers have found it necessary to introduce violence, bondage, torture, and aggressive physical destruction to an extraordinary degree. The same sort of bloody escalation may very well happen in the pure pornography of violence. Even such able craftsmen as Truman Capote, Ian Fleming, NBC, and CBS may not suffice. Fortunately, there are historical models to rescue us from this frustration. In the latter days of the Roman Empire, the Emperor Commodus became jealous of the celebrity of the great gladiators. He took to the arena himself, with his sword, and began dispatching suitably screened cripples and hobbled fighters. Audience participation became so popular that soon various *illuminati* of the Commodus set, various boys and girls of the year, were out there, suited up, gaily cutting a sequence of dwarfs and feebles down to short ribs. Ah, swinging generations, what new delights await?

Questions for Discussion

1. What is the thesis of this essay? Do you find Wolfe's support for the thesis convincing? Why or why not?

2. From Wolfe's perspective, what characteristics of his subject earn it the label *pornoviolence*? How does pornoviolence differ from ordinary violence?

3. In his essay, to what extent — if any — is Wolfe guilty of the sensationalism he accuses the newspapers of fostering?

4. Wolfe says "the television networks have schooled us in the view from Oswald's rifle." What do you think he means by this statement? Do you agree with him?

5. Compare Wolfe's use of etymology in his definition of "pornography" with Krutch's use of it in his definition of "normal." Whose use do you prefer? Why?

6. What is the tone of this essay? How is it created? Do you find it effective?

Suggested Activities

1. List the distinctions Wolfe makes between what he calls the "old" pornography and pornoviolence. Do you find the distinctions convincing?

2. Compare the headlines used by four or five different newspapers to introduce stories on the same sensational event. What differences do you find in them? Do they all support Wolfe's contention that daily newspapers have adopted *The Enquirer*'s techniques?

3. Write an essay that discusses the role of violence in a sport or other social activity.

Apple Pie

M. F. K. FISHER

M. F. K. Fisher (b. 1908), noted culinary expert, is the author of a dozen books on subjects as diverse as California wines and French provincial towns. Both her wit and her wide-ranging culinary interests are reflected in the titles of two of her books: *Consider the Oyster* (1941) and *How to Cook a Wolf* (1942). In the essay reprinted here, Fisher combines historical facts, anecdotes, and recipes to create an extended definition of America's best-loved dessert.

It is as meaningless to say that something is "as American as apple pie" as it is to assert proudly that a Swedish or Irish grandfather who emigrated to Minnesota was "a first American." Both the pie and the parent sprang from other cultures, and neither got here before the Indian.

Be that as it is, and nonetheless, most of us today would fight staunchly to defend the rights and honors of what we choose to consider our own dish . . . or at least one of our own *great* dishes. The fact that it came here from England, with the Pilgrims up North and the Cavaliers down South, long before we were a nation, and that it was probably brought in recognizable form to England by William the Conqueror in 1066 or so, cannot mar the fine polish of how we feel about apple pie as a part of our comparatively youthful heritage.

There are as many opinions about perfection in this national dish as there are about hangover cures. A man-on-the-street survey, no matter who conducts it nor how nor where, will turn up firm contradictions based on knowledge or prejudice or plain wishful thinking. A lot of people have never really had the chance to eat a decent apple pie, but after a minute's sensual reflection will know positively what they would expect if they did. They can taste it on their mind's tongue: thin flaky pastry and hunks of sweet apples bathed in a syrup; rich but sturdy dough filled with finely sliced tart apples seasoned with cinnamon; an upper and lower crust in a traditional pie pan; an upper crust only, in a deep dish; a bottom crust with crosses of dough over the filling. . . .

It is all a dream, unless one has a quaint old-country grandma or an equally rare bakery. We order apple pie doggedly in everything from expensive steak houses to the corner drugstore, and gallantly disguise it with vanilla ice cream "a la mode," or eat packaged ersatz "Cheddar" alongside, or even tolerate it (in what can only be a form of chauvinism) with cheese baked under the top crust, or raisins added, or some other such heinous desecration of what apple pie can be.

It can be very very good, like the little girl with the curl in the middle of her forehead. Since the possibilities for its being equally horrid have been hinted at, and no mention at all has been made of bad bakery products and tasteless but somewhat less dangerous frozen goods, I'll try a more positive look at what *can* happen to this adopted beauty of a dish.

Like anything fit to be put on the table, it cannot be whipped out in a few minutes from bad supplies and a bored heart. A really good apple pie takes perhaps an hour and a half to get from the peelings to the table. This does not count buying the apples and seeing that the other supplies are on hand . . . and even having a kitchen and an oven! If the pie smells as good as it should, people will want to eat it immediately, but it should wait for a while and be served gently warm. It is almost as easy to make two or six as one, and some of the batch can be frozen or stored. In simpler days, extra pies were put outside the kitchen window, safe from four-legged friends of course, or down in the icy cellar. A two-crust pie risks becoming soggy if not eaten soon, and pioneer cooks found that, for keeping, it was wise to bake one or two deep-dish pies with only a top crust.

So, given the ingredients and the essentials — like pan, stove, oven — one goes calmly about the game, which can become as skilled as eye surgery or Wimbledon, of concocting an apple pie to fit the sensual expectations and requirements of its eaters. It should leave them happy but expectant of the next time and with excellent digestion.

A woman who is eminent in this branch of gastronomical therapy tells me:

Peel, core, and slice about six tart apples into a bowl. Sugar them, add a little cinnamon and a jigger of good brandy or bourbon, and stir them well. While they sit, make a light rich dough, and roll it out (never back and forth but *out*). Have the oven at 450°. Line the pan(s), heap in the apples, dot generously with butter. Cover with top crust, seal edges, and cut a slash in the top. Bake fast for ten minutes, and then reduce heat to 350° for about thirty to forty minutes or until the apples feel tender when speared through the peekhole.

She adds a few casual asides to this basically plain procedure: if the apples are too mild, stir a little lemon juice into them; add a couple of tablespoonsful of cornstarch if you think the pie will be too soupy . . . and if it runs over, throw salt onto the juice in the oven; don't mention the brandy if Aunt Jenny, who is president of the W.C.T.U., asks why the pie is so tasty, since she wouldn't admit that all the alcohol has long since evaporated. . . .

There is a surprising scarcity of such fundamental recipes in our old kitchen manuals, because in early America any cook worth his or her salt knew perforce how to produce a pie by puberty, so that there was no need to write the rules. Many of the existing directions are, of course, impractical by now, but even a modern amateur can take a good look at a standard guide like Mrs. Rombauer or Fanny Farmer and roll out a decent crust. And there are real apples almost always in the markets. There is sugar, cinnamon, even lemon juice in an emergency. Margarine is procurable if butter is not.

To sound realistic rather than wishful for a minute, a "homemade" pie that might bring some joy to a person used to drugstore offerings can be fabricated with a bought crust and a can of "pie apples," if rather heavily seasoned and gussied. It tastes fairly good, perhaps because it is actually made in the home (which is where the oven is). But comparisons are said to be odious. . . .

Possibly our national appetite for apple pie could be called a syndrome, or even a mystique, and perhaps we can blame a lot of it on a very nice quiet religious eccentric named John Chapman. He was a New Englander (1774–1845) who spent the last forty years of his life wandering around what is now Ohio-Indiana-Illinois, planting apple seeds, yes, "Planting the trees that would march/ In his name to the great Pacific,/ Like Birnam Wood to Dunsinane,/ Johnny Appleseed swept on." That is what Carl Sandburg sang about Johnny, and another poet wrote,"Let all unselfish spirits heed/The story of Johnny Appleseed," and my own grandfather is said to have rested under Johnny's bending orchard boughs on his way to survey the Iowa territory for Mr. Lincoln. That was in about 1864. He said that the trees were half wild but fruitful and that people still talked affectionately of the crazy gentle man as if he were still there.

Apple trees have grown in temperate zones for as long as we can tell (how about the Garden of Eden?), and they are a tough rich beautiful tree, a boon to us all in spite of Eve's slip of the tongue. They are intricately woven into our legends and myths and religious fantasies, from Aphrodite to William Tell. There are said to be about 7,600 varieties of them, almost all edible in one form or another. They will live a long time even in high places but not on deserts.

Apples keep well in cool cellars and can be partially or wholly cooked and used in preserves and sauces, or dried, as pioneer Americans found. (A fine pie can be made of dried apple slices let swell to their right size in warm water overnight. Then the pie can be baked in time for breakfast, while the men are at their first chores. Pie for breakfast is as American as . . .) An apple a day is said to keep the doctor away, and certainly it should, if the eater has a good stomach and strong teeth and can breathe good air and a few other things that otherwise might bring the pill boys hurrying in. The best apples now available, unless there is a venerable orchard nearby, are marketed as Rome Beauties, mostly for cooking; Northern Spies, McIntoshes, Jonathans for eating; Gravensteins for both. This is a northern California estimate, and I know there are countless other choices in our country and that I would blush to make this one anywhere but here.

A pie is always a baked dish with a crust on top for me. It can have a top and bottom crust, especially if filled with fruit. But if it has only a bottom crust it is a tart. This simplifies life. In England, where our pies came from, they can be either tarts or pies, depending on what is in them; that is, fruit can be topless or bottomless, but meat is always with a top and is called a pie and not a tart. (A pasty, usually with meat and vegetables in it, is what we call a turnover.) In France a *tarte* is a tart, topless and unashamed, except for a slight lacing of strips of pastry and a hint of a blush from the sweet glaze over it.

(It is interesting or even significant that Mrs. Irma Rombauer, whose *Joy of Cooking* is as staunchly American as Mrs. Isabella Beeton's *Book of Household Management* is British, states flatly of her French apple pie — really an open-face *tarte* on *galette* crust — that it is "the prince"! Her Gallic recipe is as *echt* as *Apfelkuchen*, although I feel patriotically that her rule for plain Midwestern apple pie is equally noble.)

I try to stay positive about several American institutions, including apple pie, but it is hard not to make firm and even derisive statements about what is fobbed off on us just because we seem to have a compulsive craving for the dish. How dare the local U-Help Drugs display, much less sell, what I see boldly cut onto plates on glass shelves behind the fair-tressed serving maid? What good will a scoop of vanilla ice cream lend it? But I may *need* some quick energy from sugar or glucose, the taste of ex-fruit, the sustenance of dead fat and emasculated flour. . . . The crust is inedible, like slippery cardboard on the bottom and sugared newsprint on top. The apples are canned vintage, embalmed for posterity in a rare chemical syrup. As for the scoop of . . . Back to the wall, I can dig between the two crusts and eat some shiny lumps and think of other days.

Perhaps it is true that national surveys show that American males now prefer chocolate pie to apple, and although I can understand, I refuse to believe it. Myself, I have never eaten chocolate pie in a good restaurant or coffee shop, much less in my own home, but once I was served a chocolate meringue pie in a New York apartment that had been "decorated" in browns and blacks to match the pet dachshund, and it was an experience in nothingness, except perhaps calorically. The flavor was so delicately un-chocolate as to vanish within the frothy high-piled filling, and the crust was equally discreet and neither light nor heavy, flaky nor rich, nor . . . *crusty*. The little dog had much more character, and a forthright approximation of our national dish, even from a stylish caterer, would have matched him better.

Vanilla ice cream is the best camouflage of outrage at the local U-Helps, but if an honorable, decent, healthy, respectable apple pie is at hand, I would send it down my happy gullet either unassisted or with one of two special things: a piece of good Cheddar cheese, English or American. (It can be called rat-trap, where I came from.) The other is plain thick cream, poured from a pitcher and preferably into a soup plate over the piece of pie.

Once I stayed for a time in southern Illinois and lived from one Sunday-noon invitation to the next, less aware of the elegant old house, a station of the Underground on the Mason-Dixon line in the Civil War, than of the fact that not only one pie would be served for dessert but *two*. They were mince and apple, and both were just hot enough to melt the ice cream served from a chilled bowl. The ice cream was made with maple sugar, to pile on top of the slices of pie, each on a separate plate. This was a dizzying reward to a half-starved college student. It was as near as I ever came to New England, where shaved maple sugar and plain cream are eaten now as in the seventeenth century with apple dumplings, pies, pandowdies, anything with a good crust.

Myself, given such a crusty pie made with tart apples and the right sugar-cinnamon-butter, that is all I need for a whole meal, a private sensual satisfying supper. I agree with Robert Louis Stevenson's seemingly infantile prattling in *A Child's Garden of Verses*: "The friendly cow all red and white,/ I love with all my heart./ She gives me cream with all her might,/ To eat with apple tart."

In other words, apple pie as we make it now, whether at a U-Help or in an Idaho cabin or a New York kitchenette-studio, is unique to America. It assumes ethnic tinges depending on where we live and who bore us there, but the shape is formally *ours*: a two-crust round baked shallow dish or pan, containing sliced apples, spices, sugar and butter (with perhaps lemon juice or brandy).

I'll eat it anytime I can find a good one. Or, I'll stay home and bake one, which is probably what we all should do.

Questions for Discussion

1. What elements of this essay suggest that Fisher is a cooking expert? Is her expertise important to the essay? Why or why not?

2. In the beginning of the essay Fisher says it is "meaningless to say that something is 'as American as apple pie'. . . ." At the end she says the "apple pie as we make it now . . . is unique to America." Do these two statements contradict each other?

3. Does Fisher seem more concerned with what apple pie is or with what she thinks it ought to be? Explain.

4. At the end of her essay Fisher says we probably all should stay home and bake an apple pie. Do you think she means this statement literally? Why or why not?

5. Fisher uses a number of "homely" images and comparisons throughout this essay. Do they seem deliberate? appropriate? Explain.

6. How would you describe Fisher's attitude toward her subject matter in this essay?

Suggested Activities

1. Compare your favorite foods with those of other members of the class. To what extent are your differences in taste the result of differences in ethnic background and upbringing?

2. Write an essay examining the significance of a custom or symbol we now think of as "unique to America."

3. Write a paragraph describing the taste and texture of a food item served in a fast-food restaurant.

Kitsch

GILBERT HIGHET

Gilbert Highet (1906-78), a Scottish-born naturalized citizen of the United States, was professor of classics at Columbia University from 1937 to 1972. He is the author of a number of scholarly books on ancient life and literature, including *The Classical Tradition* (1949) and *The Anatomy of Satire* (1962). In the selection reprinted here, from *A Clerk at Oxenford* (1954), Highet departs from his usual subject matter to reveal the pleasure that can be found in unintentionally bad writing.

If you have ever passed an hour wandering through an antique shop (not looking for anything exactly, but simply looking), you must have noticed how your taste gradually grows numb, and then — if you stay — becomes perverted. You begin to see unsuspected charm in those hideous pictures of plump girls fondling pigeons, you develop a psychopathic desire for spinning wheels and cobblers' benches, you are apt to pay out good money for a bronze statuette of Otto von Bismarck, with a metal hand inside a metal frock coat and metal pouches under his metallic eyes. As soon as you take the things home, you realize that they are revolting. And yet they have a sort of horrible authority; you don't like them; you know how awful they are; but it is a tremendous effort to drop them in the garbage, where they belong.

To walk along a whole street of antique shops — that is an experience which shakes the very soul. Here is a window full of bulbous Chinese deities; here is another littered with Zulu assegais, Indian canoe paddles, and horse pistols which

KITSCH   From *A Clerk at Oxenford* by Gilbert Highet, published by Oxford University Press. Copyright © 1954 by Gilbert Highet. Reprinted by permission of Curtis Brown, Ltd.

won't fire; the next shopfront is stuffed with gaudy Italian majolica vases, and the next, even worse, with Austrian pottery — tiny ladies and gentlemen sitting on lace cushions and wearing lace ruffles, with every frill, every wrinkle and reticulation translated into porcelain: pink; stiff; but fortunately not unbreakable. The nineteenth century produced an appalling amount of junky art like this, and sometimes I imagine that clandestine underground factories are continuing to pour it out like illicit drugs.

There is a name for such stuff in the trade, a word apparently of Russian origin, kitsch[1]: it means vulgar showoff, and it is applied to anything that took a lot of trouble to make and is quite hideous.

It is paradoxical stuff, kitsch. It is obviously bad: so bad that you can scarcely understand how any human being would spend days and weeks making it, and how anybody else would buy it and take it home and keep it and dust it and leave it to her heirs. It is terribly ingenious, and terribly ugly, and utterly useless; and yet it has one of the qualities of good art — which is that, once seen, it is not easily forgotten. Of course it is found in all the arts: think of Milan Cathedral, or the statues in Westminster Abbey, or Liszt's settings of Schubert songs. There is a lot of it in the United States — for instance, the architecture of Miami, Florida, and Forest Lawn Cemetery in Los Angeles. Many of Hollywood's most ambitious historical films are superb kitsch. Most Tin Pan Alley love songs are perfect 100 per cent kitsch.

There is kitsch in the world of books also. I collect it. It is horrible, but I enjoy it.

The gem of my collection is the work of the Irish novelist Mrs. Amanda McKittrick Ros, whose masterpiece, *Delina Delaney*, was published about 1900. It is a stirringly romantic tale, telling how Delina, a fisherman's daughter from Erin Cottage, was beloved by Lord Gifford, the heir of Columba Castle, and — after many trials and even imprisonment — married him. The story is dramatic, not to say impossible; but it is almost lost to view under the luxuriant style. Here, for example, is a sentence in which Mrs. Ros explains that her heroine used to earn extra cash by doing needlework.

> She tried hard to assist in keeping herself a stranger to her poor old father's slight income by the use of the finest production of steel, whose blunt edge eyed the reely covering with marked greed, and offered its sharp dart to faultless fabrics of flaxen fineness.

Revolting, but distinctive: what Mr. Polly called 'rockockyo' in manner. For the baroque vein, here is Lord Gifford saying goodby to his sweetheart:

> My darling virgin! my queen! my Delina! I am just in time to hear the toll of a parting bell strike its heavy weight of appalling softness against the weakest fibers of a heart of love, arousing and tickling its dormant action,

[1]The Russian verb *keetcheetsya* means 'to be haughty and puffed up.'

thrusting the dart of evident separation deeper into its tubes of tenderness, and fanning the flame, already unextinguishable, into volumes of blaze.

Mrs. Ros had a remarkable command of rhetoric, and could coin an unforgettable phrase. She described her hero's black eyes as 'glittering jet revolvers.' When he became ill, she said he fell 'into a state of lofty fever' — doubtless because commoners have high fever, but lords have lofty fever. And her reflections on the moral degeneracy of society have rarely been equaled, in power and penetration:

> Days of humanity, whither hast thou fled? When bows of compulsion, smiles for the deceitful, handshakes for the dogmatic, and welcome for the tool of power live under your objectionable, unambitious beat, not daring to be checked by the tongue of candour because the selfish world refuses to dispense with her rotten policies. The legacy of your forefathers, which involved equity, charity, reason, and godliness, is beyond the reach of their frivolous, mushroom offspring — deceit, injustice, malice, and unkindness — and is not likely to be codiciled with traits of harmony so long as these degrading vices of mock ambition fester the human heart.

Perhaps one reason I enjoy this stuff is because it so closely resembles a typical undergraduate translation of one of Cicero's finest perorations: sound and fury, signifying nothing. I regret only that I have never seen Mrs. Ros's poetry. One volume was called *Poems of Puncture* and another *Bayonets of Bastard Sheen:* alas, jewels now almost unprocurable. But at least I know the opening of her lyric written on first visiting St. Paul's Cathedral:

> Holy Moses, take a look,
> Brain and brawn in every nook!

Such genius is indestructible. Soon, soon now, some earnest researcher will be writing a Ph.D. thesis on Mrs. Amanda McKittrick Ros, and thus (as she herself might put it) conferring upon her dewy brow the laurels of concrete immortality.

Next to Mrs. Ros in my collection of kitsch is the work of the Scottish poet William McGonagall. This genius was born in 1830, but did not find his vocation until 1877. Poor and inadequate poets pullulate in every tongue, but (as the *Times Literary Supplement* observes) McGonagall 'is the only truly memorable bad poet in our language.' In his command of platitude and his disregard of melody, he was the true heir of William Wordsworth as a descriptive poet.

In one way his talents, or at least his aspirations, exceeded those of Wordsworth. He was at his best in describing events he had never witnessed, such as train disasters, shipwrecks, and sanguinary battles, and in picturing magnificent scenery he had never beheld except with the eye of the imagination. Here is his unforgettable Arctic landscape:

> Greenland's icy mountains are fascinating and grand,
> And wondrously created by the Almighty's command;

And the works of the Almighty there's few can understand:
Who knows but it might be a part of Fairyland?

Because there are churches of ice, and houses glittering like glass,
And for scenic grandeur there's nothing can it surpass,
Besides there's monuments and spires, also ruins,
Which serve for a safe retreat from the wild bruins.

The icy mountains they're higher than a brig's topmast,
And the stranger in amazement stands aghast
As he beholds the water flowing off the melted ice
Adown the mountain sides, that he cries out, Oh! how nice!

McGonagall also had a strong dramatic sense. He loved to tell of agonizing adventures, more drastic perhaps but not less moving than that related in Wordsworth's 'Vaudracour and Julia.' The happy ending of one of his 'Gothic' ballads is surely unforgettable:

So thus ends the story of Hanchen, a heroine brave,
That tried hard her master's gold to save,
And for her bravery she got married to the miller's eldest son,
And Hanchen on her marriage night cried Heaven's will be done.

These scanty selections do not do justice to McGonagall's ingenuity as a rhymester. His sound effects show unusual talent. Most poets would be baffled by the problem of producing rhymes for the proper names *General Graham* and *Osman Digna*, but McGonagall gets them into a single stanza, with dazzling effect:

Ye sons of Great Britain, I think no shame
To write in praise of brave General Graham!
Whose name will be handed down to posterity without any stigma,
Because, at the battle of El-Tab, he defeated Osman Digna.

One of McGonagall's most intense personal experiences was his visit to New York. Financially, it was not a success. In one of his vivid autobiographical sketches, he says, 'I tried occasionally to get an engagement from theatrical proprietors and music-hall proprietors, but alas! 'twas all in vain, for they all told me they didn't encourage rivalry!' However, he was deeply impressed by the architecture of Manhattan. In eloquent verses he expressed what many others have felt, although without adequate words to voice their emotion:

Oh! Mighty City of New York, you are wonderful to behold,
Your buildings are magnificent, the truth be it told;
They were the only thing that seemed to arrest my eye,
Because many of them are thirteen stories high.

> And the tops of the houses are all flat,
> And in the warm weather the people gather to chat;
> Besides on the house-tops they dry their clothes,
> And also many people all night on the house-tops repose.

Yet McGonagall felt himself a stranger in the United States. And here again his close kinship with Wordsworth appears. The Poet Laureate, in a powerful sonnet written at Calais, once reproached the English Channel for delaying his return by one of those too frequent storms in which (reckless tyrant!) it will indulge itself:

> Why cast ye back upon the Gallic shore,
> Ye furious waves! a patriotic Son
> Of England?

In the same vein McGonagall sings with rapture of his return to his 'ain countree':

> And with regard to New York, and the sights I did see,
> One street in Dundee is more worth to me,
> And, believe me, the morning I sailed from New York,
> For bonnie Dundee — my heart it felt as light as a cork.

Indeed, New York is a challenging subject for ambitious poets. Here, from the same shelf, is a delicious poem on the same theme, by Ezra Pound:

> My City, my beloved,
> Thou art a maid with no breasts
> Thou art slender as a silver reed.
> Listen to me, attend me!
> And I will breathe into thee a soul,
> And thou shalt live for ever.

The essence of this kind of trash is incongruity. The kitsch writer is always sincere. He really means to say something important. He feels he has a lofty spiritual message to bring to an unawakened world, or else he has had a powerful experience which he must communicate to the public. But either his message turns out to be a majestic platitude, or else he chooses the wrong form in which to convey it — or, most delightful of all, there is a fundamental discrepancy between the writer and his subject, as when Ezra Pound, born in Idaho, addresses the largest city in the world as a maid with no breasts, and enjoins it to achieve inspiration and immortality by listening to him. This is like climbing Mount Everest in order to carve a head of Mickey Mouse in the east face.

Bad love poetry, bad religious poetry, bad mystical prose, bad novels both autobiographical and historical — one can form a superb collection of kitsch simply by reading with a lively and awakened eye. College songs bristle with it. The

works of Father Divine are full of it — all the more delightful because in him it
is usually incomprehensible. One of the Indian mystics, Sri Ramakrishna,
charmed connoisseurs by describing the Indian scriptures (in a phrase which
almost sets itself to kitsch-music) as

> fried in the butter of knowledge and steeped
> in the honey of love.

Bad funeral poetry is a rich mine of the stuff. Here, for example, is the opening
of a jolly little lament, 'The Funeral' by Stephen Spender, apparently written during his pink period:

> Death is another milestone on their way.
> With laughter on their lips and with winds blowing round them
> They record simply
> How this one excelled all others in making driving belts.

Observe the change from humanism to communism. Spender simply took Brown-
ing's 'Grammarian's Funeral,' threw away the humor and the marching rhythm,
and substituted wind and the Stakhanovist speed-up. Such also is a delicious cou-
plet from Archibald MacLeish's elegy on the late Harry Crosby:

> He walks with Ernest in the streets in Saragossa
> They are drunk their mouths are hard they say *qué cosa.*

From an earlier romantic period, here is a splendid specimen. Coleridge
attempted to express the profound truth that men and animals are neighbors in
a hard world; but he made the fundamental mistake of putting it into a mono-
logue address to a donkey:

> Poor Ass! Thy master should have learnt to show
> Pity — best taught by fellowship of Woe!
> Innocent foal! thou poor despised forlorn!
> I hail thee brother . . .

Once you get the taste for this kind of thing it is possible to find pleasure in
hundreds of experiences which you might otherwise have thought either anes-
thetic or tedious: bad translations, abstract painting, grand opera . . . Dr. Johnson,
with his strong sense of humor, had a fancy for kitsch, and used to repeat a poem
in celebration of the marriage of the Duke of Leeds, composed by 'an inferiour
domestick . . . in such homely rhimes as he could make':

> When the Duke of Leeds shall married be
> To a fine young lady of high quality,
> How happy will that gentlewoman be
> In his Grace of Leed's good company.

> She shall have all that's fine and fair,
> And the best of silk and sattin shall wear;
> And ride in a coach to take the air,
> And have a house in St. James's Square.

Folk poetry is full of such jewels. Here is the epitaph on an old gentleman from Vermont who died in a sawmill accident:

> How shocking to the human mind
> The log did him to powder grind.
> God did command his soul away
> His summings we must all obey.

Kitsch is well known in drama, although (except for motion pictures) it does not usually last long. One palmary instance was a play extolling the virtues of the Boy Scout movement, called *Young England*. It ran for a matter of years during the 1930's, to audiences almost wholly composed of kitsch-fanciers, who eventually came to know the text quite as well as the unfortunate actors. I can still remember the opening of one magnificent episode. Scene: a woodland glade. Enter the hero, a Scoutmaster, riding a bicycle, and followed by the youthful members of his troop. They pile bicycles in silence. Then the Scoutmaster raises his finger, and says (accompanied fortissimo by most of the members of the audience):

> Fresh water must be our first consideration!

In the decorative arts kitsch flourishes, and is particularly widespread in sculpture. One of my favorite pieces of bad art is a statue in Rockefeller Center, New York. It is supposed to represent Atlas, the Titan condemned to carry the sky on his shoulders. That is an ideal of somber, massive tragedy: greatness and suffering combined as in Hercules or Prometheus. But this version displays Atlas as a powerful moron, with a tiny little head, rather like the pan-fried young men who appear in the health magazines. Instead of supporting the heavens, he is lifting a spherical metal balloon: it is transparent, and quite empty; yet he is balancing insecurely on one foot like a furniture mover walking upstairs with a beach ball; and he is scowling like a mad baboon. If he ever gets the thing up, he will drop it; or else heave it onto a Fifth Avenue bus. It is a supremely ridiculous statue, and delights me every time I see it.

Perhaps you think this is a depraved taste. But really it is an extension of experience. At one end, Homer. At the other, Amanda McKittrick Ros. At one end, *Hamlet*. At the other, McGonagall, who is best praised in his own inimitable words:

> The poetry is moral and sublime
> And in my opinion nothing could be more fine.
> True genius there does shine so bright
> Like unto the stars of night.

Questions for Discussion

1. This essay uses many examples to define its subject. Does this technique seem effective Why or why not?

2. What audience do you think would most appreciate this essay? Explain.

3. In speaking of popular music, Highet says that "most Tin Pan Alley love songs are perfect 100 per cent kitsch." Do you agree?

4. Highet says that kitsch "is horrible, but I enjoy it." Do you also enjoy things that you know are in bad taste? What seems to be the cause of such enjoyment?

5. William Wordsworth, Ezra Pound, Stephen Spender, Archibald MacLeish, and Samuel Taylor Coleridge are all famous poets. Why do you think Highet cites examples of kitsch from their works?

6. On the basis of this essay, what is your impression of Gilbert Highet? Do you think he is a snob? What evidence can you cite in justification of your view?

Suggested Activities

1. Not all kitsch was created in the distant past. Discuss current examples from magazines, movies, and television with other members of your class. How closely does your taste agree with theirs?

2. Write an essay that defines through the use of multiple examples. Choose your own topic.

3. Using your own language, write brief, formal definitions for the following words used in "Kitsch": bulbous, assegais, reticulation, perorations, pullulate, sanguinary, palmary.

4. A book called *Mom, the Flag, and Apple Pie* contains an essay by Gerald Nachman called "Cornball." Find this book in the library and write an essay comparing Nachman's and Highet's views of bad taste.

classification

In 1948, William Faulkner was putting together a collection of his short stories. After struggling for some time with the problem of how to group the stories, he finally came upon a solution. Here is how he described his discovery to his editor:

> On the way down yesterday, I kept on thinking about the table of contents page; something about it nagged at me. I kept on thinking, why *Indians* when we had never said the Country *people* and the Village *people,* but only the *Country* and the *Village.* Then I thought, not *Indians* but *Wilderness,* and then suddenly the whole page stood right, each noun in character and tone and tune with every other. . . .[1]

"Each noun in character and tone and tune with every other"—Faulkner's phrase perfectly expresses the delight we all feel when we suddenly see the right way to classify something. This delight is deeply rooted in us, for the impulse to sort and classify is inherent in human beings. Infants do it, when they arrange their blocks by color and size. At the age of eight or nine, children temporarily become obsessed with the process: they collect something—bottle caps or baseball cards or beads—and then spend hours grouping and regrouping the items, almost as if they were being unconsciously impelled to practice

[1]William Faulkner, *Selected Letters,* ed. Joseph Blotner (New York: Random House, 1977), p. 227.

a basic human skill. And when we grow up, the impulse stays with us. We sort laundry and canned goods and pictures and books and money, and we use other people's classifications as well, relying on them to provide us with sensible groupings of things as diverse as the groceries in a supermarket, the stories in a newspaper, and the listings in a television guide.

However widely we use classification in our daily lives, though, using it well in writing may take a bit of practice. The classifications we encounter in every-day situations are frequently informal, self-contradictory, and incomplete. If these deficiencies don't usually bother us, it's because we've grown accustomed to them. Why is the kitty litter stacked next to the charcoal and the fireplace logs in the supermarket? What difference does it make? That's where it's always been, we know it, and we can find it there if we need to.

But classification in writing is a different matter. When we use a classificatory scheme in an essay, our readers are seeing it for the first time as they read. If it is arbitrary or logically inconsistent, they may be confused—and they will almost certainly lose some of their faith in our ability to organize and present information. Fortunately, though, there are three fairly easy steps we can take to ensure that the classifications we use in our writing will be clear and useful.

1. Use only one principle of division at each level of classification. Think back for a moment to the example of Faulkner and his short stories. What was wrong with his initial classification of them into the categories "Indians-Country-Village"? Well, as Faulkner himself suggests, this classification illogically combines two different principles of division: type of characters involved (Indians) and setting (Country and Village). Only when he substitutes another setting term, "Wilderness," for "Indians" does he arrive at a self-consistent system of classification.

This example illustrates the basic requirement that we group things according to a single principle. Note, though, that we can change principles when we change levels of classification. Suppose Faulkner had decided to subdivide two of his categories in the following manner:

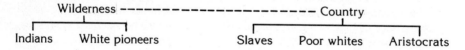

Here he would again be classifying his stories by the two principles of setting and type of character involved, but this time he would be doing so in a self-consistent manner. (Observe that if he had decided to subdivide the "Village" category as well, he would have needed to use the same principle of division for it as for the other two categories.)

2. Use mutually exclusive classes. Once we've decided on the single principle of division we're going to use at each level, we then need to make sure that our classes don't overlap with each other. Say you're planning to write a paper on the relationship between the political attitudes of college freshmen and their places of birth. You might sketch out the following classification: "farm-country-suburb-city-ghetto." But this clearly won't do, because your categories aren't exclusive: farm dwellers live in the country, and ghetto dwellers live in the city.

In order to solve this problem, you need to find categories that don't overlap. In this case, "country," "suburb," and "city" would do. In cutting back to non-overlapping categories, though, you may feel that you're losing some valuable distinctions. If so, reintroduce them as subdivisions:

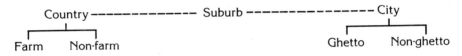

Country ─────────── Suburb ──────────── City

Farm   Non-farm   Ghetto   Non-ghetto

3. Cover all significant possibilities. In setting up a system of classification, we need to make sure that we don't inadvertently omit any significant possibilities. In order to classify students by their living arrangements, for example, we might set up the following categories: "dorm dwellers-apartment dwellers-students who live with their parents." These classes may seem to cover all the possibilities, and at one time they probably would have. But now that colleges are admitting increasing numbers of older students, a fourth category, "homeowner," is surely needed. Or take another example. Say we're classifying sports by the seasons in which they occur. We know where to put football and baseball and basketball. But where should we put such traditionally female sports as field hockey and archery? Or did we even remember that we needed to put them somewhere?

Both these examples illustrate that failure to cover all possibilities is often the result of *stereotyping*. If we automatically think that "college student" means "young person" or that "sport" means "male activity," we're likely to overlook significant possibilities. It's a good idea, then, to ask yourself what assumptions you're making whenever you set up a system of classification. On the other hand, setting up classes to cover every possibility, no matter how remote, is usually unnecessary. The basic question is whether you've covered all the possibilities that might reasonably occur to your readers. If you have, then it's pedantic to go further. In classifying sports by seasons, it's probably safe to leave out lawn bowling.

If you follow the three guidelines we've just discussed, your classificatory schemes will be self-consistent. But is there any way to give them a persuasive edge as well? In a few cases, unfortunately, the answer has to be no. If the classification a person is using is the only one that fits a subject, then there may not be much flexibility in the way he or she can use it. Writers of dictionaries have to classify words by the letters of the alphabet, and that's that. They can't rearrange them just because they would like to achieve a particular rhetorical effect.

But most situations aren't this rigid. Usually, a writer selects his classificatory scheme from among several possibilities. Which one he *chooses,* how he *names* its parts, and how he *orders* them can all have considerable persuasive impact. Look, for example, at the set of classes used by John Holt in an essay entitled "Three Kinds of Discipline."[2]

The Discipline —————— The Discipline —————— The Discipline
of Nature   of Culture, of Society,   of Superior
or of Reality   of What People Really Do   Force

Obviously, this three-part arrangement isn't the only way one could classify "discipline." One could, for example, classify it by who receives it (prisoner, student, athlete, child), by who gives it (judge, teacher, coach, parent), or by the form it takes (physical, verbal, mental). Nor is there anything inherent in the subject to force a writer to use one type of classification rather than another.

Because of this freedom, Holt's decision to choose the pattern he does takes on rhetorical force. How he divides his subject helps to express his attitude toward it. So too does the way he names and orders his classes. In the first one, he uses words with a strongly positive connotation ("Nature," "Reality"); in the second, words that are still positive, though less so ("Culture," "Society"); and in the third, a word ("Force") that has a negative connotation when used in relation to discipline. The order of the three classes exhibits a movement from more attractive to less attractive kinds of discipline—a movement that, as a matter of fact, exactly parallels the pattern of development Holt uses for his argument as a whole.

Classification, then, isn't just a neutral process of putting things into boxes. It's a way of viewing and evaluating the world. As such, it challenges writers to find fresh, inventive, and convincing ways of grouping things together. As you read the essays that follow in this chapter, ask yourself how their authors have met this challenge. Why have they chosen, named, and ordered their classes in the way they have? As you seek answers to these questions, you'll be discovering how to use classification effectively as a means of persuasion.

[2]From John Holt's *Freedom and Beyond* (New York: E. P. Dutton, 1975), adapted in William Herman, *Reading, Writing, Rhetoric* (New York: Holt, Rinehart & Winston, 1977), pp. 81–84.

The Technology
of Medicine

LEWIS THOMAS

Lewis Thomas (b. 1913) is president of the Memorial Sloan-Kettering Cancer Center. Before assuming this post, he was chairman of the Department of Pathology and dean of the Yale Medical School. He is the author of two popular books on biology and related subjects: *The Lives of a Cell* (1974), for which he won the National Book Award, and *The Medusa and the Snail* (1979). In the following chapter from *The Lives of a Cell*, Thomas classifies medical technologies as a way of demonstrating the need for more basic research in the biological sciences.

Technology assessment has become a routine exercise for the scientific enterprises on which the country is obliged to spend vast sums for its needs. Brainy committees are continually evaluating the effectiveness and cost of doing various things in space, defense, energy, transportation, and the like, to give advice about prudent investments for the future.

Somehow medicine, for all the $80-odd billion that it is said to cost the nation, has not yet come in for much of this analytical treatment. It seems taken for granted that the technology of medicine simply exists, take it or leave it, and the only major technologic problem which policy-makers are interested in is how to deliver today's kind of health care, with equity, to all the people.

When, as is bound to happen sooner or later, the analysts get around to the technology of medicine itself, they will have to face the problem of measuring the relative cost and effectiveness of all the things that are done in the management of disease. They make their living at this kind of thing, and I wish them well, but I imagine they will have a bewildering time. For one thing, our methods of managing disease are constantly changing — partly under the influence of new bits of information brought in from all corners of biologic science. At the same time, a great many things are done that are not so closely related to science, some not related at all.

In fact, there are three quite different levels of technology in medicine, so unlike each other as to seem altogether different undertakings. Practitioners of medicine and the analysts will be in trouble if they are not kept separate.

1. First of all, there is a large body of what might be termed "nontechnology," impossible to measure in terms of its capacity to alter either the natural course of disease or its eventual outcome. A great deal of money is spent on this. It is valued highly by the professionals as well as the patients. It consists of what is sometimes call "supportive therapy." It tides patients over through diseases that are not, by and large, understood. It is what is meant by the phrases "caring for" and "standing by." It is indispensable. It is not, however, a technology in any real sense, since it does not involve measures directed at the underlying mechanism of disease.

It includes the large part of any good doctor's time that is taken up with simply providing reassurance, explaining to patients who fear that they have contracted one or another lethal disease that they are, in fact, quite healthy.

It is what physicians used to be engaged in at the bedside of patients with diphtheria, meningitis, poliomyelitis, lobar pneumonia, and all the rest of the infectious diseases that have since come under control.

It is what physicians must now do for patients with intractable cancer, severe rheumatoid arthritis, multiple sclerosis, stroke, and advanced cirrhosis. One can think of at least twenty major diseases that require this kind of supportive medical care because of the absence of an effective technology. I would include a large amount of what is called mental disease, and most varieties of cancer, in this category.

The cost of this nontechnology is very high, and getting higher all the time. It requires not only a great deal of time but also very hard effort and skill on the part of physicians; only the very best of doctors are good at coping with this kind of defeat. It also involves long periods of hospitalization, lots of nursing, lots of involvement of nonmedical professionals in and out of the hospital. It represents, in short, a substantial segment of today's expenditures for health.

2. At the next level up is a kind of technology best termed "halfway technology." This represents the kinds of things that must be done after the fact, in efforts to compensate for the incapacitating effects of certain diseases whose course one is unable to do very much about. It is a technology designed to make up for disease, or to postpone death.

The outstanding examples in recent years are the transplantations of hearts, kidneys, livers, and other organs, and the equally spectacular inventions of artificial organs. In the public mind, this kind of technology has come to seem like the equivalent of the high technologies of the physical sciences. The media tend to present each new procedure as though it represented a breakthrough and therapeutic triumph, instead of the makeshift that it really is.

In fact, this level of technology is, by its nature, at the same time highly sophisticated and profoundly primitive. It is the kind of thing that one must continue to do until there is a genuine understanding of the mechanisms involved in disease. In chronic glomerulonephritis, for example, a much clearer insight will be needed into the events leading to the destruction of glomeruli by the immunologic reactants that now appear to govern this disease, before one will know how to intervene intelligently to prevent the process, or turn it around. But when this level of understanding has been reached, the technology of kidney replacement will not be much needed and should no longer pose the huge problem of logistics, cost, and ethics that it poses today.

An extremely complex and costly technology for the management of coronary heart disease has evolved—involving specialized ambulances and hospital units, all kinds of electronic gadgetry, and whole platoons of new professional personnel—to deal with the end results of coronary thrombosis. Almost everything offered today for the treatment of heart disease is at this level of technology, with the transplanted and artificial hearts as ultimate examples. When enough has been learned to know what really goes wrong in heart disease, one ought to be in a position to figure out ways to prevent or reverse the process, and when this happens the current elaborate technology will probably be set to one side.

Much of what is done in the treatment of cancer, by surgery, irradiation, and chemotherapy, represents halfway technology, in the sense that these measures are directed at the existence of already established cancer cells, but not at the mechanisms by which cells become neoplastic.

It is a characteristic of this kind of technology that it costs an enormous amount of money and requires a continuing expansion of hospital facilities. There is no end to the need for new, highly trained people to run the enterprise. And there is really no way out of this, at the present state of knowledge. If the installation of specialized coronary-care units can result in the extension of life for only a few patients with coronary disease (and there is no question that this technology is effective in a few cases), it seems to me an inevitable fact of life that as many of these as can be will be put together, and as much money as can be found will be spent. I do not see that anyone has much choice in this. The only thing that can move medicine away from this level of technology is new information, and the only imaginable source of this information is research.

3. The third type of technology is the kind that is so effective that it seems to attract the least public notice; it has come to be taken for granted. This is the genuinely decisive technology of modern medicine, exemplified best by modern methods for immunization against diphtheria, pertussis, and the childhood virus diseases, and the contemporary use of antibiotics and chemotherapy for bacterial infections. The capacity to deal effectively with syphilis and tuberculosis represents a milestone in human endeavor, even though full use of this potential has

not yet been made. And there are, of course, other examples: the treatment of endocrinologic disorders with appropriate hormones, the prevention of hemolytic disease of the newborn, the treatment and prevention of various nutritional disorders, and perhaps just around the corner the management of Parkinsonism and sickle-cell anemia. There are other examples, and everyone will have his favorite candidates for the list, but the truth is that there are nothing like as many as the public has been led to believe.

The point to be made about this kind of technology — the real high technology of medicine — is that it comes as the result of a genuine understanding of disease mechanisms, and when it becomes available, it is relatively inexpensive, and relatively easy to deliver.

Offhand, I cannot think of any important human disease for which medicine possesses the outright capacity to prevent or cure where the cost of the technology is itself a major problem. The price is never as high as the cost of managing the same diseases during the earlier stages of no-technology or halfway technology. If a case of typhoid fever had to be managed today by the best methods of 1935, it would run to a staggering expense. At, say, around fifty days of hospitalization, requiring the most demanding kind of nursing care, with the obsessive concern for details of diet that characterized the therapy of that time, with daily laboratory monitoring, and, on occasion, surgical intervention for abdominal catastrophe, I should think $10,000 would be a conservative estimate for the illness, as contrasted with today's cost of a bottle of chloramphenicol and a day or two of fever. The halfway technology that was evolving for poliomyelitis in the early 1950s, just before the emergence of the basic research that made the vaccine possible, provides another illustration of the point. Do you remember Sister Kenny, and the cost of those institutes for rehabilitation, with all those ceremonially applied hot fomentations, and the debates about whether the affected limbs should be totally immobilized or kept in passive motion as frequently as possible, and the masses of statistically tormented data mobilized to support one view or the other? It is the cost of that kind of technology, and its relative effectiveness, that must be compared with the cost and effectiveness of the vaccine.

Pulmonary tuberculosis had similar episodes in its history. There was a sudden enthusiasm for the surgical removal of infected lung tissue in the early 1950s, and elaborate plans were being made for new and expensive installations for major pulmonary surgery in tuberculosis hospitals, and then INH and streptomycin came along and the hospitals themselves were closed up.

It is when physicians are bogged down by their incomplete technologies, by the innumerable things they are obliged to do in medicine when they lack a clear understanding of disease mechanisms, that the deficiencies of the health-care system are most conspicuous. If I were a policy-maker, interested in saving money for health care over the long haul, I would regard it as an act of high prudence to give high priority to a lot more basic research in biologic science. This is the only way to get the full mileage that biology owes to the science of medicine, even though it seems, as used to be said in the days when the phrase still had some meaning, like asking for the moon.

Questions for Discussion

1. What is Thomas' stated purpose in setting up his three categories? How well does his system fulfill that purpose?

2. Thomas suggests that the third of his three classes of medical technology is the most valuable. Do you agree?

3. Thomas announces his thesis at the end of the essay. Would his argument have been as convincing if he had stated his thesis at the beginning? Explain your answer.

4. The vocabulary of this essay suggests that Thomas is writing for a specialized audience, yet his essays enjoy a relatively wide popularity. In your opinion, what accounts for this popularity?

5. Did this essay offer you a new understanding of the technology of medicine? Be prepared to discuss your answer in class.

Suggested Activities

1. List two or three alternative ways of classifying medical technology. Compare your alternatives with those of other members of your class.

2. Write a classification essay in which you evaluate competing brands of a consumer product. Some possibilities: pickup trucks, skis, stereos, roller skates, mopeds.

3. Using resources in your library, write a short report about one of the diseases mentioned in the essay. Suggested topics: chronic glomerulonephritis, coronary thrombosis, parkinsonism, sickle-cell anemia. Does what you learned from your research help you understand why Thomas assigned the disease to the category he did?

Realms
of the Soil

RACHEL CARSON

For many years, Rachel Carson (1907-64) combined authorship
of books on oceanography with a full-time career with the U.S.
Bureau of Fisheries. Her first major success, *The Sea Around
Us,* won the National Book Award in 1951 and prompted her to
devote all her time to her writing. In 1962, she published *Silent
Spring,* a controversial and highly influential study of the effect
of pesticides on the environment. In the chapter from this book
reprinted here, Carson uses classification to demonstrate the
complexity of the soil and to argue against the indiscriminate
use of pesticides.

The thin layer of soil that forms a patchy covering over the continents controls
our own existence and that of every other animal of the land. Without soil, land
plants as we know them could not grow, and without plants no animals could
survive.

Yet if our agriculture-based life depends on the soil, it is equally true that
soil depends on life, its very origins and the maintenance of its true nature being
intimately related to living plants and animals. For soil is in part a creation of life,
born of a marvelous interaction of life and nonlife long eons ago. The parent
materials were gathered together as volcanoes poured them out in fiery streams,
as waters running over the bare rocks of the continents wore away even the hard-
est granite, and as the chisels of frost and ice split and shattered the rocks. Then

REALMS OF THE SOIL   From *Silent Spring* by Rachel Carson, published by Houghton Mifflin Company. Copyright © 1962 by Rachel L. Carson. Reprinted by permission of the publisher.

living things began to work their creative magic and little by little these inert materials became soil. Lichens, the rocks' first covering, aided the process of disintegration by their acid secretions and made a lodging place for other life. Mosses took hold in the little pockets of simple soil — soil formed by crumbling bits of lichen, by the husks of minute insect life, by the debris of a fauna beginning its emergence from the sea.

Life not only formed the soil, but other living things of incredible abundance and diversity now exist within it; if this were not so the soil would be a dead and sterile thing. By their presence and by their activities the myriad organisms of the soil make it capable of supporting the earth's green mantle.

The soil exists in a state of constant change, taking part in cycles that have no beginning and no end. New materials are constantly being contributed as rocks disintegrate, as organic matter decays, and as nitrogen and other gases are brought down in rain from the skies. At the same time other materials are being taken away, borrowed for temporary use by living creatures. Subtle and vastly important chemical changes are constantly in progress, converting elements derived from air and water into forms suitable for use by plants. In all these changes living organisms are active agents.

There are few studies more fascinating, and at the same time more neglected, than those of the teeming populations that exist in the dark realms of the soil. We know too little of the threads that bind the soil organisms to each other and to their world, and to the world above.

Perhaps the most essential organisms in the soil are the smallest — the invisible hosts of bacteria and of threadlike fungi. Statistics of their abundance take us at once into astronomical figures. A teaspoonful of topsoil may contain billions of bacteria. In spite of their minute size, the total weight of this host of bacteria in the top foot of a single acre of fertile soil may be as much as a thousand pounds. Ray fungi, growing in long threadlike filaments, are somewhat less numerous than the bacteria, yet because they are larger their total weight in a given amount of soil may be about the same. With small green cells called algae, these make up the microscopic plant life of the soil.

Bacteria, fungi, and algae are the principal agents of decay, reducing plant and animal residues to their component minerals. The vast cyclic movements of chemical elements such as carbon and nitrogen through soil and air and living tissue could not proceed without these microplants. Without the nitrogen-fixing bacteria, for example, plants would starve for want of nitrogen, though surrounded by a sea of nitrogen-containing air. Other organisms form carbon dioxide, which, as carbonic acid, aids in dissolving rock. Still other soil microbes perform various oxidations and reductions by which minerals such as iron, manganese, and sulfur are transformed and made available to plants.

Also present in prodigious numbers are microscopic mites and primitive wingless insects called springtails. Despite their small size they play an important part in breaking down the residues of plants, aiding in the slow conversion of the litter of the forest floor to soil. The specialization of some of these minute creatures for their task is almost incredible. Several species of mites, for example, can begin life only within the fallen needles of a spruce tree. Sheltered here, they digest out the inner tissues of the needle. When the mites have completed their development only the outer layer of cells remains. The truly staggering task of dealing with the tremendous amount of plant material in the annual leaf fall belongs to some of the small insects of the soil and the forest floor. They macerate and digest the leaves, and aid in mixing the decomposed matter with the surface soil.

Besides all this horde of minute but ceaselessly toiling creatures there are of course many larger forms, for soil life runs the gamut from bacteria to mammals. Some are permanent residents of the dark subsurface layers; some hibernate or spend definite parts of their life cycles in underground chambers; some freely come and go between their burrows and the upper world. In general the effect of all this habitation of the soil is to aerate it and improve both its drainage and the penetration of water throughout the layers of plant growth.

Of all the larger inhabitants of the soil, probably none is more important than the earthworm. Over three quarters of a century ago, Charles Darwin published a book titled *The Formation of Vegetable Mould, through the Action of Worms, with Observations on Their Habits*. In it he gave the world its first understanding of the fundamental role of earthworms as geologic agents for the transport of soil — a picture of surface rocks being gradually covered by fine soil brought up from below by the worms, in annual amounts running to many tons to the acre in most favorable areas. At the same time, quantities of organic matter contained in leaves and grass (as much as 20 pounds to the square yard in six months) are drawn down into the burrows and incorporated in soil. Darwin's calculations showed that the toil of earthworms might add a layer of soil an inch to an inch and a half thick in a ten-year period. And this is by no means all they do: their burrows aerate the soil, keep it well drained, and aid the penetration of plant roots. The presence of earthworms increases the nitrifying powers of the soil bacteria and decreases putrifaction of the soil. Organic matter is broken down as it passes through the digestive tracts of the worms and the soil is enriched by their excretory products.

This soil community, then, consists of a web of interwoven lives, each in some way related to the others — the living creatures depending on the soil, but the soil in turn a vital element of the earth only so long as this community within it flourishes.

The problem that concerns us here is one that has received little consideration: What happens to these incredibly numerous and vitally necessary inhabitants of the soil when poisonous chemicals are carried down into their world, either introduced directly as soil "sterilants" or borne on the rain that has picked up a lethal contamination as it filters through the leaf canopy of forest and orchard and cropland? Is it reasonable to suppose that we can apply a broad-spectrum insecticide to kill the burrowing larval stages of a crop-destroying insect, for example, without also killing the "good" insects whose function may be the essential one of breaking down organic matter? Or can we use a nonspecific fungicide without also killing the fungi that inhabit the roots of many trees in a beneficial association that aids the tree in extracting nutrients from the soil?

The plain truth is that this critically important subject of the ecology of the soil has been largely neglected even by scientists and almost completely ignored by control men. Chemical control of insects seems to have proceeded on the assumption that the soil could and would sustain any amount of insult via the introduction of poisons without striking back. The very nature of the world of the soil has been largely ignored.

From the few studies that have been made, a picture of the impact of pesticides on the soil is slowly emerging. It is not surprising that the studies are not always in agreement, for soil types vary so enormously that what causes damage in one may be innocuous in another. Light sandy soils suffer far more heavily than humus types. Combinations of chemicals seem to do more harm than separate applications. Despite the varying results, enough solid evidence of harm is accumulating to cause apprehension on the part of many scientists.

Under some conditions, the chemical conversions and transformations that lie at the very heart of the living world are affected. Nitrification, which makes atmospheric nitrogen available to plants, is an example. The herbicide 2,4-D causes a temporary interruption of nitrification. In recent experiments in Florida, lindane, heptachlor, and BHC (benzene hexachloride) reduced nitrification after only two weeks in soil; BHC and DDT had significantly detrimental effects a year after treatment. In other experiments BHC, aldrin, lindane, heptachlor, and DDD all prevented nitrogen-fixing bacteria from forming the necessary root nodules on leguminous plants. A curious but beneficial relation between fungi and the roots of higher plants is seriously disrupted.

Sometimes the problem is one of upsetting that delicate balance of populations by which nature accomplishes far-reaching aims. Explosive increases in some kinds of soil organisms have occurred when others have been reduced by insecticides, disturbing the relation of predator to prey. Such changes could easily alter the metabolic activity of the soil and affect its productivity. They could also mean that potentially harmful organisms, formerly held in check, could escape from their natural controls and rise to pest status.

One of the most important things to remember about insecticides in soil is their long persistence, measured not in months but in years. Aldrin has been recovered after four years, both as traces and more abundantly as converted to dieldrin. Enough toxaphene remains in sandy soil ten years after its application to kill termites. Benzene hexachloride persists at least eleven years, heptachlor or a more toxic derived chemical, at least nine. Chlordane has been recovered twelve years after its application, in the amount of 15 per cent of the original quantity.

Seemingly moderate applications of insecticides over a period of years may build up fantastic quantities in soil. Since the chlorinated hydrocarbons are persistent and long-lasting, each application is merely added to the quantity remaining from the previous one. The old legend that "a pound of DDT to the acre is harmless" means nothing if spraying is repeated. Potato soils have been found to contain up to 15 pounds of DDT per acre, corn soils up to 19. A cranberry bog under study contained 34.5 pounds to the acre. Soils from apple orchards seem to reach the peak of contamination, with DDT accumulating at a rate that almost keeps pace with its rate of annual application. Even in a single season, with orchards sprayed four or more times, DDT residues may build up to peaks of 30 to 50 pounds. With repeated spraying over the years the range between trees is from 26 to 60 pounds to the acre; under trees, up to 113 pounds.

Arsenic provides a classic case of the virtually permanent poisoning of the soil. Although arsenic as a spray on growing tobacco has been largely replaced by the synthetic organic insecticides since the mid-'40's, *the arsenic content of cigarettes made from American-grown tobacco increased more than 300 per cent* between the years 1932 and 1952. Later studies have revealed increases of as much as 600 per cent. Dr. Henry S. Satterlee, an authority on arsenic toxicology, says that although organic insecticides have been largely substituted for arsenic, the tobacco plants continue to pick up the old poison, for the soils of tobacco plantations are now thoroughly impregnated with residues of a heavy and relatively insoluble poison, arsenate of lead. This will continue to release arsenic in soluble form. The soil of a large proportion of the land planted to tobacco has been subjected to "cumulative and well-nigh permanent poisoning," according to Dr. Satterlee. Tobacco grown in the eastern Mediterranean countries where arsenical insecticides are not used has shown no such increase in arsenic content.

We are therefore confronted with a second problem. We must not only be concerned with what is happening to the soil; we must wonder to what extent insecticides are absorbed from contaminated soils and introduced into plant tissues. Much depends on the type of soil, the crop, and the nature and concentration of the insecticide. Soil high in organic matter releases smaller quantities of poisons than others. Carrots absorb more insecticide than any other crop studied; if the chemical used happens to be lindane, carrots actually accumulate higher concentrations than are present in the soil. In the future it may become necessary to analyze soils for insecticides before planting certain food crops. Otherwise even unsprayed crops may take up enough insecticide merely from the soil to render them unfit for market.

This very sort of contamination has created endless problems for at least one leading manufacturer of baby foods who has been unwilling to buy any fruits or vegetables on which toxic insecticides have been used. The chemical that caused him the most trouble was benzene hexachloride (BHC), which is taken up by the roots and tubers of plants, advertising its presence by a musty taste and odor. Sweet potatoes grown on California fields where BHC had been used two years earlier contained residues and had to be rejected. In one year, in which the firm had contracted in South Carolina for its total requirements of sweet potatoes, so large a proportion of the acreage was found to be contaminated that the company was forced to. buy in the open market at a considerable financial loss. Over the years a variety of fruits and vegetables, grown in various states, have had to be rejected. The most stubborn problems were concerned with peanuts. In the southern states peanuts are usually grown in rotation with cotton, on which BHC is extensively used. Peanuts grown later in this soil pick up considerable amounts of the insecticide. Actually, only a trace is enough to incorporate the telltale musty odor and taste. The chemical penetrates the nuts and cannot be removed. Processing, far from removing the mustiness, sometimes accentuates it. The only course open to a manufacturer determined to exclude BHC residues is to reject all produce treated with the chemical or grown on soils contaminated with it.

Sometimes the menace is to the crop itself — a menace that remains as long as the insecticide contamination is in the soil. Some insecticides affect sensitive plants such as beans, wheat, barley, or rye, retarding root development or depressing growth of seedlings. The experience of the hop growers in Washington and Idaho is an example. During the spring of 1955 many of these growers undertook a large-scale program to control the strawberry root weevil, whose larvae had become abundant on the roots of the hops. On the advice of agricultural experts and insecticide manufacturers, they chose heptachlor as the control agent. Within a year after the heptachlor was applied, the vines in the treated yards were wilting and dying. In the untreated fields there was no trouble; the damage stopped at the border between treated and untreated fields. The hills were replanted at great expense, but in another year the new roots, too, were found to be dead. Four years later the soil still contained heptachlor, and scientists were unable to predict how long it would remain poisonous, or to recommend any procedure for correcting the condition. The federal Department of Agriculture, which as late as March 1959 found itself in the anomalous position of declaring heptachlor to be acceptable for use on hops in the form of a soil treatment, belatedly withdrew its registration for such use. Meanwhile, the hop growers sought what redress they could in the courts.

As applications of pesticides continue and the virtually indestructible residues continue to build up in the soil, it is almost certain that we are heading for trouble. This was the consensus of a group of specialists who met at Syracuse University in 1960 to discuss the ecology of the soil. These men summed up the hazards of using "such potent and little-understood tools" as chemicals and radiation: "A few false moves on the part of man may result in destruction of soil productivity and the arthropods may well take over."

Questions for Discussion

1. In the course of this essay, Carson moves from strict scientific observation and description to evaluation. How effective is this method of development? Why do you think she chose to develop her essay in this manner?

2. At a transitional point in this essay (pp. 120–21), Carson poses a series of questions. Does her essay answer these questions satisfactorily? Be prepared to support your response with specific evidence from the essay.

3. Carson uses an informal system of classification in this essay. Do you find it effective?

4. In what ways is Carson adapting her subject to the needs and interests of a general (rather than scientifically trained) audience?

5. One of Carson's most extensive examples in this essay concerns a manufacturer of baby food. Why do you think she chose this particular example?

6. Carson's book created a sensation when it was first published. Do you think the problems she addresses are still relevant today, or have they mainly been solved?

Suggested Activities

1. Write a topic outline of the basic points Carson makes in her argument. On the basis of this outline, what conclusions can you draw about the way she organizes and develops her material?

2. In this essay, Carson is explaining a process that is often too slow or too minute to be observed by the unaided eye. Write a paper analyzing her techniques for making the process "visible."

3. Write an essay in which you discuss an environmental issue that particularly interests you.

Eastern Cults
and Western Culture

HARVEY COX

Harvey Cox (b. 1929) is an ordained minister in the American Baptist Church and Victor Thomas Professor of Divinity at Harvard University. His interest in the place of religion in modern society led to his most famous book, *The Secular City: Secularization and Urbanization in Theological Perspective* (1965; revised edition, 1966). The selection reprinted here appears in a different form in Cox's most recent book, *Turning East: The Promise and Peril of Orientalism* (1977). In the selection, Cox explores the reasons for the popularity of Eastern religions among college students.

An old Zen story tells of a pilgrim who mounted his horse and crossed formidable mountains and swift rivers seeking a famous roshi, or wise man, in order to ask him how to find true enlightenment. After months of searching, the pilgrim located the teacher in a cave. The roshi listened to the question, and said nothing. The seeker waited. Finally, after hours of silence, the roshi looked at the steed on which the pilgrim had arrived, and asked the pilgrim why he was not looking for a horse instead of enlightenment. The pilgrim responded that obviously he already had a horse. The roshi smiled, and retreated to his cave.

In the past decade, this country has seen dozens of Eastern religious cults and movements spring up and flourish, attracting thousands of American youths who are searching for truth, brotherhood, and authority. What has provoked this neo-Oriental religious revival? Who are the people caught up in it? Why have they left some more conventional religious life — or none at all — to become seekers or adherents in these new spiritual movements? What does it all mean for American culture?

Large numbers of people are involved in this quest, not just a fringe group. And the extent of their interest has no precedent in American religious history. Although overall estimates vary widely — partly because the movements themselves tend to overstate their membership — I would guess that by now several million Americans have been touched one way or another by some form of neo-Oriental thought or devotional practice. I base this guess not only on the number of actual adherents, but also on those who practice — regularly or sporadically — various forms of meditation, or whose practice of karate or the martial arts goes beyond self-defense to their underlying Buddhist philosophy.

To learn why people join these movements and practice these disciplines, I and some of my students at Harvard Divinity School spent three years informally studying dozens of such groups currently operating in Cambridge, Massachusetts. Some of the students were already involved in the movements, while most of them were just curious about what meaning they had to their adherents, why people had joined, and what they were looking for.

To find out, we visited the centers to observe, participate in the meetings and the rituals, and talk with the devotees.

Cambridge is known throughout the country primarily as the home of Harvard University. But in recent years it has also become a thriving center of Eastern religious cults and movements, prompting one of my friends to call it "Benares-on-the-Charles."

Within walking distance of Harvard Square, one can find dozens of different neo-Oriental religious movements. A few blocks away stands the Zen center, furnished with black silk cushions, bells, an appropriately wizened and wise-looking resident master, and a visiting Zen swordplay instructor. In the basement of a nearby Episcopal church, the Sufi dancers meet twice a week to twist and turn like the legendary whirling dervishes in a ritual circle, chanting verses from the Koran. Down the street is the Ananda Marga center, specializing in a combination of meditation and community action.

A few blocks south sits the headquarters of the Hare Krishnas, officially known as the International Society for Krishna Consciousness. There, the devotees hold a weekly feast of savory Indian food and a somewhat less piquant introductory lecture on the mysteries of the Krishna devotion. The clean-shaven followers of the chubby young guru, the Maharaj Ji, have a meeting place near Central Square. A group of self-styled Sikhs, immaculately clad in white robes, turbans, and daggers, have opened a vegetarian restaurant called the Golden Temple of Conscious Cookery. Nearby is the International Student Meditation Center, founded several years ago by the Maharishi Mahesh Yoga, the best known of the swamis of the late '60s, where one can learn the art of "transcendental meditation." Recent arrivals include the followers of guru Sri Chinmoy, a former postal clerk living in Queens; the Dharma House, founded by Chogyam Trungpa Rinpoche, the Tibetan Buddhist lama; and dozens of smaller, less stable groups devoted to yoga, Tai Chi, and other exotic pursuits.

I knew that no matter how hard I tried to maintain scholarly objectivity, my inner distrust for all "opiates of the people" might continue to influence me. But I decided to do the study anyway. Although my prejudice against some of the movements was undeniable, I was at least fully aware of it.

During the first several weeks of the study my students and I all had a marvelous time. Together and separately we attended dozens of meditation sessions, feasts, satsangs, introductory lectures, inquirers' meetings, worship services, and study circles. The groups we visited were invariably hospitable. We asked questions, read stacks of tracts and pamphlets, watched, listened, and filled up stacks of tape cartridges. For once we were getting something straight from the source instead of from textbooks.

With all our research, however, I felt something was lacking. As the notebooks piled up, I began to wonder what it would feel like to be on the inside of one of the movements. No one can hope to experience another person's faith as he does. And as a Christian and a professional theologian I realized I was neither a genuine Oriental pilgrim nor an authentic seeker. I was intrigued, curious, fascinated, but not a devotee. Still, I realized I would have to pursue some kind of "inside" knowing and feeling if I were going to understand the disciples I was studying. So I tried to become as much of a participant as I could. I did not merely observe the Sufi dancers; I whirled too. I did not just read about Zen, or visit centers; I "sat." I chanted with the Hare Krishnas. I stood on my head, stretched my torso, and breathed deeply with the yoga practitioners. I spent hours softly intoning a mantra to myself in a favorite form of Hindu devotional practice.

I became a participant not because I thought there was actually something in it for me, but because I wanted to nourish my capacity for empathy. I wanted to find out what I could about the lure of the East on the visceral level. This participant-observer phase of my inquiry took me far away from Benares-on-the-Charles. It led me to spiritual centers in California, Colorado, Texas, and Vermont, and into conversations with Zen abbots, Sufi drummers, and Divine Light devotees.

Only after my search became personal did I finally hit on an approach which seemed both faithful to the movements, and helpful in interpreting them to other people. I had become interested in Eastern spirituality for personal reasons, with a host of internal reservations. My purposes were clearly different from those advanced by the teachers themselves. I was quite sure that mine was a most unusual case. I soon discovered, however, it was not. Once I got to know them, nearly all the people I met turned out to have personal reasons that often had little to do with the official teaching of the movement's leaders. This discovery provided me with the clue I needed. I decided to concentrate not on what the movements and their leaders claim to offer, but on what the individuals who turn to them actually find.

The "East turners" we found in these movements have not moved to India to live in an ashram. They have not left home for the Orient to dwell in a Tibetan temple or a Zen monastery. They still live in Texas or Ohio or New York or somewhere else in the United States. They have not *gone* East, they have *turned* East. There are true seekers and frivolous dilettantes, converts and fellow travelers. Their interest comes in widely varying degrees of seriousness and persistence: some merely sneak a glance at a paperback edition of the *I Ching* or try some yoga postures; others find that one of the Eastern practices becomes important to them; others leave everything behind and sleep on mats in a Hare Krishna temple.

One way to find out what kind of people join these movements is to determine the standard sociological data of their social class, age, race, sex, education, and ethnic background. Such studies have been done, but they leave much unsaid. The participants tend to be young, in their late teens or early 20s. Although some early teen-agers learn how to do yoga, or read a little Eastern philosophy, few become seriously involved until late adolescence. The 20s are the prime turning time.

The Eastern religious movements are made up almost exclusively of white, educated, middle- and upper-middle-class young people. Most have at least begun college, although some have dropped out after a year or two. Men and women seem to participate in fairly equal numbers, but men control the leadership groups. There is no predominance of any particular regional background, although more of the devotees seem to come from urban than from rural areas, probably because the movements are generally based in cities.

These young people come from all religious denominations, with relatively more from liberal Protestant and reform Jewish backgrounds than the proportion of these groups in the general population would suggest. This is not surprising, considering the urban, middle-class, educated milieu in which these groups recruit most of their members. Few come from strongly atheistic or unusually pious homes. They seem to have received some religion from their parents, but not enough to satisfy them.

Despite all these statistics and data and categories, we still don't know much about the actual human beings who have made this decisive choice. So my students and I asked the people themselves to tell us in their own words what they found in the groups they belonged to. Their answers varied, but as we sorted through them, several definite patterns emerged.

1. Most of the members of these movements seem to be looking for simple human *friendship*. The reply we heard most often, especially from those actually living in religious communes or ashrams, told a story of loneliness, isolation, and the search for a supportive community. To paraphrase a large number of replies:

> They seem to care for me here. I was bummed out, confused, just wandering around. When I first came here I didn't know what they were talking about. They all seemed crazy, and I told them so. But that didn't seem to bother them. They took me in. They made me feel at home. Now I feel like I'm a part of it, an important part, too. I belong here. It's where I was meant to be.

The newer the convert, the more likely this reply. After a few weeks, however, the novices begin to learn a more theologically proper answer, such as, *Krishna called me here*, or *It was my karma*. Many seekers who drift into such movements looking for intimacy quickly learn to express their reasons in the group argot. But the need for plain friendship is clearly their chief motivation. They are looking for warmth, affection, and close ties of feeling. They don't find it at work, at school, in churches they attend, or even at home. But they do seem to find it, at least for a while, in the community of devotees. The groups we visited provide an island of companionship in what the adherents feel is a world devoid of fraternity.

2. The East turners are also looking for a way to experience life directly, without the intervention of ideas and concepts. They seek a kind of *immediacy* they have not been able to find elsewhere. Even though some young people drift from movement to movement, they do not seem to be looking for just another kick or "trip" to add to their collection.

Most are serious, and want a real, personal encounter with God, or simply with life, nature, and other people:

> *All I got at any church I ever went to were sermons or homilies about God, about "the peace that passes understanding." Words, words, words. It was all up in the head. I never really felt it. It was all abstract, never direct, always somebody else's account of it. It was dull and boring. I'd sit or kneel or stand. I'd listen to or read prayers. But it seemed lifeless. It was like reading the label instead of eating the contents.*
>
> *But here it really happened to me. I experienced it myself. I don't have to take someone else's word for it.*

This testimony of direct experience became more understandable when we noticed that nearly all the neo-Oriental movements include instruction in some form of spiritual discipline. Initiates learn the primary techniques of prayer, chanting, contemplation, or meditation. Teachers rely not only on words, as in most Western religious training, but also on actual techniques—either quite simple, as in transcendental meditation, or complex, as in Zen—for inducing the desired forms of consciousness. At the local Zen center, for example, the teachers sit you down immediately to face a blank wall, and smilingly refuse to answer all but the most elementary questions until you have taken the practical step of trying to meditate. Even after that they keep the ideas to a minimum. Practice and direct exposure are the keys to the kingdom.

3. Some East turners are looking for *authority*. They have turned East to find truth, to lay hold on a message or teaching they can believe and trust. They join these groups as refugees from uncertainty and doubt. They often stress the role of the particular swami or guru whose wisdom or charismatic power has caused such a change in their lives:

> *I tried everything. I read all the books, went to lectures, listened to different teachers. But all that happened was that I got more con-*

*fused. I couldn't think straight any more. I couldn't get myself
together or make any decisions. Then I met him, and what he said
finally made sense. Everything finally clicked. I knew he was for real.
I could tell just from the way he spoke that he knew. Now my confusion is over.*

The quest for authority results from a wide range of factors documented by
dozens of sociologists: the dissolution of conventional moral codes; the erosion of
traditional authorities; the emergence of what Alvin Toffler, the author of *Future
Shock,* once called "over-choice." As a result, large numbers of people have begun
to suffer a kind of choice-fatigue. They hunger for an authority that will simplify,
straighten out, assure; something or somebody that will make their choices fewer
and less arduous. For some, the search for authority ends at the swami's feet.

4. A smaller number of people told us in one way or another that they had
turned to the East because somehow it seemed more *natural.* These people also
seem to have changed their faith-orientation more self-consciously than others,
and with deliberate rejection of what they consider the effete, corrupt, or outworn
religious tradition of the West. They see in Eastern spirituality a kind of
unspoiled purity. In contrast to Western faith, the East seems artless, simple, and
fresh. They could often tell us why they had turned *from* some Western religion
more clearly than they could say why they had turned *toward* the East.

> *Western civilization is shot. It is nothing but technology and power
> and rationalization, corrupted to its core by power and money. It has
> no contact with nature, feeling, spontaneity. What we need to do
> now is learn from the Oriental peoples who have never been ruined
> by machines and science, who have kept close to their ancestors' sim-
> plicity. Western religion has invalidated itself. Now only the East is
> possible.*

The people who talked to us in this vein were often the most widely read
and best educated of the East turners. They could often cite evidence more specifically and phrase their arguments more clearly than the others. Though they
did not put it this way themselves, to me their decision to turn East often seemed
to have some of the quality of a purification ritual. It was as though they were
going through the Western equivalent of a bath in the Ganges, shedding the
tainted and the impure.

These then are the reasons most East turners cite for their choice: they seek
friendship; a direct experience of God and the world; a way out of intellectual
and moral confusion; and a kind of innocence, or a way of life unmarred by technological overkill. This list of goals shows that East turners are really not very
different from anyone else. They are looking for what many other people in
America are looking for today. They have merely chosen a more visible and dramatic way of looking. The real question, of course, is will they find it?

The ironic aspect of the Turn East is that it is occurring just as many millions
of Asians are involved in an epochal "Turn West" toward Western science and

technology, Western political systems, and Western cultural forms. Just as this great awakening to history has begun to occur in the real Asia, millions of Americans have fallen in love with an Asia that is disappearing, or maybe never existed: the "mysterious Orient" of the old Western myth. In fact, those who yearn for what they call an "Oriental" approach today are really opting for an archaic rather than a historical way of life. They may be turning back instead of turning East.

Two kinds of replies from East turners disturb me because they reveal a quest that will lead not just to disillusionment but to frustration and bitterness. One can sympathize with those who hope to regain a lost innocence — a world free of complications, a world of black and white choices. But eventually they will find out that no such world will ever be found. For maturity means learning to live in a complex, shades-of-gray world.

I feel similar qualms about those who long for an authority so unquestionable and total that they would not have to make hard decisions or chew through choices on their own.

At first, converts to these movements often do seem to find a kind of new innocence. They are "blissed out" with their hassle-free life. The emphasis many of these groups place on the inner life, plus their relegation of secular society to an inferior form of reality, means that adhering to their teachings will remove the uncomfortable tensions of school, work, or home. Since money, power, and, in some cases, even the capacity to make choices are viewed as illusory or insignificant, the causes of most political tussles disappear. The problem is that the nasty issues of work, politics, and the rest do not really disappear, and even East turners must eventually grapple with them. But as devotees they must do so with a world view that gives them little help, because it refuses to recognize that the problems even exist.

I am also troubled by the pursuit of an absolute religious and moral authority that will relieve the discomfort of making decisions. People who hunger for this kind of authority over them suffer from the wounds dealt out by parents, schools, and jobs where they have never been encouraged to flex their decision-making capabilities. But in order to mature, the last thing they need is one more perfect master to solve their problems for them.

They need friends and families and larger settings in which their confidence in their own capacities will be strengthened.

What the East turners are doing is hardly a prescription for a general cure; rather, it is a symptom of a malaise with which we must all contend. Religious remedies to the ills of a culture take two basic forms: One tries to get at the underlying causes of the malady; the other provides a way for people to live in spite of the illness, usually by providing them with an alternative miniworld, sufficiently removed from the one outside so that its perils are kept away from the gate. The East turners have almost all chosen this second form. The only solution they offer to other people is to join them in their miniworld.

But if we all join them, it would soon be a maxiworld with all the problems back again. Part of the answer is that these movements cannot be the answer for everyone. Some East turners have found a haven from the impersonality and vacuousness of the larger society, and, some would say, of its churches. They have rightly located the most severe symptoms of our ailing era. But their solution, though it may work for them individually, at least for a while, is ultimately no solution for the rest of us.

As for the movements themselves, I also worry about their future. For the business of America is business, and that includes the religion business. The greatest irony of the Eastern religious movements is that in their effort to present an alternative to the Western way of life, most have succeeded in adding only one more line of spiritual products to the American religious marketplace. They have become a part of the consumer culture they set out to call in question.

This consumerization of the new religious movements should not surprise us. After all, the genius of any consumer society is its capacity for changing anything, including its critics, into items for distribution and sale. Religious teachings and disciplines — Eastern or Western — can be transformed into commodities, assigned prices, packaged attractively, and made available to prospective buyers.

Conspicuous consumption is no longer a mark of distinction. What we have in its place is something I call the new gluttony, which transforms the entire range of human ideas and emotions into a well-stocked pantry. Today, only the old-fashioned glutton still stuffs his mouth with too many entrees. The new glutton craves experiences: in quantity and variety, more and better, increasingly exotic, and even spiritual. Today's money does not lust after houses, cars, and clothes, but travel, drugs, unusual sights and sounds, exotic tastes, therapies, and new emotional states. If disgrace haunts the affluent, it is not apt to be for failing to *have* something, but rather for failing to have *tried* something. The very thought that out there lurks an experience one has not had now sends the affluent into panic.

No doubt economists as well as theologians could advance explanations for why we are moving from a greed for things to a gluttony of experience. In a system based on encouraging greed, people eventually become sated. It is hard to sell still another television set to the family that already has one in every room. There is a limit somewhere to what most people can stack up.

With experiences, however, there seems to be no such limit, and the experience merchants do not need to plan obsolescence or invent style changes. Their product self-destructs immediately, except for one's memory. Last year's model is unusable not for any reason as trivial as changing hemlines but because it is gone.

Economists can explain the new gluttony in the classical terms of a movement from goods to services. It is the old story of expanding markets, finding new resources and developing novel products. But now the product is an experience that can be sold and delivered to a customer. The resources are virtually infinite for the imaginative entrepreneur, and the market is that growing group of people whose hunger for accumulating mere things has begun to decline.

I think there is an element of spiritual gluttony in the current fascination with Oriental spirituality. We should not blame this on the Oriental traditions themselves, most of which are highly sensitive to the pitfalls of spiritual pride. Nor can we blame the often anguished people who are driven by forces they can neither control nor understand toward searching out more and more exhilarating spiritual experiences.

If there is any fault to be allocated, it lies not with the victims but with the buyer-seller nexus within which the new religious wave is marketed. Despite what may be good intentions all around, the consumer mentality can rot the fragile fruits of Eastern spirituality as soon as they are unpacked. The process is both ironic and pathetic. What begins in Benares as a protest against possessiveness ends up in Boston as still another possession.

No deity, however terrible, no devotion, however deep, no ritual, however splendid, is exempt from the voracious process of trivialization. The smiling Buddha himself and the worldly wise Krishna can be transformed by the new gluttony into collectors' trinkets. It was bad enough for King Midas that everything he touched turned to gold. The acquisition-accumulation pattern of the new gluttony does even more. Reversing the alchemist's course, it transforms rubies and emeralds into plastic, the sacred into the silly, the holy into the hokey.

The gods of the Orient mean one thing there, and something quite different here. This is not to be blamed either on the gods themselves, or on their original devotees, or on their new seekers. It happens because when the gods migrate, or are transported to a civilization where everything is to some extent a commodity, they become commodities too.

The culture barrier that a commodity culture erects against the possibility of genuine interreligious exchange is formidable. It raises the question of whether we in the West can ever hear the voice of the East, can ever learn about the Buddhist or Hindu paths without corrupting them in the process.

Although America today *seems* uncommonly receptive to spiritual ideas and practices from the East, the truth is that we are not really receptive to them at all. True, no stone walls have been erected to keep the pagans out. No orders of Knights Templar have ridden forth to hurl back the infidels. The gates are open, and the citizens seem ready to listen. No wonder many Eastern teachers view America as a fertile ground in which to sow their seeds.

But curiously it is precisely America's receptivity, its eagerness to hear, explore, and experience, that creates the most difficult barrier to our actually learning from Eastern spirituality. The very insatiable hunger for novelty, for intimacy, even for a kind of spirituality that motivates so many Americans to turn toward the East also virtually guarantees that the turn will ultimately fail.

The final paradox is that Easterners have never claimed to be able to save the West. Frequently they deny having any interest in doing so, even if they could. They rarely send missionaries here, and they accept Western novices with reluctance. Although the Western versions of Eastern faiths often claim to bring salvation to the West, at this point they betray the spirit of their sources, and actually worsen the Western dilemma by advertising more than they can deliver.

The spiritual crisis of the West will not be resolved by spiritual importations or individual salvation. It is the crisis of a whole civilization, and one of its major symptoms is the belief that the answer must come from Elsewhere. The crisis can be met only when the West sets aside myths of the Orient, and returns to its own primal roots.

Eventually the spiritual disciplines of the Orient will make a profound contribution to our consciousness and our way of life. Some day, somewhere, we will hear the message the East has for us. But we can only begin to know the real Orient when we are willing to let go of the mythical one. And we can only begin to hear the message of the Oriental religious traditions when we are willing to confront the inner dislocations in our own civilization that caused us to invent the myth of the East in the first place. And when we are willing to do that, we may realize, like the truth seeker in the Zen parable, that what we are seeking so frantically elsewhere may turn out to be the horse we have been riding all along.

Questions for Discussion

1. At the beginning of this essay Cox poses four questions. How do they relate to the organization of the rest of the essay?

2. In the sixth and seventh paragraphs of his essay, Cox describes the different Eastern cults that can be found within "walking distance of Harvard Square." Discuss his use of concrete detail in these paragraphs.

3. Cox admits that he has prejudices against some of the Eastern religious movements. What evidence, if any, do you see of prejudice in this essay? Do you think he is fair in his treatment of Eastern religion?

4. Cox refers to himself frequently and interjects his opinions freely throughout the essay. What is your opinion of this way of writing? Would you have preferred him to make himself less visible? Why or why not?

5. According to Cox, "The Eastern religious movements are made up almost exclusively of white, educated, middle- and upper-middle-class young people." Why do you think this is so?

6. Toward the end of his essay, Cox says that "what begins in Benares as a protest against possessiveness ends up in Boston as still another possession." Do you agree with this statement?

Suggested Activities

1. Make a list of Cox's reasons for being concerned about young Americans' interest in Eastern religions. Which of these reasons for concern would also apply to their interest in *Western* religions? Which would not?

2. Write a paragraph defining a religious movement with which you happen to be familiar. Be objective; don't show your readers whether you approve or disapprove of the movement.

3. Write an essay exploring a current form of social protest. Some possibilities: punk rock, the anti-draft movement, the anti–nuclear power movement.

Thinking
as a Hobby

WILLIAM GOLDING

William Golding was born in 1911 in St. Columb Manor, Corn-
wall, England, and was educated at Brasenose College, Oxford.
A renowned novelist, he is the author of such works as *Lord of
the Flies* (1954), *The Inheritors* (1955), *Free Fall* (1960), and *The
Pyramid* (1967). After a ten-year silence, he recently published
an ambitious new novel, *Darkness Visible* (1979). His nonfiction
has been collected in *The Hot Gates, and Other Occasional
Pieces* (1965). In the essay reprinted below, Golding uses nov-
elistic techniques to enliven his description of three classes of
thinkers.

While I was still a boy, I came to the conclusion that there were three grades of
thinking; and since I was later to claim thinking as my hobby, I came to an even
stranger conclusion — namely, that I myself could not think at all.

I must have been an unsatisfactory child for grownups to deal with. I remember how incomprehensible they appeared to me at first, but not, of course, how
I appeared to them. It was the headmaster of my grammar school who first
brought the subject of thinking before me — though neither in the way, nor with
the result he intended. He had some statuettes in his study. They stood on a high
cupboard behind his desk. One was a lady wearing nothing but a bath towel. She
seemed frozen in an eternal panic lest the bath towel slip down any farther; and

since she had no arms, she was in an unfortunate position to pull the towel up again. Next to her, crouched the statuette of a leopard, ready to spring down at the top drawer of a filing cabinet labeled A-AH. My innocence interpreted this as the victim's last, despairing cry. Beyond the leopard was a naked, muscular gentleman, who sat; looking down, with his chin on his fist and his elbow on his knee. He seemed utterly miserable.

Some time later, I learned about these statuettes. The headmaster had placed them where they would face delinquent children, because they symbolized to him the whole of life. The naked lady was the Venus of Milo. She was Love. She was not worried about the towel. She was just busy being beautiful. The leopard was Nature, and he was being natural. The naked, muscular gentleman was not miserable. He was Rodin's Thinker, an image of pure thought. It is easy to buy small plaster models of what you think life is like.

I had better explain that I was a frequent visitor to the headmaster's study, because of the latest thing I had done or left undone. As we now say, I was not integrated. I was, if anything, disintegrated; and I was puzzled. Grownups never made sense. Whenever I found myself in a penal position before the headmaster's desk, with the statuettes glimmering whitely above him, I would sink my head, clasp my hands behind my back and writhe one shoe over the other.

The headmaster would look opaquely at me, through flashing spectacles.

"What are we going to do with you?"

Well, what *were* they going to do with me? I would writhe my shoe some more and stare down at the worn rug.

"Look up, boy! Can't you look up?"

Then I would look up at the cupboard, where the naked lady was frozen in her panic and the muscular gentleman contemplated the hindquarters of the leopard in endless gloom. I had nothing to say to the headmaster. His spectacles caught the light so that you could see nothing human behind them. There was no possibility of communication.

"Don't you ever think at all?"

No, I didn't think, wasn't thinking, couldn't think — I was simply waiting in anguish for the interview to stop.

"Then you'd better learn — hadn't you?"

On one occasion the headmaster leaped to his feet, reached up and plonked Rodin's masterpiece on the desk before me.

"That's what a man looks like when he's really thinking."

I surveyed the gentleman without interest or comprehension.

"Go back to your class."

Clearly there was something missing in me. Nature had endowed the rest of the human race with a sixth sense and left me out. This must be so, I mused, on my way back to the class, since whether I had broken a window, or failed to remember Boyle's Law, or been late for school, my teachers produced me one, adult answer: "Why can't you think?"

As I saw the case, I had broken the window because I had tried to hit Jack

Arney with a cricket ball and missed him; I could not remember Boyle's Law because I had never bothered to learn it; and I was late for school because I preferred looking over the bridge into the river. In fact, I was wicked. Were my teachers, perhaps, so good that they could not understand the depths of my depravity? Were they clear, untormented people who could direct their every action by this mysterious business of thinking? The whole thing was incomprehensible. In my earlier years, I found even the statuette of the Thinker confusing. I did not believe any of my teachers were naked, ever. Like someone born deaf, but bitterly determined to find out about sound, I watched my teachers to find out about thought.

There was Mr. Houghton. He was always telling me to think. With a modest satisfaction, he would tell me that he had thought a bit himself. Then why did he spend so much time drinking? Or was there more sense in drinking than there appeared to be? But if not, and if drinking were in fact ruinous to health — and Mr. Houghton was ruined, there was no doubt about that — why was he always talking about the clean life and the virtues of fresh air? He would spread his arms wide with the action of a man who habitually spent his time striding along mountain ridges.

"Open air does me good, boys — I know it!"

Sometimes, exalted by his own oratory, he would leap from his desk and hustle us outside into a hideous wind.

"Now, boys! Deep breaths! Feel it right down inside you — huge draughts of God's good air!"

He would stand before us, rejoicing in his perfect health, an open-air man. He would put his hands on his waist and take a tremendous breath. You could hear the wind, trapped in the cavern of his chest and struggling with all the unnatural impediments. His body would reel with shock and his ruined face go white at the unaccustomed visitation. He would stagger back to his desk and collapse there, useless for the rest of the morning.

Mr. Houghton was given to high-minded monologues about the good life, sexless and full of duty. Yet in the middle of one of these monologues, if a girl passed the window, tapping along on her neat little feet, he would interrupt his discourse, his neck would turn of itself and he would watch her out of sight. In this instance, he seemed to me ruled not by thought but by an invisible and irresistible spring in his nape.

His neck was an object of great interest to me. Normally it bulged a bit over his collar. But Mr. Houghton had fought in the First World War alongside both Americans and French, and had come — by who knows what illogic? — to a settled detestation of both countries. If either country happened to be prominent in current affairs, no argument could make Mr. Houghton think well of it. He would bang the desk, his neck would bulge still further and go red. "You can say what you like," he would cry, "but I've thought about this — and I know what I think!"

Mr. Houghton thought with his neck.

There was Miss Parsons. She assured us that her dearest wish was our welfare, but I knew even then, with the mysterious clairvoyance of childhood, that what she wanted most was the husband she never got. There was Mr. Hands — and so on.

I have dealt at length with my teachers because this was my introduction to the nature of what is commonly called thought. Through them I discovered that thought is often full of unconscious prejudice, ignorance and hypocrisy. It will lecture on disinterested purity while its neck is being remorselessly twisted toward a skirt. Technically, it is about as proficient as most businessmen's golf, as honest as most politicians' intentions, or — to come near my own preoccupation — as coherent as most books that get written. It is what I came to call grade-three thinking, though more properly, it is feeling, rather than thought.

True, often there is a kind of innocence in prejudices, but in those days I viewed grade-three thinking with an intolerant contempt and an incautious mockery. I delighted to confront a pious lady who hated the Germans with the proposition that we should love our enemies. She taught me a great truth in dealing with grade-three thinkers; because of her, I no longer dismiss lightly a mental process which for nine-tenths of the population is the nearest they will ever get to thought. They have immense solidarity. We had better respect them, for we are outnumbered and surrounded. A crowd of grade-three thinkers, all shouting the same thing, all warming their hands at the fire of their own prejudices, will not thank you for pointing out the contradictions in their beliefs. Man is a gregarious animal, and enjoys agreement as cows will graze all the same way on the side of a hill.

Grade-two thinking is the detection of contradictions. I reached grade two when I trapped the poor, pious lady. Grade-two thinkers do not stampede easily, though often they fall into the other fault and lag behind. Grade-two thinking is a withdrawal, with eyes and ears open. It became my hobby and brought satisfaction and loneliness in either hand. For grade-two thinking destroys without having the power to create. It set me watching the crowds cheering His Majesty the King and asking myself what all the fuss was about, without giving me anything positive to put in the place of that heady patriotism. But there were compensations. To hear people justify their habit of hunting foxes and tearing them to pieces by claiming that the foxes liked it. To hear our Prime Minister talk about the great benefit we conferred on India by jailing people like Pandit Nehru and Gandhi. To hear American politicians talk about peace in one sentence and refuse to join the League of Nations in the next. Yes, there were moments of delight.

But I was growing toward adolescence and had to admit that Mr. Houghton was not the only one with an irresistible spring in his neck. I, too, felt the compulsive hand of nature and began to find that pointing out contradiction could be costly as well as fun. There was Ruth, for example, a serious and attractive girl. I was an atheist at the time. Grade-two thinking is a menace to religion and knocks down sects like skittles. I put myself in a position to be converted by her with an hypocrisy worthy of grade three. She was a Methodist — or at least, her parents were, and Ruth had to follow suit. But, alas, instead of relying on the Holy Spirit to convert me, Ruth was foolish enough to open her pretty mouth in argument. She claimed that the Bible (King James Version) was literally inspired. I countered by saying that the Catholics believed in the literal inspiration of Saint Jerome's *Vulgate*, and the two books were different. Argument flagged.

At last she remarked that there were an awful lot of Methodists, and they couldn't be wrong, could they — not all those millions? That was too easy, said I restively (for the nearer you were to Ruth, the nicer she was to be near to) since there were more Roman Catholics than Methodists anyway; and they couldn't be wrong, could they — not all those hundreds of millions? An awful flicker of doubt appeared in her eyes. I slid my arm round her waist and murmured breathlessly that if we were counting heads, the Buddhists were the boys for my money. But Ruth had *really* wanted to do me good, because I was so nice. She fled. The combination of my arm and those countless Buddhists was too much for her.

That night her father visited my father and left, red cheeked and indignant. I was given the third degree to find out what had happened. It was lucky we were both of us only fourteen. I lost Ruth and gained an undeserved reputation as a potential libertine.

So grade-two thinking could be dangerous. It was in this knowledge, at the age of fifteen, that I remember making a comment from the heights of grade two, on the limitations of grade three. One evening I found myself alone in the school hall, preparing it for a party. The door of the headmaster's study was open. I went in. The headmaster had ceased to thump Rodin's Thinker down on the desk as an example to the young. Perhaps he had not found any more candidates, but the statuettes were still there, glimmering and gathering dust on top of the cupboard. I stood on a chair and rearranged them. I stood Venus in her bath towel on the filing cabinet, so that now the top drawer caught its breath in a gasp of sexy excitement. "A-ah!" The portentous Thinker I placed on the edge of the cupboard so that he looked down at the bath towel and waited for it to slip.

Grade-two thinking, though it filled life with fun and excitement, did not make for content. To find out the deficiencies of our elders bolsters the young ego but does not make for personal security. I found that grade two was not only the power to point out contradictions. It took the swimmer some distance from the shore and left him there, out of his depth. I decided that Pontius Pilate was a typical grade-two thinker. "What is truth?" he said, a very common grade-two thought, but one that is used always as the end of an argument instead of the beginning. There is a still higher grade of thought which says, "What is truth?" and sets out to find it.

But these grade-one thinkers were few and far between. They did not visit my grammar school in the flesh though they were there in books. I aspired to them, partly because I was ambitious and partly because I now saw my hobby as an unsatisfactory thing if it went no further. If you set out to climb a mountain, however high you climb, you have failed if you cannot reach the top.

I *did* meet an undeniably grade-one thinker in my first year at Oxford. I was looking over a small bridge in Magdalen Deer Park, and a tiny mustached and hatted figure came and stood by my side. He was a German who had just fled from the Nazis to Oxford as a temporary refuge. His name was Einstein.

But Professor Einstein knew no English at that time and I knew only two words of German. I beamed at him, trying wordlessly to convey by my bearing all the affection and respect that the English felt for him. It is possible — and I have to make the admission — that I felt here were two grade-one thinkers standing side by side; yet I doubt if my face conveyed more than a formless awe. I would have given my Greek and Latin and French and a good slice of my English for enough German to communicate. But we were divided; he was as inscrutable as my headmaster. For perhaps five minutes we stood together on the bridge, undeniable grade-one thinker and breathless aspirant. With true greatness, Professor Einstein realized that any contact was better than none. He pointed to a trout wavering in midstream.

He spoke: *"Fisch."*

My brain reeled. Here I was, mingling with the great, and yet helpless as the veriest grade-three thinker. Desperately I sought for some sign by which I might convey that I, too, revered pure reason. I nodded vehemently. In a brilliant flash I used up half my German vocabulary.

"Fisch. Ja. Ja."

For perhaps another five minutes we stood side by side. Then Professor Einstein, his whole figure still conveying good will and amiability, drifted away out of sight.

I, too, would be a grade-one thinker. I was irreverent at the best of times. Political and religious systems, social customs, loyalties and traditions, they all came tumbling down like so many rotten apples off a tree. This was a fine hobby and a sensible substitute for cricket, since you could play it all the year round. I came up in the end with what must always remain the justification for grade-one thinking, its sign, seal and charter. I devised a coherent system for living. It was a moral system, which was wholly logical. Of course, as I readily admitted, conversion of the world to my way of thinking might be difficult, since my system did away with a number of trifles, such as big business, centralized government, armies, marriage. . . .

It was Ruth all over again. I had some very good friends who stood by me, and still do. But my acquaintances vanished, taking the girls with them. Young women seemed oddly contented with the world as it was. They valued the meaningless ceremony with a ring. Young men, while willing to concede the chaining sordidness of marriage, were hesitant about abandoning the organizations which they hoped would give them a career. A young man on the first rung of the Royal Navy, while perfectly agreeable to doing away with big business and marriage, got as red-necked as Mr. Houghton when I proposed a world without any battleships in it.

Had the game gone too far? Was it a game any longer? In those prewar days, I stood to lose a great deal, for the sake of a hobby.

Now you are expecting me to describe how I saw the folly of my ways and came back to the warm nest, where prejudices are so often called loyalties, where pointless actions are hallowed into custom by repetition, where we are content to say we think when all we do is feel.

But you would be wrong. I dropped my hobby and turned professional.

If I were to go back to the headmaster's study and find the dusty statuettes still there, I would arrange them differently. I would dust Venus and put her aside, for I have come to love her and know her for the fair thing she is. But I would put the Thinker, sunk in his desperate thought, where there were shadows before him — and at his back, I would put the leopard, crouched and ready to spring.

Questions for Discussion

1. What do you understand Golding to mean when he calls thinking his "hobby"? What do you take his meaning to be at the end of his essay when he says he abandoned his hobby and "turned professional"?

2. In light of what Golding has shown us in the essay, do you agree with his final placement of the statuettes? In what way is his arrangement an appropriate one? Why does he set one statuette aside?

3. Why do you suppose there are so few grade-one thinkers, as Golding defines them? Why would he purposely create a category with so few members?

4. How would you describe the tone of this essay? Is it appropriate to the subject matter? Inappropriate?

5. What seems to be Golding's *present* attitude toward Mr. Houghton, Miss Parsons, and Ruth? Does he still have some of the characteristics of a grade-two thinker?

6. What grade of thinker are you? Are you satisfied with the category you're in?

Suggested Activities

1. Golding might have given his categories more descriptive names. Create three titles for his categories that describe the characteristics of each. Compare your titles with those of your classmates.

2. Expand Golding's three categories of thinkers by creating appropriate subcategories for each type. Be sure your subcategories are parallel and non-overlapping.

3. Write an essay in which you use three objects to symbolize your attitudes toward some segment of your life. Suggested topics: education, work, entertainment, politics.

comparison and contrast

If you spent very many of your preschool afternoons watching *Sesame Street*, then you're familiar with the following lyric:

> One of these things is not like the others
> One of these things just doesn't belong
> Can you tell which thing is not like the others,
> By the time I finish my song?

The activity this song may have helped you practice—comparing and contrasting—is fundamental to human life. We use it continually, to decide matters as minor as which television program to watch and as major as where to go to college and whom (or whether) to marry. Without it, no one could tell the difference between a mushroom that's safe to eat and a toadstool that isn't.

Because we begin comparing (the one term can be used for both processes) so early in life and do it so often, it may seem that there's not much left to learn about it. And as a matter of fact, most people do find comparison to be an easy, comfortable way of thinking about things. Still, there are three guidelines you should bear in mind as you move from the casual comparisons of everyday life to the writing of formal comparison-and-contrast essays.

1. Choose a clear basis for comparison and stick to it. Almost any two things can be compared in more than one way. Take cars, for example. If you want to compare a Mustang and a Mercedes-Benz, what term are you going to use? Performance? Cost? Fuel economy? Style? Or some combination of the four? If you don't decide on the basis of your comparison before you begin writing, you may get lost—and lose your audience—halfway through your essay. This is especially true when your comparison involves broad concepts, such as styles of life or systems of religion. Matters as large as these can be compared in so many different ways that it's crucially important for you to decide on the terms you're going to limit yourself to before you begin.

Remember, too, to use the *same* basis throughout the comparison. It isn't fair, or enlightening, to talk about the Mercedes's cost and then switch to the Mustang's fuel economy. And if you decide to use several terms for your comparison, make sure you don't lose any of them along the way. If it's performance, style, and fuel economy for the one car, then it should be performance, style, and fuel economy for the other.

2. Only compare things that are significantly similar or different.   Everything in the world is similar to everything else in some ways and different in others, but not all these resemblances and differences are worth pointing out. Little is to be gained by demonstrating the similarities between things we all agree are similar, or by pointing out the differences between things we know are different. It *is* important, however, to show how apparently different ideas or events in fact resemble one another, or how things that initially seem the same are actually different. The key to deciding whether a comparison is worth making is to think of it in relation to your audience. If the comparison will be obvious to most of your readers, then it isn't worth making. If it will seem trivial to them once you've pointed it out, then again it isn't worth making. Worthwhile comparisons are those—and only those—that your readers will think are interesting and important.

3. Choose a logical organizational pattern.   Once you've settled on the terms of your comparison and decided that it is a worthwhile one to make, you need to choose the organizational pattern you're going to use. For most essays, there are two clear-cut alternatives. You can use either a *point-by-point* or a *subject-by-subject* pattern. In the first of these, you look at both subjects together, first in terms of one point of comparison and then in terms of another, until all the points have been considered. In the second, you look at the two subjects separately, first considering all the points of comparison in relation to the one subject and only afterwards considering them in relation to the other.

An easy way to see the difference between these two organizational patterns is through examples. Here is a *point-by-point* comparison of Ian Fleming (the author of the James Bond novels) and Ernest Hemingway:

> . . . their careers have certain resemblances. Both were romantically inclined
> to the life of action while being constantly hauled back from it by too much

imagination and sensibility and even intellectual discipline: both had their moments of being men of action in the late war (Fleming in Germany, Hemingway in France) while otherwise relying on sport—golf, cards, skiing and underwater fishing for one; shooting, hunting and spectator bull-fighting for the other. Both had dominating mothers and experienced woman trouble: both made large fortunes and were dragged protesting by the Bitch Goddess into ever larger areas of limelight. Both died prematurely. In fact, I began to imagine a composite character, Ernest Flemingway, author of a macabre thriller, *The Scum also Rises.*[1]

And here is a *subject-by-subject* comparison of two other men, Floyd Dominy and David Brower. At the time this comparison was written, Dominy was head of the Bureau of Reclamation, the federal agency mainly responsible for the development of dams and other water-control projects. Brower was the head of Friends of the Earth, a vehemently pro-environmental group. The two of them were taking a raft trip down the Colorado River:

> Dominy is wearing a blue yachting cap with gold braid, and above its visor in gold letters are the words "LAKE POWELL." His skin is rouge brown. His nose is peeling. He wears moccasins, and a frayed cotton shirt in dark, indeterminate tartan, and long trousers secured by half a pound of silver buckle. He has with him a couple of small bags and a big leather briefcase on which is painted the great seal of the Bureau of Reclamation—snow-capped mountains, a reservoir, a dam, and irrigated fields, all within the framing shape of a big drop of water. . . .
>
> Brower is also wearing an old tartan shirt, basically orange, and faded. He wears shorts and sneakers. The skin of his legs and face is bright red. Working indoors and all but around the clock, he has been too long away from the sun. He protects his head with a handkerchief knotted at the corners and soaked in the river, but his King Lear billowing white hair is probably protection enough. He travels light. A miniature duffelbag, eight inches in diameter and a foot long—standard gear for the river—contains all that he has with him, most notably his Sierra Club cup, without which he would be incomplete.[2]

And now here are the organizational patterns of the two passages in outline form:

FLEMING/HEMINGWAY	DOMINY/BROWER
Point 1: Life of action	A. Dominy
A. Fleming	Point 1: Style of dress
B. Hemingway	Point 2: Skin color

[1]Cyril Connolly, "Ian Fleming," in *The Evening Colonnade* (London: David Bruce and Watson, 1973), p. 389.

[2]John McPhee, *Encounters with the Archdruid* (New York: Farrar, Straus & Giroux, 1971), pp. 174-75.

Point 2: Relations with women
    A. Fleming
    B. Hemingway
Point 3: Money and fame
    A. Fleming
    B. Hemingway
Point 4: Early death
    A. Fleming
    B. Hemingway

Point 3: Further aspects of dress
Point 4: Luggage
  B. Brower
Point I: Style of dress
Point 2: Skin color
Point 3: Further aspects of dress
Point 4: Luggage

As the Fleming/Hemingway outline makes clear, in a point-by-point comparison each point about the one subject is immediately followed by a corresponding point about the other. But in a subject-by-subject comparison, as we have said, the two subjects are treated separately. When a writer uses this pattern, he or she writes what amounts to a miniature essay about each subject, and then joins the two together. Note that the two halves of a subject-by-subject comparison should have the same structure. The same points need to be considered for each subject, and they should be presented in the same order.

Each of these patterns has its advantages and disadvantages. In general, the subject-by-subject pattern is more flexible than the point-by-point one, since it allows you to expand on particular points of comparison if you wish. Using it, you can give fuller attention to a point in relation to one subject than in relation to the other without throwing your comparison out of balance. By contrast, the point-by-point pattern usually works better in long essays, since the wide separation between points that the subject-by-subject pattern entails may cause readers to lose sight of specific comparisons. Also, long subject-by-subject comparisons can tend to be repetitious if they're not carefully handled. To a large extent, your specific writing situation will help you decide which of the patterns to use. Be aware, though, that there isn't always a single right choice to be made, and that writers sometimes find themselves choosing between the two patterns simply on the basis of personal preference.

In any case, you'll probably find that your main purpose in using either pattern is to persuade. Next to argumentation itself, comparison is the rhetorical mode most clearly concerned with persuasion. Although we sometimes compare things simply to *explain* one in terms of the other, we more often do so in order to *evaluate* them. This should not surprise us. Choosing is a basic human activity, and the very structure of comparison, with its placement of similar things side by side, is an invitation to evaluate them and to choose one in preference to the other.

When we use comparison in this evaluative way in our writing, our aim should be to convince our readers that we've made the right judgment about the merits of the items being compared. Here, it is important to be fair in the use of evidence and argument. The truly persuasive comparison will treat both of its subjects evenhandedly. It will not suppress some aspects of the comparison and emphasize others unduly, but will instead rely on the merits of the items themselves to convince the reader.

Beyond this explicit use of comparison to persuade lies a subtler purpose. To use an old-fashioned phrase, comparison can lead us to wonder and delight. The world is a varied place, full of odd and arresting things. One of the main powers of comparison is to put this variety on display by juxtaposing things in a way that lets us see just how interesting they really are. Look back, for example, at the selection of detail in McPhee's comparison of Dominy and Brower. Note the contrast between Dominy's Lake Powell hat and Brower's handkerchief (Lake Powell was a Bureau of Reclamation project strenuously opposed by environmentalists), between Dominy's briefcase and Brower's duffelbag, and between Brower's Sierra Club cup and Dominy's "half a pound" silver buckle.

More than any of these contrasts, though, it is Dominy's "rouge brown" skin and Brower's sunburn that most readers carry away from the passage. Here, surprisingly, it is the bureaucrat who is tanned and the environmentalist who is pale from too many days spent indoors at a desk. By including these details McPhee shows himself finally to be less concerned with the differences between Dominy and Brower than with the complexity of both of them. When comparison is directed to such an end, it ceases to be simply a rhetorical mode and instead becomes a form of art.

Education

E. B. WHITE

The most renowned and highly respected of modern American
essayists, E. B. White was born in 1899 in Mt. Vernon, New
York, and now lives in Maine. His works include *Is Sex Necessary?* (coauthored with James Thurber, 1927), *One Man's Meat*
(1942), *The Second Tree from the Corner* (1954), and two
famous children's books, *Stuart Little* (1945) and *Charlotte's
Web* (1952). Master of a supple and evocative prose style,
White has been the recipient of numerous honors and awards,
including the Presidential Medal of Freedom (1963) and a special citation from the Pulitzer Prize Committee (1978). The
selection reprinted here originally appeared in the "Talk of the
Town" section of *The New Yorker*. In it, White compares two
schools and, by implication, two philosophies of education.

I have an increasing admiration for the teacher in the country school where we
have a third-grade scholar in attendance. She not only undertakes to instruct her
charges in all the subjects of the first three grades, but she manages to function
quietly and effectively as a guardian of their health, their clothes, their habits,
their mothers, and their snowball engagements. She has been doing this sort of
Augean task for twenty years, and is both kind and wise. She cooks for the children on the stove that heats the room, and she can cool their passions or warm
their soup with equal competence. She conceives their costumes, cleans up their
messes, and shares their confidences. My boy already regards his teacher as his
great friend, and I think tells her a great deal more than he tells us.

    The shift from city school to country school was something we worried

EDUCATION   Excerpt from pages 52–54 in "Education," from *One Man's Meat* by E. B. White.
Copyright 1939 by E. B. White. Reprinted by permission of Harper & Row, Publishers, Inc.

about quietly all last summer. I have always rather favored public school over private school, if only because in public school you meet a greater variety of children. This bias of mine, I suspect, is partly an attempt to justify my own past (I never knew anything but public schools) and partly an involuntary defense against getting kicked in the shins by a young ceramist on his way to the kiln. My wife was unacquainted with public schools, never having been exposed (in her early life) to anything more public than the washroom of Miss Winsor's. Regardless of our backgrounds, we both knew that the change in schools was something that concerned not us but the scholar himself. We hoped it would work out all right. In New York our son went to a medium-priced private institution with semi-progressive ideas of education, and modern plumbing. He learned fast, kept well, and we were satisfied. It was an electric, colorful, regimented existence with moments of pleasurable pause and giddy incident. The day the Christmas angel fainted and had to be carried out by one of the Wise Men was educational in the highest sense of the term. Our scholar gave imitations of it around the house for weeks afterward, and I doubt if it ever goes completely out of his mind.

His days were rich in formal experience. Wearing overalls and an old sweater (the accepted uniform of the private seminary), he sallied forth at morn accompanied by a nurse or a parent and walked (or was pulled) two blocks to a corner where the school bus made a flag stop. This flashy vehicle was as punctual as death: seeing us waiting at the cold curb, it would sweep to a halt, open its mouth, suck the boy in, and spring away with an angry growl. It was a good deal like a train picking up a bag of mail. At school the scholar was worked on for six or seven hours by half a dozen teachers and a nurse, and was revived on orange juice in mid-morning. In a cinder court he played games supervised by an athletic instructor, and in a cafeteria he ate lunch worked out by a dietitian. He soon learned to read with gratifying facility and discernment and to make Indian weapons of a semi-deadly nature. Whenever one of his classmates fell low of a fever the news was put on the wires and there were breathless phone calls to physicians, discussing periods of incubation and allied magic.

In the country all one can say is that the situation is different, and somehow more casual. Dressed in corduroys, sweatshirt, and short rubber boots, and carrying a tin dinner-pail, our scholar departs at crack of dawn for the village school, two and a half miles down the road, next to the cemetery. When the road is open and the car will start, he makes the journey by motor, courtesy of his old man. When the snow is deep or the motor is dead or both, he makes it on the hoof. In the afternoons he walks or hitches all or part of the way home in fair weather, gets transported in foul. The schoolhouse is a two-room frame building, bungalow type, shingles stained a burnt brown with weather-resistant stain. It has a chemical toilet in the basement and two teachers above stairs. One takes the first three grades, the other the fourth, fifth, and sixth. They have little or no time for individual instruction, and no time at all for the esoteric. They teach what they know themselves, just as fast and as hard as they can manage. The pupils sit still at their desks in class, and do their milling around outdoors during recess.

There is no supervised play. They play cops and robbers (only they call it "Jail") and throw things at one another—snowballs in winter, rose hips in fall. It seems to satisfy them. They also construct darts, pinwheels, and "pick-up sticks" (jackstraws), and the school itself does a brisk trade in penny candy, which is for sale right in the classroom and which contains "surprises." The most highly prized surprise is a fake cigarette, made of cardboard, fiendishly lifelike.

The memory of how apprehensive we were at the beginning is still strong. The boy was nervous about the change too. The tension, on that first fair morning in September when we drove him to school, almost blew the windows out of the sedan. And when later we picked him up on the road, wandering along with his little blue lunch-pail, and got his laconic report "All right" in answer to our inquiry about how the day had gone, our relief was vast. Now, after almost a year of it, the only difference we can discover in the two school experiences is that in the country he sleeps better at night—and *that* probably is more the air than the education. When grilled on the subject of school-in-country *vs.* school-in-city, he replied that the chief difference is that the day seems to go so much quicker in the country. "Just like lightning," he reported.

Questions for Discussion

1. What examples of heightened diction can you find in "Education"? What effect do they have on the tone of the essay?

2. In his first paragraph, White says that the teacher in the country school guards the children's "health, their clothes, their habits, their mothers, and their snowball engagements." What impression does this statement create of the teacher's duties?

3. Consider White's claim that "the day the Christmas angel fainted . . . was educational in the highest sense of the term." What definition of "educational" is implied here? What is the relationship between the view White expresses here and his reasons for preferring public schools?

4. At the beginning of his third paragraph, White says that in the private school his son's "days were rich in formal experience." What view of "formal experience" does he create in the rest of this paragraph? How does he create it?

5. White concludes by saying that the only discernible difference between the two school experiences is his son's sounder sleep in the country. Does this statement seem to be warranted by the rest of the essay? Do you see any other differences between the two experiences?

6. What is your attitude toward private schools? Does White's essay confirm or undercut your view of them?

Suggested Activities

1. Using this essay and "Once More to the Lake" (pp. 295–300) as your sources of information, write a paragraph characterizing E. B. White. What can you say about his living

situation, his educational status, his moral and intellectual attitudes? Cite specific details from the essays in support of your assertions.

2. Write an essay arguing the need for more (or less) "formal experience" in America's elementary schools.

3. Compare your recollections of the third grade with those of your friends. Is there any common pattern to your memories? What do you recall with the most pleasure? the most displeasure?

4. Using a subject of your own choice, write two or three stylistic imitations of the following sentence from "Education": "She cooks for the children on the stove that heats the room, and she can cool their passions or warm their soup with equal competence." What seems to be the secret of the sentence's effectiveness?

Two Clowns

EDWARD HOAGLAND

After an early career as a novelist, Edward Hoagland (b. 1922) turned in the late 1960s to the writing of nonfiction. He is now widely known for his travel notes, nature reportage, and vignettes of life in New York City. His books include *The Courage of Turtles* (1970), *Walking the Dead Diamond River* (1973), *Red Wolves and Black Bears* (1976), and, most recently, *African Calliope: A Journey to the Sudan* (1979). The following selection, taken from *Walking the Dead Diamond River*, is a spare, precise comparison of two masters of an unusual profession.

Clowning is the one profession in the circus which has no limits on what can be done, and where youth and physique don't count for much. A man may start late in it or may operate in the realm of hallucination if he wants. Usually clowns take a role which is close to the earth — a plowman-pieman-tinker type, a barefoot sprite whose sex is uncertain because he's infantile. They're overly tall or small or in some way out of it — innocent and light of heart, yet stuck with some disfigurement which is an extension of what the rest of us are supposed to want: a nose with "character," for instance, or tously hair and a fair skin. But these possibilities, ample for the average rather passive though contentious fellow who makes clowning his career, are trivial detail in the persona of the few great clowns. After apprenticing in paleface as a simpleton for a few years, with a thick, giddy, up-arching, imprinted smile, such men will gradually start to draw a more scored and complicated personality with the greasepaint, developing a darker role.

Otto Griebling,[1] who is the best American clown, wears a rag heap that has grown so shapeless as to seem mountainous. His nose, instead of bulbous, is bent and decomposing in a face the color of a frying pan. His resentful stare, eaten up with grievances, is as calculating as a monkey's. He plays a bum whose universe has been so mutilated and circumscribed that all he knows is that he's free to sit where he is sitting or walk where he is going to walk, and any impulse we may feel to try and cheer him up is itself cause for outrage, not worth even a bitter laugh. He hasn't lost so much that he isn't afraid of further blows, but as he shuffles along with a notebook, compiling a blacklist, marking people in the audience down, all his grudges blaze in his face. Like a sore-footed janitor (he's seventy-four), he climbs into the crowd to put the heat on selected guests — begins perversely dusting their chairs, falling in love at close quarters, gazing at some squirming miss with his whole soul, leaning closer still, until, inexplicably furious, he slaps her with his cleaning cloth — she may try kissing him but it won't work. Now that in actual life his vocal cords have been removed, Griebling has inaugurated a "broadcast," too. Wearing a headset and a microphone, he follows the rest of the clowns, whispering a commentary on their fate, on each mishap. His role is madder, more paranoid and ruined, than Emmett Kelly's famous tramp was; less lachrymose, it fits the times. With faded baggage tickets pinned to his cloak, he tries to powder his scorched face, looks for old enemies in the crowd. Obviously long past attempting to cope, he simply wants revenge; yet he's so small-time that instead of being fearful we laugh at him.

Added to Griebling's troubles is the same seething irritant that seems to bother all clowns. Nobody likes these ovations which are bestowed on the man in the center ring. Suddenly he loses patience, grabs three tin plates, clacks them together and insists that the audience hail *him*. He juggles perfunctorily, since what he's interested in is not the juggling but the applause, and signals with his hands for a real crescendo. Setting two sides of the arena against each other, he works them up almost to the level the trapeze troupe achieved. But he isn't a bit satisfied. It never quite reaches the imagined pitch. Besides, it is too late for consolation now — too much of his life already has gone by!

Pio Nock is the Swiss master clown. He's old enough to have a daughter who romps on the single trapeze, dangling her yellow hair, wriggling from side to side, looking like butterfat in the strong lights. Nock confronted big cats and the flying trapeze when he was young and now is a high-wire clown, although he does some conventional clowning as well. He plays a sort of country cousin, a man floundering past the prime of life with nothing to show for it except his scars, not even an ironic viewpoint or the pleasure of vindictiveness. Where Griebling stands in baffled fury, past tears or shouting, torn between petulance and outraged astonishment, Nock is a man who doesn't look for root causes, doesn't even suspect that he has enemies or that the odds might be stacked against him.

From every misfortune he simply goes on trying to learn. And for this characterization he doesn't rely much on greasepaint or costumes; instead, he makes

---

[1]Otto Griebling died in New York City, April 19, 1972.

queer hollow hoots, like the sounds in a birdhouse. As a trademark they have the advantage over costumes that the kids also can imitate them. They troop out of the auditorium parroting him.

Whenever Nock's country bumpkin gets slapped around, he's always willing to forgive the prankster if only the fellow will teach him how to do that particular trick so that Nock will never be slapped around quite the same way again. Of course, during the show we discover that there are more pranks on the earth than Nock will ever become proof against. We learn that life has limited its gifts to him to these few satisfactions — after the fact. After all, if the world appears upside down it must only be because he is standing on his head. Punishment follows each blunder; yet when he sees a nice girl — his daughter — up on the high wire, he decides that he wants to make an endeavor at that also. At first the ringmaster stops him, but escaping the ringmaster's grasp, he climbs a rope ladder and in pantomime is instructed by her in the rudiments of wire-walking, cheeping eagerly at every lesson learned. The next thing he knows, he is out on the wire, terrified, alone, all the tips forgotten, whistling if he can. Whistling in the dark, a man in a jam, he teeters, steps on his own feet, gaining experience by trial and error, keeping his courage up with those strange hoots, which seem to epitomize how absurdly fragile life is, how often we see a tragedy in the making, as well as its end. The band plays music representing the wry look we wear while watching a stranger's funeral procession pass.

Nock stumbles on the wire and slips to his knees; wobbling, he looks downward, giving an unforgettable peep of fear. He's a short man with long legs and one of those wedgelike noses that even without makeup poke out starkly. His hoot is really like a sigh distilled — the sigh that draws on one's own resources as being the only source from which to draw. A man in the wrong place, again he jerks and nearly falls, giving his peep of mortality, and casts all his hopes just on the process of being methodical, doing what he's been taught as if by rote, which is what most of us do when we are in over our heads. But now he discovers he's learning! His obtuseness has shielded him from the danger a little, and suddenly he finds that he is getting the knack. He lets out a tombstone-chiseler's hoot. Now comes the moment when he can enjoy himself after having learned a particular dodge.

Pio Nock and Otto Griebling are great stars, and the image they leave in my head is so accessible that I don't miss them after the circus moves on. In the case of those performers who do mere heroics the memory does not survive as vividly.

Questions for Discussion

1. Hoagland says that the characteristic "disfigurement" in a clown's appearance is "an extension of what the rest of us are supposed to want." What do you think he means by this statement? Is his claim here consistent with his interpretation of Griebling's and Nock's performances? Why or why not?

2. In his first paragraph, Hoagland distinguishes between "the average ... fellow who makes clowning his career" and "the few great clowns." What does he say the difference is? How do Griebling and Nock exemplify it?

3. Why do you think Hoagland uses the present tense in describing the two performances? How effective do you find his use of it to be?

4. What do you think is the basic difference between Griebling's and Nock's approaches to clowning? Be prepared to defend your answer.

5. Hoagland says that Griebling's resentment-laden performance "fits the times." Would it still? Or have the times changed since the early 1970s, when this essay was written?

6. What view of life does Nock's performance express? Is it a view you agree with? Why or why not?

Suggested Activities

1. At the end of his essay, Hoagland speaks of how much more memorable these two clowns are than are "performers who do mere heroics." Is his account of Griebling's and Nock's performances also memorable? Make a note on your calendar to recall this essay a month from today. Exactly what do you remember about it? Compare your memories with those of your classmates. What conclusions can you draw?

2. Write a paragraph describing the kind of clown you would like to be.

3. Write an essay comparing two people performing the same job. Choose people and work you know well.

4. Do you believe that great comedy necessarily has tragic undertones? Write an essay expressing your point of view on this question. Draw on novels, movies, or the work of particular comedians for examples.

Allen Ginsberg
and Louis Ginsberg

JANE KRAMER

After beginning her career as a reporter for *The Village Voice*, Jane Kramer formed an enduring association with *The New Yorker*. Her books include *The Unsettling of Europe* (1980) and *The Last Cowboy* (1977), a powerful depiction of a man frustrated in his desire to be a "proper cowboy" by the demands of a technological society. The selection reprinted here comes from *Allen Ginsberg in America* (1969), a book about the most famous poet of the Beat Generation. In it, Kramer describes one of Ginsberg's visits to his father's house in Paterson, New Jersey. Full of sly humor, Kramer's account conveys both the differences between Ginsberg and his father and their mutual underlying affection.

On a snowy Sunday morning in Paterson, Allen Ginsberg and his father settled into a pair of plumped chintz armchairs in Mr. Ginsberg's living room to look at the *New York Times* together and talk over the schedule for a father-and-son poetry reading that they were going to give that night at Paterson State. Ginsberg's stepmother, Edith, was in the kitchen fixing a big breakfast of bagels, bialys, lox, cream cheese, and scrambled eggs, and Maretta, who had come home with Ginsberg for the weekend, was still asleep. It was Ginsberg's first visit to the house since early fall, when a warrant had been issued in Paterson for his arrest on a marijuana charge. The mayor of Paterson, who was on his way out of office, had ordered the arrest after Ginsberg informed the audience at another family reading, at the local Young Men's Hebrew Association, that he had "heightened the experience" of a poetic pilgrimage that morning with his father to the Passaic Falls. Paterson's policemen had thereupon combed the city for Ginsberg, who had last been seen carrying his purple woven book bag and wearing horn-rimmed glasses, his tan hiking boots, rumpled khaki pants, his unmatching gray socks, a relatively threadbare brown tweed jacket, an old white button-down, finger cymbals, and an oracle's ring, and after a few days they located a likely-looking beard near a bar downtown. By the time the gentleman with the beard was released as a sartorial follower of Ginsberg, but by no means the genuine poetic article, Ginsberg was safely across the state line in New York. He thought about returning to Paterson, with a phalanx of reporters, to be arrested publicly as a first move in a marijuana-law test case, but he abandoned the scheme as "too embarrassing" to his father, and left for the West Coast, to teach at Berkeley, instead. While Ginsberg was away, a new and friendlier mayor took office, and when he finally came home, a few weeks ago, the case against him was dismissed, on the ground of insufficient evidence, by the Paterson Municipal Court.

Ginsberg's five months as the poet who was "wanted in Paterson" reminded him of one of the letters he had written to William Carlos Williams, from San Francisco, over ten years ago:

> . . . I have NOT absconded from Paterson. I do have a whitmanic mania & nostalgia for cities and detail & panorama and isolation in jungle and pole, like the images you pick up. When I've seen enough I'll be back to splash in the Passaic again only with a body so naked and happy City Hall will have to call out the Riot Spad [sic]. When I come back I'll make big political speeches in the mayoralty campaign like I did when I was 16 only this time I'll have W. C. Fields on my left and Jehovah on my right. Why not? Paterson is only a big sad poppa who needs compassion . . . In any case Beauty is where I hang my hat. And reality. And America . . . I mean to say Paterson is not a task like Milton going down to hell, it's a flower to the mind too . . .

He mentioned the letter to his father, who was peering at him over the top of the "News of the Week in Review." Mr. Ginsberg said that he remembered it. At seventy-one, Louis Ginsberg was compact and jaunty, with quizzical, popping eyes, a scrubbed-to-gleaming forehead, and a favorite expression of slightly oppressed seniority. For forty years he had taught English in the Paterson public high schools, and for fifty he had been writing and steadily publishing lyric poems. At the moment he was stagestruck, according to Mrs. Ginsberg, who dated this new passion of her husband's from the night of the first Ginsberg reading, *père et fils*, in March of 1966.

"You *did* bring home some good clothes for the reading tonight, didn't you, Allen?" Mr. Ginsberg, who was already dressed for the event in a new polka-dot bow tie and a blue-serge suit, asked his son.

Ginsberg looked up from Section I, which he was scouring for hippie news, and laughed. "Yeah, I've got *my* suit, too," he said.

Mr. Ginsberg sighed. "We'll show them that the Ginsberg names means [*sic*] poetry," he said, and he added, philosophically, "You know, Allen, you're popular with the college crowd, but with a real audience you need me for balance. I'm like the stamp to your letter."

Ginsberg shook his head.

"I told you that one," Mr. Ginsberg said. "The one where the stamp says to the letter, 'I may be square, but I send you.'"

Ginsberg groaned.

His father, who had long been known in the Passaic County press as "the Paterson pun-dit" or, alternatively, "the Paterson punny man," went on to say that he had just recatalogued his pun collection by subjects, such as "Flirtation," "Love," "Automobiles," and "Alcoholics," and now had a comprehensive folder just on beatniks. He stood up to get it from his desk, in the sunroom, but Ginsberg waved him down.

"You know, Louis, I think you secretly dig my poetry," Ginsberg said.

Louis Ginsberg shrugged. "You're a new generation, Allen," he said. "I believe in poetic coexistence, but you young people — you don't like a nice, regular, flexible meter. You don't like discipline. You don't like rhyme. You say it's not natural. I ask you, what could be more natural than rhyme? Rhymes are so enchanting, so instinctive. Children make rhymes as soon as they can speak." Mr. Ginsberg sighed again, and went right on. "And you've got such new mores. For instance, you use four-letter words that I was brought up not to use in company. And the way you live. You don't have to live like that, Allen. You're a world-famous poet."

Ginsberg made a mudra to assure his father that he recognized and respected the soul of another sentient being in the living room. Then he said "*Om*," signifying the ultimate oneness of all views.

"And these odd religions," Mr. Ginsberg said. He seemed to be warming to the chance at hand, and Ginsberg chuckled, listening to him. In December, he had taken his father to a birthday party for his friend Swami Satchidananda, the Hindu yoga and holy man who lived on West End Avenue. Mr. Ginsberg had had indigestion after three spoonfuls of the Swami's party food, and had ever since displayed a certain impatience with the customs of the East.

"I bet it was that curry, Louis," Ginsberg said.

Mr. Ginsberg shook his head. He said it was really Maretta that was bothering him. She had arrived at the house last night with a sack of equipment for her rather unnerving meditations — a tattered paperback copy of the *Tibetan Book of the Dead*, a pair of finger cymbals, Ginsberg's big metal dorje, her own faceted gazing crystal, and a packet of incense sticks — and had emptied it out on the living-room couch for the Ginsbergs to see. Then, just before bed, she had informed Mr. Ginsberg that her sadhana was hashish. "What's with this Maretta?" Mr. Ginsberg asked. "Why can't you bring home a nice Jewish girl?"

Ginsberg, laughing, threw up his hands. "For the love of God, Louis," he said, "here for years you've been saying, 'Please, just bring home a *girl* for a change,' and now that I do, you want a *Jewish* one?"

"You're such an *experimenter*, Allen," Mr. Ginsberg said. "Tibetan Buddhist girl friends. Swamis. Drugs. All this talk from you about pot — 'It's so elevating, Louis. So ecstatic. My soul is outside my body. I see ultimate reality.'" Mr. Ginsberg frowned. "You know what *I* say? I say, 'Allen, take it easy.'"

Ginsberg, who had removed his shoes and was sitting in the lotus position in the chintz chair, leaned forward and took his father's hand. "*You* should take it easy, Louis," he said. "You'll wear yourself out straightening me out."

"Look, Allen, it's been a long time since I've been able to get you to the old homestead," Mr. Ginsberg said. "Your father waits, counts the days."

"Well, the troubles are over now," Ginsberg said. "Was it bad for you here? With the trial?"

Mr. Ginsberg shook his head. "You know, some people talk," he said. "You hear all sorts of odd things." He shuffled through a pile of papers on an end table by his chair and handed a clipping to Ginsberg. It was a letter to the editor of the Paterson *Call:* "In reference to Allen Ginsberg, whom your reporter, George James, described as a poet, living legend, and international traveler. So what! I was extremely disgusted with your paper's continuously shielding and glorifying this poet. One would think that you were trying to defend a moral saintly man instead of a person who openly admitted that he was smoking marijuana, which is unlawful . . . I was a student at Central High School and remember his father, Louis Ginsberg, who taught there. Being a parent myself I do not condemn him because of his son, but I am shocked that he has joined his son as a team in the poetry readings. It seems that he must certainly enjoy all this publicity, despite what kind it may be . . ."

Ginsberg tossed the clipping back on the table.

"Some people are like that," Mr. Ginsberg said. "I've got no axiom to grind."

"I was just wondering what the gossip in the coffee shops was, that's all," Ginsberg said.

"Allen, I *told* you," Mr. Ginsberg said. "Everybody thought that it was pretty silly of the previous mayor to make a fuss. That the evidence was flimsy. Everybody's glad it turned out fine. Still . . ." Mr. Ginsberg looked up.

"Go ahead," Ginsberg said.

"Well, *my* feeling," Mr. Ginsberg said, "is really that you should obey the law, and then when the law is changed, you can go ahead and smoke all you want."

Maretta walked into the living room, yawning.

"I felt I didn't need the drugs," Mr. Ginsberg told her. "I felt that with my *own* imagination I could receive the majesty and grandeur of the Falls."

Maretta nodded, and began poking her hair into a new fringed shawl which she had wrapped around her head. She was dressed for breakfast in baggy black ski pants and purple sari cloth. The dorje and the crystal were both on strings around her neck. Mr. Ginsberg stared, speechless, as she arranged herself on his brown-slipcovered couch.

"Well, young lady, how do you like it here?" Mr. Ginsberg asked, finally, with a sweep of his hand.

Maretta contemplated the small, tidy living room. It was painted a rosy tan and had beige carpeting and silvery nylon curtains at the windows. There were urns of bright green plastic leaves in a fireplace at one end and, at the other, a gilded white secretary and an enormous television set. Photographs of various Ginsberg grandchildren were displayed along the walls, and above the brown couch there were two Montmartre flower market scenes, which Mr. Ginsberg pointed to proudly, telling Maretta that he had picked them out himself.

Maretta, however, was busy scrutinizing a lampshade through her crystal bead.

"I imagine you're meditating," Mr. Ginsberg said, finally. "Do you meditate often?"

"I've sat in a few caves," Maretta said.

"And have you been grazing and ciphering ancient Buddhist texts?" Mr. Ginsberg went on. "Are you wiser now than before?"

"Yeah," Maretta said.

Mr. Ginsberg put down his paper. "With you young people," he said, "it's like the one about children — you can love them in the abstract, but it's hard in the concrete."

"Maretta speaks Tibetan," Ginsberg said.

"So what's wrong with English?" Mr. Ginsberg said.

Questions for Discussion

1. Kramer uses a number of little-known Hindu words in this essay. Do you think she should have defined them? How would their effect have differed if she had?

2. Kramer says that the mayor who issued the warrant for Allen Ginsberg's arrest "was on his way out of office." Why do you think she includes this detail?

3. Do the attitudes toward marijuana in this essay seem dated? Why or why not?

4. Compare this essay to Hoagland's "Two Clowns." How do the two essays differ in their use of the techniques of comparison and contrast?

5. Kramer introduces her paragraph describing the living room with the sentence, "Maretta contemplated the small, tidy living room." Why do you think she links the description to Maretta?

6. How does Mr. Ginsberg's view of the nature of poetry differ from his son's? Which view do you tend to agree with?

Suggested Activities

1. Give a brief report on Allen Ginsberg to the class. To prepare the report, seek out additional biographical information in the library and read some of Ginsberg's poetry and published letters.

2. Write an essay analyzing a continuing difference of opinion between you and one or both of your parents. How have you adjusted your relationship to accommodate this difference?

3. Write a brief essay comparing the styles of the two letters quoted in this selection. In what ways are the styles consistent with the points of view expressed?

4. Write a brief essay comparing Mr. Ginsberg's attitude toward Eastern religion with Harvey Cox's (as expressed in "Eastern Cults and Western Culture," pp. 125–34).

The Prisoner's
Dilemma

STEPHEN CHAPMAN

Formerly a staff writer for *The New Republic*, Stephen Chapman is now that magazine's associate editor. In the selection
reprinted here, published in 1980 in *The New Republic*, Chapman compares American penal practices with those prevailing
in Islamic countries and arrives at some startling conclusions.

If the punitive laws of Islam were applied for only one year, all the devastating
injustices would be uprooted. Misdeeds must be punished by the law of retal-
iation: cut off the hands of the thief; kill the murderers; flog the adulterous
woman or man. Your concerns, your "humanitarian" scruples are more childish than reasonable. Under the terms of Koranic law, any judge fulfilling the
seven requirements (that he have reached puberty, be a believer, know the
Koranic laws perfectly, be just, and not be affected by amnesia, or be a bastard,
or be of the female sex) is qualified to be a judge in any type of case. He can
thus judge and dispose of twenty trials in a single day, whereas the Occidental
justice might take years to argue them out.

— From *Sayings of the Ayatollah Khomeini* (Bantam Books)

One of the amusements of life in the modern West is the opportunity to observe
the barbaric rituals of countries that are attached to the customs of the dark ages.
Take Pakistan, for example, our newest ally and client state in Asia. Last October

THE PRISONER'S DILEMMA   From *The New Republic*, March 8, 1980. Reprinted by permission of the
publisher, © 1980 The New Republic, Inc.

President Zia, in harmony with the Islamic fervor that is sweeping his part of the world, revived the traditional Moslem practice of flogging lawbreakers in public. In Pakistan, this qualified as mass entertainment, and no fewer than 10,000 law-abiding Pakistanis turned out to see justice done to 26 convicts. To Western sensibilities the spectacle seemed barbaric — both in the sense of cruel and in the sense of pre-civilized. In keeping with Islamic custom each of the unfortunates — who had been caught in prostitution raids the previous night and summarily convicted and sentenced — was stripped down to a pair of white shorts, which were painted with a red stripe across the buttocks (the target). Then he was shackled against an easel, with pads thoughtfully placed over the kidneys to prevent injury. The floggers were muscular, fierce-looking sorts — convicted murderers, as it happens — who paraded around the flogging platform in colorful loincloths. When the time for the ceremony began, one of the floggers took a running start and brought a five-foot stave down across the first victim's buttocks, eliciting screams from the convict and murmurs from the audience. Each of the 26 received from five to 15 lashes. One had to be carried from the stage unconscious.

Flogging is one of the punishments stipulated by Koranic law, which has made it a popular penological device in several Moslem countries, including Pakistan, Saudi Arabia, and, most recently, the ayatollah's Iran. Flogging, or *ta'zir*, is the general punishment prescribed for offenses that don't carry an explicit Koranic penalty. Some crimes carry automatic *hadd* punishments — stoning or scourging (a severe whipping) for illicit sex, scourging for drinking alcoholic beverages, amputation of the hands for theft. Other crimes — as varied as murder and abandoning Islam — carry the death penalty (usually carried out in public). Colorful practices like these have given the Islamic world an image in the West, as described by historian G. H. Jansen, "of blood dripping from the stumps of amputated hands and from the striped backs of malefactors, and piles of stones barely concealing the battered bodies of adulterous couples." Jansen, whose book *Militant Islam* is generally effusive in its praise of Islamic practices, grows squeamish when considering devices like flogging, amputation, and stoning. But they are given enthusiastic endorsement by the Koran itself.

Such traditions, we all must agree, are no sign of an advanced civilization. In the West, we have replaced these various punishments (including the death penalty in most cases) with a single device. Our custom is to confine criminals in prison for varying lengths of time. In Illinois, a reasonably typical state, grand theft carries a punishment of three to five years; armed robbery can get you from six to 30. The lowest form of felony theft is punishable by one to three years in prison. Most states impose longer sentences on habitual offenders. In Kentucky, for example, habitual offenders can be sentenced to life in prison. Other states are less brazen, preferring the more genteel sounding "indeterminate sentence," which allows parole boards to keep inmates locked up for as long as life. It was under an indeterminate sentence of one to 14 years that George Jackson served 12 years in California prisons for committing a $70 armed robbery. Under a Texas law imposing an automatic life sentence for a third felony conviction, a man was sent to jail for life last year because of three thefts adding up to less than $300 in property value. Texas also is famous for occasionally imposing extravagantly long sentences, often running into hundreds or thousands of years. This gives Texas a leg up on Maryland, which used to sentence some criminals to life plus a day — a distinctive if superfluous flourish.

The punishment *intended* by Western societies in sending their criminals to prison is the loss of freedom. But, as everyone knows, the actual punishment in most American prisons is of a wholly different order. The February 2 [1980] riot at New Mexico's state prison in Santa Fe, one of several bloody prison riots in the nine years since the Attica bloodbath, once again dramatized the conditions of life in an American prison. Four hundred prisoners seized control of the prison before dawn. By sunset the next day 33 inmates had died at the hands of other convicts and another 40 people (including five guards) had been seriously hurt. Macabre stories came out of prisoners being hanged, murdered with blowtorches, decapitated, tortured, and mutilated in a variety of gruesome ways by drug-crazed rioters.

The Santa Fe penitentiary was typical of most maximum-security facilities, with prisoners subject to overcrowding, filthy conditions, and routine violence. It also housed first-time, non-violent offenders, like check forgers and drug dealers, with murderers serving life sentences. In a recent lawsuit, the American Civil Liberties Union called the prison "totally unfit for human habitation." But the ACLU says New Mexico's penitentiary is far from the nation's worst.

That American prisons are a disgrace is taken for granted by experts of every ideological stripe. Conservative James Q. Wilson has criticized our "[c]rowded, antiquated prisons that require men and women to live in fear of one another and to suffer not only deprivation of liberty but a brutalizing regimen." Leftist Jessica Mitford has called our prisons "the ultimate expression of injustice and inhumanity." In 1973 a national commission concluded that "the American correctional system today appears to offer minimum protection to the public and maximum harm to the offender." Federal courts have ruled that confinement in prisons in 16 different states violates the constitutional ban on "cruel and unusual punishment."

What are the advantages of being a convicted criminal in an advanced culture? First there is the overcrowding in prisons. One Tennessee prison, for example, has a capacity of 806, according to accepted space standards, but it houses 2,300 inmates. One Louisiana facility has confined four and five prisoners in a single six-foot-by-six-foot cell. Then there is the disease caused by overcrowding, unsanitary conditions, and poor or inadequate medical care. A federal appeals court noted that the Tennessee prison had suffered frequent outbreaks of infectious diseases like hepatitis and tuberculosis. But the most distinctive element of American prison life is its constant violence. In his book *Criminal Violence, Criminal Justice*, Charles Silberman noted that in one Louisiana prison, there were 211 stabbings in only three years, 11 of them fatal. There were 15 slayings in a prison in Massachusetts between 1972 and 1975. According to a federal court, in Alabama's penitentiaries (as in many others), "robbery, rape, extortion, theft and assault are everyday occurrences."

At least in regard to cruelty, it's not at all clear that the system of punishment that has evolved in the West is less barbaric than the grotesque practices of Islam. Skeptical? Ask yourself: would you rather be subjected to a few minutes of intense pain and considerable public humiliation, or be locked away for two or three years in a prison cell crowded with ill-tempered sociopaths? Would you rather lose a hand or spend 10 years or more in a typical state prison? I have taken my own survey on this matter. I have found no one who does not find the Islamic system hideous. And I have found no one who, given the choices mentioned above, would not prefer its penalties to our own.

The great divergence between Western and Islamic fashions in punishment is relatively recent. Until roughly the end of the 18th century, criminals in Western countries rarely were sent to prison. Instead they were subjected to an ingenious assortment of penalties. Many perpetrators of a variety of crimes simply were executed, usually by some imaginative and extremely unpleasant method involving prolonged torture, such as breaking on the wheel, burning at the stake, or drawing and quartering. Michel Foucault's book *Discipline and Punish: The Birth of the Prison* notes one form of capital punishment in which the condemned man's "belly was opened up, his entrails quickly ripped out, so that he had time to see them, with his own eyes, being thrown on the fire; in which he was finally decapitated and his body quartered." Some criminals were forced to serve on slave galleys. But in most cases various corporal measures such as pillorying, flogging, and branding sufficed.

In time, however, public sentiment recoiled against these measures. They were replaced by imprisonment, which was thought to have two advantages. First, it was considered to be more humane. Second, and more important, prison was supposed to hold out the possibility of rehabilitation — purging the criminal of his criminality — something that less civilized punishments did not even aspire to. An 1854 report by inspectors of the Pennsylvania prison system illustrates the hopes nurtured by humanitarian reformers:

> Depraved tendencies, characteristic of the convict, have been restrained by the absence of vicious association, and in the mild teaching of Christianity, the unhappy criminal finds a solace for an involuntary exile from the comforts of social life. If hungry, he is fed; if naked, he is clothed; if destitute of the first rudiments of education, he is taught to read and write; and if he has never been blessed with a means of livelihood, he is schooled in a mechanical art, which in after life may be to him the source of profit and respectability. Employment is not his toil nor labor, weariness. He embraces them with alacrity, as contributing to his moral and mental elevation.

Imprisonment is now the universal method of punishing criminals in the United States. It is thought to perform five functions, each of which has been given a label by criminologists. First, there is simple *retribution:* punishing the lawbreaker to serve society's sense of justice and to satisfy the victims' desire for revenge. Second, there is *specific deterrence:* discouraging the offender from misbehaving in the future. Third, *general deterrence:* using the offender as an example to discourage others from turning to crime. Fourth, *prevention:* at least during the time he is kept off the streets, the criminal cannot victimize other members of society. Finally, and most important, there is *rehabilitation:* reforming the criminal so that when he returns to society he will be inclined to obey the laws and able to make an honest living.

How satisfactorily do American prisons perform by these criteria? Well, of course, they do punish. But on the other scores they don't do so well. Their effect in discouraging future criminality by the prisoner or others is the subject of much debate, but the soaring rates of the last 20 years suggest that prisons are not a dramatically effective deterrent to criminal behavior. Prisons do isolate convicted criminals, but only to divert crime from ordinary citizens to prison guards and fellow inmates. Almost no one contends anymore that prisons rehabilitate their inmates. If anything, they probably impede rehabilitation by forcing inmates into prolonged and almost exclusive association with other criminals. And prisons cost a lot of money. Housing a typical prisoner in a typical prison costs far more than a stint at a top university. This cost would be justified if prisons did the job they were intended for. But it is clear to all that prisons fail on the very grounds — humanity and hope of rehabilitation — that caused them to replace earlier, cheaper forms of punishment.

The universal acknowledgment that prisons do not rehabilitate criminals has produced two responses. The first is to retain the hope of rehabilitation but do away with imprisonment as much as possible and replace it with various forms of "alternative treatment," such as psychotherapy, supervised probation, and vocational training. Psychiatrist Karl Menninger, one of the principal critics of American penology, has suggested even more unconventional approaches, such as "a new job opportunity or a vacation trip, a course of reducing exercises, a cosmetic surgical operation or a herniotomy, some night school courses, a wedding in the family (even one for the patient!), an inspiring sermon." This starry-eyed approach naturally has produced a backlash from critics on the right, who think that it's time to abandon the goal of rehabilitation. They argue that prisons perform an important service just by keeping criminals off the streets, and thus should be used with that purpose alone in mind.

So the debate continues to rage in all the same old ruts. No one, of course, would think of copying the medieval practices of Islamic nations and experimenting with punishments such as flogging and amputation. But let us consider them anyway. How do they compare with our American prison system in achieving the ostensible objectives of punishment? First, do they punish? Obviously they do, and in a uniquely painful and memorable way. Of course any sensible person, given the choice, would prefer suffering these punishments to years of incarceration in a typical American prison. But presumably no Western penologist would criticize Islamic punishments on the grounds that they are not barbaric enough. Do they deter crime? Yes, and probably more effectively than sending convicts off to prison. Now we read about a prison sentence in the newspaper, then think no more about the criminal's payment for his crimes until, perhaps, years later we read a small item reporting his release. By contrast, one can easily imagine the vivid impression it would leave to be wandering through a local shopping center and to stumble onto the scene of some poor wretch being lustily flogged. And the occasional sight of an habitual offender walking around with a bloody stump at the end of his arm no doubt also would serve as a forceful reminder that crime does not pay.

Do flogging and amputation discourage recidivism? No one knows whether the scars on his back would dissuade a criminal from risking another crime, but it is hard to imagine that corporal measures could stimulate a higher rate of recidivism than already exists. Islamic forms of punishment do not serve the favorite new right goal of simply isolating criminals from the rest of society, but they may achieve the same purpose of making further crimes impossible. In the movie *Bonnie and Clyde*, Warren Beatty successfully robs a bank with his arm in a sling, but this must be dismissed as artistic license. It must be extraordinarily difficult, at the very least, to perform much violent crime with only one hand.

Do these medieval forms of punishment rehabilitate the criminal? Plainly not. But long prison terms do not rehabilitate either. And it is just as plain that typical Islamic punishments are no crueler to the convict than incarceration in the typical American state prison.

Of course there are other reasons besides its bizarre forms of punishment that the Islamic system of justice seems uncivilized to the Western mind. One is the absence of due process. Another is the long list of offenses — such as drinking, adultery, blasphemy, "profiteering," and so on — that can bring on conviction and punishment. A third is all the ritualistic mumbo-jumbo in pronouncements of Islamic law (like that talk about puberty and amnesia in the ayatollah's quotation at the beginning of this article). Even in these matters, however, a little cultural modesty is called for. The vast majority of American criminals are convicted and sentenced as a result of plea bargaining, in which due process plays almost no role. It has been only half a century since a wave of religious fundamentalism stirred this country to outlaw the consumption of alcoholic beverages. Most states also still have laws imposing austere constraints on sexual conduct. Only two weeks ago the *Washington Post* reported that the FBI had spent two and a half years and untold amounts of money to break up a nationwide pornography ring. Flogging the clients of prostitutes, as the Pakistanis did, does seem silly. But only a few months ago Mayor Koch of New York was proposing that clients caught in his own city have their names broadcast by radio stations. We are not so far advanced on such matters as we often like to think. Finally, my lawyer friends assure me that the rules of jurisdiction for American courts contain plenty of petty requirements and bizarre distinctions that would sound silly enough to foreign ears.

Perhaps it sounds barbaric to talk of flogging and amputation, and perhaps it is. But our system of punishment also is barbaric, and probably more so. Only cultural smugness about their system and willful ignorance about our own make it easy to regard the one as cruel and the other as civilized. We inflict our cruelties away from public view, while nations like Pakistan stage them in front of 10,000 onlookers. Their outrages are visible; ours are not. Most Americans can live their lives for years without having their peace of mind disturbed by the knowledge of what goes on in our prisons. To choose imprisonment over flogging and amputation is not to choose human kindness over cruelty, but merely to prefer that our cruelties be kept out of sight, and out of mind.

Public flogging and amputation may be more barbaric forms of punishment than imprisonment, even if they are not more cruel. Society may pay a higher price for them, even if the particular criminal does not. Revulsion against officially sanctioned violence and infliction of pain derives from something deeply ingrained in the Western conscience, and clearly it is something admirable. Grotesque displays of the sort that occur in Islamic countries probably breed a greater tolerance for physical cruelty, for example, which prisons do not do precisely because they conceal their cruelties. In fact it is our admirable intolerance for calculated violence that makes it necessary for us to conceal what we have not been able to do away with. In a way this is a good thing, since it holds out the hope that we may eventually find a way to do away with it. But in another way it is a bad thing, since it permits us to congratulate ourselves on our civilized humanitarianism while violating its norms in this one area of our national life.

Questions for Discussion

1. Why do you think Chapman gives such a graphic description of flogging in his first paragraph?

2. Examine Chapman's use of concession. How effectively does he deal with potential objections to his argument?

3. In his third paragraph, Chapman refers to George Jackson. Who was Jackson? Why do you think Chapman uses this specific example?

4. Most people would agree that Chapman's thesis comes at the beginning of his eighth paragraph, when he says, "At least in regard to cruelty, it's not at all clear that the system of punishment that has evolved in the West is less barbaric than the grotesque practices of Islam." Why do you think he delays presenting his thesis until this point?

5. In response to the question of whether Islamic punishments deter crime, Chapman says, "Yes, and probably more effectively than sending convicts off to prison." Do you agree? Why or why not?

6. Is Chapman advocating replacement of American penal practices with Islamic ones? On what evidence do you base your answer?

Suggested Activities

1. Have you had a brush with the law? If so, write a narrative account of it.

2. Chapman is only one of many writers concerned about the effectiveness of our prison system. Give a report to the class on one of the following books on this subject: Jessica Mitford, *Women in Cages;* Eldridge Cleaver, *Soul on Ice;* Tom Wicker, *A Time to Die.*

3. Write an essay replacing a popular view with a less popular one. Some possibilities: why hamburger is better than steak; why —— is a better spectator sport than football; why professors should grade harder.

Examsmanship
and the Liberal Arts

WILLIAM G. PERRY, Jr.

For many years director of the Bureau of Study Council at Harvard University, William G. Perry, Jr. (b. 1913) is an educational psychologist whose special field of study is late adolescent intellectual and moral development. In the witty essay reprinted here, Perry uses comparison and contrast to differentiate between two kinds of intellectual activity, "cowing" and "bulling."

"But sir, I don't think I really deserve it, it was mostly bull, really." This disclaimer from a student whose examination we have awarded a straight "A" is wondrously depressing. Alfred North Whitehead invented its only possible rejoinder: "Yes sir, what you wrote is nonsense, utter nonsense. But ah! Sir! It's the right *kind* of nonsense!"

Bull, in this university [Harvard], is customarily a source of laughter, or a problem in ethics. I shall step a little out of fashion to use the subject as a take-off point for a study in comparative epistemology. The phenomenon of bull, in all the honor and opprobrium with which it is regarded by students and faculty, says something, I think, about our theories of knowledge. So too, the grades which we assign on examinations communicate to students what these theories may be.

We do not have to be out-and-out logical-positivists to suppose that we have something to learn about "what we think knowledge is" by having a good look at "what we do when we go about measuring it." We know the straight "A"

EXAMSMANSHIP AND THE LIBERAL ARTS   Reprinted by permission of the publishers from *Examining in Harvard College: A Collection of Essays by Members of the Harvard Faculty*, Cambridge, Mass.: Harvard University Press, 1963.

examination when we see it, of course, and we have reason to hope that the student will understand why his work receives our recognition. He doesn't always. And those who receive lesser honor? Perhaps an understanding of certain anomalies in our customs of grading good bull will explain the students' confusion.

I must beg patience, then, both of the reader's humor and of his morals. Not that I ask him to suspend his sense of humor but that I shall ask him to go beyond it. In a great university the picture of a bright student attempting to outwit his professor while his professor takes pride in not being outwitted is certainly ridiculous. I shall report just such a scene, for its implications bear upon my point. Its comedy need not present a serious obstacle to thought.

As for the ethics of bull, I must ask for a suspension of judgment. I wish that students could suspend theirs. Unlike humor, moral commitment is hard to think beyond. Too early a moral judgment is precisely what stands between many able students and a liberal education. The stunning realization that the Harvard Faculty will often accept, as evidence of knowledge, the cerebrations of a student who has little data at his disposal, confronts every student with an ethical dilemma. For some it forms an academic focus for what used to be thought of as "adolescent disillusion." It is irrelevant that rumor inflates the phenomenon to mythical proportions. The students know that beneath the myth there remains a solid and haunting reality. The moral "bind" consequent on this awareness appears most poignantly in serious students who are reluctant to concede the competitive advantage to the bullster and who yet feel a deep personal shame when, having succumbed to "temptation," they themselves receive a high grade for work they consider "dishonest."

I have spent many hours with students caught in this unwelcome bitterness. These hours lend an urgency to my theme. I have found that students have been able to come to terms with the ethical problem, to the extent that it is real, only after a refined study of the true nature of bull and its relation to "knowledge." I shall submit grounds for my suspicion that we can be found guilty of sharing the students' confusion of moral and epistemological issues.

I

I present as my "premise," then, an amoral *fabliau*. Its hero-villain is the Abominable Mr. Metzger '47. Since I celebrate his virtuosity, I regret giving him a pseudonym, but the peculiar style of his bravado requires me to honor also his modesty. Bull in pure form is rare; there is usually some contamination by data. The community has reason to be grateful to Mr. Metzger for having created an instance of laboratory purity, free from any adulteration by matter. The more credit is due him, I think, because his act was free from premeditation, deliberation, or hope of personal gain.

Mr. Metzger stood one rainy November day in the lobby of Memorial Hall. A junior, concentrating in Mathematics, he was fond of diverting himself by taking part in the drama, a penchant which may have had some influence on the events of the next hour. He was waiting to take part in a rehearsal in Sanders Theatre, but, as sometimes happens, no other players appeared. Perhaps the rehearsal had been cancelled without his knowledge? He decided to wait another five minutes.

Students, meanwhile, were filing into the Great Hall opposite, and taking seats at the testing tables. Spying a friend crossing the lobby toward the Great Hall's door, Metzger greeted him and extended appropriate condolences. He inquired, too, what course his friend was being tested in. "Oh, Soc. Sci. something-or-other." "What's it all about?" asked Metzger, and this, as Homer remarked of Patroclus, was the beginning of evil for him.

"It's about Modern Perspectives on Man and Society and All That," said his friend. "Pretty interesting, really."

"Always wanted to take a course like that," said Metzger. "Any good reading?"

"Yeah, great. There's this book" — his friend did not have time to finish.

"Take your seats please," said a stern voice beside them. The idle conversation had somehow taken the two friends to one of the tables in the Great Hall. Both students automatically obeyed; the proctor put blue books before them; another proctor presented them with copies of the printed hour-test.

Mr. Metzger remembered afterwards a brief misgiving that was suddenly overwhelmed by a surge of curiosity and puckish glee. He wrote "George Smith" on the blue book, opened it, and addressed the first question.

I must pause to exonerate the Management. The Faculty has a rule that no student may attend an examination in a course in which he is not enrolled. To the wisdom of this rule the outcome of this deplorable story stands witness. The Registrar, charged with the enforcement of the rule, has developed an organization with procedures which are certainly the finest to be devised. In November, however, class rosters are still shaky, and on this particular day another student, named Smith, was absent. As for the culprit, we can reduce his guilt no further than to suppose that he was ignorant of the rule, or, in the face of the momentous challenge before him, forgetful.

We need not be distracted by Metzger's performance on the "objective" or "spot" questions on the test. His D on these sections can be explained by those versed in the theory of probability. Our interest focuses on the quality of his essay. It appears that when Metzger's friend picked up his own blue book a few days later, he found himself in company with a large proportion of his section in having received on the essay a C+. When he quietly picked up "George Smith's" blue book to return it to Metzger, he observed that the grade for the essay was A−. In the margin was a note in the section man's hand. It read "Excellent work. Could you have pinned these observations down a bit more closely? Compare . . . in . . . pp. . . ."

Such news could hardly be kept quiet. There was a leak, and the whole scandal broke on the front page of Tuesday's *Crimson*. With the press Metzger was modest, as becomes a hero. He said that there had been nothing to it at all, really. The essay question had offered a choice of two books, Margaret Mead's *And Keep Your Powder Dry* or Geoffrey Gorer's *The American People*. Metzger reported that having read neither of them, he had chosen the second "because the title gave me some notion as to what the book might be about." On the test, two critical comments were offered on each book, one favorable, one unfavorable. The students were asked to "discuss." Metzger conceded that he had played safe in throwing his lot with the more laudatory of the two comments, "but I did not forget to be balanced."

I do not have Mr. Metzger's essay before me except in vivid memory. As I recall, he took his first cue from the name Geoffrey, and committed his strategy to the premise that Gorer was born into an "Anglo Saxon" culture, probably English, but certainly "English speaking." Having heard that Margaret Mead was a social anthropologist, he inferred that Gorer was the same. He then entered upon his essay, centering his inquiry upon what he supposed might be the problems inherent in an anthropologist's observation of a culture which was his own, or nearly his own. Drawing in part from memories of table-talk on cultural relativity[1] and in part from creative logic, he rang changes on the relation of observer to observed, and assessed the kind and degree of objectivity which might accrue to an observer through training as an anthropologist. He concluded that the book in question did in fact contribute a considerable range of "'objective', and even 'fresh'," insights into the nature of our culture. "At the same time," he warned, "these observations must be understood within the context of their generation by a person only partly freed from his embeddedness in the culture he is observing, and limited in his capacity to transcend those particular tendencies and biases which he has himself developed as a personality in his interaction with this culture since his birth. In this sense the book portrays as much the character of Geoffrey Gorer as it analyzes that of the American people." It is my regrettable duty to report that at this moment of triumph Mr. Metzger was carried away by the temptations of parody and added, "We are thus much the richer."

In any case, this was the essay for which Metzger received his honor grade and his public acclaim. He was now, of course, in serious trouble with the authorities.

I shall leave him for the moment to the mercy of the Administrative Board of Harvard College and turn the reader's attention to the section man who ascribed the grade. He was in much worse trouble. All the consternation in his immediate area of the Faculty and all the glee in other areas fell upon his unprotected head. I shall now undertake his defense.

I do so not simply because I was acquainted with him and feel a respect for his intelligence; I believe in the justice of his grade! Well, perhaps "justice" is the wrong word in a situation so manifestly absurd. This is more a case in "equity." That is, the grade is equitable if we accept other aspects of the situation which are equally absurd. My proposition is this: if we accept as valid those C grades which were accorded students who, like Metzger's friend, demonstrated a thorough familiarity with the details of the book without relating their critique to

[1]"An important part of Harvard's education takes place during meals in the Houses." An Official Publication.

the methodological problems of social anthropology, then "George Smith" deserved not only the same, but better.

The reader may protest that the C's given to students who showed evidence only of diligence were indeed not valid and that both these students and "George Smith" should have received E's. To give the diligent E is of course not in accord with custom. I shall take up this matter later. For now, were I to allow the protest, I could only restate my thesis: that "George Smith's" E would, in a college of liberal arts, be properly a "better" E.

At this point I need a short-hand. It is a curious fact that there is no academic slang for the presentation of evidence of diligence alone. "Parroting" won't do; it is possible to "parrot" bull. I must beg the reader's pardon, and, for reasons almost too obvious to bear, suggest "cow."

Stated as nouns, the concepts look simple enough:

> cow (pure): data, however relevant, without relevancies.

> bull (pure): relevancies, however relevant, without data.

The reader can see all too clearly where this simplicity would lead. I can assure him that I would not have imposed on him this way were I aiming to say that knowledge in this university is definable as some neuter compromise between cow and bull, some infertile hermaphrodite. This is precisely what many diligent students seem to believe: that what they must learn to do is to "find the right mean" between "amounts" of detail and "amounts" of generalities. Of course this is not the point at all. The problem is not quantitative, nor does its solution lie on a continuum between the particular and the general. Cow and bull are not poles of a single dimension. A clear notion of what they really are is essential to my inquiry, and for heuristic purposes I wish to observe them further in the celibate state.

When the pure concepts are translated into verbs, their complexities become apparent in the assumptions and purposes of the students as they write:

To cow *(v. intrans.)* or the act of cowing:

> To list data (or perform operations) without awareness of, or comment upon, the contexts, frames of reference, or points of observation which determine the origin, nature, and meaning of the data (or procedures). To write on the assumption that "a fact is a fact." To present evidence of hard work as a substitute for understanding, without any intent to deceive.

To bull *(v. intrans.)* or the act of bulling:

> To discourse upon the contexts, frames of reference and points of observation which would determine the origin, nature, and meaning of data if one had any. To present evidence of an understanding of

form in the hope that the reader may be deceived into supposing a familiarity with content.

At the level of conscious intent, it is evident that cowing is more moral, or less immoral, than bulling. To speculate about unconscious intent would be either an injustice or a needless elaboration of my theme. It is enough that the impression left by cow is one of earnestness, diligence, and painful naiveté. The grader may feel disappointment or even irritation, but these feelings are usually balanced by pity, compassion, and a reluctance to hit a man when he's both down and moral. He may feel some challenge to his teaching, but none whatever to his one-ups-manship. He writes in the margin: "See me."

We are now in a position to understand the anomaly of custom: As instructors, we always assign bull an E, *when we detect it;* whereas we usually give cow a C, *even though it is always obvious.*

After all, we did not ask to be confronted with a choice between morals and understanding (or did we?). We evince a charming humanity, I think, in our decision to grade in favor of morals and pathos. "I simply *can't* give this student an E after he has *worked* so hard." At the same time we tacitly express our respect for the bullster's strength. We recognize a colleague. If he knows so well how to dish it out, we can be sure that he can also take it.

Of course it is just possible that we carry with us, perhaps from our own school-days, an assumption that if a student is willing to work hard and collect "good hard facts" he can always be taught to understand their relevance, whereas a student who has caught on to the forms of relevance without working at all is a lost scholar.

But this is not in accord with our experience.

It is not in accord either, as far as I can see, with the stated values of a liberal education. If a liberal education should teach students "how to think," not only in their own fields but in fields outside their own — that is, to understand "how the other fellow orders knowledge," then bulling, even in its purest form, expresses an important part of what a pluralist university holds dear, surely a more important part than the collecting of "facts that are facts" which schoolboys learn to do. Here then, good bull appears not as ignorance at all but as an aspect of knowledge. It is both relevant and "true." In a university setting good bull is therefore of more value than "facts," which, without a frame of reference, are not even "true" at all.

Perhaps this value accounts for the final anomaly: as instructors, we are inclined to reward bull highly, *where we do not detect its intent*, to the consternation of the bullster's acquaintances. And often we do not examine the matter too closely. After a long evening of reading blue books full of cow, the sudden meeting with a student who at least understands the problems of one's field provides a lift like a draught of refreshing wine, and a strong disposition toward trust.

This was, then, the sense of confidence that came to our unfortunate section man as he read "George Smith's" sympathetic considerations.

II

In my own years of watching over students' shoulders as they work, I have come to believe that this feeling of trust has a firmer basis than the confidence generated by evidence of diligence alone. I believe that the theory of a liberal education holds. Students who have dared to understand man's real relation to his knowledge have shown themselves to be in a strong position to learn content rapidly and meaningfully, and to retain it. I have learned to be less concerned about the education of a student who has come to understand the nature of man's knowledge, even though he has not yet committed himself to hard work, than I am about the education of the student who, after one or two terms at Harvard, is working desperately hard and still believes that collected "facts" constitute knowledge. The latter, when I try to explain to him, too often understands me to be saying that he "doesn't *put in enough generalities.*" Surely he has "put in *enough* facts."

I have come to see such quantitative statements as expressions of an entire, coherent epistemology. In grammar school the student is taught that Columbus discovered America in 1492. The *more* such items he gets "right" on a given test, the more he is credited with "knowing." From years of this sort of thing it is not unnatural to develop the conviction that knowledge consists of the accretion of hard facts by hard work.

The student learns that the more facts and procedures he can get "right" in a given course, the better will be his grade. The more courses he takes, the more subjects he has "had," the more credits he accumulates, the more diplomas he will get, until, after graduate school, he will emerge with his doctorate, a member of the community of scholars.

The foundation of this entire life is the proposition that a fact is a fact. The necessary correlate of this proposition is that a fact is either right or wrong. This implies that the standard against which the rightness or wrongness of a fact may be judged exists *someplace* — perhaps graven upon a tablet in a Platonic world outside and above *this* cave of tears. In grammar school it is evident that the tablets which enshrine the spelling of a word or the answer to an arithmetic problem are visible to my teacher who need only compare my offerings to it. In high school I observe that my English teachers disagree. This can only mean that the tablets in such matters as the goodness of a poem are distant and obscured by clouds. They surely exist. The pleasing of befuddled English teachers degenerates into assessing their prejudices, a game in which I have no protection against my competitors more glib of tongue. I respect only my science teachers, authorities who *really know.* Later I learn from them "This is only what we think *now.*" But eventually, surely. . . . Into this epistemology of education, apparently shared by teachers, in such terms as "credits," "semester hours" and "years of French" the student may invest his ideals, his drive, his competitiveness, his safety, his self-esteem, and even his love.

College raises other questions: by whose calendar is it proper to say that Columbus discovered America in 1492? How, when and by whom was the year

1 established in this calendar? What of other calendars? In view of the evidence for Leif Ericson's previous visit (and the American Indians), what historical ethnocentrism is suggested by the use of the word "discover" in this sentence? As for Leif Ericson, in accord with what assumptions do *you* order the evidence?

These questions and their answers are not "more" knowledge. They are devastation. I do not need to elaborate upon the epistemology, or rather epistemologies, they imply. A fact has become at last "an observation or an operation performed in a frame of reference." A liberal education is founded in an awareness of frame of reference even in the most immediate and empirical examination of data. Its acquirement involves relinquishing hope of absolutes and of the protection they afford against doubt and the glib-tongued competitor. It demands an ever widening sophistication about systems of thought and observation. It leads, not away from, but *through* the arts of gamesmanship to a new trust.

This trust is in the value and integrity of systems, their varied character, and the way their apparently incompatible metaphors enlighten, from complementary facets, the particulars of human experience. As one student said to me: "I used to be cynical about intellectual games. Now I want to know them thoroughly. You see I came to realize that it was only when I knew the rules of the game cold that I could tell whether what I was saying was tripe."

We too often think of the bullster as cynical. He can be, and not always in a light-hearted way. We have failed to observe that there can lie behind cow the potential of a deeper and more dangerous despair. The moralism of sheer work and obedience can be an ethic that, unwilling to face a despair of its ends, glorifies its means. The implicit refusal to consider the relativity of both ends and means leaves the operator in an unconsidered proprietary absolutism. History bears witness that in the pinches this moral superiority has no recourse to negotiation, only to force.

A liberal education proposes that man's hope lies elsewhere: in the negotiability that can arise from an understanding of the integrity of systems and of their origins in man's address to his universe. The prerequisite is the courage to accept such a definition of knowledge. From then on, of course, there is nothing incompatible between such an epistemology and hard work. Rather the contrary.

I can now at last let bull and cow get together. The reader knows best how a productive wedding is arranged in his own field. This is the nuptial he celebrates with a straight A on examinations. The masculine context must embrace the feminine particular, though itself "born of woman." Such a union is knowledge itself, and it alone can generate new contexts and new data which can unite in their turn to form new knowledge.

In this happy setting we can congratulate in particular the Natural Sciences, long thought to be barren ground to the bullster. I have indeed drawn my examples of bull from the Social Sciences, and by analogy from the Humanities. Essay-writing in these fields has long been thought to nurture the art of bull to its prime. I feel, however, that the Natural Sciences have no reason to feel slighted. It is perhaps no accident that Metzger was a mathematician. As part of my researches for this paper, furthermore, a student of considerable talent has recently honored me with an impressive analysis of the art of amassing "partial credits" on examinations in advanced physics. Though beyond me in some respects, his presentation confirmed my impression that instructors of Physics frequently honor on examinations operations structurally similar to those requisite in a good essay.

The very qualities that make the Natural Sciences fields of delight for the eager gamesman have been essential to their marvelous fertility.

III

As priests of these mysteries, how can we make our rites more precisely expressive? The student who merely cows robs himself, without knowing it, of his education and his soul. The student who only bulls robs himself, as he knows full well, of the joys of inductive discovery — that is, of engagement. The introduction of frames of reference in the new curricula of Mathematics and Physics in the schools is a hopeful experiment. We do not know yet how much of these potent revelations the very young can stand, but I suspect they may rejoice in them more than we have supposed. I can't believe they have never wondered about Leif Ericson and that word "discovered," or even about 1492. They have simply been too wise to inquire.

Increasingly in recent years better students in the better high schools and preparatory schools *are* being allowed to inquire. In fact they appear to be receiving both encouragement and training in their inquiry. I have the evidence before me.

Each year for the past five years all freshmen entering Harvard and Radcliffe have been asked in freshman week to "grade" two essays answering an examination question in History. They are then asked to give their reasons for their grades. One essay, filled with dates, is 99% cow. The other, with hardly a date in it, is a good essay, easily mistaken for bull. The "official" grades of these essays are, for the first (alas!) C+ "because he has worked so hard," and for the second (soundly, I think) B+. Each year a larger majority of freshmen evaluate these essays as would the majority of the faculty, and for the faculty's reasons, and each year a smaller minority give the higher honor to the essay offering data alone. Most interesting, a larger number of students each year, while not over-rating the second essay, award the first the straight E appropriate to it in a college of liberal arts.

For us who must grade such students in a university, these developments imply a new urgency, did we not feel it already. Through our grades we describe for the students, in the showdown, what we believe about the nature of knowledge. The subtleties of bull are not peripheral to our academic concerns. That they penetrate to the center of our care is evident in our feelings when a student whose good work we have awarded a high grade reveals to us that he does not feel he deserves it. Whether he disqualifies himself because "there's too much bull in it," or worse because "I really don't think I've worked that hard," he presents a serious educational problem. Many students feel this sleasiness; only a few reveal it to us.

We can hardly allow a mistaken sense of fraudulence to undermine our students' achievements. We must lead students beyond their concept of bull so that they may honor relevancies that are really relevant. We can willingly acknowledge that, in lieu of the date 1492, a consideration of calendars and of the word "discovered," may well be offered with intent to deceive. We must insist that this does not make such considerations intrinsically immoral, and that, contrariwise, the date 1492 may be no substitute for them. Most of all, we must convey the impression that we grade understanding qua understanding. To be convincing, I suppose we must concede to ourselves in advance that a bright student's understanding is understanding even if he achieved it by osmosis rather than by hard work in our course.

These are delicate matters. As for cow, its complexities are not what need concern us. Unlike good bull, it does not represent partial knowledge at all. It belongs to a different theory of knowledge entirely. In our theories of knowledge it represents total ignorance, or worse yet, a knowledge downright inimical to understanding. I even go so far as to propose that we award no more C's for cow. To do so is rarely, I feel, the act of mercy it seems. Mercy lies in clarity.

IV

The reader may be afflicted by a lingering curiosity about the fate of Mr. Metzger. I hasten to reassure him. The Administrative Board of Harvard College, whatever its satanic reputation, is a benign body. Its members, to be sure, were on the spot. They delighted in Metzger's exploit, but they were responsible to the Faculty's rule. The hero stood in danger of probation. The debate was painful. Suddenly one member, of a refined legalistic sensibility, observed that the rule applied specifically to "examinations" and that the occasion had been simply an hour-test. Mr. Metzger was merely "admonished."

Questions for Discussion

1. In his fifth paragraph, Perry says, "Too early a moral judgment is precisely what stands between many able students and a liberal education." Do you agree with this assertion? With what arguments does Perry support it in the body of his essay?

2. When Perry talks about the mating of "cow" and "bull," he is using an *extended metaphor*. What other extended metaphors does he use? How effective is his use of them?

3. Discuss the construction of the following sentence: "As for the culprit, we can reduce his guilt no further than to suppose that he was ignorant of the rule, or, in the face of the momentous challenge before him, forgetful." What other examples of unusually constructed sentences can you find in this essay? What is their effect on you as a reader?

4. Although Perry calls Mr. Metzger a "culprit" in the sentence quoted in question 3 above, elsewhere he repeatedly refers to him as a hero. Why? Would he be a hero to you? Why or why not?

5. Perry says that "cow" contains "the potential of a deeper and more dangerous despair"

than does "bull." What is this deeper despair? How does Perry's belief in its existence help to explain his preference for "bull"?

6. What is your overall assessment of the style of this essay? Do you think the essay is overwritten? Why or why not?

Suggested Activities

1. In speaking to other teachers, Perry says, "Through our grades we describe for the students . . . what we believe about the nature of knowledge." Assuming this statement to be true, what have your teachers' grades revealed them to believe about the nature of knowledge? Compare your answer to this question with those of other members of your class.

2. Write an extended definition of a college slang term.

3. Perry says, "it is evident that cowing is more moral, or less immoral, than bulling." Write an essay either supporting or opposing this assertion.

process analysis

If you've ever built a model airplane or sewn from a pattern, then you're already familiar with one kind of process analysis: *step-by-step instruction.* The distinguishing feature of this type of writing is its practical intent. Its aim is to teach someone how to do something, and its effectiveness can be simply tested: if by following the steps exactly a reader can arrive at the intended outcome, then the instructions are good ones.

This sort of "how to" process analysis has a number of uses. Any time you leave a note telling a friend how to find your apartment, or write down a recipe, or write a lab report recounting the steps you followed in performing an experiment, you're using the technique. So learning how to write clear and accurate instructions can be a valuable undertaking. In your college career, though, you'll more often find yourself writing a second sort of process analysis. This type, which we'll call *explanatory analysis,* does not instruct (at least not directly). Instead, it explains a process that neither the author nor the readers expect the readers to engage in. In "The Moose on the Wall," for example, Edward Hoagland uses explanatory analysis to demonstrate how a taxidermist reconstructs the head of an animal out of wax, wood, and putty. His intention clearly is not to enable us to repeat the procedure, as it would be in step-by-step instruction, but to have us *understand* it and *appreciate* its intricacies.

Explanatory analysis also differs from step-by-step instruction in the frequency with which it has a persuasive purpose. In step-by-step instruction, the writer need not convince us that the steps are worth following. Presumably, we already think they are, or we wouldn't be reading the instructions. But in explanatory analysis, the writer's attempt to bring us to an understanding and appreciation of a process often has the further aim of helping us form an opinion of it. In "The Moose on the Wall," for instance, Hoagland is not content merely to have us understand how animal heads are mounted; he also wishes us to confront the larger question of the worth of the process. Is taxidermy a craft we should admire? Or has it come to be outmoded in recent years by our heightened environmental awareness? In much the same way, John McPhee's "Oranges" raises questions about our food processing practices, and Joan Didion's "Bureaucrats" asks us to decide on the worth of a particularly striking form of governmental involvement in people's daily lives.

Whether your purpose when you write a process analysis is to teach someone a skill, to explain a process, or to persuade your readers to hold a particular point of view, there are three suggestions that you should bear in mind.

1. Determine the characteristics of your audience before you begin to write. No other rhetorical mode demands as completely as process analysis that you know the characteristics of your audience in advance. This is especially true if you're writing step-by-step instructions. If you assume your reader is a skilled craftsman but it turns out he doesn't know the difference between a crescent wrench and a pipe wrench, then you're in trouble. Conversely, instructions that would serve quite well to guide beginners through their first engine tune-up would bore and frustrate a trained mechanic. So it is important to keep the characteristics of your audience clearly in mind at all times.

Well and good, but how do you adapt your writing to this awareness of audience? In part, the level of difficulty of the process you're describing can serve as a guide. If you're giving instructions for a simple process, like cooking an omelet, it's fairly safe to assume that your audience will be people who have little or no knowledge of even basic skills in the area. If, however, you're describing a complex task, like making a Baked Alaska, you can assume that your audience has command of the basic skills involved and only needs instruction in the specific task itself.

If you're writing an explanatory analysis, it's usually best to imagine a reader very much like yourself or your classmates—someone who has a general interest in the process you're describing but who does not have specialized knowledge of it. Once you've imagined this sort of reader, it's a good idea to examine the terms pertinent to your topic and decide which of them you'll need to define in a word or two as they come up. Look, for example, at how Alexander Petrunkevitch keeps his audience in mind in the following passage from "The Spider and the Wasp":

> The trichobothria, very fine hairs growing from disklike membranes on the legs, were once thought to be the spider's hearing organs, but we now know that they have nothing to do with sound. They are sensitive only to air

movement. A light breeze makes them vibrate slowly without disturbing the common hair. When one blows gently on the trichobothria, the tarantula reacts with a quick jerk of its four front legs.

Because Petrunkevitch wrote his essay for publication in *Scientific American,* rather than in a scholarly journal on entomology, he could assume that he would have an audience of nonspecialists. He therefore briefly defines "trichobothria" when it first appears. Once he has done so, he feels free to use the term again without further comment. He is thus doubly respectful of his readers.

2. Follow chronological order.   This suggestion applies to both step-by-step instruction and explanatory analysis. If, for example, you're showing someone how to prepare for a camping trip, you should let them know what they need to do in the order in which they need to do it. It can be very frustrating to be told at the end of a set of instructions that something—making a reservation, say— needed to be done at the beginning of the sequence.

In the case of explanatory analysis, following chronological order doesn't have this sort of practical urgency, but it is nonetheless important. Here, just as in step-by-step instruction, we're dealing with how something happens in time, and our readers will soon become disoriented if our account jumps capriciously from place to place. If we're explaining a complex process, though, we may find that more than one sequence of events is taking place simultaneously. Even though we may not be able to maintain overall chronological order in such a situation, we can—and should—maintain it *within* each sequence. Look, for example, at how Berton Roueché handles this problem in his discussion of the variety of factors that affect the speed with which alcohol is absorbed into the bloodstream. He first gives us an overview of the absorptive process with none of these factors present. Then as he takes up each mitigating factor in turn— speed of consumption, ingestion of food and water, ingestion of carbon dioxide—he moves back to the beginning point of the process and retraces it in strict chronological sequence.

3. Vary your pace.   In our comments on narration in the introduction to Chapter 3, we warned against using an "and then . . . and then . . ." narrative pattern. The same warning applies even more strongly to process analysis. Since in process analysis you don't have much freedom to use flashbacks, you must be especially alert to opportunities to vary your pace in other ways. As with narration, you should look for situations where you can either shift from detailed analysis to summary or interrupt your chronological report with paragraphs of reflection and interpretation. A good aid here is to divide the process you're describing into its main segments before you begin writing about it. Doing this will allow you to determine where the logical stopping points are and will help you to see whether some parts of the sequence can be either summarized or omitted.

One last observation: To hold your reader's attention, you need to not only vary your pace but also to depict each step of the process as vividly as possible. Here a judicious use of metaphor and simile can be of great assistance. When you read McPhee's "Oranges," for example, look for a hard-breathing McIntosh apple. When you find it, ask yourself how much it has done to make a potentially mundane topic vivid and memorable.

The Neutral Spirit:
A Portrait of Alcohol

BERTON ROUECHÉ

Berton Roueché (b. 1911) began his distinguished career in journalism as a reporter for the *Kansas City Star* in 1934. For many
years a staff writer for *The New Yorker*, Roueché has been the
recipient of the annual award from the American Medical Writers Association, the Lasker Journalism award for medical
reporting, and the Journalism award of the American Medical
Association. His popular books on medicine include *Eleven
Blue Men, and Other Narratives of Medical Detection* (1953);
The Neutral Spirit: A Portrait of Alcohol (1960); and *Curiosities
of Medicine: An Assembly of Medical Diversions,1552-1962*
(1963). In the following chapter from *The Neutral Spirit*,
Roueché uses graphic examples to explain how alcohol is
absorbed by the human body.

Much of the misbelief with which emotion has fantasied alcohol derives from a
cloudy conception of its general metabolism. No aspect of its nature, however, is
more nearly transparent, and none has been so well established for so many years.
A rough but accurate description of the way the body disposes of alcohol has been
on conspicuous record since the second quarter of the nineteenth century.

It was inscribed there in 1842 by the prodigious German chemist Justus von
Liebig (whose other triumphs include the discovery of chloroform, the detection
of the importance of protein substances, and, with Friedrich Wöhler, the creation

of modern physiological chemistry). Prior to that time, as the American ency-
clopedist Ernest Hurst Cherrington has noted, it was universally assumed that
"alcohol leaves the body unchanged through the lungs, skin, and kidneys, that
within the organism it is neither transformed nor destroyed, [and] that it is
ejected from the body in its original form and condition." Von Liebig demolished
this traditional supposition with a series of definitive experiments, which he
crisply summarized in *Die Tierchemie oder Organische Chemie in Ihrer Anwen-
dung auf Physiologie und Pathologie*, the most monumental of his many monumental works. "According to all observations made," he reported, "there is no
trace of alcohol in the breath, in the sweat, or in the urine after the consumption
of alcoholic liquors." He then, just as crisply, proclaimed the truth of the matter.
The process involved, he wrote, was the familiar physiological phenomenon
known as oxidation. "There can be no doubt that alcohol's constituent elements
have become fused with oxygen in the body, that its carbon and hydrogen leave
the body as carbonic acid [carbon dioxide and water]." This being the case, he
added, it was possible, if not desirable, to consider alcohol a food, for oxidation is
invariably accompanied by the release of heat and energy. Subsequent investigators have found it necessary to correct von Liebig's elucidation in only one detail.
It is not quite true that alcohol undergoes a total combustion in the body. A variable fraction (from two to possibly ten per cent) escapes through the lungs, the
kidneys, and the skin as unaltered alcohol.

The susceptibility of ethyl (or beverage) alcohol to oxidation is probably its
most distinctive trait. For one thing, it makes ethyl alcohol, alone among the
many alcohols, a generally acceptable beverage. Contrary to common conviction,
ethyl alcohol is not inherently the least toxic of alcohols. It is merely the least
intractably toxic. The other alcohols, being all but incombustible, can, at best, be
broken down and expelled from the body only after long and racking physiological exertion. They thus tend inevitably to accumulate in the blood stream, and
when ingested in more than small amounts, they swiftly reach an unwieldy concentration. "A man who drinks, say, a pint of whisky in one day has no ethyl
alcohol left in his body the next day," the late Howard W. Haggard, director of
the Laboratory of Applied Physiology at Yale, noted, "but a man who drinks this
amount of methyl [or wood] alcohol does not get rid of it completely for perhaps
a week. He not only has a long period of intoxication, but if he drinks [again]
within the week, he [places himself] in great danger." The danger includes blind-
ness, for one of the oxidation products of methyl alcohol is formic acid (the protective venom of ants), which has the power to destroy the optic nerve. Ethyl
alcohol's ready oxidation also distinguishes it from the majority of other foods,
including all fats and proteins and most carbohydrates. Their molecular structure
is too complex for immediate combustibility. They must first be radically remod-
eled by prolonged (from one to several hours) immersion in the various digestive
acids and enzyme catalysts that are secreted for that purpose in the mouth, the
stomach, and the small intestine. Only then can their essential elements be assimilated into the body. Alcohol needs no such preparation. It is as naturally assim-
ilable as water.

Most foods are absorbed into the body from the small intestine. So, it seems probable, are the many essential salts and minerals. Even water, though almost incomparably diffusible, is confined to a single entrance. It can be assimilated solely through the walls of the large intestine. Alcohol is more versatile. Although the small intestine constitutes its principal port of entry, it can also be absorbed directly from the stomach, through the rectum (by enema), and, most remarkably, through the lungs (by inhalation). The fact that alcohol can be absorbed from the stomach is sometimes assumed to explain its galvanic initial impact. This assumption, though superficially plausible, is just the reverse of the truth. The amount of alcohol that is assimilated into the body through the walls of the stomach is relatively small, being hardly twenty per cent of the total quantity ingested. Moreover, its passage, while metronomically regular, is lethargically slow, and the principles of diffusion that control the process are largely impervious to interference.

This ability of the stomach to circumspectly admit alcohol directly into the body would thus appear to be a defensive mechanism. It has, at any rate, the effect of protecting the body from a paralyzing inundation. A further safeguard is the valvular link between the stomach and the small intestine known as the pyloric sphincter. The pyloric sphincter has as its primary purpose the retention of food in the stomach until the digestive action that takes place there is complete, but it also tends to trip and close at the repeated touch of any irritating substance. Alcohol can create such a spasm. The maximum movement of alcohol through the pylorus occurs with the first drink. With the second, the rate abruptly decreases. If that is soon followed by a third, the controlling mechanism comes fully into play, and the flow into the small intestine is practically halted; the alcohol thus trapped in the stomach is eventually released at a rate determined by a complexity of forces. Unlike the stomach, the small intestine is incapable of exercising any control over the absorption of alcohol. Absorption there is rapid, constant, and complete. It continues without remission until all alcohol has been eliminated from the gastrointestinal tract.

Among the various factors that variously influence the rate of alcohol absorption by the stomach and the small intestine, the speed with which it is drunk is of crucial importance. Although the absorption of alcohol directly from the stomach is almost flawlessly controlled, the effect on the body of a quick succession of highly alcoholic drinks (whiskey, gin, rum, brandy) is often swift and shattering. It can, as barroom athletes are occasionally inspired to demonstrate, be fatal. One conclusive demonstration occurred in Chicago in 1954. A commuter informed a group of friends in a tavern there that he could drink seventeen dry Martinis in something less than one hour. He did, but as he emptied the final glass, he toppled off his stool. He was dead when he hit the floor. (That he chose to prove his strength with dry Martinis is, of course, irrelevant. Despite the almost mystical awe in which the Martini is commonly held, it is not an intoxicating drink of unique powers. Alcohol, and alcohol alone, is what produces intoxication. The other elements that are present in, or added to, alcoholic drinks contribute only flavor, aroma, and color. A Martini is no more, and no less, intoxicating than any other drink that contains the same amount of alcohol. If the number and variety of spirits in a drink increased its power to intoxicate, the most potent drink in the bartender's manual would be, perhaps, a pousse-café. The supposed brute virility of the Martini lies not in the glass but in the conditioned mind of the drinker.) More recently, on Christmas Day, 1958, a seven-year-old New Jersey boy slipped back to the dining room after a family dinner, emptied a bottle containing about ten ounces of wine, went into convulsions, and died within an hour.

The chief deterrent to the prompt absorption of alcohol is food. Eating while drinking perceptibly slows absorption, and the effect of even several drinks can be substantially retarded if they are soon followed by a meal. (In a recent monograph, *The Neurology of Alcoholism*, J. M. Nielsen, clinical professor of neurology at the University of California at Los Angeles, describes a drinking bout he witnessed in a neighboring bar between two alcoholics. "The wager stated that he who first became unable to stand would pay the bill," he reports. "One of the contestants ordered the bartender to put a raw egg into each drink; the other protested, but in vain, and took his 'straight.' The man who took the eggs won and was able to walk home, while the other became helpless.") In general, the larger the meal, the more slowly absorption proceeds. Quantity is not, however, the only factor involved. Some foods are much more effective than others in hobbling both alcohol's absorption from the stomach and its passage through the pylorus. Milk is perhaps the most widely celebrated member of this group, but its inhibitory powers are equaled by butter, cheese, meat, eggs — in fact, by all foods rich in protein. For protein, being the most chemically complicated of foods, lingers longest in the stomach, and alcohol caught in its deliberate embrace is held there until the completion of the digestive process.

Water is also capable of perceptibly delaying alcohol absorption. When taken with or just after a drink, it notably blunts its thrust. As a rule — though one to which there are striking exceptions — it is the concentration of alcohol in a drink that determines the rate of absorption. An ounce or two of whiskey well diluted with water, as in a conventional highball, is absorbed less rapidly than the same amount poured over ice. This would seem to suggest (and did for many years to many investigators) that alcohol is absorbed most quickly in its least diluted form. But such, paradoxically, is not the case. Absorption is most rapid when the alcohol is diluted to a concentration of between ten and thirty-five per cent. "Concentrations of alcohol of fifty per cent (a hundred proof) or greater exert a depressant effect on absorption," Harold E. Himwich, director of research at the Galesburg State Research Hospital, in Illinois, has recently noted. "[They produce] a sort of local narcosis. In addition, high concentrations are irritating to the mucosa and evoke the secretion of mucus, which also delays absorption."

Another factor that has a bearing on absorption is the nature of the dilutent. Milk (as in eggnog), tomato juice (as in the Bloody Mary cocktail), melted butter (as in hot buttered rum), and other liquids rich in food substances are firmer curbs than water. Soda water, on the other hand, quickens the absorption rate, because carbon dioxide, which forms the effervescent essence of all animated beverages, sweeps imperiously through the stomach, and alcohol caught up in its rush is flung directly into the small intestine. It is this vivacious element that gives champagne and sparkling Burgundy the headiness that distinguishes them from sedentary wines.

Questions for Discussion

1. Does Roueché simply report on his subject in as objective a manner as possible, or does he convey an attitude toward it? On what specific details in the selection do you base your answer?

2. What common beliefs about alcohol does Roueché attempt to disprove? Did you hold any of these beliefs before reading his essay? Do you still?

3. If you had a younger brother or sister just beginning to experiment with alcohol, what information from this essay would you want to pass along to him or her? Why?

4. Examine Roueché's illustrations and examples. How effective do you find his use of them to be?

5. As our headnote indicates, *The Neutral Spirit* is the title of the book from which the selection reprinted here is taken. What irony is there in naming a book on alcohol *The Neutral Spirit?* How does the selection you have just read manifest this irony?

6. At one point Roueché uses the phrase "barroom athletes." Is this metaphor an apt one? On the basis of your own observations, what role does competition play in drinking?

Suggested Activities

1. Together with your friends, draw up a list of common beliefs about alcohol not mentioned by Roueché. Which of these beliefs do you suspect may be false? Why?

2. There are a number of common mistaken beliefs about the following subjects: dieting, birth control, sleep, physical fitness. Choose one of these subjects and write a brief essay dispelling one or more of the misunderstandings associated with it.

3. Write a narrative essay recounting your most memorable experience with alcohol. Note that the experience need not involve drinking on your part.

Oranges

JOHN McPHEE

For biographical information on John McPhee, see page 55. The following selection from his book *Oranges* (1967) explains how citrus packing houses alter the color of oranges to satisfy the buying public. Especially noteworthy is the way McPhee uses concrete examples to vivify the technical aspects of the process.

One day, I went into an Indian River [Florida] packinghouse to watch [oranges] being readied for market. Citrus packinghouses are much the same wherever they are. In a sense, they are more like beauty parlors than processing plants. To make their oranges marketably orange, packers can do two things, one of which is, loosely speaking, natural and the other wholly artificial. The first is a process that was once known as "gassing," but the unpleasant connotations of that word have caused it to be generally suppressed, and most people now say "de-greening" instead. Green or partly green oranges are put into chambers where, for as much as four days, ethylene gas is circulated among them. The gas helps eliminate the chlorophyll in the flavedo, or outer skin, which is, in a sense, tiled with cells that contain both orange and green pigments. The orange ones are carotenoids, the green ones are chlorophylls, and the chlorophylls are so much more intense that, while they are there, the orange color will not show through. Both of these pigments are floating around in a clear, colorless enzyme called chlorophyllase, which will destroy chlorophyll on contact but has no effect on anything else. The chlorophyll is protected from the enzyme by a thin membrane called a tonoplast. In chilly weather, the tonoplast loses its strength and breaks down, and the enzyme gets at the chlorophyll and destroys it. The orange becomes orange. It would seem to be simple enough to pick a green orange and put it in a refrigerator until it turns orange, but, unfortunately, the membrane that protects the chlorophyll from the enzyme will no longer react in the same way once an orange is picked. In the early years of this century, Californians noticed that oranges tended to become more orange in rooms where kerosene stoves were burning. Assuming that the heat was responsible, orange men on both coasts erected vast wooden ovens called "sweat rooms," installed banks of kerosene stoves, and turned out vividly colored petroleum-smoked oranges. The more enthusiastic they got, the more stoves they put in. The emerging oranges were half dehydrated. And, with alarming frequency, whole packinghouses would burst into flame. That era closed when it was discovered that the ethylene gas produced in the combustion of the kerosene was the actual agent that was affecting the color of the oranges. Ethylene appears to anesthetize, or at least to relax, the membrane that protects the chlorophyll. All fruits take in oxygen and give off carbon dioxide through their skins, and some fruits, interestingly enough, give off ethylene gas as well when they breathe. A pile of green oranges will turn color if stored in a room with enough bananas. One McIntosh apple, puffing hard, can turn out enough ethylene to de-green a dozen oranges in a day or two.

Oranges are gassed in both California and Florida, often merely to improve an already good color. A once-orange orange which has turned green again on the tree will not react to it. Neither will an orange that is not ripe.

The second method of affecting the color of oranges is more direct: they can be bathed, at times, in a dye whose chemical name is 1-(2, 5-dimethoxyphenylazo)-2 napthol, popularly known as Citrus Red No. 2. This is the only dye permitted by federal law. The use of it is against California law, and the law of Florida, as a kind of safeguard against criticism, requires that dyed oranges be labeled as such and that they contain ten per cent more juice than the established minimum for undyed oranges. In practice, this regulation affects only the Ridge, because Indian River packinghouses are, almost without exception, too proud to dye their oranges. Citrus Red No. 2 is an aggressive and unnerving pink, but, applied to the green and yellow-green and yellow-orange surfaces of oranges, it produces an acceptable color. How acceptable seems to differ with individuals, and, in a more remarkable way, with geography. Judging by sales figures, people in New England instinctively reject oranges that have the purple letters "COLOR ADDED" stamped on their skins. In the Middle West, though, color-added oranges are in demand. Stores have even put advertisements in Chicago newspapers announcing when color-added oranges were available. Distributors there say they could sell many more oranges if the packinghouses would intensify the dye. In Florida, citrus men sometimes say of Midwesterners, "These people don't want oranges. They want tomatoes."

Questions for Discussion

1. McPhee says the processors of oranges prefer to say they "de-green" them rather than "gas" them. Why would they choose the one term over the other? Which term does McPhee himself use?

2. Does McPhee's comparison of citrus packinghouses to beauty parlors seem appropriate? Explain.

3. Why do you think some packinghouses are "too proud" to dye their oranges, but not to "gas" them?

4. The word "orange" can refer either to the fruit or to the color. How does McPhee play on these two meanings in this selection?

5. To personify an inanimate object is to ascribe to it the characteristics of a living being. Where and why does McPhee use personification in this selection?

6. Compare McPhee's style in this selection to his style in "The Pinball Philosophy." How do the two styles differ? How do you account for the differences?

Suggested Activities

1. John McPhee is the author of a number of books on a wide variety of subjects. If you enjoyed "Oranges," prepare a report on one of these books for presentation in class.

2. Almost everyone has some unusual eating habits. Write an essay describing one or two of yours and analyzing their causes.

3. The food snob is a recurrent human type. Write an essay in which you draw on your own observations to characterize the type.

The Spider
and the Wasp

ALEXANDER PETRUNKEVITCH

Alexander Petrunkevitch (1875-1964), a Russian-born naturalized citizen of the United States, earned world-wide fame as a
zoologist. Affiliated with a number of universities, including Harvard, Indiana University, and Yale, Petrunkevitch devoted more
than fifty years to the study of spiders. He was also a translator
of Russian and English poetry. His writings include *Index Catalogue of Spiders of North, Central, and South America* (1911),
Choice and Responsibility (1947), and *Principles of Classification* (1952). Petrunkevitch's popular essay, "The Spider and the
Wasp," reprinted from *Scientific American*, explains the
remarkable process whereby one species of insect provides
food for its progeny.

To hold its own in the struggle for existence, every species of animal must have
a regular source of food, and if it happens to live on other animals, its survival
may be very delicately balanced. The hunter cannot exist without the hunted; if
the latter should perish from the earth, the former would, too. When the hunted
also prey on some of the hunters, the matter may become complicated.

This is nowhere better illustrated than in the insect world. Think of the
complexity of a situation such as the following: There is a certain wasp, *Pimpla
inquisitor*, whose larvae feed on the larvae of the tussock moth. *Pimpla* larvae in
turn serve as food for the larvae of a second wasp, and the latter in their turn

nourish still a third wasp. What subtle balance between fertility and mortality must exist in the case of each of these four species to prevent the extinction of all of them! An excess of mortality over fertility in a single member of the group would ultimately wipe out all four.

This is not a unique case. The two great orders of insects, Hymenoptera and Diptera, are full of such examples of interrelationship. And the spiders (which are not insects but members of a separate order of arthropods) also are killers and victims of insects.

The picture is complicated by the fact that those species which are carnivorous in the larval stage have to be provided with animal food by a vegetarian mother. The survival of the young depends on the mother's correct choice of a food which she does not eat herself.

In the feeding and safeguarding of their progeny the insects and spiders exhibit some interesting analogies to reasoning and some crass examples of blind instinct. The case I propose to describe here is that of the tarantula spiders and their arch-enemy, the digger wasps of the genus Pepsis. It is a classic example of what looks like intelligence pitted against instinct — a strange situation in which the victim, though fully able to defend itself, submits unwittingly to its destruction.

Most tarantulas live in the Tropics, but several species occur in the temperate zone and a few are common in the southern U.S. Some varieties are large and have powerful fangs with which they can inflict a deep wound. These formidable looking spiders do not, however, attack man; you can hold one in your hand, if you are gentle, without being bitten. Their bite is dangerous only to insects and small mammals such as mice; for a man it is no worse than a hornet's sting.

Tarantulas customarily live in deep cylindrical burrows, from which they emerge at dusk and into which they retire at dawn. Mature males wander about after dark in search of females and occasionally stray into houses. After mating, the male dies in a few weeks, but a female lives much longer and can mate several years in succession. In a Paris museum is a tropical specimen which is said to have been living in captivity for 25 years.

A fertilized female tarantula lays from 200 to 400 eggs at a time; thus it is possible for a single tarantula to produce several thousand young. She takes no care of them beyond weaving a cocoon of silk to enclose the eggs. After they hatch, the young walk away, find convenient places in which to dig their burrows and spend the rest of their lives in solitude. Tarantulas feed mostly on insects and millepedes. Once their appetite is appeased, they digest the food for several days before eating again. Their sight is poor, being limited to sensing a change in the intensity of light and to the perception of moving objects. They apparently have little or no sense of hearing, for a hungry tarantula will pay no attention to a loudly chirping cricket placed in its cage unless the insect happens to touch one of its legs.

But all spiders, and especially hairy ones, have an extremely delicate sense of touch. Laboratory experiments prove that tarantulas can distinguish three types of touch: pressure against the body wall, stroking of the body hair and riffling of certain very fine hairs on the legs called trichobothria. Pressure against the body, by a finger or the end of a pencil, causes the tarantula to move off slowly for a short distance. The touch excites no defensive response unless the approach is from above where the spider can see the motion, in which case it rises on its hind legs, lifts its front legs, opens its fangs and holds this threatening posture as long as the object continues to move. When the motion stops, the spider drops back to the ground, remains quiet for a few seconds and then moves slowly away.

The entire body of a tarantula, especially its legs, is thickly clothed with hair. Some of it is short and woolly, some long and stiff. Touching this body hair produces one of two distinct reactions. When the spider is hungry, it responds with an immediate and swift attack. At the touch of a cricket's antennae the tarantula seizes the insect so swiftly that a motion picture taken at the rate of 64 frames per second shows only the result and not the process of capture. But when the spider is not hungry, the stimulation of its hairs merely causes it to shake the touched limb. An insect can walk under its hairy belly unharmed.

The trichobothria, very fine hairs growing from disklike membranes on the legs, were once thought to be the spider's hearing organs, but we now know that they have nothing to do with sound. They are sensitive only to air movement. A light breeze makes them vibrate slowly without disturbing the common hair. When one blows gently on the trichobothria, the tarantula reacts with a quick jerk of its four front legs. If the front and hind legs are stimulated at the same time, the spider makes a sudden jump. This reaction is quite independent of the state of its appetite.

These three tactile responses — to pressure on the body wall, to moving of the common hair and to flexing of the trichobothria — are so different from one another that there is no possibility of confusing them. They serve the tarantula adequately for most of its needs and enable it to avoid most annoyances and dangers. But they fail the spider completely when it meets its deadly enemy, the digger wasp Pepsis.

These solitary wasps are beautiful and formidable creatures. Most species are either a deep shiny blue all over, or deep blue with rusty wings. The largest have a wing span of about four inches. They live on nectar. When excited, they give off a pungent odor — a warning that they are ready to attack. The sting is much worse than that of a bee or common wasp, and the pain and swelling last longer. In the adult stage the wasp lives only a few months. The female produces but a few eggs, one at a time at intervals of two or three days. For each egg the mother must provide one adult tarantula, alive but paralyzed. The tarantula must be of the correct species to nourish the larva. The mother wasp attaches the egg to the paralyzed spider's abdomen. Upon hatching from the egg, the larva is many hundreds of times smaller than its living but helpless victim. It eats no other food and drinks no water. By the time it has finished its single gargantuan meal and become ready for wasphood, nothing remains of the tarantula but its indigestible chitinous skeleton.

The mother wasp goes tarantula-hunting when the egg in her ovary is almost ready to be laid. Flying low over the ground late on a sunny afternoon, the wasp looks for its victim or for the mouth of a tarantula burrow, a round hole edged by a bit of silk. The sex of the spider makes no difference, but the mother is highly discriminating as to species. Each species of Pepsis requires a certain species of tarantula, and the wasp will not attack the wrong species. In a cage with a tarantula which is not its normal prey the wasp avoids the spider, and is usually killed by it in the night.

Yet when a wasp finds the correct species, it is the other way about. To identify the species the wasp apparently must explore the spider with her antennae. The tarantula shows an amazing tolerance to this exploration. The wasp crawls under it and walks over it without evoking any hostile response. The molestation is so great and so persistent that the tarantula often rises on all eight legs, as if it were on stilts. It may stand this way for several minutes. Meanwhile the wasp, having satisfied itself that the victim is of the right species, moves off a few inches to dig the spider's grave. Working vigorously with legs and jaws, it excavates a hole 8 to 10 inches deep with a diameter slightly larger than the spider's girth. Now and again the wasp pops out of the hole to make sure that the spider is still there.

When the grave is finished, the wasp returns to the tarantula to complete her ghastly enterprise. First she feels it all over once more with her antennae. Then her behavior becomes more aggressive. She bends her abdomen, protruding her sting, and searches for the soft membrane at the point where the spider's leg joins its body — the only spot where she can penetrate the horny skeleton. From time to time, as the exasperated spider slowly shifts ground, the wasp turns on her back and slides along with the aid of her wings, trying to get under the tarantula for a shot at the vital spot. During all this maneuvering, which can last for several minutes, the tarantula makes no move to save itself. Finally the wasp corners it against some obstruction and grasps one of its legs in her powerful jaws. Now at last the harassed spider tries a desperate but vain defense. The two contestants roll over and over on the ground. It is a terrifying sight and the outcome is always the same. The wasp finally manages to thrust her sting into the soft spot and holds it there for a few seconds while she pumps in the poison. Almost immediately the tarantula falls paralyzed on its back. Its legs stop twitching; its heart stops beating. Yet it is not dead, as is shown by the fact that if taken from the wasp it can be restored to some sensitivity by being kept in a moist chamber for several months.

After paralyzing the tarantula, the wasp cleans herself by dragging her body along the ground and rubbing her feet, sucks the drop of blood oozing from the wound in the spider's abdomen, then grabs a leg of the flabby, helpless animal in her jaws and drags it down to the bottom of the grave. She stays there for many minutes, sometimes for several hours, and what she does all that time in the dark we do not know. Eventually she lays her egg and attaches it to the side of the spider's abdomen with a sticky secretion. Then she emerges, fills the grave with soil carried bit by bit in her jaws, and finally tramples the ground all around to hide any trace of the grave from prowlers. Then she flies away, leaving her descendant safely started in life.

In all this the behavior of the wasp evidently is qualitatively different from that of the spider. The wasp acts like an intelligent animal. This is not to say that instinct plays no part or that she reasons as man does. But her actions are to the point; they are not automatic and can be modified to fit the situation. We do not know for certain how she identifies the tarantula — probably it is by some olfactory or chemo-tactile sense — but she does it purposefully and does not blindly tackle a wrong species.

On the other hand, the tarantula's behavior shows only confusion. Evidently the wasp's pawing gives it no pleasure, for it tries to move away. That the wasp is not simulating sexual stimulation is certain, because male and female tarantulas react in the same way to its advances. That the spider is not anesthetized by some odorless secretion is easily shown by blowing lightly at the tarantula and making it jump suddenly. What, then, makes the tarantula behave as stupidly as it does?

No clear, simple answer is available. Possibly the stimulation by the wasp's antennae is masked by a heavier pressure on the spider's body, so that it reacts as when prodded by a pencil. But the explanation may be much more complex. Initiative in attack is not in the nature of tarantulas; most species fight only when cornered so that escape is impossible. Their inherited patterns of behavior apparently prompt them to avoid problems rather than attack them. For example, spiders always weave their webs in three dimensions, and when a spider finds that there is insufficient space to attach certain threads in the third dimension, it leaves the place and seeks another, instead of finishing the web in a single plane. This urge to escape seems to arise under all circumstances, in all phases of life and to take the place of reasoning. For a spider to change the pattern of its web is as impossible as for an inexperienced man to build a bridge across a chasm obstructing his way.

In a way the instinctive urge to escape is not only easier but often more efficient than reasoning. The tarantula does exactly what is most efficient in all cases except in an encounter with a ruthless and determined attacker dependent for the existence of her own species on killing as many tarantulas as she can lay eggs. Perhaps in this case the spider follows its usual pattern of trying to escape, instead of seizing and killing the wasp, because it is not aware of its danger. In any case, the survival of the tarantula species as a whole is protected by the fact that the spider is much more fertile than the wasp.

Questions for Discussion

1. Why do you think Petrunkevitch takes such care to classify the tarantula's three types of tactile responses? Is his care justified later in the essay?

2. What does Petrunkevitch seem to assume is the primary difference between "reasoning" and "instinct"? Do you draw the same distinction between the two terms?

3. Which of the activities the wasp engages in best illustrates Petrunkevitch's contention that she is able to reason? Why?

4. The term "protagonist" designates the character in a work of literature with whom we most sympathize. Who is the protagonist of "The Spider and the Wasp"?

5. Petrunkevitch tells us the outcome of the conflict between the spider and the wasp in advance. How does he nevertheless manage to create a sense of drama in his account of their confrontation?

6. Compare Petrunkevitch's description of the demise of the spider with Dillard's description of the moth's death in "The Death of a Moth" (pp. 17–19). Which do you find more engaging? Why?

Suggested Activities

1. Find a close-up photograph of a tarantula and write a one-paragraph description of it. How does your description compare to Petrunkevitch's? What details has he omitted as irrelevant to his purpose?

2. Examine a few recent issues of *Scientific American*, then write an essay describing the magazine. What columns regularly appear in the magazine? What sorts of advertising does it carry? How long are its articles? How are they illustrated? What audience is the magazine aimed at? How closely do the characteristics of Petrunkevitch's essay conform to the characteristics of other essays in the magazine?

3. Write a process essay analyzing the way a species of insect or animal cares for its young. Whenever possible, rely on your own observations for your information, but supplement them with appropriate research where necessary. Be sure to give full credit to your sources.

The Moose
on the Wall

EDWARD HOAGLAND

For biographical information on Edward Hoagland, see page
152. In "The Moose on the Wall," Hoagland pays a visit to a
neighboring taxidermist in his home state of Vermont. Someday, Hoagland suggests, the products of the taxidermist's craft
may be all that remain of the major wildlife of northern New
England.

Since it is likely that the last wild animals of large size and dignity that people
will see will be stuffed ones, I paid a visit to my neighborhood taxidermist in
northern Vermont to learn how he does his work, and what precisely it is: by
what means these few crick-necked and powdery phantoms of the great game
confluxes of the past will be preserved. The area where I live still has a smattering
of black bear, and plenty of deer, some bobcats, and an occasional coyote migrat-
ing in from westerly parts. The beaver are beginning to come back, now that
nobody traps them, and the groundhogs and skunks and porcupines are flourish-
ing as the farms become summer places, where they aren't shot as varmints. The
moose, cougar, wolves and wolverines are long gone, but the humbler animals,
meek, elusive, adaptable, are doing all right for the moment—in fact, my friend
the taxidermist says that when he was a boy and this was farm country, people
would travel for miles just to set eyes on a bear's track, if one was reported. The

wildlife left will probably continue to prosper until the seasonal owners break up their properties into smaller and smaller tracts as land values rise.

My friend is a likable man with white hair, a quiet, spacious, mild face well used by his sixty years, a farmer's suspenders, a carpenter's arms, and an acumen in the woods, or a love for the woods, that no doubt exceeds my own, though my bias and his are opposed. We are allies nevertheless, because hunting and non-hunting naturalists when taken together are only a dot in the populace, at least when wildlife conservation is involved. Clean air and water, provision for beaches and lakes and parks — these causes draw a dependable measure of support from good men everywhere, but animals unseen, whose wish is to steer clear of mankind, get less attention. Hunters do fret about them, however, keeping tabs on the toll the winter snows take, and the relentless shrinkage of open land. Hunters miss the moose and mountain lions and pass along rumors that a handful still somehow survive here in the Northeast. Besides, hunters are folk who like to walk half-a-dozen miles before having lunch, to get their feet wet, pant up the ledges and draws, cook over a fire, and perhaps finally haul a load of meat home on their backs; and they take their ration of blood as they find it, in a natural fashion, not transmogrified onto the TV. Hunters are as attentive as the predator animals to the habits of what they are after; and some of them want visible proof on the wall of what they got for their trouble — the taxidermist does this for them. In some ways his work resembles an undertaker's, with the congenial difference that he needn't hurry or pretend to be sad.

In the window of his shop is an old display of two newborn bear cubs, bleached white by the sun, sitting in a tiny boat on a pond. The pond is represented by a sheet of plastic, with realistic-looking trout underneath. There are also some dusty pheasants and ducks, their colors dead now. But the splendor inside is undeniable — deep, virile black hides of bears seized at the prime, just before they would have dug in for a winter's sleep. These are stacked in piles, glossy, blue-black, and there are other mounds of orange and caribou-colored deer hides. Visiting, I was surprised at the number of tools along the workbench: fleshing and cartilage knives, saws and scalpels in rows, pliers, pincers, hammers and mallets, bone snippers and scrapers, curved sewing needles, forceps, punches, drills, picking tools, tweezers, stiff wires. The plywood tables are big enough for him to stretch out a nine-foot skin to dry after it has been soaked in the tanning tub and washed in fresh water. The soaking goes on for six weeks or so — he has sacks of alum, which is the main ingredient in the pickling acid. There is salt in quantity too, for drying the flesh side of the skins when they first arrive, and plaster of Paris, and sacks of a grainy roof-insulation material which is used to thicken the plaster of Paris.

Ideally, the taxidermist is given the skull of the animal along with the hide, if a head job is wanted, not simply the flat tanned skin. After boiling the skull until all the meat has fallen away, he rebuilds the original shape of the head by thumbing plaster into the grooves and cavities on the skull so that the skin fits over it again as neatly as before. For deer, whose jaws and teeth are not to be emphasized, he doesn't need more than the skull's top plate, where the antlers attach, but a carnivore is most realistically mounted when the teeth that you see are the real teeth, not hoked up from wax in an oversized jaw. He restructures the underpart of a deer's face by whittling a small block of cedar or basswood, though of course he could buy entire preformed heads made of papier mâché from the wholesalers — heads of moose, deer, or the numerous and various African antelopes. A ready-made jaguar's wax mouth and paper skull costs only about $12, for instance; a set of artificial porcelain teeth is $5.95 for a tiger and $1.95 for a coyote, because these are higher quality.

He could buy rubber noses by the gross as well, but usually he moulds the animal's nose out of putty, attaching it to the snout that he shaped from wood or from plaster of Paris and painting it black. Each ear is a piece of soft lead bent so that the skin slips onto it alertly. The eyes are glass; and he has a watchmaker's cabinet of compartments and drawers filled with fox eyes, owl eyes, loon eyes, lynx eyes, coon eyes, lion eyes, snake eyes. Some are veined or show lifelike white corners and carefully differentiate iris and pupil. The catalogue lists twenty-eight sizes, from a buffalo's down to a hummingbird's, and there are cheapjack economy grades, eight pairs for a dollar. He can buy rubber tongues, set into a roll like a wolf's tongue, but unless he is rushed he carves his from wood. He glues the tongue inside the skull, and the lips, gums and roof of the mouth he forms out of wax and then paints them the correct color. Next, he sews and pins the eyelids and cheeks into an appropriate expression and whittles a frame for the neck. He likes to whittle — that basic craft — first using a drawknife, later a delicate spokeshaver, such as wagon wheels used to be carved with. When only wadding is needed, as for stuffing squirrels and birds, excelsior serves very well, or cotton batting. A bad craftsman would insert the filler as if he were stuffing a cushion, but it's best to wind it tightly first into a credible stance and tie it with thread for permanence. He polishes and lacquers the hooves of the deer and blows with a bellows at the game birds to clean their feathers. Songbirds are wired into a pert pose, wings outspread or beak pointed left; wires bore down through their legs to the varnished perch.

Many droll requests come from customers, surpassing the sort of ideas an undertaker encounters. Some people want blinking lights installed in the eyeholes of the lynx that they've shot. Or they'll put their house thermometer in a deer's leg; they'll want a fat mother porcupine stuffed conventionally but with the fetuses found inside her embalmed in a talcum powder bottle like little rolled-up human babies. A local minister who had served as a missionary in Africa brought back the ears and a foot of an elephant he had shot, and a souvenir strip of leg skin like hard bark. Sometimes a hotel man will buy a pair of bear cubs a farmer has killed and, under the general umbrella of humor, ask that they be preserved in a standing position on their hind legs to hold the ash trays in the lobby. ("Oh, pardon me, little sir, may I use you?")

Understand that I'm making a figurative investigation — the animals native to Vermont which have survived so far are not in danger of quick extinction. The end of subsistence farming has worked to their advantage, and, paradoxically, before the farmers appeared and cleared the land, the Indians of nearby Canada had called this section of New England The Desert because the unfelled timber grew so thick that game was scarce. Still, these modest creatures — flittering does fleeing with a peahen's squawking cry, a pony's hoofbeats, and a carousel motion; porcine black bear rooting for mushrooms, rooting for grubs; and all the parade of back-field inhabitants, like the varying hares which explode through the ferns and the fire cherry and in winter turn white and nibble ironwood nuts — represent the much bigger ghosts of creatures gone.

Taxidermy, or the notion of saving the scalp, horns and teeth of game, goes along with a fairly advanced stage of settlement. The frontiersmen and home-steaders hunted for meat — it was labor to them, it was feeding the family; other than furs to dress themselves in, they didn't often keep tokens. The Indians, having evolved a game-oriented religion and culture, were more likely to save an especially superb big skull, but they also killed for use and didn't go in for tricking the animal up as a mannequin. The practice of mounting heads to hang on the wall developed only as the white towns became county seats, long after the first artisans like blacksmiths and carpenters had arrived, when hunters became "sportsmen." Earlier, a fellow might throw a phenomenal skin embodying the memories of real risk and adventure up on the cabin roof to freeze and dry; he might even salt it. By and by the sun would convert the flesh side to a brown board, and it would be tacked in the entryway — that was the taxidermy.

Once in the old gold town of Barkerville, British Columbia, I was talking to a prospector and his wife, both over seventy-five. Their serenity and good cheer were plain; wilderness gardening had obviously agreed with them, so had the solitude, and there was no counting the tonnage of creek sand that they must have panned in a lifetime. But what brought the sense of their achievement home to me as they talked was suddenly to notice two antediluvian grizzly hides hanging in the hallway just behind them: from floor to ceiling, a plush chestnut-brown with darker shades. A basketball player could have enveloped himself in either one with room to spare. Apparently both husband and wife had shot other bears, but had happened to save these. They didn't mention them until I did, and as with every other keepsake they had, didn't stress or boast about the circumstances, just said that the bears had strayed within range on their creek in different years and had seemed to be taking up a settled abode. On a whole host of topics that we touched on, the skins completed what was unsaid.

I'm not against keeping trophies if they define or somehow enlarge the possessor, if they're taken seriously, and if they memorialize the animal world, besieged and warranted for an early death as it surely is. Old dirt farmers and mild-mannered old taxidermists are outdated too; they will go the way of the wildlife soon. (There is another taxidermist in town, a retired fellow with pouchy cheeks, an upright posture and a face like a squirrel, who keeps his first-prize ribbons from the state fairs of 1911 and 1913 under glass.) This business of my friend's employs three generations. All day outdoorsmen, wearing red shirts or hip boots, drop in and talk, and he and his son and the young boy, scraping the flesh from a black wolf's legs, listen in. They throw sawdust on the floor and handle the beasts that arrive as farmers do their own butchered stock — it lives to live but it lives to be shot. The older man has hunted moose in northern Quebec that put all these little buck deer in the shade, so he's got photographs of the vanished big stuff. When he talks it's always of hunting and game: knolls and ledges to scale, ravines to bypass, and openings which open up as you reach them. Game is like vastly enlivened farm stock; you study it, wish it well, go for the prize.

Along the walls there are shelves of skulls, tagged for insertion into the bear skulls which are being prepared. When the skins are tanned, repairs are made — holes sewn up, bald spots touched over with paint or patched with scraps from another skin. The claws are cleaned, the blemishes concealed, and the obligatory pained-looking snarl, which the animal seldom wore while it was alive, is inscribed on the face. Bear rugs cost the clientele $25 per square foot nowadays, and in a year the shop gets up to seventy of them to work on, though last fall was an unlucky one for hunters because the mast crop was sparse and scattered and a heavy, early snowfall put all the bears in Vermont to bed ahead of time (an estimated thirty-five hundred live in the state). Also, by late November upwards of two hundred deer have been brought in, the floor is heaped high with salted skins, antlers are lying all over the place. Some people want the deer's feet mounted on a plaque under the head and set with an upward poke, to be utilized as a gun rack. The workroom has samples of this arrangement nailed to the walls, and big moose feet, and a great moose head is exhibited, with its pendulous bell, long-suffering ears, and primeval superstructure, bony, leaf-shaped. There's a lovely gray bobcat hanging head down, and a stuffed horned owl, a goshawk, some quail, some black ducks, a Canada goose, a pouter pigeon, two mink, a fox skin, beaver kits, the unfinished head of a coyote with its lips and eyes intricately pinned, and a yearling bear posed standing up, holding a pair of field glasses, as if to help it see better next time.

Snapshots of big men and downed bear, of deer sprawled on the ground and hunters squatting, are tacked on the wall. About fifteen thousand deer a year are killed in Vermont, almost two per square mile, although only one hunter in ten who buys a license is successful in making a kill. The out-of-state hunters do a little bit better statistically, strangely enough, maybe they're at it full time while they're here. Then during the winter perhaps just as many deer starve to death. The deer that we see in the north are still healthy-looking, though there are very few predators left who can prune the herds in a natural fashion, taking the weaker individuals so that the wintering areas are not overgrazed. Bobcats have become scarce because they are hunted year-round, and bobcats aren't really up to the task anyway. Eventually our deer are expected to shrink to the wizened proportions of some of their cousins in southern Vermont or southerly New England, where often the bucks can't even muster the strength to sprout antlers and the fawns that they father are comparably frail — most being shot within the first two or three years of life, in any case. What with the game diminishing in grandeur, the short hunting seasons and complicated regulations, a talented, old-fashioned hunter finds his style crimped. For want of any other game, he exercises himself by hunting coons or the few small surviving predators. One fellow in town, who runs the schoolbuses, a lanky, devoted, preeminent hunter who probably was born too late, goes after bobcats with dogs every weekend all winter, patrolling the snowy deer yards, believing that he is protecting the deer. Bobcats have diminutive chests; they can dash in a burst of speed but soon must get into a tree if the hounds are close, not being equipped for a distance race. A photo shows him with seventeen of the creatures hammered frozen to the side of his house, each with clenched paws and a grimace. He collected the $10 bounty on each, cut off the bobbed tails, and threw the bodies on the town dump.

There is a furred compendium on the tables, a dukedom in furs, not only raccoons and otter and bucks, but skins from the West — grizzly and cougar — as if the supply would never run out. All around the top of the room are fastened dozens of black and white tails — these the whitetail deer tails which they flip up to warn one another when they have cause to bolt, and which they wag vigorously in the fly season, just as a horse does. Almost every evening I watch deer in my field, their coats as red as a red fox. They snort with the sharp sound of a box dropped. Sometimes you only see their tall ears, in a V, the late sunlight shining through pinkly. Originally, a hundred or more years ago, only a moose trail and horse trail wound past where I live. It is exceptionally moosey country, with ponds, mountains, lakes and bogs — country that cries out for moose, in fact. Moose love water. When hard-pressed by wolves, they will spend the whole winter knee-deep in a pond, standing close to where a spring comes in and the water won't freeze; and in the summer, browsing on the bottom, they wade out so far in search of water plants that they finally get in over their heads and push up the tips of their noses every few minutes. The huge bulls, however, are a sight surpassing the vision one had of them, surpassing the mind's inventions. You would think that when they caught sight of themselves reflected on the surface of a smooth lake they would be frightened.

Even the bank in town has the head of a moose fixed to the wall, as a remembrance of the old days. It looks like the head of a horse or a cow poking through the half-door of a stable. And looking at it, I get the benign sense of good existing in the world that I have sometimes when I look at a cow — those big ears thrust forward, and those big eyes, as if we all have at least two ways of communicating with each other in this world: sound and sight. A youngster came into the bank while I was there and stared for a long time at the moose head. After a while he went to the door and tried to go through to the other side so that he could see the rest of the animal. To begin with, they had to tell him it wasn't alive.

Questions for Discussion

1. Examine Hoagland's descriptions of the taxidermist and his workshop. How do these descriptions contribute to the view Hoagland creates of taxidermy?

2. Hoagland compares the taxidermist's work to an undertaker's. In your judgment, is this comparison an apt one? Why or why not?

3. Why do you think Hoagland includes the example of the old prospector and his wife? What do you understand him to mean when he says that the grizzly bear hides on the wall of their cabin "brought the sense of their achievement home"?

4. What seems to be Hoagland's attitude toward hunters? In what ways is Hoagland's own status as a nonhunter an important element in this essay?

5. Why does Hoagland include the final anecdote about the boy and the moose head? Did you find it to be an effective conclusion to the essay?

6. What examples of the taxidermist's art does Hoagland find most attractive? least attractive? Is his taste in styles of taxidermy consistent with his overall attitude toward the craft?

Suggested Activities

1. After doing some library research, write an essay extending (or correcting) Hoagland's account of the early American history of taxidermy.

2. Write an analysis of some process of a craft you know well. Your purpose should not be to instruct your readers in the techniques of the craft but to lead them to appreciate its complexity and worth.

3. Compare your classmates' attitudes toward hunting with their attitudes toward fishing. How do you explain the differences, if any, between the two?

Bureaucrats

JOAN DIDION

For biographical information on Joan Didion, see page 84. In "Bureaucrats," reprinted from *The White Album* (1979), Didion shows how the California Department of Transportation attempted to make "it harder for drivers to use freeways." She also suggests why so many drivers reacted violently to the attempt.

The closed door upstairs at 120 South Spring Street in downtown Los Angeles is marked OPERATIONS CENTER. In the windowless room beyond the closed door a reverential hush prevails. From six A.M. until seven P.M. in this windowless room men sit at consoles watching a huge board flash colored lights. "There's the heart attack," someone will murmur, or "we're getting the gawk effect." 120 South Spring is the Los Angeles office of Caltrans, or the California Department of Transportation, and the Operations Center is where Caltrans engineers monitor what they call "the 42-Mile Loop." The 42-Mile Loop is simply the rough triangle formed by the intersections of the Santa Monica, the San Diego and the Harbor freeways, and 42 miles represents less than ten per cent of freeway mileage in Los Angeles County alone, but these particular 42 miles are regarded around 120 South Spring with a special veneration. The Loop is a "demonstration system," a phrase much favored by everyone at Caltrans, and is part of a "pilot project," another two words carrying totemic weight on South Spring.

The Loop has electronic sensors embedded every half-mile out there in the pavement itself, each sensor counting the crossing cars every twenty seconds. The Loop has its own mind, a Xerox Sigma V computer which prints out, all day and

BUREAUCRATS   From *The White Album* by Joan Didion. Copyright © 1979 by Joan Didion. Reprinted by permission of Simon & Schuster, a Division of Gulf & Western Corporation.

night, twenty-second readings on what is and is not moving in each of the Loop's eight lanes. It is the Xerox Sigma V that makes the big board flash red when traffic out there drops below fifteen miles an hour. It is the Xerox Sigma V that tells the Operations crew when they have an "incident" out there. An "incident" is the heart attack on the San Diego, the jackknifed truck on the Harbor, the Camaro just now tearing out the Cyclone fence on the Santa Monica. "Out there" is where incidents happen. The windowless room at 120 South Spring is where incidents get "verified." "Incident verification" is turning on the closed-circuit TV on the console and watching the traffic slow down to see (this is "the gawk effect") where the Camaro tore out the fence.

As a matter of fact there is a certain closed-circuit aspect to the entire mood of the Operations Center. "Verifying" the incident does not after all "prevent" the incident, which lends the enterprise a kind of tranced distance, and on the day recently when I visited 120 South Spring it took considerable effort to remember what I had come to talk about, which was that particular part of the Loop called the Santa Monica Freeway. The Santa Monica Freeway is 16.2 miles long, runs from the Pacific Ocean to downtown Los Angeles through what is referred to at Caltrans as "the East-West Corridor," carries more traffic every day than any other freeway in California, has what connoisseurs of freeways concede to be the most beautiful access ramps in the world, and appeared to have been transformed by Caltrans, during the several weeks before I went downtown to talk about it, into a 16.2-mile parking lot.

The problem seemed to be another Caltrans "demonstration," or "pilot," a foray into bureaucratic terrorism they were calling "The Diamond Lane" in their promotional literature and "The Project" among themselves. That the promotional literature consisted largely of schedules for buses (or "Diamond Lane Expresses") and invitations to join a car pool via computer ("Commuter Computer") made clear not only the putative point of The Project, which was to encourage travel by car pool and bus, but also the actual point, which was to eradicate a central Southern California illusion, that of individual mobility, without anyone really noticing. This had not exactly worked out. "FREEWAY FIASCO," the *Los Angeles Times* was headlining page-one stories. "THE DIA-MOND LANE: ANOTHER BUST BY CALTRANS." "CALTRANS PILOT EFFORT ANOTHER IN LONG LIST OF FAILURES." "OFFICIAL DIAMOND LANE STANCE: LET THEM HOWL."

All "The Diamond Lane" theoretically involved was reserving the fast inside lanes on the Santa Monica for vehicles carrying three or more people, but in practice this meant that 25 per cent of the freeway was reserved for 3 per cent of the cars, and there were other odd wrinkles here and there suggesting that Caltrans had dedicated itself to making all movement around Los Angeles as arduous as possible. There was for example the matter of surface streets. A "surface street" is anything around Los Angeles that is not a freeway ("going surface" from one part of town to another is generally regarded as idiosyncratic), and surface streets do not fall directly within the Caltrans domain, but now the engineer in charge of surface streets was accusing Caltrans of threatening and intimidating him. It appeared that Caltrans wanted him to create a "confused and congested situation" on his surface streets, so as to force drivers back to the freeway, where they would meet a still more confused and congested situation and decide to stay home, or take a bus. "We are beginning a process of deliberately making it harder for drivers to use freeways," a Caltrans director had in fact said at a transit conference some months before. "We are prepared to endure considerable public outcry in order to pry John Q. Public out of his car.... I would emphasize that this is a political decision, and one that can be reversed if the public gets sufficiently enraged to throw us rascals out."

Of course this political decision was in the name of the greater good, was in the interests of "environmental improvement" and "conservation of resources," but even there the figures had about them a certain Caltrans opacity. The Santa Monica normally carried 240,000 cars and trucks every day. These 240,000 cars and trucks normally carried 260,000 people. What Caltrans described as its ultimate goal on the Santa Monica was to carry the same 260,000 people, "but in 7,800 fewer, or 232,200 vehicles." The figure "232,200" had a visionary precision to it that did not automatically create confidence, especially since the only effect so far had been to disrupt traffic throughout the Los Angeles basin, triple the number of daily accidents on the Santa Monica, prompt the initiation of two lawsuits against Caltrans, and cause large numbers of Los Angeles County residents to behave, most uncharacteristically, as an ignited and conscious proletariat. Citizen guerrillas splashed paint and scattered nails in the Diamond Lanes. Diamond Lane maintenance crews expressed fear of hurled objects. Down at 120 South Spring the architects of the Diamond Lane had taken to regarding "the media" as the architects of their embarrassment, and Caltrans statements in the press had been cryptic and contradictory, reminiscent only of old communiqués out of Vietnam.

To understand what was going on it is perhaps necessary to have participated in the freeway experience, which is the only secular communion Los Angeles has. Mere driving on the freeway is in no way the same as participating in it. Anyone can "drive" on the freeway, and many people with no vocation for it do, hesitating here and resisting there, losing the rhythm of the lane change, thinking about where they came from and where they are going. Actual participants think only about where they are. Actual participation requires a total surrender, a concentration so intense as to seem a kind of narcosis, a rapture-of-the-freeway. The mind goes clean. The rhythm takes over. A distortion of time occurs, the same distortion that characterizes the instant before an accident. It takes only a few seconds to get off the Santa Monica Freeway at National-Overland, which is a difficult exit requiring the driver to cross two new lanes of traffic streamed in from the San Diego Freeway, but those few seconds always seem to me the longest part of the trip. The moment is dangerous. The exhilaration is in doing it. "As you acquire the special skills involved," Reyner Banham observed in an extraordinary chapter about the freeways in his 1971 *Los Angeles: The Architecture of Four Ecologies*, "the freeways become a special way of being alive . . . the extreme concentration required in Los Angeles seems to bring on a state of heightened awareness that some locals find mystical."

Indeed some locals do, and some nonlocals too. Reducing the number of lone souls careering around the East-West Corridor in a state of mechanized rapture may or may not have seemed socially desirable, but what it was definitely not going to seem was easy. "We're only seeing an initial period of unfamiliarity," I was assured the day I visited Caltrans. I was talking to a woman named Eleanor Wood and she was thoroughly and professionally grounded in the diction of "planning" and it did not seem likely that I could interest her in considering the freeway as regional mystery. "Any time you try to rearrange people's daily habits, they're apt to react impetuously. All this project requires is a certain re-arrangement of people's daily planning. That's really all we want."

It occurred to me that a certain rearrangement of people's daily planning might seem, in less rarefied air than is breathed at 120 South Spring, rather a great deal to want, but so impenetrable was the sense of higher social purpose there in the Operations Center that I did not express this reservation. Instead I changed the subject, mentioned an earlier "pilot project" on the Santa Monica: the big electronic message boards that Caltrans had installed a year or two before. The idea was that traffic information transmitted from the Santa Monica to the Xerox Sigma V could be translated, here in the Operations Center, into suggestions to the driver, and flashed right back out to the Santa Monica. This operation, in that it involved telling drivers electronically what they already knew empirically, had the rather spectral circularity that seemed to mark a great many Caltrans schemes, and I was interested in how Caltrans thought it worked.

"Actually the message boards were part of a larger pilot project," Mrs. Wood said. "An ongoing project in incident management. With the message boards we hoped to learn if motorists would modify their behavior according to what we told them on the boards."

I asked if the motorists had.

"Actually no," Mrs. Wood said finally. "They didn't react to the signs exactly as we'd hypothesized they would, no. *But*. If we'd *known* what the motorist would do . . . then we wouldn't have needed a pilot project in the first place, would we."

The circle seemed intact. Mrs. Wood and I smiled, and shook hands. I watched the big board until all lights turned green on the Santa Monica and then I left and drove home on it, all 16.2 miles of it. All the way I remembered that I was watched by the Xerox Sigma V. All the way the message boards gave me the number to call for CAR POOL INFO. As I left the freeway it occurred to me that they might have their own rapture down at 120 South Spring, and it could be called Perpetuating the Department. Today the California Highway Patrol reported that, during the first six weeks of the Diamond Lane, accidents on the Santa Monica, which normally range between 49 and 72 during a six-week period, totaled 204. Yesterday plans were announced to extend the Diamond Lane to other freeways at a cost of $42,500,000.

Questions for Discussion

1. What different processes are explained in this essay? What seems to be Didion's reason for explaining them?

2. What is the rhetorical purpose of the repetition of the phrase "out there" in the second paragraph? Does this repetition work for you as a reader? Explain.

3. Look at the sentence beginning "The Santa Monica Freeway is 16.2 miles long . . ." in the third paragraph of "Bureaucrats." What is stylistically distinctive about this sentence? What is its function in the essay as a whole?

4. Didion calls freeway driving "the only secular communion Los Angeles has." What does the phrase "secular communion" mean here? Do you agree that driving can be a form of secular communion?

5. Didion says that Eleanor Wood "was thoroughly and professionally grounded in the diction of 'planning'." How is this diction exemplified in the conversation between the two of them? Where else does it occur in the essay? How does it differ from Didion's own diction?

6. In your opinion, is Didion fair to the California Department of Transportation? Explain your answer.

Suggested Activities

1. Make a list of the stylistic similarities this essay shares with Didion's "The Santa Ana." Do the same for Hoagland's two essays and for White's. Which writer do you think has the most consistent style? Why?

2. Write an essay explaining the strengths and weaknesses of the way in which an organization you know well is managed. Some possibilities: a dormitory or apartment building, a fraternity or sorority, a place where you've worked, a school cafeteria.

3. Write an essay explaining the significance that some form of driving holds for you.

4. Didion's essay was first published in 1976. Do some library research on what has happened to the Diamond Lanes project since then, and write an essay reporting your findings.

cause and effect

Like narration (Chapter 3) and process analysis (Chapter 7), cause-and-effect analysis is concerned with events in sequence. But where narration and process analysis are content merely to show *how* something happens, cause-and-effect writing seeks to explain *why* it does. It's a way of thinking almost as natural to us as breathing. As your parents undoubtedly can affirm, you began practicing it around the age of three, when you started asking a seemingly endless string of questions about why we can see our breath when it's cold, and why things fall down instead of up, and why the sky is blue.

In children's uses of it, cause-and-effect analysis usually consists of lining up a single, distinct cause with a single, distinct effect. For adults, too, it is sometimes no more than this: if your car won't start, you often need search no further than the battery to find the exclusive cause. A moment's reflection, though, will show that this simple, one-to-one sort of cause-and-effect relationship is only one possibility among many. Three factors work together to create more complex (and more interesting) causal relationships.

1. Both causes and effects may be multiple in number. Sometimes your car won't start because the battery is dead. But say you have an old car that has been starting only reluctantly for some time now. The battery isn't dead, but it's low; the spark plugs are old; the engine is losing compression. On the morning when the car finally won't start, to what do you assign the blame? Probably no one factor was alone responsible: it took the three of them working together to stop you in your tracks. Here we have an example of multiple causes producing a single effect. Note that the opposite is equally possible. A single cause, such as a stalled car, can result in multiple effects: missed work, an angry boss, frayed nerves. And of course, multiple causes can easily combine to produce multiple effects as well.

2. Causes can be either immediate or remote.   In our example of the old car, the multiple ailments that prevented it from running are all *immediate* causes, in that they contributed directly to the effect. But there exist *remote* causes as well. These are causes that are removed from the effect in space or time but that nonetheless can be seen to have helped produce it. In the case of the stalled car, not having enough money for a tuneup would be a remote cause, as would a deficiency in the car's design that made it hard to start.

All effects, in fact, have both immediate and remote causes—and writers must often decide which of the two to concentrate on. In "The Care and Prevention of Disaster," for example, John Kenneth Galbraith focuses his attention exclusively on remote causes. The immediate cause of the stock market crash—loss of investor confidence—interests him only insofar as it is itself something to be explained by the remote causes. In Berton Roueché's "Eleven Blue Men," by contrast, the focus is exclusively on determining the immediate cause of the old men's illness. The larger social and economic causes that would explain why the old men were in a situation where they could be poisoned lie beyond the scope of Roueché's concern.

3. Effects can also be causes.   As our example of the stalled car suggests, effects can also be causes. This is so because all events exist within *causal chains:* they result from events that precede them, and they lead to others that follow after. In "Politics and the English Language" (reprinted in Chapter 9), George Orwell gives a particularly telling example of this process. In his words: " . . . an effect can become a cause, reinforcing the original cause and producing the same effect in an intensified form, and so on indefinitely. A man may take to drink because he feels himself to be a failure, and then fail all the more completely because he drinks."

As with immediate and remote causes, the ability of an event to be simultaneously an effect and a cause requires writers to decide where to place their emphasis. In "Life in the Streets," for example, the street surveillance that Jane Jacobs describes is both a cause of safe streets and an effect of certain architectural and social conditions. Since Jacobs is interested in tracing the causal chain that links architectural design to safety in the city, she chooses to give equal weight to both dimensions of the surveillance. In "Shooting an Elephant," by contrast, George Orwell is primarily interested in explaining what caused him to shoot the elephant. He therefore only briefly mentions the effects of its death on its owner and the other people involved in the narrative.

How a causal analysis functions as a form of persuasion is determined by how complex it is. In the simple sort of cause-and-effect analysis that we use to determine why a car won't start, there's little or no room for differences of opinion. When this sort of analysis occurs in your writing, your aim can be to convince your readers that you've found the one right analysis of the matter, and you can expect them to accept your claim completely if it is a valid one.

When we turn to the more complex sorts of cause-and-effect relationships, though, the possibility of a single, indisputable analysis disappears. In a complex situation there are simply too many causes and effects, and the causal chains are too long and intricate for any one analysis to achieve absolute authority. In this circumstance, your aim can no longer be to convince your readers of the exclusive validity of your analysis. Instead, you should seek to show them that your view of the matter is an *important* and *plausible* one. You want them to agree that you've examined a significant causal relationship, not a trivial one, and that you've made correct decisions about which causes (or effects) to emphasize.

In order to achieve these aims, take a detailed look at your subject before you begin writing about it. If you're going to be discussing a causal chain, for example, you need to decide how far back along the chain to carry your analysis, and whether any steps in the sequence of causes and effects should be summarized or passed over in silence. If the relationship you're examining involves either multiple causes or multiple effects (or both), you need to decide which of them are significant enough to merit separate consideration and which are not. Also, it's a good idea to experiment with different orders of presentation before beginning to write. Will your essay be most effective if you move from the least important cause to the most important one, or vice versa? Or can you find, as John Kenneth Galbraith did in "The Care and Prevention of Disaster," a distinctive order of presentation suited to your subject alone?

Finally, as a last step before beginning to write, examine your causal analysis to see that it doesn't contain any *post hoc* reasoning. The term "post hoc" is a shorthand version of the Latin expression *post hoc, ergo propter hoc,* which translates as "after this, therefore because of this." The expression refers to the common human tendency to assume that if B happens *after* A it happens *because* of A. You can help yourself avoid this kind of mistaken reasoning if you ask two questions any time you wish to claim that A is the cause of B:

1. Does A have to happen for B to happen?

2. Does B happen every time A happens?

If the answer to both questions is "yes," then you can be confident that you're working with a valid cause-and-effect relationship. Be aware, though, that a "no" answer to one or the other question doesn't necessarily mean the relationship is invalid. It just means you should take a close second look at your analysis to make sure it is correct before including it in your essay.

Life
in the Streets

JANE JACOBS

After graduating from high school in Scranton, Pennsylvania, Jane Jacobs (b. 1916) moved to New York City, where she worked for a number of years as a stenographer, free-lance writer, and editor of the magazine *Architectural Forum*. A determined foe of conventional forms of city planning, Jacobs wrote her first book, *The Death and Life of Great American Cities* (1961), to suggest alternative ways of looking at city life. She has since written *The Economy of Cities* (1969), and *The Question of Separatism* (1980). In the selection from *Death and Life* reprinted here, Jacobs argues that a number of easily overlooked factors determine whether or not city streets are safe.

This is something everyone already knows: A well-used city street is apt to be a safe street. A deserted city street is apt to be unsafe. But how does this work, really? And what makes a city street well used or shunned? Why is the sidewalk mall in Washington Houses, which is supposed to be an attraction, shunned? Why are the sidewalks of the old city just to its west not shunned? What about streets that are busy part of the time and then empty abruptly?

A city street equipped to handle strangers, and to make a safety asset, in itself, out of the presence of strangers, as the streets of successful city neighborhoods always do, must have three main qualities:

First, there must be a clear demarcation between what is public space and what is private space. Public and private spaces cannot ooze into each other as they do typically in suburban settings or in projects.

Second, there must be eyes upon the street, eyes belonging to those we might call the natural proprietors of the street. The buildings on a street equipped to handle strangers and to insure the safety of both residents and strangers, must be oriented to the street. They cannot turn their backs or blank sides on it and leave it blind.

And third, the sidewalk must have users on it fairly continuously, both to add to the number of effective eyes on the street and to induce the people in buildings along the street to watch the sidewalks in sufficient numbers. Nobody enjoys sitting on a stoop or looking out a window at an empty street. Almost nobody does such a thing. Large numbers of people entertain themselves, off and on, by watching street activity.

In settlements that are smaller and simpler than big cities, controls on acceptable public behavior, if not on crime, seem to operate with greater or lesser success through a web of reputation, gossip, approval, disapproval and sanctions, all of which are powerful if people know each other and word travels. But a city's streets, which must control not only the behavior of the people of the city but also of visitors from suburbs and towns who want to have a big time away from the gossip and sanctions at home, have to operate by more direct, straightforward methods. It is a wonder cities have solved such an inherently difficult problem at all. And yet in many streets they do it magnificently.

It is futile to try to evade the issue of unsafe city streets by attempting to make some other features of a locality, say interior courtyards, or sheltered play spaces, safe instead. By definition again, the streets of a city must do most of the job of handling strangers for this is where strangers come and go. The streets must not only defend the city against predatory strangers, they must protect the many, many peaceable and well-meaning strangers who use them, insuring their safety too as they pass through. Moreover, no normal person can spend his life in some artificial haven, and this includes children. Everyone must use the streets.

On the surface, we seem to have here some simple aims: To try to secure streets where the public space is unequivocally public, physically unmixed with private or with nothing-at-all space, so that the area needing surveillance has clear and practicable limits; and to see that these public street spaces have eyes on them as continuously as possible.

But it is not so simple to achieve these objects, especially the latter. You can't make people use streets they have no reason to use. You can't make people watch streets they do not want to watch. Safety on the streets by surveillance and mutual policing of one another sounds grim, but in real life it is not grim. The safety of the street works best, most casually, and with least frequent taint of hostility or suspicion precisely where people are using and most enjoying the city streets voluntarily and are least conscious, normally, that they are policing.

The basic requisite for such surveillance is a substantial quantity of stores and other public places sprinkled along the sidewalks of a district; enterprises and public places that are used by evening and night must be among them especially.

Stores, bars and restaurants, as the chief examples, work in several different and complex ways to abet sidewalk safety.

First, they give people — both residents and strangers — concrete reasons for using the sidewalks on which these enterprises face.

Second, they draw people along the sidewalks past places which have no attractions to public use in themselves but which become traveled and peopled as routes to somewhere else; this influence does not carry very far geographically, so enterprises must be frequent in a city district if they are to populate with walkers those other stretches of street that lack public places along the sidewalk. Moreover, there should be many different kinds of enterprises, to give people reasons for crisscrossing paths.

Third, storekeepers and other small businessmen are typically strong proponents of peace and order themselves; they hate broken windows and holdups; they hate having customers made nervous about safety. They are great street watchers and sidewalk guardians if present in sufficient numbers.

Fourth, the activity generated by people on errands, or people aiming for food or drink, is itself an attraction to still other people.

This last point, that the sight of people attracts still other people, is something that city planners and city architectural designers seem to find incomprehensible. They operate on the premise that city people seek the sight of emptiness, obvious order and quiet. Nothing could be less true. People's love of watching activity and other people is constantly evident in cities everywhere. This trait reaches an almost ludicrous extreme on upper Broadway in New York, where the street is divided by a narrow central mall, right in the middle of traffic. At the cross-street intersections of this long north-south mall, benches have been placed behind big concrete buffers and on any day when the weather is even barely tolerable these benches are filled with people at block after block after block, watching the pedestrians who cross the mall in front of them, watching the traffic, watching the people on the busy sidewalks, watching each other. Eventually Broadway reaches Columbia University and Barnard College, one to the right, the other to the left. Here all is obvious order and quiet. No more stores, no more activity generated by the stores, almost no more pedestrians crossing — and no more watchers. The benches are there but they go empty in even the finest weather. I have tried them and can see why. No place could be more boring. Even the students of these institutions shun the solitude. They are doing their outdoor loitering, outdoor homework and general street watching on the steps overlooking the busiest campus crossing.

It is just so on city streets elsewhere. A lively street always has both its users and pure watchers. Last year I was on such a street in the Lower East Side of Manhattan, waiting for a bus. I had not been there longer than a minute, barely long enough to begin taking in the street's activity of errand goers, children playing, and loiterers on the stoops, when my attention was attracted by a woman who opened a window on the third floor of a tenement across the street and vigorously yoo-hooed at me. When I caught on that she wanted my attention and responded, she shouted down, "The bus doesn't run here on Saturdays!" Then by a combination of shouts and pantomime she directed me around the corner. This woman was one of thousands upon thousands of people in New York who casually take care of the streets. They notice strangers. They observe everything going on. If they need to take action, whether to direct a stranger waiting in the wrong place or to call the police, they do so. Action usually requires, to be sure, a certain self-assurance about the actor's proprietorship of the street and the support he will get if necessary. . . . But even more fundamental than the action, and necessary to the action, is the watching itself.

Not everyone in cities helps to take care of the streets, and many a city resident or city worker is unaware of why his neighborhood is safe. The other day an incident occurred on the street where I live, and it interested me because of this point.

My block of the street, I must explain, is a small one, but it contains a remarkable range of buildings, varying from several vintages of tenements to three- and four-story houses that have been converted into low-rent flats with stores on the ground floor, or returned to single-family use like ours. Across the street there used to be mostly four-story brick tenements with stores below. But twelve years ago several buildings, from the corner to the middle of the block, were converted into one building with elevator apartments of small size and high rents.

The incident that attracted my attention was a suppressed struggle going on between a man and a little girl of eight or nine years old. The man seemed to be trying to get the girl to go with him. By turns he was directing a cajoling attention to her, and then assuming an air of nonchalance. The girl was making herself rigid, as children do when they resist, against the wall of one of the tenements across the street.

As I watched from our second-floor window, making up my mind how to intervene if it seemed advisable, I saw it was not going to be necessary. From the butcher shop beneath the tenement had emerged the woman who, with her husband, runs the shop; she was standing within earshot of the man, her arms folded and a look of determination on her face. Joe Cornacchia, who with his sons-in-law keeps the delicatessen, emerged about the same moment and stood solidly to the other side. Several heads poked out of the tenement windows above, one was withdrawn quickly and its owner reappeared a moment later in the doorway behind the man. Two men from the bar next to the butcher shop came to the doorway and waited. On my side of the street, I saw that the locksmith, the fruit man and the laundry proprietor had all come out of their shops and that the scene was also being surveyed from a number of windows besides ours. That man did not know it, but he was surrounded. Nobody was going to allow a little girl to be dragged off, even if nobody knew who she was.

I am sorry — sorry purely for dramatic purposes — to have to report that the little girl turned out to be the man's daughter.

Throughout the duration of the little drama, perhaps five minutes in all, no eyes appeared in the windows of the high-rent, small-apartment building. It was the only building of which this was true. When we first moved to our block, I

used to anticipate happily that perhaps soon all the buildings would be rehabili-
tated like that one. I know better now, and can only anticipate with gloom and
foreboding the recent news that exactly this transformation is scheduled for the
rest of the block frontage adjoining the high-rent building. The high-rent tenants,
most of whom are so transient we cannot even keep track of their faces,[1] have not
the remotest idea of who takes care of their street, or how. A city neighborhood
can absorb and protect a substantial number of these birds of passage, as our neighborhood does. But if and when the neighborhood finally *becomes* them, they will
gradually find the streets less secure; they will be vaguely mystified about it, and
if things get bad enough they will drift away to another neighborhood which is
mysteriously safer.

In some rich city neighborhoods, where there is little do-it-yourself surveillance, such as residential Park Avenue or upper Fifth Avenue in New York, street
watchers are hired. The monotonous sidewalks of residential Park Avenue, for
example, are surprisingly little used; their putative users are populating, instead,
the interesting store-, bar- and restaurant-filled sidewalks of Lexington Avenue
and Madison Avenue to east and west, and the cross streets leading to these. A
network of doormen and superintendents, of delivery boys and nursemaids, a
form of hired neighborhood, keeps residential Park Avenue supplied with eyes.
At night, with the security of the doormen as a bulwark, dog walkers safely ven-
ture forth and supplement the doormen. But this street is so blank of built-in
eyes, so devoid of concrete reasons for using or watching it instead of turning the
first corner off of it, that if its rents were to slip below the point where they could
support a plentiful hired neighborhood of doormen and elevator men, it would
undoubtedly become a woefully dangerous street.

Once a street is well equipped to handle strangers, once it has both a good,
effective demarcation between private and public spaces and has a basic supply
of activity and eyes, the more strangers the merrier.

Strangers become an enormous asset on the street on which I live, and the
spurs off it, particularly at night when safety assets are most needed. We are fortunate enough, on the street, to be gifted not only with a locally supported bar
and another around the corner, but also with a famous bar that draws continuous
troops of strangers from adjoining neighborhoods and even from out of town. It
is famous because the poet Dylan Thomas used to go there, and mentioned it in
his writing. This bar, indeed, works two distinct shifts. In the morning and early
afternoon it is a social gathering place for the old community of Irish longshore-
men and other craftsmen in the area, as it always was. But beginning in midafternoon it takes on a different life, more like a college bull session with beer,
combined with a literary cocktail party, and this continues until the early hours
of the morning. On a cold winter's night, as you pass the White Horse, and the
doors open, a solid wave of conversation and animation surges out and hits you;
very warming. The comings and goings from this bar do much to keep our street
reasonably populated until three in the morning, and it is a street always safe to
come home to. The only instance I know of a beating in our street occurred in

---

[1]Some, according to the storekeepers, live on beans and bread and spend their sojourn looking for a
place to live where all their money will not go for rent.

the dead hours between the closing of the bar and dawn. The beating was halted by one of our neighbors who saw it from his window and, unconsciously certain that even at night he was part of a web of strong street law and order, intervened.

A friend of mine lives on a street uptown where a church youth and community center, with many night dances and other activities, performs the same service for his street that the White Horse bar does for ours. Orthodox planning is much imbued with puritanical and Utopian conceptions of how people should spend their free time, and in planning, these moralisms on people's private lives are deeply confused with concepts about the workings of cities. In maintaining city street civilization, the White Horse bar and the church-sponsored youth center, different as they undoubtedly are, perform much the same public street civilizing service. There is not only room in cities for such differences and many more in taste, purpose and interest of occupation; cities also have a need for people with all these differences in taste and proclivity. The preferences of Utopians, and of other compulsive managers of other people's leisure, for one kind of legal enterprise over others is worse than irrelevant for cities. It is harmful. The greater and more plentiful the range of all legitimate interests (in the strictly legal sense) that city streets and their enterprises can satisfy, the better for the streets and for the safety and civilization of the city.

Questions for Discussion

1. At one point, Jacobs speaks disparagingly of city planners and city architectural designers. From her point of view, what mistakes do they make when trying to provide for the safety of city residents?

2. Jacobs says that "thousands upon thousands of people in New York . . . casually take care of the streets." Does this assertion agree with your impression of New York City? If not, how do you account for the disagreement?

3. Compare Jacobs' paragraphing with Hoagland's in "The Moose on the Wall" (pp. 199–204). Whose do you prefer? Why?

4. Jacobs says that the block on which she lives is fortunate in the number and variety of bars it has. Do your own observations support her view that bars contribute to the safety of city streets?

5. What restrains criminal activity in suburban neighborhoods? Do you prefer the kinds of restraints in effect there to the ones described in this essay?

6. Does this selection suggest that Jacobs may be nostalgic for an earlier form of city life? Why or why not?

Suggested Activities

1. Make up a list of the attractive and unattractive features of the neighborhood where you presently live. Compare your list with those of your classmates. What common patterns emerge?

2. Someone once said that in the twentieth century the center of American social life has

moved from the front porch to the back patio. Write an essay discussing the significance of this shift.

3. Write an essay describing the formal and informal controls on children's behavior in the neighborhood where you grew up. How were you protected? How were others protected from you?

4. Write a short essay describing the role played by one of the following institutions in the social life of your home town or neighborhood:

A drugstore   A movie theater

A park   A schoolyard

A Little League diamond   A restaurant

The Care and
Prevention of Disaster

JOHN KENNETH GALBRAITH

John Kenneth Galbraith (b. 1908), for many years Paul M. War-
burg Professor of Economics at Harvard University, is an
extraordinarily prolific writer. Author of over forty books on
subjects as diverse as the Great Depression, Indian art, and his
own Scottish ancestry, Galbraith is especially noted for his
trenchant economic and social analyses. Among his best-known
books are *The Affluent Society* (1958), *The New Industrial
State* (1967), and *Ambassador's Journal: A Personal Account
of the Kennedy Years* (1969). When questioned about his widely
admired style, Galbraith is reported to have said that to complete a work he writes four drafts, then writes a fifth one to "put
in the spontaneity everybody likes."

The selection reprinted here, which comes from *The Liberal Hour* (1960), is a compelling account of some of the major
causes of the stock market crash of 1929. Readers interested in
a fuller analysis of the crash should read Galbraith's book *The
Great Crash, 1929* (1955).

The decade of the twenties, or more precisely the eight years between the postwar
depression of 1920–21 and the stock market crash in October of 1929, were prosperous ones in the United States. The total output of the economy increased by
more than 50 per cent. The preceding decades had brought the automobile; now

THE CARE AND PREVENTION OF DISASTER   From *The Liberal Hour* by John Kenneth Galbraith, published by Houghton Mifflin Company. Copyright © 1960 by John Kenneth Galbraith. Reprinted by
permission of the publisher.

came many more automobiles and also roads on which they could be driven with reasonable reliability and comfort. The downtown section of the mid-continent city — Des Moines, Omaha, Minneapolis — dates to these years. It was then, more likely than not, that what is still the leading hotel, the tallest office building, and the biggest department store went up.

These years were also remarkable in another respect, for as time passed, it became increasingly evident that the prosperity could not last. Contained within it were the seeds of its own destruction. Herein lies the peculiar fascination of the period for a study in the problem of leadership. For almost no steps were taken during these years to arrest tendencies which were obviously leading, and which did lead, to disaster.

At least four things were seriously wrong, and they worsened as the decade passed. And knowledge of them does not depend on the always brilliant assistance of hindsight. At least three of these flaws were highly visible and widely discussed. In ascending order, not of importance but of visibility, they were as follows:

First, income in these prosperous years was being distributed with marked inequality. Although output per worker rose steadily during the period, wages were fairly stable as also were prices. As a result, business profits increased rapidly and so did incomes of the wealthy and the well-to-do. This tendency was nurtured by the assiduous and successful efforts of Secretary of the Treasury Andrew W. Mellon to reduce income taxes with special attention to the higher brackets. In 1929 the 5 per cent of the people with the highest incomes received perhaps a third of all personal income, and those at the very top were increasing their share. This meant that the economy was heavily and increasingly dependent on the luxury consumption of the well-to-do and on their willingness to reinvest what they did not or could not spend on themselves. Anything that shocked the confidence of the rich either in their personal or in their business future would have a bad effect on total spending and hence on the behavior of the economy.

This was the least visible flaw. To be sure farmers, who were not participating in the general advance, were making themselves heard; and twice during the period the Congress passed far-reaching farm relief legislation which was vetoed by Coolidge. But other groups were much less vocal. Income distribution in the United States had long been unequal. The inequality of these years did not seem exceptional. The trade union movement was also far from strong, and labor was little heard from. In the early twenties the steel industry was still working a twelve-hour day and a seven-day week. (Every two weeks, when the shift changed, a man worked twice around the clock.) Workers lacked the organization or the organizing power to deal even with conditions like this, and the twelve-hour day was, in fact, ended as the result of personal pressure by President Harding on the steel companies.[1] In all these circumstances the increasingly lopsided

[1]In particular on Judge Elbert H. Gary, the lawyer who was head of the United States Steel Corporation. Judge Gary's personal acquaintance with these working conditions was thought to be slight, and this gave rise to Benjamin Stolberg's classic sally that the Judge "never saw a blast furnace until his death."

income did not excite much comment or alarm. Perhaps it would have been surprising if it had.

But the other three flaws in the economy were far less subtle. During World War I the United States ceased to be the world's greatest debtor country and became its greatest creditor. The consequences of this change have been so often described that they have the standing of a cliché. A debtor country could export a greater value of goods than it imported and use the difference for interest and debt repayment. This was what we did before the First World War. But a creditor must import a greater value than it exports if those who owe it money are to have the wherewithal to pay interest and principal. Otherwise the creditor must either forgive the debts or make new loans to pay off the old.[2]

During the twenties the balance was maintained by making new foreign loans. Their promotion was profitable to domestic investment houses. And when the supply of honest and competent foreign borrowers ran out, dishonest, incompetent or fanciful borrowers were invited to borrow and, on occasion, bribed to do so. In 1927 Juan Leguia, the son of the current dictator of Peru, was paid $450,000 by the National City Company, an affiliate of the National City Bank, and by J. & W. Seligman for his services in promoting a $50,000,000 loan to Peru which these houses marketed. Americans lost and the Peruvians didn't gain much. Other Latin American republics got equally dubious loans by equally dubious devices. And for reasons that now tax the imagination, so did a large number of German cities and municipalities. Obviously, once investors awoke to the character of these loans, or there was any other shock to confidence, they would no longer be made. There would be nothing with which to pay the old loans. Given this arithmetic, there would be either a sharp reduction in exports, or a wholesale default on the outstanding loans, or more likely both. Wheat and cotton farmers and others who depended on exports would suffer. So would those who owned the bonds. The buying power of both would be reduced. These consequences were freely predicted at the time.

The second weakness of the economy was the large-scale corporate thimblerigging that was going on. This took a variety of forms of which by far the most common was the organization of corporations to hold stock in yet other corporations which, in turn, held stock in yet other corporations. In the case of the railroad and the utilities, the purpose of this pyramid of holding companies was to obtain control of a very large number of operating companies with a very small investment in the ultimate holding company. A hundred million dollar electric utility, of which the capitalization was represented half by bonds and half by common stock, could be controlled with an investment of a little over twenty-five million — the value of just over half the common stock. Were a company then formed with the same capital structure to hold *this* twenty-five million worth of common stock, it could be controlled with an investment of $6.25 million. On the next round the amount required would be less than two million. That two million would still control the entire hundred million dollar edifice. By

[2]In modern times two new correctives of imbalance have come into extensive use. These are government loans and gifts. In the twenties government loans were not yet a peacetime commonplace, and large-scale public gifts as yet uninvented, at least by the United States.

the end of the twenties holding company structures six or eight tiers high were commonplace. Some of them — the utility pyramid of Insull and Associated Gas & Electric, and the railroad pyramid of the Van Sweringens — were marvelously complex. It is unlikely that anyone fully understood them or could.

In other cases companies were organized to hold securities in other companies and thus to manufacture more securities to sell to the public. This was true of the great investment trusts. During 1929 one investment house, Goldman, Sachs & Company, organized and sold nearly a billion dollars worth of securities in three interconnected investment trusts — Goldman, Sachs Trading Corporation, Shenandoah Corporation, and the Blue Ridge Corporation. All eventually depreciated virtually to nothing. This was, perhaps, the greatest financial fiasco in our history.

This corporate insanity was also highly visible. So was the damage. The pyramids would last only so long as earnings of the company at the bottom were secure. If anything happened to the dividends of the underlying company, there would be trouble for upstream companies that had issued bonds (or in practice sometimes preferred stock) against the dividends on the stock of the downstream companies. Once the earnings stopped, the bonds would go into default or the preferred stock would take over and the pyramid would collapse. Such a collapse would have a bad effect not only on the orderly prosecution of business and investment by the operating companies but also on confidence, investment, and spending by the community at large. The likelihood was increased because in a number of cities — Cleveland, Detroit, and Chicago were notable examples — the banks were deeply committed to these pyramids or had fallen under the control of the pyramiders.

Finally, and most evident of all, was the stock market boom. Month after month and year after year, prices rose and people became increasingly preoccupied with the market. In May of 1924 the *New York Times* industrials stood at 106; by the end of the year they were 134; by the end of 1925 they were up to 181. In 1927 the advance began in earnest — to 245 by the end of that year and on to 331 by the end of 1928. There were some setbacks in early 1929, but then came the fantastic summer explosion when in a matter of three months the averages went up another 110 points. This was perhaps the most frantic summer in our financial history. By its end stock prices had quadrupled as compared with four years earlier. Transactions on the New York Stock Exchange regularly ran to five million or more shares a day. Radio (adjusted) went to 505 without ever having paid a dividend. Only the old-fashioned or the eccentric held securities for their income. What counted was the increase in capital values.

And since capital gains were what counted, one could vastly increase his opportunities by extending his holdings with borrowed funds — by buying on margin. Margin accounts expanded enormously, and from all over the country, indeed from all over the world, money poured into New York to finance these transactions. During the summer of 1929 brokers' loans increased at the rate of $400,000,000 a month. By September they totaled more than $7,000,000,000. The rate of interest on these loans varied from 7 to 12 per cent and went as high as 15.

The boom was also inherently self-liquidating. It could last only as long as new people, or at least new money, was pouring into the market in pursuit of the capital gains. This new demand bid up the stocks and made the capital gains. Once the supply of new customers began to falter, the market would cease to rise. Once the market stopped rising there would be no more gains and some, perhaps a good many, would start to cash in. If you are concerned with capital gains, you must get them while the getting is good. But the getting will start the market down, and this would one day be the signal for much more selling — both by those who were trying to get out and those who were being forced to sell securities that were no longer safely margined. Thus the market was certain one day to go down and far more rapidly than it went up. Down it went with a thunderous crash in October of 1929. In a series of terrible days, of which Thursday, October 24, and Tuesday, October 29, were the most terrifying, billions in values were lost, and thousands of speculators — they had been called investors — were utterly and totally ruined.

This too had far-reaching effects. Economists have rather deprecated the tendency to attribute too much to the great stock market collapse of 1929. That was the drama. The causes of the subsequent depression really lay deeper. In fact, the stock market crash was very important. It exposed the other weakness of the economy. The overseas loans on which the payments balance depended came to an end. The jerry-built holding company structures came tumbling down. The investment trust stocks collapsed. The crash put a marked crimp on borrowing for investment and therewith on business spending. It also removed from the economy some billions of consumer spending that was either based on, sanctioned by, or encouraged by stock market gains. The crash was an intensely damaging thing.

And this damage, too, was not only foreseeable but foreseen. For months the speculative frenzy had all but dominated American life. Many times before in history — the South Sea Bubble, John Law's speculations, the recurrent real estate booms of the Nineteenth Century, the Florida land boom earlier in the same decade — there had been similar frenzy. And the end had always come not with a whimper but a bang. Many men, including in 1929 the President of the United States, knew it would again be so.

Questions for Discussion

1. Galbraith presents the four things that were wrong with the economy in the 1920s in an "ascending order . . . of visibility." Why do you think he chose this order of presentation? How effective is his use of it?

2. Near the outset of this selection, Galbraith says that although people in the 1920s knew a crash was imminent, they did little to avert it. How does his analysis of the situation help to explain why people failed to act more decisively?

3. When Galbraith says "thousands of speculators — they had been called investors — were utterly and totally ruined," he juxtaposes a term of his own with one used by the par-

ticipants in the "speculative frenzy" of the 1920s. How do the connotations of the two terms differ?

4. Discuss the title of this selection. What does it reveal about Galbraith's attitude toward his subject?

5. Discuss Galbraith's use of technical terms from the field of economics. What assumptions do you think he is making about the nature of his audience?

6. Would you agree or disagree if someone described this selection as a study in mass psychology? Why?

Suggested Activities

1. Have two or three of your acquaintances who are conversant with the current economic situation read this essay; then ask them if they believe anything of equivalent seriousness is going wrong now. Compare their responses with those gathered by your classmates.

2. Make a report to the class on one of the following individuals or events mentioned in this selection:

> Juan Leguia   The Goldman, Sachs & Company collapse
>
> Samuel Insull   The South Sea Bubble
>
> John Law

3. Write an essay describing your troubles with money. If you wish, make it a humorous one.

4. When Galbraith uses the phrase "not with a whimper but a bang" near the end of this selection, he is alluding to T. S. Eliot's poem "The Hollow Men." Read this poem and write a paragraph analyzing the significance of the allusion.

Eleven
Blue Men

BERTON ROUECHÉ

For biographical information on Berton Roueché, see page 185. "Eleven Blue Men," the selection reprinted here, was first published in book form in Rauché's *Eleven Blue Men, and Other Narratives of Medical Detection* (1953); it was recently republished in *The Medical Detectives* (1980). The essay is a fascinating account of how a team of epidemiologists determined the cause of a mysterious outbreak of illness among a group of derelicts.

At about eight o'clock on Monday morning, September 25, 1944, a ragged, aimless old man of eighty-two collapsed on the sidewalk on Dey Street, near the Hudson Terminal. Innumerable people must have noticed him, but he lay there alone for several minutes, dazed, doubled up with abdominal cramps, and in an agony of retching. Then a policeman came along. Until the policeman bent over the old man, he may have supposed that he had just a sick drunk on his hands; wanderers dropped by drink are common in that part of town in the early morning. It was not an opinion that he could have held for long. The old man's nose, lips, ears, and fingers were sky-blue. The policeman went to a telephone and put in an ambulance call to Beekman-Downtown Hospital, half a dozen blocks away. The old man was carried into the emergency room there at eight-thirty. By that time, he was unconscious and the blueness had spread over a large part of his body.

The examining physician attributed the old man's morbid color to cyanosis, a condition that usually results from an insufficient supply of oxygen in the blood, and also noted that he was diarrheic and in a severe state of shock. The course of treatment prescribed by the doctor was conventional. It included an instant gastric lavage, heart stimulants, bed rest, and oxygen therapy. Presently, the old man recovered an encouraging, if painful, consciousness and demanded, irascibly and in the name of God, to know what had happened to him. It was a question that, at the moment, nobody could answer with much confidence.

For the immediate record, the doctor made a free-hand diagnosis of carbon-monoxide poisoning — from what source, whether an automobile or a gas pipe, it was, of course, pointless even to guess. Then, because an isolated instance of gas poisoning is something of a rarity in a section of the city as crammed with human beings as downtown Manhattan, he and his colleagues in the emergency room braced themselves for at least a couple more victims. Their foresight was promptly and generously rewarded. A second man was rolled in at ten-twenty-five. Forty minutes later, an ambulance drove up with three more men. At eleven-twenty, two others were brought in. An additional two arrived during the next fifteen minutes. Around noon, still another was admitted. All of these nine men were also elderly and dilapidated, all had been in misery for at least an hour, and all were rigid, cyanotic, and in a state of shock. The entire body of one, a bony, seventy-three-year-old consumptive named John Mitchell, was blue. Five of the nine, including Mitchell, had been stricken in the Globe Hotel, a sunless, upstairs flophouse at 190 Park Row, and two in a similar place, called the Star Hotel, at 3 James Street. Another had been found slumped in the doorway of a condemned building on Park Row, not far from City Hall Park, by a policeman. The ninth had keeled over in front of the Eclipse Cafeteria, at 6 Chatham Square. At a quarter to seven that evening, one more aged blue man was brought in. He had been lying, too sick to ask for help, on his cot in a cubicle in the Lion Hotel, another flophouse, at 26 Bowery, since ten o'clock that morning. A clerk had finally looked in and seen him.

By the time this last blue man arrived at the hospital, an investigation of the case by the Department of Health, to which all outbreaks of an epidemiological nature must be reported, had been under way for five hours. Its findings thus far had not been illuminating. The investigation was conducted by two men. One was the Health Department's chief epidemiologist, Dr. Morris Greenberg, a small, fragile, reflective man of fifty-seven, who is now acting director of the Bureau of Preventable Diseases; the other was Dr. Ottavio Pellitteri, a field epidemiologist, who, since 1946, has been administrative medical inspector for the Bureau. He is thirty-six years old, pale, and stocky, and has a bristling black mustache. One day, when I was in Dr. Greenberg's office, he and Dr. Pellitteri told me about the case. Their recollection of it is, understandably, vivid. The derelicts were the victims of a type of poisoning so rare that only ten previous outbreaks of it had been recorded in medical literature. Of these, two were in the United States and two in Germany; the others had been reported in France, England, Switzerland, Algeria, Australia, and India. Up to September 25, 1944, the largest number of people stricken in a single outbreak was four. That was in Algeria, in 1926.

The Beekman-Downtown Hospital telephoned a report of the occurrence to the Health Department just before noon. As is customary, copies of the report were sent to all the Department's administrative offices. "Mine was on my desk when I got back from lunch," Dr. Greenberg said to me. "It didn't sound like much. Nine persons believed to be suffering from carbon-monoxide poisoning had been admitted during the morning, and all of them said that they had eaten breakfast at the Eclipse Cafeteria, at 6 Chatham Square. Still, it was a job for us. I checked with the clerk who handles assignments and found that Pellitteri had gone out on it. That was all I wanted to know. If it amounted to anything, I knew he'd phone me before making a written report. That's an arrangement we have here. Well, a couple of hours later I got a call from him. My interest perked right up."

"I was at the hospital," Dr. Pellitteri told me, "and I'd talked to the staff and most of the men. There were ten of them by then, of course. They were sick as dogs, but only one was in really bad shape."

"That was John Mitchell," Dr. Greenberg put in. "He died the next night. I understand his condition was hopeless from the start. The others, including the old boy who came in last, pulled through all right. Excuse me, Ottavio, but I just thought I'd get that out of the way. Go on."

Dr. Pellitteri nodded. "I wasn't at all convinced that it was gas poisoning," he continued. "The staff was beginning to doubt it, too. The symptoms weren't quite right. There didn't seem to be any of the headache and general dopiness that you get with gas. What really made me suspicious was this: Only two or three of the men had eaten breakfast in the cafeteria at the same time. They had straggled in all the way from seven o'clock to ten. That meant that the place would have had to be full of gas for at least three hours, which is preposterous. It also indicated that we ought to have had a lot more sick people than we did. Those Chatham Square eating places have a big turnover. Well, to make sure, I checked with Bellevue, Gouverneur, St. Vincent's, and the other downtown hospitals. None of them had seen a trace of cyanosis. Then I talked to the sick men some more. I learned two interesting things. One was that they had all got sick right after eating. Within thirty minutes. The other was that all but one had eaten oatmeal, rolls, and coffee. He ate just oatmeal. When ten men eat the same thing in the same place on the same day and then all come down with the same illness . . . I told Greenberg that my hunch was food poisoning."

"I was willing to rule out gas," Dr. Greenberg said. A folder containing data on the case lay on the desk before him. He lifted the cover thoughtfully, then let it drop. "And I agreed that the oatmeal sounded pretty suspicious. That was as far as I was willing to go. Common, ordinary, everyday food poisoning—I gathered that was what Pellitteri had in mind—wasn't a very satisfying answer. For one thing, cyanosis is hardly symptomatic of that. On the other hand, diarrhea and severe vomiting are, almost invariably. But they weren't in the clinical picture, I found, except in two or three of the cases. Moreover, the incubation periods—the time lapse between eating and illness—were extremely short. As you probably know, most food poisoning is caused by eating something that has been contaminated by bacteria. The usual offenders are the staphylococci—they're mostly responsible for boils and skin infections and so on — and the salmonella. The latter are related to the typhoid organism. In a staphylococcus case, the first symptoms rarely develop in under two hours. Often, it's closer to five. The incubation period in the other ranges from twelve to thirty-six hours. But here we were with something that hit in thirty minutes or less. Why, one of the men had got only as far as the sidewalk in front of the cafeteria before he was knocked out. Another fact that Pellitteri had dug up struck me as very significant. All of the men told him that the illness had come on with extraordinary suddenness. One minute they were feeling fine, and the next minute they were practically helpless. That was another point against the ordinary food-poisoning theory. Its onset is never that fast. Well, that suddenness began to look like a lead. It led me to suspect that some drug might be to blame. A quick and sudden reaction is characteristic of a great many drugs. So is the combination of cyanosis and shock."

"None of the men were on dope," Dr. Pellitteri said. "I told Greenberg I was sure of that. Their pleasure was booze."

"That was O.K.," Dr. Greenberg said. "They could have got a toxic dose of some drug by accident. In the oatmeal, most likely. I couldn't help thinking that the oatmeal was relevant to our problem. At any rate, the drug idea was very persuasive."

"So was Greenberg," Dr. Pellitteri remarked with a smile. "Actually, it was the only explanation in sight that seemed to account for everything we knew about the clinical and environmental picture."

"All we had to do now was prove it," Dr. Greenberg went on mildly. "I asked Pellitteri to get a blood sample from each of the men before leaving the hospital for a look at the cafeteria. We agreed he would send the specimens to the city toxicologist, Dr. Alexander O. Gettler, for an overnight analysis. I wanted to know if the blood contained methemoglobin. Methemoglobin is a compound that's formed only when any one of several drugs enters the blood. Gettler's report would tell us if we were at least on the right track. That is, it would give us a yes-or-no answer on drugs. If the answer was yes, then we could go on from there to identify the particular drug. How we would go about that would depend on what Pellitteri was able to turn up at the cafeteria. In the meantime, there was nothing for me to do but wait for their reports. I'd theorized myself hoarse."

Dr. Pellitteri, having attended to his bloodletting with reasonable dispatch, reached the Eclipse Cafeteria at around five o'clock. "It was about what I'd expected," he told me. "Strictly a horse market, and dirtier than most. The sort of place where you can get a full meal for fifteen cents. There was a grind house on one side, a cigar store on the other, and the 'L' overhead. Incidentally, the Eclipse went out of business a year or so after I was there, but that had nothing to do with us. It was just a coincidence. Well, the place looked deserted and the door was locked. I knocked, and a man came out of the back and let me in. He was one of our people, a health inspector for the Bureau of Food and Drugs, named Weinberg. His bureau had stepped into the case as a matter of routine, because of the reference to a restaurant in the notification report. I was glad to see him and to have his help. For one thing, he had put a temporary embargo on everything in the cafeteria. That's why it was closed up. His main job, though, was to check the place for violations of the sanitation code. He was finding plenty."

"Let me read you a few of Weinberg's findings," Dr. Greenberg said, extracting a paper from the folder on his desk. "None of them had any direct bearing on our problem, but I think they'll give you a good idea of what the Eclipse was like — what too many restaurants are like. This copy of his report lists fifteen specific violations. Here they are: 'Premises heavily infested with roaches. Fly infestation throughout premises. Floor defective in rear part of dining room. Kitchen walls and ceiling encrusted with grease and soot. Kitchen floor encrusted with dirt. Refuse under kitchen fixtures. Sterilizing facilities inadequate. Sink defective. Floor and walls at serving tables and coffee urns encrusted with dirt. Kitchen utensils encrusted with dirt and grease. Storage-cellar walls, ceiling, and floor encrusted with dirt. Floor and shelves in cellar covered with refuse and useless material. Cellar ceiling defective. Sewer pipe leaking. Open sewer line in cellar.' Well . . ." He gave me a squeamish smile and stuck the paper back in the folder.

"I can see it now," Dr. Pellitteri said. "And smell it. Especially the kitchen, where I spent most of my time. Weinberg had the proprietor and the cook out there, and I talked to them while he prowled around. They were very coöperative. Naturally. They were scared to death. They knew nothing about gas in the place and there was no sign of any, so I went to work on the food. None of what had been prepared for breakfast that morning was left. That, of course, would have been too much to hope for. But I was able to get together some of the kind of stuff that had gone into the men's breakfast, so that we could make a chemical determination at the Department. What I took was ground coffee, sugar, a mixture of evaporated milk and water that passed for cream, some bakery rolls, a five-pound carton of dry oatmeal, and some salt. The salt had been used in preparing the oatmeal. That morning, like every morning, the cook told me, he had prepared six gallons of oatmeal, enough to serve around a hundred and twenty-five people. To make it, he used five pounds of dry cereal, four gallons of water — regular city water — and a handful of salt. That was his term — a handful. There was an open gallon can of salt standing on the stove. He said the handful he'd put in that morning's oatmeal had come from that. He refilled the can on the stove every morning from a big supply can. He pointed out the big can — it was up on a shelf — and as I was getting it down to take with me, I saw another can, just like it, nearby. I took that one down, too. It was also full of salt, or, rather, something that looked like salt. The proprietor said it wasn't salt. He said it was saltpetre — sodium nitrate — that he used in corning beef and in making pastrami. Well, there isn't any harm in saltpetre; it doesn't even act as an anti-aphrodisiac, as a lot of people seem to think. But I wrapped it up with the other loot and took it along, just for fun. The fact is, I guess, everything in that damn place looked like poison."

After Dr. Pellitteri had deposited his loot with a Health Department chemist, Andrew J. Pensa, who promised to have a report ready by the following afternoon, he dined hurriedly at a restaurant in which he had confidence and returned to Chatham Square. There he spent the evening making the rounds of the lodging houses in the neighborhood. He had heard at Mr. Pensa's office that an eleventh blue man had been admitted to the hospital, and before going home he wanted to make sure that no other victims had been overlooked. By midnight, having covered all the likely places and having rechecked the downtown hospitals, he was satisfied. He repaired to his office and composed a formal progress report for Dr. Greenberg. Then he went home and to bed.

The next morning, Tuesday, Dr. Pellitteri dropped by the Eclipse, which was still closed but whose proprietor and staff he had told to return for questioning. Dr. Pellitteri had another talk with the proprietor and the cook. He also had a few inconclusive words with the rest of the cafeteria's employees — two dishwashers, a busboy, and a counterman. As he was leaving, the cook, who had apparently passed an uneasy night with his conscience, remarked that it was possible that he had absent-mindedly refilled the salt can on the stove from the one that contained saltpetre. "That was interesting," Dr. Pellitteri told me, "even though such a possibility had already occurred to me, and even though I didn't know whether it was important or not. I assured him that he had nothing to worry about. We had been certain all along that nobody had deliberately poisoned the old men." From the Eclipse, Dr. Pellitteri went on to Dr. Greenberg's office, where Dr. Gettler's report was waiting.

"Gettler's test for methemoglobin was positive," Dr. Greenberg said. "It had to be a drug now. Well, so far so good. Then we heard from Pensa."

"Greenberg almost fell out of his chair when he read Pensa's report," Dr. Pellitteri observed cheerfully.

"That's an exaggeration," Dr. Greenberg said. "I'm not easily dumfounded. We're inured to the incredible around here. Why, a few years ago we had a case involving some numskull who stuck a fistful of potassium-thiocyanate crystals, a very nasty poison, in the coils of an office water cooler, just for a practical joke. However, I can't deny that Pensa rather taxed our credulity. What he had found was that the small salt can and the one that was supposed to be full of sodium nitrate both contained sodium *nitrite*. The other food samples, incidentally, were O.K."

"That also taxed my credulity," Dr. Pellitteri said.

Dr. Greenberg smiled. "There's a great deal of difference between nitrate and nitrite," he continued. "Their only similarity, which is an unfortunate one, is that they both look and taste more or less like ordinary table salt. Sodium nitrite isn't the most powerful poison in the world, but a little of it will do a lot of harm. If you remember, I said before that this case was almost without precedent — only ten outbreaks like it on record. Ten is practically none. In fact, sodium-nitrite poisoning is so unusual that some of the standard texts on toxicology don't even mention it. So Pensa's report was pretty startling. But we accepted it, of course, without question or hesitation. Facts are facts. And we were glad to. It seemed to explain everything very nicely. What I've been saying about sodium-nitrite poisoning doesn't mean that sodium nitrite itself is rare. Actually, it's fairly common. It's used in the manufacture of dyes and as a medical drug. We use it in treating certain heart conditions and for high blood pressure. But it also has another important use, one that made its presence at the Eclipse sound plausible. In recent years, and particularly during the war, sodium nitrite has been used as a substitute for sodium nitrate in preserving meat. The government permits it but stipulates that the finished meat must not contain more than one part of sodium nitrite per five thousand parts of meat. Cooking will safely destroy enough of that small quantity of the drug." Dr. Greenberg shrugged. "Well, Pellitteri had had the cook pick up a handful of salt — the same amount, as nearly as possible, as went into the oatmeal — and then had taken this to his office and found that it weighed approximately a hundred grams. So we didn't have to think twice to realize that the proportion of nitrite in that batch of cereal was considerably higher than one to five thousand. Roughly, it must have been around one to about eighty before cooking destroyed part of the nitrite. It certainly looked as though Gettler, Pensa, and the cafeteria cook between them had given us our answer. I called up Gettler and told him what Pensa had discovered and asked him to run a specific test for nitrites on his blood samples. He had, as a matter of course, held some blood back for later examination. His confirmation came through in a couple of hours. I went home that night feeling pretty good."

Dr. Greenberg's serenity was a fugitive one. He awoke on Wednesday morning troubled in mind. A question had occurred to him that he was unable to ignore. "Something like a hundred and twenty-five people ate oatmeal at the Eclipse that morning," he said to me, "but only eleven of them got sick. Why? The undeniable fact that those eleven old men were made sick by the ingestion of a toxic dose of sodium nitrite wasn't enough to rest on. I wanted to know exactly how much sodium nitrite each portion of that cooked oatmeal had contained. With Pensa's help again, I found out. We prepared a batch just like the one the cook had made on Monday. Then Pensa measured out six ounces, the size of the average portion served at the Eclipse, and analyzed it. It contained two and a half grains of sodium nitrite. That explained why the hundred and fourteen other people did not become ill. The toxic dose of sodium nitrite is three grains. But it didn't explain how each of our eleven old men had received an additional half grain. It seemed extremely unlikely that the extra touch of nitrite had been in the oatmeal when it was served. It had to come in later. Then I began to get a glimmer. Some people sprinkle a little salt, instead of sugar, on hot cereal. Suppose, I thought, that the busboy, or whoever had the job of keeping the table salt shakers filled, had made the same mistake that the cook had. It seemed plausible. Pellitteri was out of the office — I've forgotten where — so I got Food and Drugs to step over to the Eclipse, which was still under embargo, and bring back the shakers for Pensa to work on. There were seventeen of them, all good-sized, one for each table. Sixteen contained either pure sodium chloride or just a few inconsequential traces of sodium nitrite mixed in with the real salt, but the other was point thirty-seven per cent nitrite. That one was enough. A spoonful of that salt contained a bit more than half a grain."

"I went over to the hospital Thursday morning," Dr. Pellitteri said. "Greenberg wanted me to check the table-salt angle with the men. They could tie the case up neatly for us. I drew a blank. They'd been discharged the night before, and God only knew where they were."

"Naturally," Dr. Greenberg said, "it would have been nice to know for a fact that the old boys all sat at a certain table and that all of them put about a spoonful of salt from that particular shaker on their oatmeal, but it wasn't essential. I was morally certain that they had. There just wasn't any other explanation. There was one other question, however. Why did they use so *much* salt? For my own peace of mind, I wanted to know. All of a sudden, I remembered Pellitteri had said they were all heavy drinkers. Well, several recent clinical studies have demonstrated that there is usually a subnormal concentration of sodium chloride in the blood of alcoholics. Either they don't eat enough to get sufficient salt or they lose it more rapidly than other people do, or both. Whatever the reasons are, the conclusion was all I needed. Any animal, you know, whether a mouse or a man, tends to try to obtain a necessary substance that his body lacks. The final question had been answered."

Questions for Discussion

1. Roueché never expresses his personal opinion of the skid-row setting of his narrative. How does his restraint in this regard affect the tone of his essay?

2. Even though the examining physician at Beekman-Downtown Hospital makes a misdiagnosis, Roueché leaves us with the impression that he is a competent physician. How does he do this?

3. Examine the use of medical terms in this essay. How does Roueché keep his definitions of these terms from being obtrusive?

4. At what point in the narrative is Dr. Greenberg certain of the solution to the mystery? Why does he continue the investigation beyond this point? How does his doing so affect your understanding of him?

5. What narrative techniques does Roueché use that you would normally expect to find in a work of fiction? How effective is his use of them?

6. Roueché follows a strict chronological order in this essay. Do you think he is right to do so? Why or why not?

Suggested Activities

1. Give a report to the class on the controversy in recent years over the use of sodium nitrate and sodium nitrite as meat preservatives. How have attitudes toward the use of these substances changed since Roueché wrote "Eleven Blue Men"?

2. Write a paragraph describing something noteworthy that happened to you in the last few weeks. Aim for the same level of specificity as Roueché achieves in the first paragraph of "Eleven Blue Men."

3. Write a cause-and-effect essay analyzing a serious mistake you once made. What caused you to make the mistake? What were its effects? Did any good come of it?

On Being
the Right Size

J. B. S. HALDANE

An Englishman, J. B. S. Haldane (1892-1964) was educated at
Eton and New College, Oxford. After spending ten years as
Reader in Biochemistry at Cambridge University (1922-32), he
became Professor of Biometry at London University, a position
he held until his retirement in 1957. His many popular books on
scientific subjects include *Possible Worlds* (1928), *Science and
Everyday Life* (1939), and *Keeping Cool* (1939). In the following
selection from *Possible Worlds,* Haldane uses imaginative
examples to demonstrate why "for every type of animal there
is a most convenient size."

The most obvious differences between different animals are differences of size,
but for some reason the zoologists have paid singularly little attention to them.
In a large textbook of zoology before me I find no indication that the eagle is
larger than the sparrow, or the hippopotamus bigger than the hare, though some
grudging admissions are made in the case of the mouse and the whale. But yet it
is easy to show that a hare could not be as large as a hippopotamus, or a whale as
small as a herring. For every type of animal there is a most convenient size, and
a large change in size inevitably carries with it a change of form.

Let us take the most obvious of possible cases, and consider a giant man sixty
feet high — about the height of Giant Pope and Giant Pagan in the illustrated
Pilgrim's Progress of my childhood. These monsters were not only ten times as

high as Christian, but ten times as wide and ten times as thick, so that their total weight was a thousand times his, or about eighty to ninety tons. Unfortunately the cross sections of their bones were only a hundred times those of Christian, so that every square inch of giant bone had to support ten times the weight borne by a square inch of human bone. As the human thigh-bone breaks under about ten times the human weight, Pope and Pagan would have broken their thighs every time they took a step. This was doubtless why they were sitting down in the picture I remember. But it lessens one's respect for Christian and Jack the Giant Killer.

To turn to zoology, suppose that a gazelle, a graceful little creature with long thin legs, is to become large, it will break its bones unless it does one of two things. It may make its legs short and thick, like the rhinoceros, so that every pound of weight has still about the same area of bone to support it. Or it can compress its body and stretch out its legs obliquely to gain stability, like the giraffe. I mention these two beasts because they happen to belong to the same order as the gazelle, and both are quite successful mechanically, being remarkably fast runners.

Gravity, a mere nuisance to Christian, was a terror to Pope, Pagan, and Despair. To the mouse and any smaller animal it presents practically no dangers. You can drop a mouse down a thousand-yard mine shaft; and, on arriving at the bottom, it gets a slight shock and walks away, provided that the ground is fairly soft. A rat is killed, a man is broken, a horse splashes. For the resistance presented to movement by the air is proportional to the surface of the moving object. Divide an animal's length, breadth, and height each by ten; its weight is reduced to a thousandth, but its surface only to a hundredth. So the resistance to falling in the case of the small animal is relatively ten times greater than the driving force.

An insect, therefore, is not afraid of gravity; it can fall without danger, and can cling to the ceiling with remarkably little trouble. It can go in for elegant and fantastic forms of support like that of the daddy-long-legs. But there is a force which is as formidable to an insect as gravitation to a mammal. This is surface tension. A man coming out of a bath carries with him a film of water of about one-fiftieth of an inch in thickness. This weighs roughly a pound. A wet mouse has to carry about its own weight of water. A wet fly has to lift many times its own weight and, as every one knows, a fly once wetted by water or any other liquid is in a very serious position indeed. An insect going for a drink is in as great danger as a man leaning out over a precipice in search of food. If it once falls into the grip of the surface tension of the water — that is to say, gets wet — it is likely to remain so until it drowns. A few insects, such as water-beetles, contrive to be unwettable; the majority keep well away from their drink by means of a long proboscis.

Of course tall land animals have other difficulties. They have to pump their blood to greater heights than a man and, therefore, require a larger blood pressure and tougher blood-vessels. A great many men die from burst arteries, especially in the brain, and this danger is presumably still greater for an elephant or a giraffe. But animals of all kinds find difficulties in size for the following reason.

A typical small animal, say a microscopic worm or rotifer, has a smooth skin through which all the oxygen it requires can soak in, a straight gut with sufficient surface to absorb its food, and a simple kidney. Increase its dimensions tenfold in every direction, and its weight is increased a thousand times, so that if it is to use its muscles as efficiently as its miniature counterpart, it will need a thousand times as much food and oxygen per day and will excrete a thousand times as much of waste products.

Now if its shape is unaltered its surface will be increased only a hundredfold, and ten times as much oxygen must enter per minute through each square millimetre of skin, ten times as much food through each square millimetre of intestine. When a limit is reached to their absorptive powers their surface has to be increased by some special device. For example, a part of the skin may be drawn out into tufts to make gills or pushed in to make lungs, thus increasing the oxygen-absorbing surface in proportion to the animal's bulk. A man, for example, has a hundred square yards of lung. Similarly, the gut, instead of being smooth and straight, becomes coiled and develops a velvety surface, and other organs increase in complication. The higher animals are not larger than the lower because they are more complicated. They are more complicated because they are larger. Just the same is true of plants. The simplest plants, such as the green algae growing in stagnant water or on the bark of trees, are mere round cells. The higher plants increase their surface by putting out leaves and roots. Comparative anatomy is largely the story of the struggle to increase surface in proportion to volume.

Some of the methods of increasing the surface are useful up to a point, but not capable of a very wide adaptation. For example, while vertebrates carry the oxygen from the gills or lungs all over the body in the blood, insects take air directly to every part of their body by tiny blind tubes called tracheae which open to the surface at many different points. Now, although by their breathing movements they can renew the air in the outer part of the tracheal system, the oxygen has to penetrate the finer branches by means of diffusion. Gases can diffuse easily through very small distances, not many times larger than the average length travelled by a gas molecule between collisions with other molecules. But when such vast journeys — from the point of view of a molecule — as a quarter of an inch have to be made, the process becomes slow. So the portions of an insect's body more than a quarter of an inch from the air would always be short of oxygen. In consequence hardly any insects are much more than half an inch thick. Land crabs are built on the same general plan as insects, but are much clumsier. Yet like ourselves they carry oxygen around in their blood, and are therefore able to grow far larger than any insects. If the insects had hit on a plan for driving air through their tissues instead of letting it soak in, they might well have become as large as lobsters, though other considerations would have prevented them from becoming as large as man.

Exactly the same difficulties attach to flying. It is an elementary principle of aeronautics that the minimum speed needed to keep an aeroplane of a given shape in the air varies as the square root of its length. If its linear dimensions are increased four times, it must fly twice as fast. Now the power needed for the minimum speed increases more rapidly than the weight of the machine. So the larger aeroplane, which weighs sixty-four times as much as the smaller, needs one hundred and twenty-eight times its horsepower to keep up. Applying the same principles to the birds, we find that the limit to their size is soon reached. An angel whose muscles developed no more power weight for weight than those of an eagle or a pigeon would require a breast projecting for about four feet to house the muscles engaged in working its wings, while to economize in weight, its legs would have to be reduced to mere stilts. Actually a large bird such as an eagle or kite does not keep in the air mainly by moving its wings. It is generally to be seen soaring, that is to say balanced on a rising column of air. And even soaring becomes more and more difficult with increasing size. Were this not the case eagles might be as large as tigers and as formidable to man as hostile aeroplanes.

But it is time that we passed to some of the advantages of size. One of the most obvious is that it enables one to keep warm. All warm-blooded animals at rest lose the same amount of heat from a unit area of skin, for which purpose they need a food-supply proportional to their surface and not to their weight. Five thousand mice weigh as much as a man. Their combined surface and food or oxygen consumption are about seventeen times a man's. In fact a mouse eats about one quarter its own weight of food every day, which is mainly used in keeping it warm. For the same reason small animals cannot live in cold countries. In the arctic regions there are no reptiles or amphibians, and no small mammals. The smallest mammal in Spitzbergen is the fox. The small birds fly away in the winter, while the insects die, though their eggs can survive six months or more of frost. The most successful mammals are bears, seals, and walruses.

Similarly, the eye is a rather inefficient organ until it reaches a large size. The back of the human eye on which an image of the outside world is thrown, and which corresponds to the film of a camera, is composed of a mosaic of 'rods and cones' whose diameter is little more than a length of an average light wave. Each eye has about half a million, and for two objects to be distinguishable their images must fall on separate rods or cones. It is obvious that with fewer but larger rods and cones we should see less distinctly. If they were twice as broad two points would have to be twice as far apart before we could distinguish them at a given distance. But if their size were diminished and their number increased we should see no better. For it is impossible to form a definite image smaller than a wave-length of light. Hence a mouse's eye is not a small-scale model of a human eye. Its rods and cones are not much smaller than ours, and therefore there are far fewer of them. A mouse could not distinguish one human face from another six feet away. In order that they should be of any use at all the eyes of small animals have to be much larger in proportion to their bodies than our own. Large animals on the other hand only require relatively small eyes, and those of the whale and elephant are little larger than our own.

For rather more recondite reasons the same general principle holds true of the brain. If we compare the brain-weights of a set of very similar animals such as the cat, cheetah, leopard, and tiger, we find that as we quadruple the body-weight the brain-weight is only doubled. The larger animal with proportionately larger bones can economize on brain, eyes, and certain other organs.

Such are a very few of the considerations which show that for every type of animal there is an optimum size. Yet although Galileo demonstrated the contrary more than three hundred years ago, people still believe that if a flea were as large as a man it could jump a thousand feet into the air. As a matter of fact the height to which an animal can jump is more nearly independent of its size than proportional to it. A flea can jump about two feet, a man about five. To jump a given height, if we neglect the resistance of the air, requires an expenditure of energy proportional to the jumper's weight. But if the jumping muscles form a constant fraction of the animal's body, the energy developed per ounce of muscle is independent of the size, provided it can be developed quickly enough in the small animal. As a matter of fact an insect's muscles, although they can contract more quickly than our own, appear to be less efficient; as otherwise a flea or grasshopper could rise six feet into the air.

And just as there is a best size for every animal, so the same is true for every human institution. In the Greek type of democracy all the citizens could listen to a series of orators and vote directly on questions of legislation. Hence their philosophers held that a small city was the largest possible democratic state. The English invention of representative government made a democratic nation possible, and the possibility was first realized in the United States, and later elsewhere. With the development of broadcasting it has once more become possible for every citizen to listen to the political views of representative orators, and the future may perhaps see the return of the national state to the Greek form of democracy. Even the referendum has been made possible only by the institution of daily newspapers.

To the biologist the problem of socialism appears largely as a problem of size. The extreme socialists desire to run every nation as a single business concern. I do not suppose that Henry Ford would find much difficulty in running Andorra or Luxembourg on a socialistic basis. He has already more men on his pay-roll than their population. It is conceivable that a syndicate of Fords, if we could find them, would make Belgium Ltd. or Denmark Inc. pay their way. But while nationalization of certain industries is an obvious possibility in the largest of states, I find it no easier to picture a completely socialized British Empire or United States than an elephant turning somersaults or a hippopotamus jumping a hedge.

Questions for Discussion

1. In the first paragraph of his essay, Haldane says, "For every type of animal there is a most convenient size." Do you think he contradicts himself when he later says "animals of all kinds find difficulties in size"? Why or why not?

2. Haldane almost always uses the word "gut" rather than "intestine." Why do you think he does so? Do you think he has made the appropriate word choice?

3. Consider the following two sentences from the essay: "The higher animals are not larger than the lower because they are more complicated. They are more complicated because they are larger." What do you understand Haldane to mean here? Why do you think he includes this distinction in his essay?

4. Personification occurs whenever a writer attributes human properties to animals, plants, or inanimate objects. Where does Haldane use personification in this essay? How does his use of it affect the tone of the essay?

5. Were you surprised by the change in subject matter in the last two paragraphs of the essay? Do you find Haldane's comparison of the animal and political worlds convincing?

6. Do you think a contemporary biologist would be comfortable with the biological speculation Haldane engages in here? Why or why not?

Suggested Activities

1. Lewis Thomas's *The Lives of a Cell* (see Chapter 5) is a recent popular book on biological topics. Make a report to the class comparing Thomas' book to Haldane's *Possible Worlds* (the book in which "On Being the Right Size" first appeared). How is the almost fifty-year difference between the dates when the books were written reflected in their style and content?

2. One physical property Haldane fails to mention is speed. Write an essay examining the significance of speed in the animal world.

3. "On Being the Right Size" is distinctive among the essays in this chapter in that it deals with hypothetical effects. Write an essay of this sort describing what you imagine the effects would be if one condition of your life were changed. Some possible changes: being heavier, lighter, shorter, or taller; being wealthier or poorer; being of a different race or sex. Be as specific as possible in your analysis.

Shooting
an Elephant

GEORGE ORWELL

George Orwell (1903-50) is the pen name of Eric Arthur Blair. Considered by many to be the most accomplished British essayist of the twentieth century, Orwell was born in Burma and educated at Eton. He joined the Imperial Police in Burma after leaving school, but soon became disenchanted with the colonial regime and returned to England to write. His first book, *Down and Out in Paris and London* (1933), describes the extreme poverty that accompanied his attempt to establish himself as a writer. After his disenchantment with British imperialism, Orwell became a lifelong socialist, though of a highly individual sort. His political opinions figure largely in a number of his books, including *The Road to Wigan Pier* (1937), *Homage to Catalonia* (1939), and his most famous book, the anti-utopian novel *1984* (1949).

In the essay reprinted here, from *Shooting an Elephant and Other Essays* (1950), Orwell recounts an experience that helped him understand his growing opposition to colonialism. A striking feature of the essay is the unflinching honesty with which Orwell examines his own motives and feelings.

In Moulmein, in Lower Burma, I was hated by large numbers of people—the only time in my life that I have been important enough for this to happen to me. I was sub-divisional police officer of the town, and in an aimless, petty kind of

SHOOTING AN ELEPHANT   From *Shooting an Elephant and Other Essays* by George Orwell, copyright 1950 by Sonia Brownell Orwell; renewed 1978 by Sonia Pitt-Rivers. Reprinted by permission of Harcourt Brace Jovanovich, Inc.

way anti-European feeling was very bitter. No one had the guts to raise a riot, but if a European woman went through the bazaars alone somebody would probably spit betel juice over her dress. As a police officer I was an obvious target and was baited whenever it seemed safe to do so. When a nimble Burman tripped me up on the football field and the referee (another Burman) looked the other way, the crowd yelled with hideous laughter. This happened more than once. In the end the sneering yellow faces of young men that met me everywhere, the insults hooted after me when I was at a safe distance, got badly on my nerves. The young Buddhist priests were the worst of all. There were several thousands of them in the town and none of them seemed to have anything to do except stand on street corners and jeer at Europeans.

All this was perplexing and upsetting. For at that time I had already made up my mind that imperialism was an evil thing and the sooner I chucked up my job and got out of it the better. Theoretically — and secretly, of course — I was all for the Burmese and all against their oppressors, the British. As for the job I was doing I hated it more bitterly than I can perhaps make clear. In a job like that you see the dirty work of Empire at close quarters. The wretched prisoners huddling in the stinking cages of the lock-ups, the grey, cowed faces of the long-term convicts, the scarred buttocks of the men who had been flogged with bamboos — all these oppressed me with an intolerable sense of guilt. But I could get nothing into perspective. I was young and ill-educated and I had had to think out my problems in the utter silence that is imposed on every Englishman in the East. I did not even know that the British Empire is dying, still less did I know that it is a great deal better than the younger empires that are going to supplant it. All I knew was that I was stuck between my hatred of the empire I served and my rage against the evil-spirited little beasts who tried to make my job impossible. With one part of my mind I thought of the British Raj as an unbreakable tyranny, as something clamped down, in *saecula saeculorum*, upon the will of prostrate peoples; with another part I thought that the greatest joy in the world would be to drive a bayonet into a Buddhist priest's guts. Feelings like these are the normal by-products of imperialism; ask any Anglo-Indian official, if you can catch him off duty.

One day something happened which in a roundabout way was enlightening. It was a tiny incident in itself, but it gave me a better glimpse than I had had before of the real nature of imperialism — the real motives for which despotic governments act. Early one morning the sub-inspector at a police station the other end of the town rang me up on the 'phone and said that an elephant was ravaging the bazaar. Would I please come and do something about it? I did not know what I could do, but I wanted to see what was happening and I got on to a pony and started out. I took my rifle, an old .44 Winchester and much too small to kill an elephant, but I thought the noise might be useful *in terrorem*. Various Burmans stopped me on the way and told me about the elephant's doings. It was not, of course, a wild elephant, but a tame one which had gone "must". It had been chained up, as tame elephants always are when their attack of "must" is due, but on the previous night it had broken its chain and escaped. Its mahout, the only person who could manage it when it was in that state, had set out in pursuit, but had taken the wrong direction and was now twelve hours' journey away, and in the morning the elephant had suddenly reappeared in the town. The Burmese population had no weapons and were quite helpless against it. It had already destroyed somebody's bamboo hut, killed a cow and raided some fruit-stalls and devoured the stock; also it had met the municipal rubbish van, and, when the driver jumped out and took to his heels, had turned the van over and inflicted violences upon it.

The Burmese sub-inspector and some Indian constables were waiting for me in the quarter where the elephant had been seen. It was a very poor quarter, a labyrinth of squalid bamboo huts, thatched with palm-leaf, winding all over a steep hillside. I remember that it was a cloudy, stuffy morning at the beginning of the rains. We began questioning the people as to where the elephant had gone, and, as usual, failed to get any definite information. That is invariably the case in the East; a story always sounds clear enough at a distance, but the nearer you get to the scene of events the vaguer it becomes. Some of the people said that the elephant had gone in one direction, some said that he had gone in another, some professed not even to have heard of any elephant. I had almost made up my mind that the whole story was a pack of lies, when we heard yells a little distance away. There was a loud, scandalized cry of "Go away, child! Go away this instant!" and an old woman with a switch in her hand came round the corner of a hut, violently shooing away a crowd of naked children. Some more women followed, clicking their tongues and exclaiming; evidently there was something that the children ought not to have seen. I rounded the hut and saw a man's dead body sprawling in the mud. He was an Indian, a black Dravidian coolie, almost naked, and he could not have been dead many minutes. The people said that the elephant had come suddenly upon him round the corner of the hut, caught him with its trunk, put its foot on his back and ground him into the earth. This was the rainy season and the ground was soft, and his face had scored a trench a foot deep and a couple of yards long. He was lying on his belly with arms crucified and head sharply twisted to one side. His face was coated with mud, the eyes wide open, the teeth bared and grinning with an expression of unendurable agony. (Never tell me, by the way, that the dead looked peaceful. Most of the corpses I have seen look devilish.) The friction of the great beast's foot had stripped the skin from his back as neatly as one skins a rabbit. As soon as I saw the dead man I sent an orderly to a friend's house nearby to borrow an elephant rifle. I had already sent back the pony, not wanting it to go mad with fright and throw me if it smelt the elephant.

The orderly came back in a few minutes with a rifle and five cartridges, and meanwhile some Burmans had arrived and told us that the elephant was in the paddy fields below, only a few hundred yards away. As I started forward practically the whole population of the quarter flocked out of the houses and followed me. They had seen the rifle and were all shouting excitedly that I was going to shoot the elephant. They had not shown much interest in the elephant when he was merely ravaging their homes, but it was different now that he was going to be shot. It was a bit of fun to them, as it would be to an English crowd; besides they wanted the meat. It made me vaguely uneasy. I had no intention of shooting the elephant — I had merely sent for the rifle to defend myself if necessary — and it is always unnerving to have a crowd following you. I marched down the hill, looking and feeling a fool, with the rifle over my shoulder and an ever-growing army of people jostling at my heels. At the bottom, when you got away from the huts, there was a metalled road and beyond that a miry waste of paddy fields a thousand yards across, not yet ploughed but soggy from the first rains and dotted with coarse grass. The elephant was standing eight yards from the road, his left side towards us. He took not the slightest notice of the crowd's approach. He was tearing up bunches of grass, beating them against his knees to clean them and stuffing them into his mouth.

I had halted on the road. As soon as I saw the elephant I knew with perfect certainty that I ought not to shoot him. It is a serious matter to shoot a working elephant — it is comparable to destroying a huge and costly piece of machinery — and obviously one ought not to do it if it can possibly be avoided. And at that distance, peacefully eating, the elephant looked no more dangerous than a cow. I thought then and I think now that his attack of "must" was already passing off; in which case he would merely wander harmlessly about until the mahout came back and caught him. Moreover, I did not in the least want to shoot him. I decided that I would watch him for a little while to make sure that he did not turn savage again, and then go home.

But at that moment I glanced round at the crowd that had followed me. It was an immense crowd, two thousand at the least and growing every minute. It blocked the road for a long distance on either side. I looked at the sea of yellow faces above the garish clothes — faces all happy and excited over this bit of fun, all certain that the elephant was going to be shot. They were watching me as they would watch a conjurer about to perform a trick. They did not like me, but with the magical rifle in my hands I was momentarily worth watching. And suddenly I realized that I should have to shoot the elephant after all. The people expected it of me and I had got to do it; I could feel their two thousand wills pressing me forward, irresistibly. And it was at this moment, as I stood there with the rifle in my hands, that I first grasped the hollowness, the futility of the white man's dominion in the East. Here was I, the white man with his gun, standing in front of the unarmed native crowd — seemingly the leading actor of the piece; but in reality I was only an absurd puppet pushed to and fro by the will of those yellow faces behind. I perceived in this moment that when the white man turns tyrant it is his own freedom that he destroys. He becomes a sort of hollow, posing dummy, the conventionalized figure of a sahib. For it is the condition of his rule that he shall spend his life in trying to impress the "natives", and so in every crisis he has got to do what the "natives" expect of him. He wears a mask, and his face grows to fit it. I had got to shoot the elephant. I had committed myself to doing it when I sent for the rifle. A sahib has got to act like a sahib; he has got to appear resolute, to know his own mind and do definite things. To come all that way, rifle in hand, with two thousand people marching at my heels, and then to trail feebly away, having done nothing — no, that was impossible. The crowd would laugh at me. And my whole life, every white man's life in the East, was one long struggle not to be laughed at.

But I did not want to shoot the elephant. I watched him beating his bunch of grass against his knees, with that preoccupied grandmotherly air that elephants have. It seemed to me that it would be murder to shoot him. At that age I was not squeamish about killing animals, but I had never shot an elephant and never wanted to. (Somehow it always seems worse to kill a *large* animal.) Besides, there was the beast's owner to be considered. Alive, the elephant was worth at least a hundred pounds; dead, he would only be worth the value of his tusks, five pounds, possibly. But I had got to act quickly. I turned to some experienced-looking Burmans who had been there when we arrived, and asked them how the elephant had been behaving. They all said the same thing: he took no notice of you if you left him alone, but he might charge if you went too close to him.

It was perfectly clear to me what I ought to do. I ought to walk up to within, say, twenty-five yards of the elephant and test his behaviour. If he charged I could shoot, if he took no notice of me it would be safe to leave him until the mahout came back. But also I knew that I was going to do no such thing. I was a poor shot with a rifle and the ground was soft mud into which one would sink at every step. If the elephant charged and I missed him, I should have about as much chance as a toad under a steam-roller. But even then I was not thinking particularly of my own skin, only of the watchful yellow faces behind. For at that moment, with the crowd watching me, I was not afraid in the ordinary sense, as I would have been if I had been alone. A white man mustn't be frightened in front of "natives"; and so, in general, he isn't frightened. The sole thought in my mind was that if anything went wrong those two thousand Burmans would see me pursued, caught, trampled on and reduced to a grinning corpse like that Indian up the hill. And if that happened it was quite probable that some of them would laugh. That would never do. There was only one alternative. I shoved the cartridges into the magazine and lay down on the road to get a better aim.

The crowd grew very still, and a deep, low, happy sigh, as of people who see the theatre curtain go up at last, breathed from innumerable throats. They were going to have their bit of fun after all. The rifle was a beautiful German thing with cross-hair sights. I did not then know that in shooting an elephant one would shoot to cut an imaginery bar running from ear-hole to ear-hole. I ought, therefore, as the elephant was sideways on, to have aimed straight at his ear-hole; actually I aimed several inches in front of this, thinking the brain would be farther forward.

When I pulled the trigger I did not hear the bang or feel the kick — one never does when a shot goes home — but I heard the devilish roar of glee that went up from the crowd. In that instant, in too short a time, one would have thought, even for the bullet to get there, a mysterious, terrible change had come over the elephant. He neither stirred nor fell, but every line of his body had altered. He looked suddenly stricken, shrunken, immensely old, as though the frightful impact of the bullet had paralysed him without knocking him down. At last, after what seemed a long time—it might have been five seconds, I dare say—he sagged flabbily to his knees. His mouth slobbered. An enormous senility seemed to have settled upon him. One could have imagined him thousands of years old. I fired again into the same spot. At the second shot he did not collapse but climbed with desperate slowness to his feet and stood weakly upright, with legs sagging and head drooping. I fired a third time. That was the shot that did for him. You could see the agony of it jolt his whole body and knock the last remnant of strength from his legs. But in falling he seemed for a moment to rise, for as his hind legs collapsed beneath him he seemed to tower upwards like a huge rock toppling, his trunk reaching skywards like a tree. He trumpeted, for the first and only time. And then down he came, his belly towards me, with a crash that seemed to shake the ground even where I lay.

I got up. The Burmans were already racing past me across the mud. It was obvious that the elephant would never rise again, but he was not dead. He was breathing very rhythmically with long rattling gasps, his great mound of a side painfully rising and falling. His mouth was wide open—I could see far down into caverns of pale pink throat. I waited a long time for him to die, but his breathing did not weaken. Finally I fired my two remaining shots into the spot where I thought his heart must be. The thick blood welled out of him like red velvet, but still he did not die. His body did not even jerk when the shots hit him, the tortured breathing continued without a pause. He was dying, very slowly and in great agony, but in some world remote from me where not even a bullet could damage him further. I felt that I had got to put an end to that dreadful noise. It seemed dreadful to see the great beast lying there, powerless to move and yet powerless to die, and not even be able to finish him. I sent back for my small rifle and poured shot after shot into his heart and down his throat. They seemed to make no impression. The tortured gasps continued as steadily as the ticking of a clock.

In the end I could not stand it any longer and went away. I heard later that it took him half an hour to die. Burmans were bringing dahs and baskets even before I left, and I was told they had stripped his body almost to the bones by the afternoon.

Afterwards, of course, there were endless discussions about the shooting of the elephant. The owner was furious, but he was only an Indian and could do nothing. Besides, legally I had done the right thing, for a mad elephant has to be killed, like a mad dog, if its owner fails to control it. Among the Europeans opinion was divided. The older men said I was right, the younger men said it was a damn shame to shoot an elephant for killing a coolie, because an elephant was worth more than any damn Coringhee coolie. And afterwards I was very glad that the coolie had been killed; it put me legally in the right and it gave me a sufficient pretext for shooting the elephant. I often wondered whether any of the others grasped that I had done it solely to avoid looking a fool.

Questions for Discussion

1. Discuss Orwell's characterization of the Burmese. How is this characterization related to his sympathy for them as members of an oppressed race?

2. Compare Orwell as narrator of the elephant's death to Orwell as participant in it. What changes have occurred in him during the time between the incident and his writing about it? How do these changes affect the tone of the essay?

3. The first, second, and last paragraphs of this essay are not part of the narrative of the shooting of the elephant. What is their function?

4. Orwell says the incident with the elephant gave him "a better glimpse" of "the real motives for which despotic governments act." In his view, what are these real motives? Do you agree with him on this point?

5. Orwell says that the white man in the East "wears a mask, and his face grows to fit it." What does this statement mean? Have you ever seen a face grow to fit a mask?

6. In describing the situation just prior to the shooting, Orwell uses a number of comparisons drawn from the world of the theater. Why do you think he does this? How effective do you find these comparisons to be?

7. In the last paragraph of his essay, Orwell says, "I was very glad that the coolie had been killed." Did this statement cause you to lose sympathy for him? Why or why not?

Suggested Activities

1. Orwell says that "when the white man turns tyrant it is his own freedom that he destroys." Ask each of your classmates what they think this statement means; also ask them to provide an example of self-enslaving tyranny from everyday life. Report the results of your survey to the class.

2. Write a narrative essay about a time when you were torn between doing what you thought was right and doing what other people expected of you. What did you learn from the experience?

3. Write an essay analyzing the causes of some act that puzzled you at the time you performed it. What allows you to understand it better now?

4. Write an essay comparing and contrasting the treatment of the themes of freedom and authority in this essay and in Frank Conroy's "Savages" (pp. 62–68.)

argumentation

More than any other form of writing, argumentation is explicitly concerned with persuasion. For many people, it is also the most satisfying form of writing in which to engage. A quick glance at the topics of the essays in this chapter can help to explain why this is so. Drug laws, pollution, women's rights, politics and the state of the language—these are subjects that generate controversy and strong feelings. They are matters that writers who enjoy the give and take of vigorous debate can approach with enthusiasm.

Yet because argumentative writing is so often concerned with emotional issues, people sometimes confuse it with the kind of argument we engage in in everyday situations. It may be useful, then, to emphasize the difference between the two. We all know how argument operates in our daily lives. When we meet with opposition on an issue we feel strongly about, often we simply respond with increased emotion. If we're interrupted, as we frequently are in verbal arguments, we raise our voices and re-interrupt in return. If we haven't learned to fight fair, we call names, drag in irrelevant issues, and insist on the exclusive correctness of our own beliefs. Our objective is to win, at whatever cost in dignity and bruised feelings.

When argumentative writing is properly done, its goal is quite different. Instead of making an all-or-nothing attempt at total conversion, argumentation aims at the more modest—but more attainable—goal of convincing readers that the point of view being presented has merit. Though writers of argumentative essays will sometimes ask their readers to change their perspective on a topic, and even to engage in concrete action as a result, more often all they seek is serious, fair-minded consideration of their point of view.

If you consult your own experience as a reader and writer, you'll probably agree that you can't attain the goal we've just described by using the written equivalent of a raised voice. But then how can you? Here are four suggestions.

1. Write to a persuadable audience.   On any controversial issue, some people will hold such firm opinions that their minds can't be changed. Some of these people will agree with your point of view and some won't. But since the ones who agree *don't* need to be persuaded and the ones who disagree *can't* be, neither group should be your intended audience. Instead, direct your attention at the readers who have yet to make up their minds on the issue. They are the ones who are open to change. If you treat them as intelligent, interested people and provide them with reasoned arguments in support of your position, then you can expect them to give your point of view a serious hearing and perhaps even to adopt it as their own.

2. Consider opposing arguments.   This second suggestion repeats a piece of advice we gave in Chapter 1. We call it to your attention again here because the themes of argumentative writing are by their nature ones for which significant opposing arguments exist. Since your readers will naturally be curious about the arguments that run counter to your point of view, it's a good idea to confront these arguments directly. This is especially true when the position you're advocating disagrees with what most people believe. Look, for example, at how George Orwell addresses a prevailing belief in "Politics and the English Language":

> . . . the decadence of our language is probably curable. Those who deny this would argue, if they produced an argument at all, that language merely reflects existing social conditions, and that we cannot influence its development by any direct tinkering with words and constructions. So far as the general tone or spirit of a language goes, this may be true, but it is not true in detail.

Both Orwell and his opponents agree that the English language has grown decadent, but they disagree on whether the causes of the decadence are controllable. Since the view that the causes cannot be controlled was the prevailing one when Orwell wrote his essay, he needed to demonstrate that he was aware of it and had considered it seriously. By doing so, he prepares his readers for his alternative analysis of the situation, and he makes them receptive to the proposed set of cures for the decadence that he later describes.

3. Take a skeptical look at your own argument.   When an argumentative essay based on a sound thesis fails to be convincing, the reason is almost always an inadequacy in the argument. Often, the writer's passionate convictions about the topic are the source of the difficulty. Believing deeply in the rightness of his or her point of view, the writer fails to see how or where the argument breaks down for other people.

The best solution to this problem is a self-induced case of skepticism. Here the concept of an audience of persuadable people can come to your aid. Imagine yourself a member of such an audience: you're open-minded, but you're not willing to be sold a bill of argumentative goods. Now ask yourself what flaws in an argument could cause such a person to remain unconvinced and check to see if any of them are present in your own argument. Have you left out any steps? Have you glossed over or ignored weaknesses in your case? Have you relied on oversimplifications, faulty generalizations, stereotypes, or overly emotional appeals? Have you spent time impugning the motives of your opponents instead of addressing the issue? If you keep reworking your argument in the light of questions like these until you're fully convinced by it, chances are it will convince your readers as well.

4. Control your tone. When people are given the advice to control their tone in argumentative writing, they often take it to mean that they should suppress their true feelings about their subject and write in a circumspect, elaborately courteous style. But the advice doesn't—or shouldn't—mean this at all. Certainly there are fundamental courtesies to be observed in writing as in life. But what "control your tone" really means is "be in command of your tone." The basic question to ask about your tone is whether it contributes to the achievement of your persuasive purpose. If your tone vents your feelings at the expense of persuading your readers, then you don't have it under control. But if expressing some righteous indignation can not only make you feel better but help convince your readers, then by all means include it in your essay.

Look, for instance, at this fine example of "throw the rascals out" rhetoric from Edward Abbey's "Second Rape of the West":

> Not only do our state politicians fail to resist these alien forces [large power plants and strip-mining operations], they bid against one another to invite them in. Our good old boys would sell their mothers' graves if they could make a quick buck out of the deal; crooked as a dog's hind-leg, tricky as a car dealer, greedy as a hog at the trough, these men will sell out the West to big industry as fast as they can, without the faintest stirrings of conscience.

Strong language, this. But when you read the essay as a whole, look at how Abbey *earns* his anger. The passage we just quoted comes at the end of several pages of strong, tough argument and factual evidence. Because Abbey first develops such a compelling case, his anger seems justified; we welcome it as a fitting reaction to the callous exploitation of the environment that he's just finished describing.

Now for a final word about argumentative writing. Throughout this book, we've been emphasizing the role of persuasion in the various rhetorical modes. In a sense, argumentation is the essence of the approach to writing we've been talking about, for it is persuasion per se. In a much larger sense, though, argumentation is central to civilized life itself. One doesn't have to be a moss-bound traditionalist to feel that our existence as civilized people is somehow dependent on our ability to engage in the free, frank exchange of ideas and opinions. Argumentative writing is a central medium of this exchange. It is both our right and our responsibility as mature human beings to engage in it.

Drugs

GORE VIDAL

Gore Vidal (b. 1925) completed his first novel, *Williwaw,* when he was only nineteen and has been appearing in print regularly ever since. His novels include *The City and the Pillar* (1948), *Julian* (1964), *Myra Breckinridge* (1968), and *1876* (1976). He is also the author of plays, short stories, book reviews, mystery stories (under the name of Edgar Box), and essays of social and political criticism. "Drugs," which first appeared in *The New York Times* in 1970, demonstrates Vidal's sardonic wit, his irreverent attitude toward traditional American pieties, and his ability to state a case forcefully.

It is possible to stop most drug addiction in the United States within a very short time. Simply make all drugs available and sell them at cost. Label each drug with a precise description of what effect — good and bad — the drug will have on the taker. This will require heroic honesty. Don't say that marijuana is addictive or dangerous when it is neither, as millions of people know — unlike "speed," which kills most unpleasantly, or heroin, which is addictive and difficult to kick.

For the record, I have tried — once — almost every drug and liked none, disproving the popular Fu Manchu theory that a single whiff of opium will enslave the mind. Nevertheless many drugs are bad for certain people to take and they should be told why in a sensible way.

Along with exhortation and warning, it might be good for our citizens to recall (or learn for the first time) that the United States was the creation of men who believed that each man has the right to do what he wants with his own life as long as he does not interfere with his neighbor's pursuit of happiness (that his neighbor's idea of happiness is persecuting others does confuse matters a bit).

This is a startling notion to the current generation of Americans. They reflect a system of public education which has made the Bill of Rights, literally, unacceptable to a majority of high school graduates (see the annual Purdue reports) who now form the "silent majority" — a phrase which that underestimated wit Richard Nixon took from Homer who used it to describe the dead.

Now one can hear the warning rumble begin: if everyone is allowed to take drugs everyone will and the GNP will decrease, the Commies will stop us from making everyone free, and we shall end up a race of Zombies, passively murmuring "groovie" to one another. Alarming thought. Yet it seems most unlikely that any reasonably sane person will become a drug addict if he knows in advance what addiction is going to be like.

Is everyone reasonably sane? No. Some people will always become drug addicts just as some people will always become alcoholics, and it is just too bad. Every man, however, has the power (and should have the legal right) to kill himself if he chooses. But since most men don't, they won't be mainliners either. Nevertheless, forbidding people things they like or think they might enjoy only makes them want those things all the more. This psychological insight is, for some mysterious reason, perennially denied our governors.

It is a lucky thing for the American moralist that our country has always existed in a kind of time-vacuum: we have no public memory of anything that happened before last Tuesday. No one in Washington today recalls what happened during the years alcohol was forbidden to the people by a Congress that thought it had a divine mission to stamp out Demon Rum — launching, in the process, the greatest crime wave in the country's history, causing thousands of deaths from bad alcohol, and creating a general (and persisting) contempt among the citizenry for the laws of the United States.

The same thing is happening today. But the government has learned nothing from past attempts at prohibition, not to mention repression.

Last year when the supply of Mexican marijuana was slightly curtailed by the Feds, the pushers got the kids hooked on heroin and deaths increased dramatically, particularly in New York. Whose fault? Evil men like the Mafiosi? Permissive Dr. Spock? Wild-eyed Dr. Leary? No.

The Government of the United States was responsible for those deaths. The bureaucratic machine has a vested interest in playing cops and robbers. Both the Bureau of Narcotics and the Mafia want strong laws against the sale and use of drugs because if drugs are sold at cost there would be no money in it for anyone.

If there was no money in it for the Mafia, there would be no friendly playground pushers, and addicts would not commit crimes to pay for the next fix. Finally, if there was no money in it, the Bureau of Narcotics would wither away, something they are not about to do without a struggle.

Will anything sensible be done? Of course not. The American people are as devoted to the idea of sin and its punishment as they are to making money — and fighting drugs is nearly as big a business as pushing them. Since the combination of sin and money is irresistible (particularly to the professional politician), the situation will only grow worse.

Questions for Discussion

1. What is your reaction to the abrupt opening of this essay? Do you think this introductory strategy is effective? Why or why not?

2. In the second paragraph, Vidal says that he has "tried — once — almost every drug and liked none . . . ." Does this admission make his argument more or less persuasive for you? Explain.

3. How would you describe the overall tone of this essay? What elements in the essay create this tone?

4. Discuss the way Vidal acknowledges opposing arguments. Do you think he is fair to his opponents?

5. In your own words, explain why Vidal thinks "the situation will only grow worse." Do you agree or disagree with his view?

6. Why does Vidal say that the government is to blame for the deaths of people hooked on heroin? Do you find his argument convincing?

Suggested Activities

1. The Purdue report on the Bill of Rights that Vidal refers to was published in 1970. Locate a copy of this report and conduct a poll of your acquaintances using the questions it contains. Are there aspects of the Bill of Rights that your acquaintances find unacceptable? Report your findings to the class.

2. Vidal says people "should have the legal right" to kill themselves. Write an argumentative essay either supporting or opposing this view.

3. Using resources in your library, locate an essay opposed to the legalization of drugs. Then write an essay of your own comparing and contrasting this essay with Vidal's. Whose argument do you find more persuasive, and why?

The Second Rape
of the West

EDWARD ABBEY

Edward Abbey (b. 1927) earned both B.A. and M.A. degrees
from the University of New Mexico. After leaving college, he
served for fifteen years as a National Park Service ranger and
fire lookout at the Arches National Monument and other loca-
tions. During this time, he developed a deep affection for the
wilderness and desert areas of the American Southwest. These
form the subject of many of his books, including the novel *Fire
on the Mountain* (1962) and the nonfiction works *Desert Soli-
taire* (1968), *Cactus Country* (1973), and *The Journey Home*
(1977), from which we have taken "The Second Rape of the
West." In this selection Abbey objects, in a sometimes bitter,
sometimes wryly humorous way, to the introduction of large-
scale power plants and strip-mining operations into undevel-
oped areas of the Southwest.

Rumbling along in my 1962 Dodge D-100, the last good truck Dodge ever made,
I tossed my empty out the window and popped the top from another can of
Schlitz. Littering the public highway? Of course I litter the public highway. Every
chance I get. After all, it's not the beer cans that are ugly; it's the highway that
is ugly. Beer cans are beautiful, and someday, when recycling becomes a serious
enterprise, the government can put one million kids to work each summer picking up the cans I and others have thoughtfully stored along the roadways.

(serious?)

THE SECOND RAPE OF THE WEST   From *The Journey Home: Some Words in Defense of the American
West* by Edward Abbey. Copyright © 1977 by Edward Abbey. Reprinted by permission of the publisher, E. P. Dutton.

Indian country. American country. Coming down out of the piny forests near Flagstaff, Arizona, headed north, you are led into one of the most exhilarating landscapes in the Southwest. On your left, the San Francisco Peaks, 12,660 feet above sea level; on your right and ahead, a group of dormant volcanoes and cinder cones, scattered over grasslands. One of those cinder cones, Sunset Crater, erupted only 910 years ago. We pray to God, my friends and I, for a little precision vulcanism once again; nothing could do our Southwest more good.

From 7,200 feet at the pass, the highway descends into the rangelands, bearing straight toward the valley of the Little Colorado and the Painted Desert. To the north, you can see the forested bulk of the Kaibab Plateau, through which the big Colorado has carved the Grand Canyon. To the northeast stand the red walls of the Echo Cliffs, the blue and sacred dome of Navajo Mountain, visible from fifty miles away. Indian ponies lounge along the highway looking for something to eat — Kleenex, hotdog buns, tumbleweed, anything more or less biodegradable. Out among the slabs of sun-burned rock the Navajo kids are herding sheep; among the scattered junipers are the hogans of The People, as they call themselves. And why not? They've been here a long time. By each dome-shaped hogan is an old car, on its back, cannibalized to keep another running, and a pickup truck, on its wheels. All seems to be in order.

Not quite. Something alien and strange has invaded the Southwest, a gigantic and inhuman power from — in effect — another world. You first notice the invaders as you approach the village of Cameron and the turnoff to Grand Canyon. They look like Martian monsters in this pastoral scene: skeleton towers of steel 90 to 120 feet tall, posted across the landscape in military file from horizon to horizon. From the crossarms of the towers hang chains of insulators, bearing power-line cables buzzing with electricity, transmitting power from Glen Canyon Dam and the new coal-fired generators near the town of Page to the burgeoning cities of Las Vegas, Phoenix, and southern California. From the silence of the desert to the clamor of Glitter Gulch, the fool's treasure of one region is transported and transmuted into the nervous neon of another. Energy, they call it, energy for growth. And what is the growth for? Ask any cancer cell.

The power lines are merely the first, outward signs of this war between the worlds. Deep in the heart of Indian country, on a plateau called Black Mesa, is the chief current battleground, a huge strip mine where walking dragline excavators 300 feet high, weighing 2,500 tons each, remove and overturn what the Peabody Coal Company calls "overburden." Blasters shatter the coal seam underneath; power shovels scoop the coal into trucks bigger than a house, trucks that look like stegosauruses on wheels. They haul it to processing plants nearby, from which it is shipped by pipeline in slurry form to a power plant in Nevada or by conveyor belt and rail to the plant at Page.

Strip mining destroys the rangeland on which the Indians once grazed their sheep and horses, and it threatens the underground water supplies that feed their few springs and wells. Strip-mined land has yet to be reclaimed successfully anywhere in the arid West. But from the point of view of the mine operators and the power companies, strip mining is cheap and profitable. A mine producing 1 million tons of coal a year may require only twenty-five workers. The machines are expensive, but machines never complain, never go on strike, never make demands for safety standards, medical insurance, retirement pensions. What about the displaced Indians and the unemployed miners back in Appalachia? Let them go on welfare; let them eat food stamps. Society at large will pay those costs. And so the strip mining goes on at an ever-growing pace and now consumes about 4,650 acres of American farm, forest, and rangeland each week. Every week of the year. An area the size of Connecticut, some 5,000 square miles, has already been strip-mined for coal alone. Can this land be reclaimed? According to the 1973 report from the National Academy of Sciences: "In the Western coal areas, complete restoration is rarely, if ever, possible." Even simple revegetation, in the West, "will require centuries."

In the case of the Black Mesa mine, what do the Indians get out of it? The Navajo tribal treasury is paid an annual royalty of $3 million, or about $25 per Navajo. The Indians also get 300 jobs paying an average of $10,000 per year. The royalty and the jobs are good for about thirty-five years, the estimated life of mine and power plant operation. Then what? No one knows for sure, but the fate of Appalachia provides a pretty good hint. Poverty, a blighted land, forced migration to the welfare slums: That has been the fate of Appalachians since King Coal moved into their homeland.

Meanwhile the Indians and everyone else living 100 miles downwind of the present and projected power plants (Warner Valley, Escalante, Caineville — all in south central Utah) will receive as a bonus a concentrated steady treatment of fly ash, sulfur dioxide, and nitrogen oxide. Even if such air-pollution-control devices as electrostatic precipitators, wet scrubbers, and baghouse filters, operating constantly at maximum theoretical efficiency, capture 99.5 percent of these pollutants at the plant smokestacks, the plants will still pump into the public air (which is all we have for breathing purposes) wastes on the order of 50,000 tons of particulates, 750,000 tons of SO_2, and 600,000 tons of NO_x per annum. These are magnitudes greater than those that now profane the Los Angeles Basin.

For those rare few who may not already be familiar with these forms of aerial garbage, a few words of explanation: Fly ash is fine black soot, the stuff that coats windowsills and car tops and other horizontal surfaces in most industrial cities of the Western world; sulfur dioxide is a gaseous poison harmful to all varieties of plant and animal life, including the human — it reacts with moisture in the atmosphere to form sulfuric acid and comes back to earth mixed with rain or snow, often causing damage to crops; nitrogen oxide is a noxious gas that combines with ozone and carbon in the air to form the eye-smarting, sun-obscuring brown haze known as smog. All these major pollutants, plus others, including trace elements of radon and mercury, are known to cause or aggravate such respiratory ailments as asthma and emphysema; all may be and probably are carcinogenic.

Only we dumb locals may suffer physically from the power plants; but all Americans who enjoy — actually or potentially — the Grand Canyon, Lake Powell, Monument Valley, Shiprock, Canyon de Chelly, Zion, Bryce Canyon, Capitol

Reef, Arches, and Canyonlands national parks will be forced to accept the degradation of the national heritage. The strip mines will tear up only a few hundred square miles; the accompanying power lines, railways, truck roads, dams, waste-disposal sites, industrial sites, and trailer-house towns will cover only a few hundred more square miles; but the filth spewed out by the power plants will smog the air for hundreds of miles in all directions, reducing visibility from the customary 50 to 100 miles to an average of something like 15. That's what you have to look forward to, tourists, next time you come west to enjoy what is, after all, *your* property.

Try to keep cool, calm, and objective, I tell myself, driving the familiar road up from Flagstaff through my favorite towns of Cameron, Tuba City, Cow Springs, and Kayenta. Don't get overagitated, Abbey, and try to keep a steady bead on the ceramic insulators that carry the lines that conduct the 50,000 volts of blue juice above the tracks of the Black Mesa and Lake Powell Railroad. Anger is bad for the aim, hard on the stomach, and makes for a nervous trigger finger. Rage is self-defeating, say all the wisest philosophers (all of whom are dead).

So much for ulcerdom. We have barely begun to discuss the difficulties that will follow mining and coal-fired power plants in the American Southwest, if the ambitious plans of the federal government and the power combines are carried to completion. We have said little, for example, of the impact on water supplies in an arid land. Every river in the Southwest is already overcommitted to agricultural and local municipal use; it was, in fact, for this purpose that the Glen Canyon Dam was built, together with secondary dams in Utah, Colorado, and New Mexico. The proposed power plants will require enormous quantities of water, primarily for cooling purposes. Since no surplus water is available, the water will have to come from sources presently allocated to agriculture. That means, of course, smaller food supplies and higher food prices. This touches on the problem; but the dislocation of groundwater supplies by mining may have more serious long-term effects, drying up some wells and streams, polluting others, on which the Indians, the farmers, and the cattle growers of the Southwest now depend.

The Four Corners Power Plant near Shiprock, New Mexico, may be the worst single industrial polluter in the world. The smog from the Four Corners plant drifts on the prevailing winds as far as Durango, Colorado, and down the Rio Grande Valley of New Mexico to obscure the skies above the historic towns of Taos, Santa Fe, and Albuquerque. This smog was the sole human artifact visible from the moon. Despite years of protest, the utility company has done almost nothing to abate this public nuisance and menace to public health. Yet several of the same companies which built and operate the Four Corners monster are now involved in the building of the Navajo Generating Station at Page, on the shore of Lake Powell, one of the most scenic and popular recreational areas in the Southwest.

With the help and/or interest of the Bureau of Reclamation, another combine consisting of Arizona Public Service Company, Southern California Edison Company, and San Diego Gas and Electric Company proposed in 1964 a third power plant in the area of the Kaiparowits Plateau, a presently uninhabited wilderness of forest and canyons within visual range of Page and Lake Powell. Though defeated in 1976, we may be sure that the power combine will attempt to revive this project when they think the political climate more favorable. You can trust your public utility about as far as you can hand roll a bulldozer.

All these Southwest power projects, actual or potential, violate the law of the land. According to the provisions of the Clean Air Act of 1971, passed by Congress and signed by the president, not only must the air of industrial regions be cleaned up to meet federal standards, but also, and equally important — perhaps *more* important — the air of nonindustrial regions, such as the Southwest, the inter-mountain West, and the northern plains, must be kept as is: clean. The intent of the act was to prevent utilities and industrial concerns from evading the law by building new plants in rural areas where the air is still reasonably clean.

Yet this violation of the act is exactly what the power companies, the mining corporations, and the public utilities hope to get away with. Although most of the energy produced will be consumed in Tucson, Phoenix, Las Vegas, and southern California, the mining and burning of the coal will take place in northern Arizona and southern Utah, where a small and docile population is being cajoled into giving up its birthright of fresh air, clear skies, and open space in exchange for a few hundred temporary jobs.

The coal could be mined and shipped by rail and truck to southern California and the big cities and burned there, at the place of need. Such a policy, while still damaging to the canyonlands and the Indian country, would at least assure the nondegradation of one of America's last large reservoirs of pure air. Local citizens who want the jobs coal mining would create but are opposed to the air pollution resulting from power plants have suggested this alternative to present policy. Their pleas go unheeded, despite the fact that the law reinforces their argument. The reason is simple: The public utilities and the oil, coal, and power combines want mine-site burning of the coal so they can escape air-quality standards imposed on the cities.

From the energy industry's point of view, it is more profitable to transport electricity long distances, via power lines, than to transport the raw coal and pay for the sophisticated technology required to clean up their urban area power plants.

The economics of the matter are more complicated than this summary indicates, involving such things as the manner in which public utility rates are set and the relative ease with which certain costs can or cannot be passed on to the consumer (fuels and power transmission costs are relatively easy to pass along, while other costs, such as improvements in pollution technology and the recovery of large-scale investments and mineral leases, are more difficult). But the core of the case is monetary profit: With profit margins fixed by state regulation at a percentage of total investment, it is more profitable for the utilities and their stockholders to develop their business to the largest scale and volume possible, no matter what the cost to the environment and the health of the citizenry.

The Environmental Protection Agency (EPA) is mandated by Congress to prevent exactly such degradation of air quality as the power combines are bringing into the Southwest. The EPA, however, blandly ignores the law and refuses to perform its clearly defined duty on the curious ground that enforcement of the law, in this case, would "retard or prevent industrial development" in presently nonindustrial areas. This may well be true; and it might well be a wise national policy to restrict or ban industrial development in areas that have a higher value for other uses, such as agriculture and human recreation.

Whether or not true, and whether or not wise, industrial development is not the concern of the EPA. The EPA's job is to protect the environment, not to assist in promoting its further industrialization. Apparently, the EPA is obeying, in this instance, not its congressional mandate but orders from higher up — from the Federal Energy Administration, the Federal Power Commission, the Department of the Interior, and the White House — that conglomerate of federal agencies and administrative powers that acts, in Ralph Nader's words, as the "indentured servant" of corporate industrialism.

The EPA has been taken to court by citizens' conservation organizations in an effort to compel it to obey the law and live up to its obligations. The federal courts have ordered the EPA to enforce the policy of nondegradation of air quality. Appealed by the EPA to the highest court, the orders of the lower courts were sustained by the Supreme Court of the United States, which ruled that the EPA may not allow "significant deterioration" of air quality anywhere.

No matter: The EPA continues to avoid, evade, and defy the law through various ruses, the latest of which is the drawing up of a complicated national map of air-quality "zones" and turning the problems of selection and enforcement over to state governments. In Utah, Arizona, Wyoming, New Mexico, and Nevada, we know well what that means: The rules will be dictated by the extractive industries — the coal, oil, and power combines.

Not only do our state politicians fail to resist these alien forces, they bid against one another to invite them in. Our good old boys would sell their mothers' graves if they could make a quick buck out of the deal; crooked as a dog's hind-leg, tricky as a car dealer, greedy as a hog at the trough, these men will sell out the West to big industry as fast as they can, without the faintest stirrings of conscience. Governors, U.S. senators, congressmen, and our chamber of commerce presidents don't give a hoot in hell for future losses; they figure, rightly, that they personally will all be dead by the time the extent of the disaster becomes clear.

So much for the canyonlands of Utah and Arizona: nothing but a barren wasteland, anyway, as any local Jaycee will tell you, nothing but sand and dust and heat and emptiness, red rock baking under the sun and hungry vultures soaring on the air. Quite so, men, quite so: nothing but canyon and desert, mountain and mesa, all too good for the likes of us.

Questions for Discussion

1. The title of this selection is "The Second Rape of the West"; when do you think the first rape occurred? How appropriate is the title, in your opinion?

2. Abbey begins this essay with a personal narrative. How does this narrative affect your attitude toward him? Did you find it an effective beginning?

3. Abbey calls the coal, oil, and power industries "alien forces." Do you agree or disagree with this characterization of them?

4. Discuss the diction of "Second Rape of the West." How does it affect the essay's tone?

5. If you were a resident of the area Abbey describes, would his essay persuade you to protest against the industrial developments he talks about? What more, if anything, would you want to know about the issues? Be prepared to argue your position in class.

6. In the last sentence of this selection, Abbey includes himself in the group of people the Western wasteland is "too good for." Did this surprise you? Why do you suppose he includes himself in this group?

Suggested Activities

1. Using the resources of your library, prepare a report for your class on the proposed Kaiparowits Plateau power plant that Abbey mentions. What is the history of the proposal? What is its present status?

2. Write an argumentative essay on an environmental issue that you feel strongly about. Suggested topics: nuclear power plants, alternative forms of energy, water pollution, preservation of wilderness areas, dam construction, protection of whales or harp seals.

3. Write an essay comparing the argumentative strategies of Vidal's "Drugs" and Abbey's "Second Rape of the West."

Professions
for Women

VIRGINIA WOOLF

Virginia Woolf (1882-1941) was a leading member of the London intellectual circle known as the Bloomsbury Group. She is
best remembered for her novels, the most famous of which are
Mrs. Dalloway (1925), *To the Lighthouse* (1927), and *The
Waves* (1931). Her long-standing interest in women's issues
manifests itself most prominently in the essay, "Professions for
Women" and the book *A Room of One's Own.* "Professions for
Women," which is reprinted here, was first given as a speech
to the Women's Service League. It is an acute analysis of the
psychological conflicts a woman faces when attempting to
become a writer. Underlying this analysis is Woolf's commitment to the struggle for increased opportunities for women in
all areas of professional life.

When your secretary invited me to come here, she told me that your Society is
concerned with the employment of women and she suggested that I might tell
you something about my own professional experiences. It is true I am a woman;
it is true I am employed; but what professional experiences have I had? It is difficult to say. My profession is literature; and in that profession there are fewer
experiences for women than in any other, with the exception of the stage — fewer,
I mean, that are peculiar to women. For the road was cut many years ago — by

Fanny Burney, by Aphra Behn, by Harriet Martineau, by Jane Austen, by George Eliot — many famous women, and many more unknown and forgotten, have been before me, making the path smooth, and regulating my steps. Thus, when I came to write, there were very few material obstacles in my way. Writing was a reputable and harmless occupation. The family peace was not broken by the scratching of a pen. No demand was made upon the family purse. For ten and sixpence one can buy paper enough to write all the plays of Shakespeare — if one has a mind that way. Pianos and models, Paris, Vienna and Berlin, masters and mistresses, are not needed by a writer. The cheapness of writing paper is, of course, the reason why women have succeeded as writers before they have succeeded in the other professions.

But to tell you my story — it is a simple one. You have only got to figure to yourselves a girl in a bedroom with a pen in her hand. She had only to move that pen from left to right — from ten o'clock to one. Then it occurred to her to do what is simple and cheap enough after all — to slip a few of those pages into an envelope, fix a penny stamp in the corner, and drop the envelope into the red box at the corner. It was thus that I became a journalist; and my effort was rewarded on the first day of the following month — a very glorious day it was for me — by a letter from an editor containing a cheque for one pound ten shillings and sixpence. But to show you how little I deserve to be called a professional woman, how little I know of the struggles and difficulties of such lives, I have to admit that instead of spending that sum upon bread and butter, rent, shoes and stockings, or butcher's bills, I went out and bought a cat — a beautiful cat, a Persian cat, which very soon involved me in bitter disputes with my neighbours.

What could be easier than to write articles and to buy Persian cats with the profits? But wait a moment. Articles have to be about something. Mine, I seem to remember, was about a novel by a famous man. And while I was writing this review, I discovered that if I were going to review books I should need to do battle with a certain phantom. And the phantom was a woman, and when I came to know her better I called her after the heroine of a famous poem, The Angel in the House. It was she who used to come between me and my paper when I was writing reviews. It was she who bothered me and wasted my time and so tormented me that at last I killed her. You who come of a younger and happier generation may not have heard of her — you may not know what I mean by the Angel in the House. I will describe her as shortly as I can. She was intensely sympathetic. She was immensely charming. She was utterly unselfish. She excelled in the difficult arts of family life. She sacrificed herself daily. If there was chicken, she took the leg; if there was a draught she sat in it — in short she was so constituted that she never had a mind or a wish of her own, but preferred to sympathize always with the minds and wishes of others. Above all — I need not say it — she was pure. Her purity was supposed to be her chief beauty — her blushes, her great grace. In those days — the last of Queen Victoria — every house had its Angel. And when I came to write I encountered her with the very first words. The shadow of her wings fell on my page; I heard the rustling of her skirts in the room. Directly, that is to say, I took my pen in hand to review that novel by a famous man, she slipped behind me and whispered: "My dear, you are a young woman. You are writing about a book that has been written by a man. Be sympathetic; be tender; flatter; deceive; use all the arts and wiles of our sex. Never let anybody guess that you have a mind of your own. Above all, be pure." And she made as if to guide my pen. I now record the one act for which I take some credit to myself, though the credit rightly belongs to some excellent ancestors of mine who left me a certain sum of money — shall we say five hundred pounds a year? — so that it was not necessary for me to depend solely on charm for my living. I turned upon her and caught her by the throat. I did my best to kill her. My excuse, if I were to be had up in a court of law, would be that I acted in self-defence. Had I not killed her she would have killed me. She would have plucked the heart out of my writing. For, as I found, directly I put pen to paper, you cannot review even a novel without having a mind of your own, without expressing what you think to be the truth about human relations, morality, sex. And all these questions, according to the Angel in the House, cannot be dealt with freely and openly by women; they must charm, they must conciliate, they must — to put it bluntly — tell lies if they are to succeed. Thus, whenever I felt the shadow of her wing or the radiance of her halo upon my page, I took up the inkpot and flung it at her. She died hard. Her fictitious nature was of great assistance to her. It is far harder to kill a phantom than a reality. She was always creeping back when I thought I had despatched her. Though I flatter myself that I killed her in the end, the struggle was severe; it took much time that had better have been spent upon learning Greek grammar; or in roaming the world in search of adventures. But it was a real experience; it was an experience that was bound to befall all women writers at that time. Killing the Angel in the House was part of the occupation of a woman writer.

But to continue my story. The Angel was dead; what then remained? You may say that what remained was a simple and common object — a young woman in a bedroom with an inkpot. In other words, now that she had rid herself of falsehood, that young woman had only to be herself. Ah, but what is "herself"? I mean, what is a woman? I assure you, I do not know. I do not believe that you know. I do not believe that anybody can know until she has expressed herself in all the arts and professions open to human skill. That indeed is one of the reasons why I have come here — out of respect for you, who are in process of showing us by your experiments what a woman is, who are in process of providing us, by your failures and successes, with that extremely important piece of information.

But to continue the story of my professional experiences. I made one pound ten and six by my first review; and I bought a Persian cat with the proceeds. Then I grew ambitious. A Persian cat is all very well, I said; but a Persian cat is not enough. I must have a motor car. And it was thus that I became a novelist — for it is a very strange thing that people will give you a motor car if you will tell them a story. It is a still stranger thing that there is nothing so delightful in the world as telling stories. It is far pleasanter than writing reviews of famous novels. And yet, if I am to obey your secretary and tell you my professional experiences as a novelist, I must tell you about a very strange experience that befell me as a novelist. And to understand it you must try first to imagine a novelist's state of mind. I hope I am not giving away professional secrets if I say that a novelist's desire is to be as unconscious as possible. He has to induce in himself a state of perpetual lethargy. He wants life to proceed with the utmost quiet and regularity. He wants to see the same faces, to read the same books, to do the same things day after day, month after month, while he is writing, so that nothing may break the illusion in which he is living — so that nothing may disturb or disquiet the mysterious nosings about, feelings round, darts, dashes and sudden discoveries of that very shy and illusive spirit, the imagination. I suspect that this state is the same both for men and women. Be that as it may, I want you to imagine me writing a novel in a state of trance. I want you to figure to yourselves a girl sitting with a pen in her hand, which for minutes, and indeed for hours, she never dips into the inkpot. The image that comes to my mind when I think of this girl is the image of a fisherman lying sunk in dreams on the verge of a deep lake with a rod held out over the water. She was letting her imagination sweep unchecked round every rock and cranny of the world that lies submerged in the depths of our unconscious being. Now came the experience, the experience that I believe to be far commoner with women writers than with men. The line raced through the girl's fingers. Her imagination had rushed away. It had sought the pools, the depths, the dark places where the largest fish slumber. And then there was a smash. There was an explosion. There was foam and confusion. The imagination had dashed itself against something hard. The girl was roused from her dream. She was indeed in a state of the most acute and difficult distress. To speak without figure she had thought of something, something about the body, about the passions which it was unfitting for her as a woman to say. Men, her reason told her, would be shocked. The consciousness of what men will say of a woman who speaks the truth about her passions had roused her from her artist's state of unconsciousness. She could write no more. The trance was over. Her imagination could work no longer. This I believe to be a very common experience with women writers — they are impeded by the extreme conventionality of the other sex. For though men sensibly allow themselves great freedom in these respects, I doubt that they realize or can control the extreme severity with which they condemn such freedom in women.

These then were two very genuine experiences of my own. These were two of the adventures of my professional life. The first — killing the Angel in the House — I think I solved. She died. But the second, telling the truth about my own experiences as a body, I do not think I solved. I doubt that any woman has solved it yet. The obstacles against her are still immensely powerful — and yet they are very difficult to define. Outwardly, what is simpler than to write books? Outwardly, what obstacles are there for a woman rather than for a man? Inwardly, I think, the case is very different; she has still many ghosts to fight, many prejudices to overcome. Indeed it will be a long time still, I think, before a woman can sit down to write a book without finding a phantom to be slain, a rock to be dashed against. And if this is so in literature, the freest of all professions for women, how is it in the new professions which you are now for the first time entering?

Those are the questions that I should like, had I time, to ask you. And indeed, if I have laid stress upon these professional experiences of mine, it is because I believe that they are, though in different forms, yours also. Even when the path is nominally open — when there is nothing to prevent a woman from being a doctor, a lawyer, a civil servant — there are many phantoms and obstacles, as I believe, looming in her way. To discuss and define them is I think of great value and importance; for thus only can the labour be shared, the difficulties be solved. But besides this, it is necessary also to discuss the ends and the aims for which we are fighting, for which we are doing battle with these formidable obstacles. Those aims cannot be taken for granted; they must be perpetually questioned and examined. The whole position, as I see it — here in this hall surrounded by women practising for the first time in history I know not how many different professions — is one of extraordinary interest and importance. You have won rooms of your own in the house hitherto exclusively owned by men. You are able, though not without great labour and effort, to pay the rent. You are earning your five hundred pounds a year. But this freedom is only a beginning; the room is your own, but it is still bare. It has to be furnished; it has to be decorated; it has to be shared. How are you going to furnish it, how are you going to decorate it? With whom are you going to share it, and upon what terms? These, I think, are questions of the utmost importance and interest. For the first time in history you are able to ask them; for the first time you are able to decide for yourselves what the answers should be. Willingly would I stay and discuss those questions and answers — but not tonight. My time is up; and I must cease.

Questions for Discussion

1. Woolf says that the "cheapness of writing paper is, of course, the reason why women have succeeded as writers before they have succeeded in the other professions." What do you think she means by this statement?

2. At the center of Woolf's essay is the metaphoric "Angel in the House." In your own words, what do you understand this metaphor to mean? To what extent do you think this self-image still remains a problem for women? Be prepared to support your answer with specific examples.

3. Discuss the ways Woolf makes her experience as a writer accessible to an audience of nonwriters.

4. The introduction and conclusion of this essay reveal that it was written to be read aloud at a women's conference. How else does the essay reveal that it was originally a speech? Do the oral techniques Woolf uses limit her ability to present an effective argument? Explain.

5. Readers have sometimes criticized Woolf for failing to answer the questions she poses

at the end of her presentation. How effective do you find the conclusion of her essay to be? Are you satisfied with her explanation of why she could not pursue the questions she raises?

6. Woolf implies in this essay that the primary obstacles women face in their efforts to obtain equality are internal, psychological ones. Do you agree? Why or why not?

Suggested Activities

1. Prepare a report for your class identifying Fanny Burney, Aphra Behn, Harriet Martineau, Jane Austen, and George Eliot and explaining their significance to Woolf's argument.

2. Woolf's phrase "Angel in the House" alludes to the title of a nineteenth-century poem by Coventry Patmore. Write an essay comparing the views of women expressed in Woolf's essay with those expressed in Patmore's poem.

3. Write a brief essay describing what you think would be the male equivalent of the "Angel in the House."

Politics and
the English Language

GEORGE ORWELL

For biographical information on George Orwell, see page 241. Orwell's "Politics and the English Language," from his *Shooting an Elephant and Other Essays* (1950), is one of the most influential assessments of the state of the language ever written. Using a sophisticated combination of political and stylistic analysis, Orwell traces the causes of our modern misuse of the language and offers shrewd advice on how it can be corrected.

Most people who bother with the matter at all would admit that the English language is in a bad way, but it is generally assumed that we cannot by conscious action do anything about it. Our civilization is decadent and our language — so the argument runs — must inevitably share in the general collapse. It follows that any struggle against the abuse of language is a sentimental archaism, like preferring candles to electric light or hansom cabs to aeroplanes. Underneath this lies the half-conscious belief that language is a natural growth and not an instrument which we shape for our own purposes.

Now, it is clear that the decline of a language must ultimately have political and economic causes: it is not due simply to the bad influence of this or that individual writer. But an effect can become a cause, reinforcing the original cause and producing the same effect in an intensified form, and so on indefinitely. A man may take to drink because he feels himself to be a failure, and then fail all the more completely because he drinks. It is rather the same thing that is happening to the English language. It becomes ugly and inaccurate because our thoughts are foolish, but the slovenliness of our language makes it easier for us to have foolish thoughts. The point is that the process is reversible. Modern English, especially written English, is full of bad habits which spread by imitation and which can be avoided if one is willing to take the necessary trouble. If one gets rid of these habits one can think more clearly, and to think clearly is a necessary first step towards political regeneration: so that the fight against bad English is not frivolous and is not the exclusive concern of professional writers. I will come back to this presently, and I hope that by that time the meaning of what I have said here will have become clearer. Meanwhile, here are five specimens of the English language as it is now habitually written.

These five passages have not been picked out because they are especially bad — I could have quoted far worse if I had chosen — but because they illustrate various of the mental vices from which we now suffer. They are a little below the average, but are fairly representative samples. I number them so that I can refer back to them when necessary:

(1) I am not, indeed, sure whether it is not true to say that the Milton who once seemed not unlike a seventeenth-century Shelley had not become, out of an experience ever more bitter in each year, more alien [*sic*] to the founder of that Jesuit sect which nothing could induce him to tolerate.

— Professor Harold Laski (essay in *Freedom of Expression*)

(2) Above all, we cannot play ducks and drakes with a native battery of idioms which prescribes such egregious collocations of vocables as the Basic *put up with* for *tolerate* or *put at a loss* for *bewilder*.

— Professor Lancelot Hogben *(Interglossa)*

(3) On the one side we have the free personality: by definition it is not neurotic, for it has neither conflict nor dream. Its desires, such as they are, are transparent, for they are just what institutional approval keeps in the forefront of consciousness; another institutional pattern would alter their number and intensity; there is little in them that is natural, irreducible, or culturally dangerous. But *on the other side*, the social bond itself is nothing but the mutual reflection of these self-secure integrities. Recall the definition of love. Is not this the very picture of a small academic? Where is there a place in this hall of mirrors for either personality or fraternity?

— Essay on psychology in *Politics* (New York)

(4) All the "best people" from the gentlemen's clubs, and all the frantic fascist captains, united in common hatred of Socialism and bestial horror of the rising tide of the mass revolutionary movement, have turned to acts of provocation, to foul incendiarism, to medieval leg-

ends of poisoned wells, to legalize their own destruction of proletarian organizations, and rouse the agitated petty-bourgeoisie to chauvinistic fervour on behalf of the fight against the revolutionary way out of the crisis.

—Communist pamphlet

(5) If a new spirit *is* to be infused into this old country, there is one thorny and contentious reform which must be tackled, and that is the humanization and galvanization of the B.B.C. Timidity here will bespeak cancer and atrophy of the soul. The heart of Britain may be sound and of strong beat, for instance, but the British lion's roar at present is like that of Bottom in Shakespeare's *Midsummer Night's Dream* — as gentle as any sucking dove. A virile new Britain cannot continue indefinitely to be traduced in the eyes or rather ears, of the world by the effete languors of Langham Place, brazenly masquerading as "standard English". When the Voice of Britain is heard at nine o'clock, better far and infinitely less ludicrous to hear aitches honestly dropped than the present priggish, inflated, inhibited, schoolma'amish arch braying of blameless bashful mewing maidens!

—Letter in *Tribune*

Each of these passages has faults of its own, but, quite apart from avoidable ugliness, two qualities are common to all of them. The first is staleness of imagery; the other is lack of precision. The writer either has a meaning and cannot express it, or he inadvertently says something else, or he is almost indifferent as to whether his words mean anything or not. This mixture of vagueness and sheer incompetence is the most marked characteristic of modern English prose, and especially of any kind of political writing. As soon as certain topics are raised, the concrete melts into the abstract and no one seems able to think of turns of speech that are not hackneyed: prose consists less and less of *words* chosen for the sake of their meaning, and more and more of *phrases* tacked together like the sections of a prefabricated hen-house. I list below, with notes and examples, various of the tricks by means of which the work of prose-construction is habitually dodged:

Dying metaphors.   A newly invented metaphor assists thought by evoking a visual image, while on the other hand a metaphor which is technically "dead" (e.g. *iron resolution*) has in effect reverted to being an ordinary word and can generally be used without loss of vividness. But in between these two classes there is a huge dump of worn-out metaphors which have lost all evocative power and are merely used because they save people the trouble of inventing phrases for themselves. Examples are: *Ring the changes on, take up the cudgels for, toe the line, ride roughshod over, stand shoulder to shoulder with, play into the hands of, no axe to grind, grist to the mill, fishing in troubled waters, on the order of the day, Achilles' heel, swan song, hotbed.* Many of these are used without knowledge of their meaning (what is a "rift", for instance?), and incompatible metaphors are frequently mixed, a sure sign that the writer is not interested in what he is saying. Some metaphors now current have been twisted out of their original meaning without those who use them even being aware of the fact. For example, *toe the line* is sometimes written *tow the line*. Another example is *the hammer and the anvil*, now always used with the implication that the anvil gets the worst of it. In real life it is always the anvil that breaks the hammer, never the other way about: a writer who stopped to think what he was saying would be aware of this, and would avoid perverting the original phrase.

Operators or *verbal false limbs.*   These save the trouble of picking out appropriate verbs and nouns, and at the same time pad each sentence with extra syllables which give it an appearance of symmetry. Characteristic phrases are: *render inoperative, militate against, make contact with, be subjected to, give rise to, give grounds for, have the effect of, play a leading part (role) in, make itself felt, take effect, exhibit a tendency to, serve the purpose of, etc., etc.* The keynote is the elimination of simple verbs. Instead of being a single word, such as *break, stop, spoil, mend, kill,* a verb becomes a *phrase,* made up of a noun or adjective tacked on to some general-purposes verb such as *prove, serve, form, play, render.* In addition, the passive voice is wherever possible used in preference to the active, and noun constructions are used instead of gerunds (*by examination of* instead of *by examining*). The range of verbs is further cut down by means of the *-ize* and *de-* formation, and the banal statements are given an appearance of profundity by means of the *not un-* formation. Simple conjunctions and prepositions are replaced by such phrases as *with respect to, having regard to, the fact that, by dint of, in view of, in the interests of, on the hypothesis that;* and the ends of sentences are saved from anticlimax by such resounding commonplaces as *greatly to be desired, cannot be left out of account, a development to be expected in the near future, deserving of serious consideration, brought to a satisfactory conclusion,* and so on and so forth.

Pretentious diction.   Words like *phenomenon, element, individual* (as noun), *objective, categorical, effective, virtual, basic, primary, promote, constitute, exhibit, exploit, utilize, eliminate, liquidate,* are used to dress up simple statement and give an air of scientific impartiality to biased judgments. Adjectives like *epoch-making, epic, historic, unforgettable, triumphant, age-old, inevitable, inexorable, veritable,* are used to dignify the sordid processes of international politics, while writing that aims at glorifying war usually takes on an archaic colour, its characteristic words being: *realm, throne, chariot, mailed fist, trident, sword, shield, buckler, banner, jackboot, clarion.* Foreign words and expressions such as *cul de sac, ancien régime, deus ex machina, mutatis mutandis, status quo, gleichschaltung, weltanschauung,* are used to give an air of culture and elegance. Except for the useful abbreviations *i.e., e.g.,* and *etc.,* there is no real need for any of the hundreds of foreign phrases now current in English. Bad writers, and especially scientific, political and sociological writers, are nearly always haunted by the notion that Latin or Greek words are grander than Saxon ones, and unnecessary words like *expedite, ameliorate, predict, extraneous, deracinated, clandestine, subaqueous* and hundreds of others constantly gain ground from their Anglo-Saxon opposite numbers.[1] The jargon peculiar to Marxist writing (*hyena, hangman, cannibal, petty bourgeois, these gentry, lacquey, flunkey, mad dog, White Guard,* etc.) consists largely of words and phrases translated from Russian, German or French; but the normal way of coining a new word is to use a Latin or Greek root with the appropriate affix and, where necessary, the -ize formation. It is often easier to make up words of this kind (*deregionalize, impermissible, extramarital, nonfragmentatory* and so forth) than to think up the English words that will cover one's meaning. The result, in general, is an increase in slovenliness and vagueness.

Meaningless words.   In certain kinds of writing, particularly in art criticism and literary criticism, it is normal to come across long passages which are almost completely lacking in meaning.[2] Words like *romantic, plastic, values, human, dead, sentimental, natural, vitality,* as used in art criticism, are strictly meaningless in the sense that they not only do not point to any discoverable object, but are hardly ever expected to so by the reader. When one critic writes, "The outstanding feature of Mr. X's work is its living quality", while another writes, "The immediately striking thing about Mr. X's work is its peculiar deadness", the reader accepts this as a simple difference of opinion. If words like *black* and *white* were involved, instead of the jargon words *dead* and *living,* he would see at once that language was being used in an improper way. Many political words are similarly abused. The word *Fascism* has now no meaning except in so far as it signifies "something not desirable". The words *democracy, socialism, freedom, patriotic, realistic, justice,* have each of them several different meanings which cannot be reconciled with one another. In the case of a word like *democracy,* not only is there no agreed definition, but the attempt to make one is resisted from all sides. It is almost universally felt that when we call a country democratic we are praising it; consequently the defenders of every kind of régime claim that it is a democracy, and fear that they might have to stop using the word if it were tied down to any one meaning. Words of this kind are often used in a consciously dishonest way. That is, the person who uses them has his own private definition, but allows his hearer to think he means something quite different. Statements like *Marshal Pétain was a true patriot, The Soviet Press is the freest in the world, The Catholic Church is opposed to persecution,* are almost always made with

---

[1]An interesting illustration of this is the way in which the English flower names which were in use till very recently are being ousted by Greek ones, *snapdragon* becoming *antirrhinum, forget-me-not* becoming *myosotis,* etc. It is hard to see any practical reason for this change of fashion: it is probably due to an instinctive turning-away from the more homely word and a vague feeling that the Greek word is scientific.

[2]Example: "Comfort's catholicity of perception and image, strangely Whitmanesque in range, almost the exact opposite in aesthetic compulsion, continues to evoke that trembling atmospheric accumulative hinting at a cruel, an inexorably serene timelessness . . . Wrey Gardiner scores by aiming at simple bull's-eyes with precision. Only they are not so simple, and through this contented sadness runs more than the surface bitter-sweet of resignation." *(Poetry Quarterly.)*

intent to deceive. Other words used in variable meanings, in most cases more or less dishonestly, are: *class*, *totalitarian*, *science*, *progressive*, *reactionary*, *bourgeois*, *equality*.

Now that I have made this catalogue of swindles and perversions, let me give another example of the kind of writing that they lead to. This time it must of its nature be an imaginary one. I am going to translate a passage of good English into modern English of the worst sort. Here is a well-known verse from *Ecclesiastes*:

"I returned and saw under the sun, that the race is not to the swift, nor the battle to the strong, neither yet bread to the wise, nor yet riches to men of understanding, nor yet favour to men of skill; but time and chance happeneth to them all."

Here it is in modern English:

"Objective consideration of contemporary phenomena compels the conclusion that success or failure in competitive activities exhibits no tendency to be commensurate with innate capacity, but that a considerable element of the unpredictable must invariably be taken into account."

This is a parody, but not a very gross one. Exhibit (3), above, for instance, contains several patches of the same kind of English. It will be seen that I have not made a full translation. The beginning and ending of the sentence follow the original meaning fairly closely, but in the middle the concrete illustrations — race, battle, bread — dissolve into the vague phrase "success or failure in competitive activities". This had to be so, because no modern writer of the kind I am discussing — no one capable of using phrases like "objective consideration of contemporary phenomena" — would ever tabulate his thoughts in that precise and detailed way. The whole tendency of modern prose is away from concreteness. Now analyse these two sentences a little more closely. The first contains forty-nine words but only sixty syllables, and all its words are those of everyday life. The second contains thirty-eight words of ninety syllables: eighteen of its words are from Latin roots, and one from Greek. The first sentence contains six vivid images, and only one phrase ("time and chance") that could be called vague. The second contains not a single fresh, arresting phrase, and in spite of its ninety syllables it gives only a shortened version of the meaning contained in the first. Yet without a doubt it is the second kind of sentence that is gaining ground in modern English. I do not want to exaggerate. This kind of writing is not yet universal, and outcrops of simplicity will occur here and there in the worst-written page. Still, if you or I were told to write a few lines on the uncertainty of human fortunes, we should probably come much nearer to my imaginary sentence than to the one from *Ecclesiastes*.

As I have tried to show, modern writing at its worst does not consist in picking out words for the sake of their meaning and inventing images in order to make the meaning clearer. It consists in gumming together long strips of words which have already been set in order by someone else, and making the results presentable by sheer humbug. The attraction of this way of writing is that it is easy. It is easier — even quicker, once you have the habit — to say *In my opinion it is a not unjustifiable assumption that* than to say *I think*. If you use ready-made phrases, you not only don't have to hunt about for words; you also don't have to bother with the rhythms of your sentences, since these phrases are generally so arranged as to be more or less euphonious. When you are composing in a hurry — when you are dictating to a stenographer, for instance, or making a public speech — it is natural to fall into a pretentious, Latinized style. Tags like *a consideration which we should do well to bear in mind* or *a conclusion to which all of us would readily assent* will save many a sentence from coming down with a bump. By using stale metaphors, similes and idioms, you save much mental effort, at the cost of leaving your meaning vague, not only for your reader but for yourself. This is the significance of mixed metaphors. The sole aim of a metaphor is to call up a visual image. When these images clash — as in *The Fascist octopus has sung its swan song, the jackboot is thrown into the melting pot* — it can be taken as certain that the writer is not seeing a mental image of the objects he is naming; in other words he is not really thinking. Look again at the examples I gave at the beginning of this essay. Professor Laski (1) uses five negatives in fifty-three words. One of these is superfluous, making nonsense of the whole passage, and in addition there is the slip *alien* for akin, making further nonsense, and several avoidable pieces of clumsiness which increase the general vagueness. Professor Hogben (2) plays ducks and drakes with a battery which is able to write prescriptions, and, while disapproving of the everyday phrase *put up with*, is unwilling to look *egregious* up in the dictionary and see what it means. (3), if one takes an uncharitable attitude toward it, is simply meaningless: probably one could work out its intended meaning by reading the whole of the article in which it occurs. In (4), the writer knows more or less what he wants to say, but an accumulation of stale phrases chokes him like tea leaves blocking a sink. In (5), words and meaning have almost parted company. People who write in this manner usually have a general emotional meaning — they dislike one thing and want to express solidarity with another — but they are not interested in the detail of what they are saying. A scrupulous writer, in every sentence that he writes, will ask himself at least four questions, thus: What am I trying to say? What words will express it? What image or idiom will make it clearer? Is this image fresh enough to have an effect? And he will probably ask himself two more: Could I put it more shortly? Have I said anything that is avoidably ugly? But you are not obliged to go to all this trouble. You can shirk it by simply throwing your mind open and letting the ready-made phrases come crowding in. They will construct your sentences for you — even think your thoughts for you, to a certain extent — and at need they will perform the important service of partially concealing your meaning even from yourself. It is at this point that the special connection between politics and the debasement of language becomes clear.

In our time it is broadly true that political writing is bad writing. Where it is not true, it will generally be found that the writer is some kind of rebel, expressing his private opinions and not a "party line". Orthodoxy, of whatever colour, seems to demand a lifeless, imitative style. The political dialects to be found in pamphlets, leading articles, manifestos, White Papers and the speeches of under-secretaries do, of course, vary from party to party, but they are all alike in that one almost never finds in them a fresh, vivid, home-made turn of speech. When one watches some tired hack on the platform mechanically repeating the familiar phrases — *bestial atrocities, iron heel, bloodstained tyranny, free peoples of the world, stand shoulder to shoulder* — one often has a curious feeling that one is not watching a live human being but some kind of dummy: a feeling which suddenly becomes stronger at moments when the light catches the speaker's spectacles and turns them into blank discs which seem to have no eyes behind them. And this is not altogether fanciful. A speaker who uses that kind of phraseology has gone some distance towards turning himself into a machine. The appropriate noises are coming out of his larynx, but his brain is not involved as it would be if he were choosing his words for himself. If the speech he is making is one that he is accustomed to make over and over again, he may be almost unconscious of what he is saying, as one is when one utters the responses in church. And this reduced state of consciousness, if not indispensable, is at any rate favourable to political conformity.

In our time, political speech and writing are largely the defence of the indefensible. Things like the continuance of British rule in India, the Russian purges and deportations, the dropping of the atom bombs on Japan, can indeed be defended, but only by arguments which are too brutal for most people to face, and which do not square with the professed aims of political parties. Thus political language has to consist largely of euphemism, question-begging and sheer cloudy vagueness. Defenceless villages are bombarded from the air, the inhabitants driven out into the countryside, the cattle machine-gunned, the huts set on fire with incendiary bullets: this is called *pacification*. Millions of peasants are robbed of their farms and sent trudging along the roads with no more than they can carry: this is called *transfer of population* or *rectification of frontiers*. People are imprisoned for years without trial, or shot in the back of the neck or sent to die of scurvy in Arctic lumber camps: this is called *elimination of unreliable elements*. Such phraseology is needed if one wants to name things without calling up mental pictures of them. Consider for instance some confortable English professor defending Russian totalitarianism. He cannot say outright, "I believe in killing off your opponents when you can get good results by doing so". Probably, therefore, he will say something like this:

"While freely conceding that the Soviet régime exhibits certain features which the humanitarian may be inclined to deplore, we must, I think, agree that a certain curtailment of the right to political opposition is an unavoidable concomitant of transitional periods, and that the rigours which the Russian people have been called upon to undergo have been amply justified in the sphere of concrete achievement."

The inflated style is itself a kind of euphemism. A mass of Latin words falls upon the facts like soft snow, blurring the outlines and covering up all the details. The great enemy of clear language is insincerity. When there is a gap between one's real and one's declared aims, one turns as it were instinctively to long words and exhausted idioms, like a cuttlefish squirting out ink. In our age there is no such thing as "keeping out of politics". All issues are political issues, and politics itself is a mass of lies, evasions, folly, hatred and schizophrenia. When the general atmosphere is bad, language must suffer. I should expect to find — this is a guess which I have not sufficient knowledge to verify — that the German, Russian and Italian languages have all deteriorated in the last ten or fifteen years, as a result of dictatorship.

But if thought corrupts language, language can also corrupt thought. A bad usage can spread by tradition and imitation, even among people who should and do know better. The debased language that I have been discussing is in some ways very convenient. Phrases like *a not unjustifiable assumption, leaves much to be desired, would serve no good purpose, a consideration which we should do well to bear in mind*, are a continuous temptation, a packet of aspirins always at one's elbow. Look back through this essay, and for certain you will find that I have again and again committed the very faults I am protesting against. By this morning's post I have received a pamphlet dealing with conditions in Germany. The author tells me that he "felt impelled" to write it. I open it at random, and here is almost the first sentence that I see: "(The Allies) have an opportunity not only of achieving a radical transformation of Germany's social and political structure in such a way as to avoid a nationalistic reaction in Germany itself, but at the same time of laying the foundations of a co-operative and unified Europe." You see, he "feels impelled" to write — feels, presumably, that he has something new to say — and yet his words, like cavalry horses answering the bugle, group themselves automatically into the familiar dreary pattern. This invasion of one's mind by ready-made phrases *(lay the foundations, achieve a radical transformation)* can only be prevented if one is constantly on guard against them, and every such phrase anaesthetizes a portion of one's brain.

I said earlier that the decadence of our language is probably curable. Those who deny this would argue, if they produced an argument at all, that language merely reflects existing social conditions, and that we cannot influence its development by any direct tinkering with words and constructions. So far as the general tone or spirit of a language goes, this may be true, but it is not true in detail. Silly words and expressions have often disappeared, not through any evolutionary process but owing to the conscious action of a minority. Two recent examples were *explore every avenue* and *leave no stone unturned*, which were killed by the jeers of a few journalists. There is a long list of flyblown metaphors which could similarly be got rid of if enough people would interest themselves in the job; and it should also be possible to laugh the *not un-* formation out of existence,[3] to reduce the amount of Latin and Greek in the average sentence, to drive out foreign phrases and strayed scientific words, and, in general, to make pretentiousness unfashionable. But all these are minor points. The defence of the English language implies more than this, and perhaps it is best to start by saying what it does *not* imply.

To begin with it has nothing to do with archaism, with the salvaging of obsolete words and turns of speech, or with the setting up of a "standard English"

---

[3]One can cure oneself of the *not un-* formation by memorizing this sentence: *A not unblack dog was chasing a not unsmall rabbit across a not ungreen field.*

which must never be departed from. On the contrary, it is especially concerned
with the scrapping of every word or idiom which has outworn its usefulness. It
has nothing to do with correct grammar and syntax, which are of no importance
so long as one makes one's meaning clear, or with the avoidance of Americanisms,
or with having what is called a "good prose style". On the other hand it is not
concerned with fake simplicity and the attempt to make written English collo-
quial. Nor does it even imply in every case preferring the Saxon word to the Latin
one, though it does imply using the fewest and shortest words that will cover
one's meaning. What is above all needed is to let the meaning choose the word,
and not the other way about. In prose, the worst thing one can do with words is
to surrender to them. When you think of a concrete object, you think wordlessly,
and then, if you want to describe the thing you have been visualizing you probably hunt about till you find the exact words that seem to fit. When you think
of something abstract you are more inclined to use words from the start, and
unless you make a conscious effort to prevent it, the existing dialect will come
rushing in and do the job for you, at the expense of blurring or even changing
your meaning. Probably it is better to put off using words as long as possible and
get one's meaning as clear as one can through pictures or sensations. Afterwards
one can choose — not simply *accept* — the phrases that will best cover the meaning, and then switch round and decide what impression one's words are likely to
make on another person. This last effort of the mind cuts out all stale or mixed
images, all prefabricated phrases, needless repetitions, and humbug and vagueness
generally. But one can often be in doubt about the effect of a word or a phrase,
and one needs rules that one can rely on when instinct fails. I think the following
rules will cover most cases:

  (i) Never use a metaphor, simile or other figure of speech which
       you are used to seeing in print.
 (ii) Never use a long word where a short one will do.
(iii) If it is possible to cut a word out, always cut it out.
 (iv) Never use the passive where you can use the active.
  (v) Never use a foreign phrase, a scientific word or a jargon word if
       you can think of an everyday English equivalent.
 (vi) Break any of these rules sooner than say anything outright
       barbarous.

   These rules sound elementary, and so they are, but they demand a deep
change of attitude in anyone who has grown used to writing in the style now
fashionable. One could keep all of them and still write bad English; but one could
not write the kind of stuff that I quoted in those five specimens at the beginning
of this article.
   I have not here been considering the literary use of language, but merely
language as an instrument for expressing and not for concealing or preventing
thought. Stuart Chase and others have come near to claiming that all abstract
words are meaningless, and have used this as a pretext for advocating a kind of

political quietism. Since you don't know what Fascism is, how can you struggle against Fascism? One need not swallow such absurdities as this, but one ought to recognize that the present political chaos is connected with the decay of language, and that one can probably bring about some improvement by starting at the verbal end. If you simplify your English, you are freed from the worst follies of orthodoxy. You cannot speak any of the necessary dialects, and when you make a stupid remark its stupidity will be obvious, even to yourself. Political language — and with variations this is true of all political parties, from Conservatives to Anarchists — is designed to make lies sound truthful and murder respectable, and to give an appearance of solidity to pure wind. One cannot change this all in a moment, but one can at least change one's own habits, and from time to time one can even, if one jeers loudly enough, send some worn-out and useless phrase — some *jackboot, Achilles' heel, hotbed, melting pot, acid test, veritable inferno* or other lump of verbal refuse — into the dustbin where it belongs.

Questions for Discussion

1. At the beginning of his second paragraph, Orwell says "it is clear that the decline of a language must ultimately have political and economic causes." Is this clear to you? Why or why not?

2. What, according to Orwell, is wrong with using ready-made phrases in written prose? Do you agree or disagree with his view on this matter?

3. How do you think political language has changed since Orwell wrote this essay in 1946? Be prepared to cite specific examples in support of your answer.

4. Orwell argues that the main cause for the misuse of language is the desire to deceive. Do you agree? What other explanations are there for unclear writing?

5. Orwell contends that the deterioration of the English language is reversible. Do you agree or disagree? What evidence can you offer in support of your view?

6. A recent report by a California state medical agency says that a patient "became deceased as a result of postsurgical complications." Using Orwell's essay as a guide, discuss the politics of this statement.

Suggested Activities

1. Find up-to-date examples of each of the four "swindles and perversions" Orwell identifies (pp. 271–74). Compare your examples with those of your classmates. Can you suggest ways to rid the language of these abuses?

2. Write an essay analyzing the diction and style of a letter you've received from a government agency or from an office of your university or college. Does the letter display any of the faults Orwell describes?

3. Write an essay criticizing or defending the use of euphemisms in relation to one of the following subjects: sex, race, death, drinking. Cite specific examples.

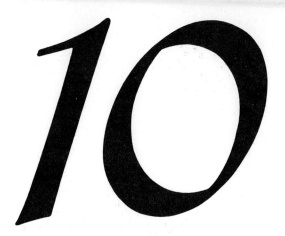

A
Modest Proposal

for Preventing the Children of Ireland from Being a Burden to Their Parents or Country

JONATHAN SWIFT

Jonathan Swift (1667-1745) was an Anglican clergyman, a brilliant satirist, and a staunch defender of individual liberties. In addition to the world-renowned satire *Gulliver's Travels* (1726), his works include *A Tale of a Tub* (1704), *The Battle of the Books* (1704), many poems, and a large number of political pamphlets. "A Modest Proposal," which was first printed in 1729, is an exercise in sustained irony. In it, Swift carries an outrageous premise to its shockingly logical conclusion. Behind his irony lies keen compassion for the plight of the Irish peasants and righteous anger at their English oppressors.

It is a melancholy object to those who walk through this great town or travel in the country, when they see the streets, the roads, and cabin-doors crowded with beggars of the female sex, followed by three, four, or six children, all in rags, and importuning every passenger for an alms. These mothers instead of being able to work for their honest livelihood, are forced to employ all their time in strolling to beg sustenance for their helpless infants, who, as they grow up, either turn thieves for want of work, or leave their dear native country, to fight for the Pretender in Spain, or sell themselves to the Barbadoes.

I think it is agreed by all parties, that this prodigious number of children in the arms, or on the backs, or at the heels of their mothers, and frequently of their fathers, is in the present deplorable state of the kingdom a very great additional grievance; and therefore whoever could find out a fair, cheap, and easy method of making these children sound and useful members of the common-wealth, would deserve so well of the public as to have his statue set up for a preserver of the nation.

But my intention is very far from being confined to provide only for the children of professed beggars; it is of a much greater extent, and shall take in the whole number of infants at a certain age, who are born of parents in effect as little able to support them, as those who demand our charity in the streets.

As to my own part, having turned my thoughts, for many years, upon this important subject, and maturely weighed the several schemes of other projectors, I have always found them grossly mistaken in their computation. It is true, a child just dropt from its dam, may be supported by her milk for a solar year with little other nourishment, at most not above the value of two shillings, which the mother may certainly get, or the value in scraps, by her lawful occupation of begging; and it is exactly at one year old that I propose to provide for them in such a manner, as, instead of being a charge upon their parents, or the parish, or wanting food and raiment for the rest of their lives, they shall, on the contrary, contribute to the feeding and partly to the clothing of many thousands.

There is likewise another great advantage in my scheme, that it will prevent those voluntary abortions, and that horrid practice of women murdering their bastard children, alas! too frequent among us — sacrificing the poor innocent babes, I doubt, more to avoid the expense than the shame — which would move tears and pity in the most savage and inhuman breast.

The number of souls in this kingdom being usually reckoned one million and a half, of these I calculate there may be about two hundred thousand couple whose wives are breeders; from which number I subtract thirty thousand couples, who are able to maintain their own children, although I apprehend there cannot be so many, under the present distresses of the kingdom; but this being granted, there will remain an hundred and seventy thousand breeders. I again subtract fifty thousand, for those women who miscarry, or whose children die by accident or disease within the year. There only remain an hundred and twenty thousand children of poor parents annually born. The question therefore is, how this num-ber shall be reared, and provided for? which, as I have already said, under the present situation of affairs, is utterly impossible by all the methods hitherto pro-posed; for we can neither employ them in handicraft or agriculture; we neither build houses, (I mean in the country) nor cultivate land. They can very seldom pick up a livelihood by stealing till they arrive at six years old, except where they are of towardly parts, although, I confess, they learn the rudiments much earlier; during which time they can however be properly looked upon only as probation-ers; as I have been informed by a principal gentleman in the county of Cavan, who protested to me, that he never knew above one or two instances under the age of six, even in a part of the kingdom so renowned for the quickest proficiency in that art.

I am assured by our merchants, that a boy or a girl before twelve years old, is no salable commodity, and even when they come to this age, they will not yield above three pounds, or three pounds and half a crown at most, on the exchange; which cannot turn to account either to the parents or kingdom, the charge of nutriment and rags having been at least four times that value.

I shall now therefore humbly propose my own thoughts, which I hope will not be liable to the least objection.

I have been assured by a very knowing American of my acquaintance in London, that a young healthy child well nursed is at a year old a most delicious, nourishing, and wholesome food, whether stewed, roasted, baked, or boiled; and I make no doubt that it will equally serve in a fricassee, or a ragout.

I do therefore humbly offer it to publick consideration, that of the hundred and twenty thousand children, already computed, twenty thousand may be reserved for breed, whereof only one fourth part to be males; which is more than we allow to sheep, black cattle, or swine; and my reason is that these children are seldom fruits of marriage, a circumstance not much regarded by our savages; therefore one male will be sufficient to serve four females. That the remaining hundred thousand may, at a year old, be offered in the sale to the persons of quality and fortune through the kingdom; always advising the mother to let them suck plentifully in the last month, so as to render them plump and fat for a good table. A child will make two dishes at an entertainment for friends; and when the family dines alone, the fore or hind quarter will make a reasonable dish, and seasoned with a little pepper or salt will be very good boiled on the fourth day, especially in winter.

I have reckoned upon a medium that a child just born will weigh 12 pounds, and in a solar year, if tolerably nursed, increaseth to 28 pounds.

I grant this food will be somewhat dear, and therefore very proper for land-lords, who, as they have already devoured most of the parents, seem to have the best title to the children.

Infants' flesh will be in season throughout the year, but more plentiful in March, and a little before and after; for we are told by a grave author, an eminent French physician, that fish being a prolific diet, there are more children born in Roman Catholic countries about nine months after Lent than at any other season; therefore, reckoning a year after Lent, the markets will be more glutted than usual, because the number of popish infants is at least three to one in this king-dom; and therefore it will have one other collateral advantage, by lessening the number of papists among us.

I have already computed the charge of nursing a beggar's child (in which list I reckon all cottagers, laborers, and four-fifths of the farmers) to be about two shillings per annum, rags included; and I believe no gentleman would repine to give ten shillings for the carcass of a good fat child, which, as I have said, will make four dishes of excellent nutritive meat, when he hath only some particular friend or his own family to dine with him. Thus the squire will learn to be a good landlord, and grow popular among his tenants; the mother will have eight shillings net profit, and be fit for work till she produces another child.

Those who are more thrifty (as I must confess the times require) may flay the carcass, the skin of which artificially dressed will make admirable gloves for ladies, and summer boots for the fine gentlemen.

As to our city of Dublin, shambles may be appointed for this purpose in the most convenient parts of it, and butchers we may be assured will not be wanting; although I rather recommend buying the children alive and dressing them hot from the knife, as we do roasting pigs.

A very worthy person, a true lover of his country, and whose virtues I highly esteem, was lately pleased in discoursing on this matter to offer a refinement upon my scheme. He said that many gentlemen of this kingdom, having of late destroyed their deer, he conceived that the want of venison might be well supplied by the bodies of young lads and maidens, not exceeding fourteen years of age nor under twelve; so great a number of both sexes in every country being now ready to starve for want of work and service; and these to be disposed of by their parents if alive, or otherwise by their nearest relations. But with due deference to so excellent a friend, and so deserving a patriot, I cannot be altogether in his sentiments; for as to the males, my American acquaintance assured me from frequent experience, that their flesh was generally tough and lean, like that of our schoolboys, by continual exercise, and their taste disagreeable, and to fatten them would not answer the charge. Then as to the females, it would, I think with humble submission, be a loss to the publick, because they soon would become breeders themselves. And besides it is not improbable that some scrupulous people might be apt to censure such a practice (although indeed very unjustly) as a little bordering upon cruelty, which, I confess, hath always been with me the strongest objection against any project, how well soever intended.

But in order to justify my friend, he confessed that this expedient was put into his head by the famous Psalmanazar, a native of the island Formosa, who came from thence to London, above twenty years ago, and in conversation told my friend, that in his country when any young person happened to be put to death, the executioner sold the carcass to persons of quality, as a prime dainty, and that, in his time, the body of a plump girl of fifteen, who was crucified for an attempt to poison the Emperor, was sold to his Imperial Majesty's prime minister of state, and other great mandarins of the court, in joints from the gibbet, at four hundred crowns. Neither indeed can I deny, that if the same use were made of several plump young girls in this town, who, without one single groat to their fortunes, cannot stir abroad without a chair, and appear at the play-house and assemblies in foreign fineries which they never will pay for, the kingdom would not be the worse.

Some persons of a desponding spirit are in great concern about that vast number of poor people, who are aged, diseased, or maimed, and I have been desired to employ my thoughts what course may be taken, to ease the nation of so grievous an encumbrance. But I am not in the least pain upon that matter, because it is very well known, that they are every day dying, and rotting, by cold, and famine, and filth, and vermin, as fast as can be reasonably expected. And as to the younger labourers, they are now in almost as hopeful a condition. They cannot get work, and consequently pine away for want of nourishment, to a degree, that if at any time they are accidentally hired to common labour, they have not strength to perform it, and thus the country and themselves are happily delivered from the evils to come.

I have too long digressed, and therefore shall return to my subject. I think the advantages by the proposal which I have made are obvious and many, as well as of the highest importance.

For *first*, as I have already observed, it would greatly lessen the number of papists, with whom we are yearly over-run, being the principal breeders of the nation, as well as our most dangerous enemies, and who stay at home on purpose with a design to deliver the kingdom to the Pretender, hoping to take their advantage by the absence of so many good Protestants, who have chosen rather to leave their country, than stay at home, and pay tithes against their conscience to an Episcopal curate.

Secondly, the poorer tenants will have something valuable of their own, which by law may be made liable to distress and help to pay their landlord's rent, their corn and cattle being already seized, and money a thing unknown.

Thirdly, whereas the maintenance of an hundred thousand children, from two years old and upward, cannot be computed at less than ten shillings apiece per annum, the nation's stock will be thereby increased fifty thousand pounds per annum, besides the profit of a new dish introduced to the tables of all gentlemen of fortune in the kingdom who have any refinement in taste. And the money will circulate among ourselves, the goods being entirely of our own growth and manufacture.

Fourthly, the constant breeders, beside the gain of eight shillings sterling per annum by the sale of their children, will be rid of the charge of maintaining them after the first year.

Fifthly, this food would likewise bring great custom to taverns, where the vintners will certainly be so prudent as to procure the best receipts for dressing it to perfection, and consequently have their houses frequented by all the fine gentlemen who justly value themselves upon their knowledge in good eating; and a skillful cook, who understands how to oblige his guests, will contrive to make it as expensive as they please.

Sixthly, this would be a great inducement to marriage, which all wise nations have either encouraged by rewards or enforced by laws and penalties. It would increase the care and the tenderness of mothers toward their chidren, when they were sure of a settlement for life to the poor babes, provided in some sort by the public, to their annual profit instead of expense. We should soon see an honest emulation among the married women, which of them could bring the fattest child to the market. Men would become as fond of their wives during the time of their pregnancy as they are now of their mares in foal, their cows in calf, their sows when they are ready to farrow; nor offer to beat or kick them (as is too frequent a practice) for fear of a miscarriage.

Many other advantages might be enumerated. For instance, the addition of some thousand carcasses in our exportation of barreled beef, the propagation of swine's flesh, and improvement in the art of making good bacon, so much wanted among us by the great destruction of pigs, too frequent at our tables; which are no way comparable in taste or magnificence to a well-grown, fat, yearling child, which roasted whole will make a considerable figure at a lord mayor's feast or any other public entertainment. But this and many others I omit, being studious of brevity.

Supposing that one thousand families in this city would be constant customers for infants' flesh, besides others who might have it at merry meetings, particularly at weddings and christenings, I compute that Dublin would take off annually about twenty thousand carcasses; and the rest of the kingdom (where probably they will be sold somewhat cheaper) the remaining eighty thousand.

I can think of no one objection that will possibly be raised against this proposal, unless it should be urged that the number of people will be thereby much lessened in the kingdom. This I freely own, and 'twas indeed one principal design in offering it to the world. I desire the reader will observe that I calculate my remedy for this one individual kingdom of Ireland, and for no other that ever was, is, or, I think, ever can be upon earth. Therefore let no man talk to me of other expedients: of taxing our absentees at five shillings a pound: of using neither clothes, nor household furniture, except what is of our own growth and manufacture: of utterly rejecting the materials and instruments that promote foreign luxury: of curing the expensiveness of pride, vanity, idleness, and gaming in our women: of introducing a vein of parsimony, prudence and temperance: of learning to love our country, wherein we differ even from Laplanders, and the inhabitants of Topinamboo: of quitting our animosities, and factions, nor act any longer like the Jews, who were murdering one another at the very moment their city was taken: of being a little cautious not to sell our country and consciences for nothing: of teaching landlords to have at least one degree of mercy towards their tenants. Lastly, of putting a spirit of honesty, industry, and skill into our shopkeepers, who, if a resolution could now be taken to buy only our native goods, would immediately unite to cheat and exact upon us in the price, the measure, and the goodness, nor could ever yet be brought to make one fair proposal of just dealing, though often and earnestly invited to it.

Therefore I repeat, let no man talk to me of these and the like expedients, till he hath at least some glimpse of hope, that there will ever be some hearty and sincere attempt to put them in practice.

But as to my self, having been wearied out for many years with offering vain, idle, visionary thoughts, and at length utterly despairing of success, I fortunately fell upon this proposal, which as it is wholly new, so it hath something solid and real, of no expense and little trouble, full in our own power, and whereby we can incur no danger in disobliging England. For this kind of commodity will not bear exportation, the flesh being of too tender a consistence, to admit a long continuance in salt, although perhaps I could name a country, which would be glad to eat up our whole nation without it.

After all, I am not so violently bent upon my own opinion, as to reject any offer, proposed by wise men, which shall be found equally innocent, cheap, easy, and effectual. But before something of that kind shall be advanced in contradiction to my scheme, and offering a better, I desire the author or authors, will be pleased maturely to consider two points. *First*, as things now stand, how they will be able to find food and raiment for a hundred thousand useless mouths and backs. And *Secondly*, there being a round million of creatures in human figure throughout this kingdom, whose whole subsistence put into a common stock would leave them in debt two millions of pounds sterling, adding those who are beggars by profession, to the bulk of farmers, cottagers and labourers, with their wives and children, who are beggars in effect; I desire those politicians, who dislike my overture, and may perhaps be so bold to attempt an answer, that they will first ask the parents of these mortals, whether they would not at this day think it a great happiness to have been sold for food at a year old, in the manner I prescribe, and thereby have avoided such a perpetual scene of misfortunes as they have since gone through, by the oppression of landlords, the impossibility of paying rent without money or trade, the want of common sustenance, with neither house nor clothes to cover them from the inclemencies of the weather, and the most inevitable prospect of entailing the like or greater miseries upon their breed forever.

I profess, in the sincerity of my heart, that I have not the least personal interest in endeavoring to promote this necessary work, having no other motive than the public good of my country, by advancing our trade, providing for infants, relieving the poor, and giving some pleasure to the rich. I have no children by which I can propose to get a single penny; the youngest being nine years old, and my wife past child-bearing.

Why I Went
to the Woods

HENRY DAVID THOREAU

A philosopher and observer of nature, Henry David Thoreau (1817-62) was born in Concord, Massachusetts, and lived there almost all his life. One of his best-known works, the essay "Civil Disobedience," is a plea for individual resistance to unjust laws. It profoundly influenced two modern advocates of nonviolent resistance, Mahatma Gandhi and Martin Luther King, Jr. Another widely known work, *Walden* (1854), is Thoreau's record of his experiment in solitary living at Walden Pond, near his native Concord. In the excerpt reprinted here, taken from "Where I Lived, and What I Lived For" in *Walden*, Thoreau gives his reasons for taking up residence in the woods. The excerpt is a good example of his allusive, metaphoric style.

I went to the woods because I wished to live deliberately, to front only the essential facts of life, and see if I could not learn what it had to teach, and not, when I came to die, discover that I had not lived. I did not wish to live what was not life, living is so dear; nor did I wish to practise resignation, unless it was quite necessary. I wanted to live deep and suck out all the marrow of life, to live so sturdily and Spartan-like as to put to rout all that was not life, to cut a broad swath and shave close, to drive life into a corner, and reduce it to its lowest terms, and, if it proved to be·mean, why then to get the whole and genuine meanness of it, and publish its meanness to the world; or if it were sublime, to know it by experience, and be able to give a true account of it in my next excursion. For most men, it appears to me, are in a strange uncertainty about it, whether it is of the devil or of God, and have *somewhat hastily* concluded that it is the chief end of man here to "glorify God and enjoy him forever."

Still we live meanly, like ants; though the fable tells us that we were long ago changed into men; like pygmies we fight with cranes; it is error upon error, and clout upon clout, and our best virtue has for its occasion a superfluous and evitable wretchedness. Our life is frittered away by detail. An honest man has hardly need to count more than his ten fingers, or in extreme cases he may add his ten toes, and lump the rest. Simplicity, simplicity, simplicity! I say, let your affairs be as two or three, and not a hundred or a thousand; instead of a million count half a dozen, and keep your accounts on your thumb nail. In the midst of this chopping sea of civilized life, such are the clouds and storms and quicksands and thousand-and-one items to be allowed for, that a man has to live, if he would not founder and go to the bottom and not make his port at all, by dead reckoning, and he must be a great calculator indeed who succeeds. Simplify, simplify. Instead of three meals a day, if it be necessary eat but one; instead of a hundred dishes, five; and reduce other things in proportion. Our life is like a German Confederacy, made up of petty states, with its boundary forever fluctuating, so that even a German cannot tell you how it is bounded at any moment. The nation itself, with all its so-called internal improvements, which, by the way, are all external and superficial, is just such an unwieldy and overgrown establishment, cluttered with furniture and tripped up by its own traps, ruined by luxury and heedless expense, by want of calculation and a worthy aim, as the million households in the land; and the only cure for it as for them is in a rigid economy, a stern and more than Spartan simplicity of life and elevation of purpose. It lives too fast. Men think that it is essential that the *Nation* have commerce, and export ice, and talk through a telegraph, and ride thirty miles an hour, without a doubt, whether *they* do or not; but whether we should live like baboons or like men, is a little uncertain. If we do not get out sleepers, and forge rails, and devote days and nights to the work, but go to tinkering upon our *lives* to improve *them*, who will build railroads? And if railroads are not built, how shall we get to heaven in season? But if we stay at home and mind our business, who will want railroads? We do not ride on the railroad; it rides upon us. Did you ever think what those sleepers are that underlie the railroad? Each one is a man, an Irishman, or a Yankee man. The rails are laid on them, and they are covered with sand, and the cars run smoothly over them. They are sound sleepers, I assure you. And every few years a new lot is laid down and run over; so that, if some have the pleasure of riding on a rail, others have the misfortune to be ridden upon. And when they run over a man that is walking in his sleep, a supernumerary sleeper in the wrong position, and wake him up, they suddenly stop the cars, and make a hue and cry about it, as if this were an exception. I am glad to know that it takes a gang of men for every five miles to keep the sleepers down and level in their beds as it is, for this is a sign that they may sometime get up again.

Why should we live with such hurry and waste of life? We are determined to be starved before we are hungry. Men say that a stitch in time saves nine, and so they take a thousand stitches today to save nine to-morrow. As for *work*, we haven't any of any consequence. We have the Saint Vitus' dance, and cannot possibly keep our heads still. If I should only give a few pulls at the parish bell-rope, as for a fire, that is, without setting the bell, there is hardly a man on his farm in the outskirts of Concord, notwithstanding that press of engagements which was his excuse so many times this morning, nor a boy, nor a woman, I might almost say, but would forsake all and follow that sound, not mainly to save property from the flames, but, if we will confess the truth, much more to see it burn, since burn it must, and we, be it known, did not set it on fire, — or to see it put out, and have a hand in it, if that is done as handsomely; yes, even if it were the parish church itself. Hardly a man takes a half hour's nap after dinner, but when he wakes he holds up his head and asks, "What's the news?" as if the rest of mankind had stood his sentinels. Some give directions to be waked every half hour, doubtless for no other purpose; and then, to pay for it, they tell what they have dreamed. After a night's sleep the news is as indispensable as the break-fast. "Pray tell me any thing new that has happened to a man any where on this globe," — and he reads it over his coffee and rolls, that a man has had his eyes gouged out this morning on the Wachito River; never dreaming the while that he lives in the dark unfathomed mammoth cave of this world, and has but the rudiment of an eye himself.

For my part, I could easily do without the post-office. I think that there are very few important communications made through it. To speak critically, I never received more than one or two letters in my life — I wrote this some years ago — that were worth the postage. The penny-post is, commonly, an institution through which you seriously offer a man that penny for his thoughts which is so often safely offered in jest. And I am sure that I never read any memorable news in a newspaper. If we read of one man robbed, or murdered, or killed by accident, or one house burned, or one vessel wrecked, or one steamboat blown up, or one cow run over on the Western Railroad, or one mad dog killed, or one lot of grasshoppers in the winter, — we never need read of another. One is enough. If you are acquainted with the principle, what do you care for a myriad instances and applications? To a philosopher all *news*, as it is called, is gossip, and they who edit and read it are old women over their tea. Yet not a few are greedy after this gossip. There was such a rush, as I hear, the other day at one of the offices to learn the foreign news by the last arrival, that several large squares of plate glass belonging to the establishment were broken by the pressure, — news which I seriously think a ready wit might write a twelvemonth or twelve years before-hand with sufficient accuracy. As for Spain, for instance, if you know how to throw in Don Carlos and the Infanta, and Don Pedro and Seville and Granada, from time to time in the right proportions, — they may have changed the names a little since I saw the papers, — and serve up a bull-fight when other entertain-ments fail, it will be true to the letter, and give us as good an idea of the exact state or ruin of things in Spain as the most succinct and lucid reports under this head in the newspapers: and as for England, almost the last significant scrap of news from that quarter was the revolution of 1649; and if you have learned the history of her crops for an average year, you never need attend to that thing again, unless your speculations are of a merely pecuniary character. If one may judge who rarely looks into the newspapers, nothing new does ever happen in foreign parts, a French revolution not excepted.

What news! how much more important to know what that is which was never old! "Kieou-he-yu (great dignitary of the state of Wei) sent a man to Khoung-tseu to know his news. Khoung-tseu caused the messenger to be seated near him, and questioned him in these terms: What is your master doing? The messenger answered with respect: My master desires to diminish the number of his faults, but he cannot accomplish it. The messenger being gone, the philosopher remarked: What a worthy messenger! What a worthy messenger!" The preacher, instead of vexing the ears of drowsy farmers on their day of rest at the end of the week, — for Sunday is the fit conclusion of an ill-spent week, and not the fresh and brave beginning of a new one, — with this one other draggletail of a sermon, should shout with thundering voice, — "Pause! Avast! Why so seeming fast, but deadly slow?"

Shams and delusions are esteemed for soundest truths, while reality is fabulous. If men would steadily observe realities only, and not allow themselves to be deluded, life, to compare it with such things as we know, would be like a fairy tale and the Arabian Nights' Entertainments. If we respected only what is inevitable and has a right to be, music and poetry would resound along the streets. When we are unhurried and wise, we perceive that only great and worthy things have any permanent and absolute existence, — that petty fears and petty pleasures are but the shadow of the reality. This is always exhilarating and sublime. By closing the eyes and slumbering, and consenting to be deceived by shows, men establish and confirm their daily life of routine and habit every where, which still is built on purely illusory foundations. Children, who play life, discern its true law and relations more clearly than men, who fail to live it worthily, but who think that they are wiser by experience, that is, by failure. I have read in a Hindoo book, that "there was a king's son, who, being expelled in infancy from his native city, was brought up by a forester, and, growing up to maturity in that state, imagined himself to belong to the barbarous race with which he lived. One of his father's ministers having discovered him, revealed to him what he was, and the misconception of his character was removed, and he knew himself to be a prince. So soul," continues the Hindoo philosopher, "from the circumstances in which it is placed, mistakes its own character, until the truth is revealed to it by some holy teacher, and then it knows itself to be *Brahme*." I perceive that we inhabitants of New England live this mean life that we do because our vision does not penetrate the surface of things. We think that that *is* which *appears* to be. If a man should walk through this town and see only the reality, where, think you, would the "Milldam" go to? If he should give us an account of the realities he beheld there, we should not recognize the place in his description. Look at a meeting-house, or a court-house, or a jail, or a shop, or a dwelling-house, and say what that thing really is before a true gaze, and they would all go to pieces in your account of them. Men esteem truth remote, in the outskirts of the system, behind the farthest star, before Adam and after the last man. In eternity there is indeed something true and sublime. But all these times and places and occasions are now and here. God himself culminates in the present moment, and will never be more divine in the lapse of all the ages. And we are enabled to apprehend at all what is sublime and noble only by the perpetual instilling and drenching of the reality that surrounds us. The universe constantly and obediently answers to our conceptions; whether we travel fast or slow, the track is laid for us. Let us spend our lives in conceiving then. The poet or the artist never yet had so fair and noble a design but some of his posterity at least could accomplish it.

Let us spend one day as deliberately as Nature, and not be thrown off the track by every nutshell and mosquito's wing that falls on the rails. Let us rise early and fast, or break fast, gently and without perturbation; let company come and let company go, let the bells ring and the children cry, — determined to make a day of it. Why should we knock under and go with the stream? Let us not be upset and overwhelmed in that terrible rapid and whirlpool called a dinner, situated in the meridian shallows. Weather this danger and you are safe, for the rest of the way is down hill. With unrelaxed nerves, with morning vigor, sail by it, looking another way, tied to the mast like Ulysses. If the engine whistles, let it whistle till it is hoarse for its pains. If the bell rings, why should we run? We will consider what kind of music they are like. Let us settle ourselves, and work and wedge our feet downward through the mud and slush of opinion, and prejudice, and tradition, and delusion, and appearance, that alluvion which covers the globe, through Paris and London, through New York and Boston and Concord, through church and state, through poetry and philosophy and religion, till we come to a hard bottom and rocks in place, which we can call *reality*, and say, This is, and no mistake; and then begin, having a *point d'appui*, below freshet and frost and fire, a place where you might found a wall or a state, or set a lamppost safely, or perhaps a gauge, not a Nilometer, but a Realometer, that future ages might know how deep a freshet of shams and appearances had gathered from time to time. If you stand right fronting and face to face to a fact, you will see the sun glimmer on both its surfaces, as if it were a cimeter, and feel its sweet edge dividing you through the heart and marrow, and so you will happily conclude your mortal career. Be it life or death, we crave only reality. If we are really dying, let us hear the rattle in our throats and feel cold in the extremities; if we are alive, let us go about our business.

Time is but the stream I go a-fishing in. I drink at it; but while I drink I see the sandy bottom and detect how shallow it is. Its thin current slides away, but eternity remains. I would drink deeper; fish in the sky, whose bottom is pebbly with stars. I cannot count one. I know not the first letter of the alphabet. I have always been regretting that I was not as wise as the day I was born. The intellect is a cleaver; it discerns and rifts its way into the secret of things. I do not wish to be any more busy with my hands than is necessary. My head is hands and feet. I feel all my best faculties concentrated in it. My instinct tells me that my head is an organ for burrowing, as some creatures use their snout and fore-paws, and with it I would mine and burrow my way through these hills. I think that the richest vein is somewhere hereabouts; so by the divining rod and thin rising vapors I judge; and here I will begin to mine.

Once More
to the Lake

E. B. WHITE

For biographical information on E. B. White, see page 148.
"Once More to the Lake" is White's account of his return to a
lake his family had vacationed at when he was a youth. By juxtaposing his experiences with those of his young son, White creates a poignant and memorable picture of the struggle of the
human imagination to transcend time.

One summer, along about 1904, my father rented a camp on a lake in Maine and
took us all there for the month of August. We all got ringworm from some kittens
and had to rub Pond's Extract on our arms and legs night and morning, and my
father rolled over in a canoe with all his clothes on; but outside of that the vacation was a success and from then on none of us ever thought there was any place
in the world like that lake in Maine. We returned summer after summer —
always on August 1st for one month. I have since become a salt-water man, but
sometimes in summer there are days when the restlessness of the tides and the
fearful cold of the sea water and the incessant wind which blows across the afternoon and into the evening make me wish for the placidity of a lake in the woods.
A few weeks ago this feeling got so strong I bought myself a couple of bass hooks
and a spinner and returned to the lake where we used to go, for a week's fishing
and to revisit old haunts.

I took along my son, who had never had any fresh water up his nose and
who had seen lily pads only from train windows. On the journey over to the lake

I began to wonder what it would be like. I wondered how time would have marred this unique, this holy spot — the coves and streams, the hills that the sun set behind, the camps and the paths behind the camps. I was sure that the tarred road would have found it out and I wondered in what other ways it would be desolated. It is strange how much you can remember about places like that once you allow your mind to return into the grooves which lead back. You remembered one thing, and that suddenly reminds you of another thing. I guess I remember clearest of all the early mornings, when the lake was cool and motionless, remembered how the bedroom smelled of the lumber it was made of and of the wet woods whose scent entered through the screen. The partitions in the camp were thin and did not extend clear to the top of the rooms, and as I was always the first up I would dress softly so as not to wake the others, and sneak out into the sweet outdoors and start out in the canoe, keeping close along the shore in the long shadows of the pines. I remembered being very careful never to rub my paddle against the gunwale for fear of disturbing the stillness of the cathedral.

The lake had never been what you would call a wild lake. There were cottages sprinkled around the shores, and it was in farming country although the shores of the lake were quite heavily wooded. Some of the cottages were owned by nearby farmers, and you would live at the shore and eat your meals at the farmhouse. That's what our family did. But although it wasn't wild, it was a fairly large and undisturbed lake and there were places in it which, to a child at least, seemed infinitely remote and primeval.

I was right about the tar: it led to within half a mile of the shore. But when I got back there, with my boy, and we settled into a camp near a farmhouse and into the kind of summertime I had known, I could tell that it was going to be pretty much the same as it had been before — I knew it, lying in bed the first morning, smelling the bedroom, and hearing the boy sneak quietly out and go off along the shore in a boat. I began to sustain the illusion that he was I, and therefore, by simple transposition, that I was my father. This sensation persisted, kept cropping up all the time we were there. It was not an entirely new feeling, but in this setting it grew much stronger. I seemed to be living a dual existence. I would be in the middle of some simple act, I would be picking up a bait box or laying down a table fork, or I would be saying something, and suddenly it would be not I but my father who was saying the words or making the gesture. It gave me a creepy sensation.

We went fishing the first morning. I felt the same damp moss covering the worms in the bait can, and saw the dragonfly alight on the tip of my rod as it hovered a few inches from the surface of the water. It was the arrival of this fly that convinced me beyond any doubt that everything was as it always had been, that the years were a mirage and there had been no years. The small waves were the same, chucking the rowboat under the chin as we fished at anchor, and the boat was the same boat, the same color green and the ribs broken in the same places, and under the floor-boards the same fresh-water leavings and débris — the dead helgramite, the wisps of moss, the rusty discarded fishhook, the dried blood from yesterday's catch. We stared silently at the tips of our rods, at the dragonflies that came and went. I lowered the tip of mine into the water, tentatively, pensively dislodging the fly, which darted two feet away, poised, darted two feet back, and came to rest again a little farther up the rod. There had been no years between the ducking of this dragonfly and the other one — the one that was part of memory. I looked at the boy, who was silently watching his fly, and it was my hands that held his rod, my eyes watching. I felt dizzy and didn't know which rod I was at the end of.

We caught two bass, hauling them in briskly as though they were mackerel, pulling them over the side of the boat in a businesslike manner without any landing net, and stunning them with a blow on the back of the head. When we got back for a swim before lunch, the lake was exactly where we had left it, the same number of inches from the dock, and there was only the merest suggestion of a breeze. This seemed an utterly enchanted sea, this lake you could leave to its own devices for a few hours and come back to, and find that it had not stirred, this constant and trustworthy body of water. In the shallows, the dark, water-soaked sticks and twigs, smooth and old, were undulating in clusters on the bottom against the clean ribbed sand, and the track of the mussel was plain. A school of minnows swam by, each minnow with its small individual shadow, doubling the attendance, so clear and sharp in the sunlight. Some of the other campers were in swimming, along the shore, one of them with a cake of soap, and the water felt thin and clear and unsubstantial. Over the years there had been this person with the cake of soap, this cultist, and here he was. There had been no years.

Up to the farmhouse to dinner through the teeming, dusty field, the road under our sneakers was only a two-track road. The middle track was missing, the one with the marks of the hooves and the splotches of dried, flaky manure. There had always been three tracks to choose from in choosing which track to walk in; now the choice was narrowed down to two. For a moment I missed terribly the middle alternative. But the way led past the tennis court, and something about the way it lay there in the sun reassured me; the tape had loosened along the backline, the alleys were green with plantains and other weeds, and the net (installed in June and removed in September) sagged in the dry noon, and the whole place steamed with midday heat and hunger and emptiness. There was a choice of pie for dessert, and one was blueberry and one was apple, and the waitresses were the same country girls, there having been no passage of time, only the illusion of it as in a dropped curtain — the waitresses were still fifteen; their hair had been washed, that was the only difference — they had been to the movies and seen the pretty girls with the clean hair.

Summertime, oh summertime, pattern of life indelible, the fadeproof lake, the woods unshatterable, the pasture with the sweetfern and the juniper forever and ever, summer without end; this was the background, and the life along the shore was the design, the cottagers with their innocent and tranquil design, their tiny docks with the flagpole and the American flag floating against the white clouds in the blue sky, the little paths over the roots of the trees leading from camp to camp and the paths leading back to the outhouses and the can of lime for sprinkling, and at the souvenir counters at the store the miniature birch-bark canoes and the post cards that showed things looking a little better than they looked. This was the American family at play, escaping the city heat, wondering whether the newcomers in the camp at the head of the cove were "common" or "nice," wondering whether it was true that the people who drove up for Sunday dinner at the farmhouse were turned away because there wasn't enough chicken.

It seemed to me, as I kept remembering all this, that those times and those summers had been infinitely precious and worth saving. There had been jollity and peace and goodness. The arriving (at the beginning of August) had been so big a business in itself, at the railway station the farm wagon drawn up, the first smell of the pine-laden air, the first glimpse of the smiling farmer, and the great importance of the trunks and your father's enormous authority in such matters, and the feel of the wagon under you for the long ten-mile haul, and at the top of the last long hill catching the first view of the lake after eleven months of not seeing this cherished body of water. The shouts and cries of the other campers when they saw you, and the trunks to be unpacked, to give up their rich burden. (Arriving was less exciting nowadays, when you sneaked up in your car and parked it under a tree near the camp and took out the bags and in five minutes it was all over, no fuss, no loud wonderful fuss about trunks.)

Peace and goodness and jollity. The only thing that was wrong now, really, was the sound of the place, an unfamiliar nervous sound of the outboard motors. This was the note that jarred, the one thing that would sometimes break the illusion and set the years moving. In those other summertimes all motors were inboard; and when they were at a little distance, the noise they made was a sedative, an ingredient of summer sleep. They were one-cylinder and two-cylinder engines, and some were make-and-break and some were jump-spark, but they all made a sleepy sound across the lake. The one-lungers throbbed and fluttered, and the twin-cylinder ones purred and purred, and that was a quiet sound too. But now the campers all had outboards. In the daytime, in the hot mornings, these motors made a petulant, irritable sound; at night, in the still evening when the afterglow lit the water, they whined about one's ears like mosquitoes. My boy loved our rented outboard, and his great desire was to achieve singlehanded mastery over it, and authority, and he soon learned the trick of choking it a little (but not too much), and the adjustment of the needle valve. Watching him I would remember the things you could do with the old one-cylinder engine with the heavy flywheel, how you could have it eating out of your hand if you got really close to it spiritually. Motor boats in those days didn't have clutches, and you would make a landing by shutting off the motor at the proper time and coasting in with a dead rudder. But there was a way of reversing them, if you learned the trick, by cutting the·switch and putting it on again exactly on the final dying revolution of the flywheel, so that it would kick back against compression and begin reversing. Approaching a dock in a strong following breeze, it was difficult to slow up sufficiently by the ordinary coasting method, and if a boy felt he had complete mastery over his motor, he was tempted to keep it running beyond its time and then reverse it a few feet from the dock. It took a cool nerve, because if you threw the switch a twentieth of a second too soon you would catch the fly-wheel when it still had speed enough to go up past center, and the boat would leap ahead, charging bull-fashion at the dock.

We had a good week at the camp. The bass were biting well and the sun shone endlessly, day after day. We would be tired at night and lie down in the accumulated heat of the little bedrooms after the long hot day and the breeze would stir almost imperceptibly outside and the smell of the swamp drift in through the rusty screens. Sleep would come easily and in the morning the red squirrel would be on the roof, tapping out his gay routine. I kept remembering everything, lying in bed in the mornings — the small steamboat that had a long rounded stern like the lip of a Ubangi, and how quietly she ran on the moonlight sails, when the older boys played their mandolins and the girls sang and we ate doughnuts dipped in sugar, and how sweet the music was on the water in the shining night, and what it had felt like to think about girls then. After breakfast we would go up to the store and the things were in the same place — the minnows in a bottle, the plugs and spinners disarranged and pawed over by the youngsters from the boys' camp, the fig newtons and the Beeman's gum. Outside, the road was tarred and cars stood in front of the store. Inside, all was just as it had always been, except there was more Coca Cola and not so much Moxie and root beer and birch beer and sarsaparilla. We would walk out with a bottle of pop apiece and sometimes the pop would backfire up our noses and hurt. We explored the streams, quietly, where the turtles slid off the sunny logs and dug their way into the soft bottom; and we lay on the town wharf and fed worms to the tame bass. Everywhere we went I had trouble making out which was I, the one walking at my side, the one walking in my pants.

One afternoon while we were there at that lake a thunderstorm came up. It was like the revival of an old melodrama that I had seen long ago with childish awe. The second-act climax of the drama of the electrical disturbance over a lake in America had not changed in any important respect. This was the big scene, still the big scene. The whole thing was so familiar, the first feeling of oppression and heat and a general air around camp of not wanting to go very far away. In midafternoon (it was all the same) a curious darkening of the sky, and a lull in everything that had made life tick; and then the way the boats suddenly swung the other way at their moorings with the coming of a breeze out of the new quarter, and the premonitory rumble. Then the kettle drum, then the snare, then the bass drum and cymbals, then crackling light against the dark, and the gods grinning and licking their chops in the hills. Afterward the calm, the rain steadily rustling in the calm lake, the return of light and hope and spirits, and the campers running out in joy and relief to go swimming in the rain, their bright cries perpetuating the deathless joke about how they were getting simply drenched, and the children screaming with delight at the new sensation of bathing in the rain, and the joke about getting drenched linking the generations in a strong indestructible chain. And the comedian who waded in carrying an umbrella.

When the others went swimming my son said he was going in too. He pulled his dripping trunks from the line where they had hung all through the shower, and wrung them out. Languidly, and with no thought of going in, I watched him, his hard little body, skinny and bare, saw him wince slightly as he pulled up around his vitals the small, soggy, icy garment. As he buckled the swollen belt suddenly my groin felt the chill of death.

Notes
of a Native Son

JAMES BALDWIN

James Baldwin was born in New York City's Harlem in 1924, the oldest of nine children and the son of a minister. Himself briefly a preacher as a teenager, he soon turned to writing as his profession. Now one of America's most distinguished writers, Baldwin is the author of several novels, including *Go Tell It on the Mountain* (1952), *Giovanni's Room* (1956), *Another Country* (1961), and *If Beale Street Could Talk* (1974). His probing, eloquent examinations of the racial situation in America are contained in three collections of essays: *Notes of a Native Son* (1955), *Nobody Knows My Name* (1961), and *The Fire Next Time* (1963). In the title essay from *Notes of a Native Son*, which is reprinted here, Baldwin uses his father's death as the occasion for a moving reflection on the debilitating power of race hatred.

On the 29th of July, in 1943, my father died. On the same day, a few hours later, his last child was born. Over a month before this, while all our energies were concentrated in waiting for these events, there had been, in Detroit, one of the bloodiest race riots of the century. A few hours after my father's funeral, while he lay in state in the undertaker's chapel, a race riot broke out in Harlem. On the morning of the 3rd of August, we drove my father to the graveyard through a wilderness of smashed plate glass.

NOTES OF A NATIVE SON   From *Notes of a Native Son* by James Baldwin. Copyright © 1955 by James Baldwin. Reprinted by permission of Beacon Press.

The day of my father's funeral had also been my nineteenth birthday. As we drove him to the graveyard, the spoils of injustice, anarchy, discontent, and hatred were all around us. It seemed to me that God himself had devised, to mark my father's end, the most sustained and brutally dissonant of codas. And it seemed to me, too, that the violence which rose all about us as my father left the world had been devised as a corrective for the pride of his eldest son. I had declined to believe in that apocalypse which had been central to my father's vision; very well, life seemed to be saying, here is something that will certainly pass for an apocalypse until the real thing comes along. I had inclined to be contemptuous of my father for the conditions of his life, for the conditions of our lives. When his life had ended I began to wonder about that life and also, in a new way, to be apprehensive about my own.

I had not known my father very well. We had got on badly, partly because we shared, in our different fashions, the vice of stubborn pride. When he was dead I realized that I had hardly ever spoken to him. When he had been dead a long time I began to wish I had. It seems to be typical of life in America, where opportunities, real and fancied, are thicker than anywhere else on the globe, that the second generation has no time to talk to the first. No one, including my father, seems to have known exactly how old he was, but his mother had been born during slavery. He was of the first generation of free men. He, along with thousands of other Negroes, came North after 1919 and I was part of that generation which had never seen the landscape of what Negroes sometimes call the Old Country.

He had been born in New Orleans and had been a quite young man there during the time that Louis Armstrong, a boy, was running errands for the dives and honky-tonks of what was always presented to me as one of the most wicked of cities — to this day, whenever I think of New Orleans, I also helplessly think of Sodom and Gomorrah. My father never mentioned Louis Armstrong, except to forbid us to play his records; but there was a picture of him on our wall for a long time. One of my father's strong-willed female relatives had placed it there and forbade my father to take it down. He never did, but he eventually maneuvered her out of the house and when, some years later, she was in trouble and near death, he refused to do anything to help her.

He was, I think, very handsome. I gather this from photographs and from my own memories of him, dressed in his Sunday best and on his way to preach a sermon somewhere, when I was little. Handsome, proud and ingrown, "like a toe-nail," somebody said. But he looked to me, as I grew older, like pictures I had seen of African tribal chieftains: he really should have been naked, with warpaint on and barbaric mementos, standing among spears. He could be chilling in the pulpit and indescribably cruel in his personal life and he was certainly the most bitter man I have ever met; yet it must be said that there was something else in him, buried in him, which lent him his tremendous power and, even, a rather crushing charm. It had something to do with his blackness, I think — he was very black — with his blackness and his beauty, and with the fact that he knew that he was black but did not know that he was beautiful. He claimed to be proud of his blackness but it had also been the cause of much humiliation and it had fixed bleak boundaries to his life. He was not a young man when we were growing up and he had already suffered many kinds of ruin; in his outrageously demanding and protective way he loved his children, who were black like him and menaced, like him; and all these things sometimes showed in his face when he tried, never to my knowledge with any success, to establish contact with any of us. When he took one of his children on his knee to play, the child always became fretful and began to cry; when he tried to help one of us with our home-work the absolutely unabating tension which emanated from him caused our minds and our tongues to become paralyzed, so that he, scarcely knowing why, flew into a rage and the child, not knowing why, was punished. If it ever entered his head to bring a surprise home for his children, it was, almost unfailingly, the wrong surprise and even the big watermelons he often brought home on his back in the summertime led to the most appalling scenes. I do not remember, in all those years, that one of his children was ever glad to see him come home. From what I was able to gather of his early life, it seemed that this inability to establish contact with other people had always marked him and had been one of the things which had driven him out of New Orleans. There was something in him, there-fore, groping and tentative, which was never expressed and which was buried with him. One saw it most clearly when he was facing new people and hoping to impress them. But he never did, not for long. We went from church to smaller and more improbable church, he found himself in less and less demand as a min-ister, and by the time he died none of his friends had come to see him for a long time. He had lived and died in an intolerable bitterness of spirit and it frightened me, as we drove him to the graveyard through those unquiet, ruined streets, to see how powerful and overflowing this bitterness could be and to realize that this bitterness now was mine.

When he died I had been away from home for a little over a year. In that year I had had time to become aware of the meaning of all my father's bitter warnings, had discovered the secret of his proudly pursed lips and rigid carriage: I had discovered the weight of white people in the world. I saw that this had been for my ancestors and now would be for me an awful thing to live with and that the bitterness which had helped to kill my father could also kill me.

He had been ill a long time—in the mind, as we now realized, reliving instances of his fantastic intransigence in the new light of his affliction and endeavoring to feel a sorrow for him which never, quite, came true. We had not known that he was being eaten up by paranoia, and the discovery that his cruelty, to our bodies and our minds, had been one of the symptoms of his illness was not, then, enough to enable us to forgive him. The younger children felt, quite simply, relief that he would not be coming home anymore. My mother's obser-vation that it was he, after all, who had kept them alive all these years meant nothing because the problems of keeping children alive are not real for children. The older children felt, with my father gone, that they could invite their friends to the house without fear that their friends would be insulted or, as had some-times happened with me, being told that their friends were in league with the devil and intended to rob our family of everything we owned. (I didn't fail to wonder, and it made me hate him, what on earth we owned that anybody else would want.)

His illness was beyond all hope of healing before anyone realized that he was ill. He had always been so strange and had lived, like a prophet, in such unimaginably close communion with the Lord that his long silences which were punctuated by moans and hallelujahs and snatches of old songs while he sat at the living-room window never seemed odd to us. It was not until he refused to eat because, he said, his family was trying to poison him that my mother was forced to accept as a fact what had, until then, been only an unwilling suspicion. When he was committed, it was discovered that he had tuberculosis and, as it turned out, the disease of his mind allowed the disease of his body to destroy him. For the doctors could not force him to eat, either, and, though he was fed intravenously, it was clear from the beginning that there was no hope for him.

In my mind's eye I could see him, sitting at the window, locked up in his terrors; hating and fearing every living soul including his children who had betrayed him, too, by reaching towards the world which had despised him. There were nine of us. I began to wonder what it could have felt like for such a man to have had nine children whom he could barely feed. He used to make little jokes about our poverty which never, of course, seemed very funny to us; they could not have seemed very funny to him, either, or else our all too feeble response to them would never have caused such rages. He spent great energy and achieved, to our chagrin, no small amount of success in keeping us away from the people who surrounded us, people who had all-night rent parties to which we listened when we should have been sleeping, people who cursed and drank and flashed razor blades on Lenox Avenue. He could not understand why, if they had so much energy to spare, they could not use it to make their lives better. He treated almost everybody on our block with a most uncharitable asperity and neither they, nor, of course, their children were slow to reciprocate.

The only white people who came to our house were welfare workers and bill collectors. It was almost always my mother who dealt with them, for my father's temper, which was at the mercy of his pride, was never to be trusted. It was clear that he felt their very presence in his home to be a violation: this was conveyed by his carriage, almost ludicrously stiff, and by his voice, harsh and vindictively polite. When I was around nine or ten I wrote a play which was directed by a young, white schoolteacher, a woman, who then took an interest in me, and gave me books to read and, in order to corroborate my theatrical bent, decided to take me to see what she somewhat tactlessly referred to as "real" plays. Theatergoing was forbidden in our house, but, with the really cruel intuitiveness of a child, I suspected that the color of this woman's skin would carry the day for me. When, at school, she suggested taking me to the theater, I did not, as I might have done if she had been a Negro, find a way of discouraging her, but agreed that she should pick me up at my house one evening. I then, very cleverly, left all the rest to my mother, who suggested to my father, as I knew she would, that it would not be very nice to let such a kind woman make the trip for nothing.

Also, since it was a schoolteacher, I imagine that my mother countered the idea of sin with the idea of "education," which word, even with my father, carried a kind of bitter weight.

Before the teacher came my father took me aside to ask *why* she was coming, what *interest* she could possibly have in our house, in a boy like me. I said I didn't know but I, too, suggested that it had something to do with education. And I understood that my father was waiting for me to say something — I didn't quite know what; perhaps that I wanted his protection against this teacher and her "education." I said none of these things and the teacher came and we went out. It was clear, during the brief interview in our living room, that my father was agreeing very much against his will and that he would have refused permission if he had dared. The fact that he did not dare caused me to despise him: I had no way of knowing that he was facing in that living room a wholly unprecedented and frightening situation.

Later, when my father had been laid off from his job, this woman became very important to us. She was really a very sweet and generous woman and went to a great deal of trouble to be of help to us, particularly during one awful winter. My mother called her by the highest name she knew: she said she was a "christian." My father could scarcely disagree but during the four or five years of our relatively close association he never trusted her and was always trying to surprise in her open, Midwestern face the genuine, cunningly hidden, and hideous motivation. In later years, particularly when it began to be clear that this "education" of mine was going to lead me to perdition, he became more explicit and warned me that my white friends in high school were not really my friends and that I would see, when I was older, how white people would do anything to keep a Negro down. Some of them could be nice, he admitted, but none of them were to be trusted and most of them were not even nice. The best thing was to have as little to do with them as possible. I did not feel this way and I was certain, in my innocence, that I never would.

But the year which preceded my father's death had made a great change in my life. I had been living in New Jersey, working in defense plants, working and living among southerners, white and black. I knew about the south, of course, and about how southerners treated Negroes and how they expected them to behave, but it had never entered my mind that anyone would look at me and expect *me* to behave that way. I learned in New Jersey that to be a Negro meant, precisely, that one was never looked at but was simply at the mercy of the reflexes the color of one's skin caused in other people. I acted in New Jersey as I had always acted, that is as though I thought a great deal of myself — I had to *act* that way — with results that were, simply, unbelievable. I had scarcely arrived before I had earned the enmity, which was extraordinarily ingenious, of all my superiors and nearly all my co-workers. In the beginning, to make matters worse, I simply did not know what was happening. I did not know what I had done, and I shortly began to wonder what *anyone* could possibly do, to bring about such unanimous, active, and unbearably vocal hostility. I knew about jim-crow but I had never experienced it. I went to the same self-service restaurant three times and stood with all the Princeton boys before the counter, waiting for a hamburger and coffee; it was always an extraordinarily long time before anything was set before me; but it was not until the fourth visit that I learned that, in fact, nothing had ever been set before me: I had simply picked something up. Negroes were not served there, I was told, and they had been waiting for me to realize that I was always the only Negro present. Once I was told this, I determined to go there all the time. But now they were ready for me and, though some dreadful scenes were subsequently enacted in that restaurant, I never ate there again.

It was the same story all over New Jersey, in bars, bowling alleys, diners, places to live. I was always being forced to leave, silently, or with mutual imprecations. I very shortly became notorious and children giggled behind me when I passed and their elders whispered or shouted—they really believed that I was mad. And it did begin to work on my mind, of course; I began to be afraid to go anywhere and to compensate for this I went places to which I really should not have gone and where, God knows, I had no desire to be. My reputation in town naturally enhanced my reputation at work and my working day became one long series of acrobatics designed to keep me out of trouble. I cannot say that these acrobatics succeeded. It began to seem that the machinery of the organization I worked for was turning over, day and night, with but one aim: to eject me. I was fired once, and contrived, with the aid of a friend from New York, to get back on the payroll; was fired again, and bounced back again. It took a while to fire me for the third time, but the third time took. There were no loopholes anywhere. There was not even any way of getting back inside the gates.

That year in New Jersey lives in my mind as though it were the year during which, having an unsuspected predilection for it, I first contracted some dread, chronic disease, the unfailing symptom of which is a kind of blind fever, a pounding in the skull and fire in the bowels. Once this disease is contracted, one can never be really carefree again, for the fever, without an instant's warning, can recur at any moment. It can wreck more important things than race relations. There is not a Negro alive who does not have this rage in his blood—one has the choice, merely, of living with it consciously or surrendering to it. As for me, this fever has recurred in me, and does, and will until the day I die.

My last night in New Jersey, a white friend from New York took me to the nearest big town, Trenton, to go to the movies and have a few drinks. As it turned out, he also saved me from, at the very least, a violent whipping. Almost every detail of that night stands out very clearly in my memory. I even remember the name of the movie we saw because its title impressed me as being so patly ironical. It was a movie about the German occupation of France, starring Maureen O'Hara and Charles Laughton and called *This Land Is Mine*. I remember the name of the diner we walked into when the movie ended: it was the "American Diner." When we walked in the counterman asked what we wanted and I remember answering with the casual sharpness which had become my habit: "We want a hamburger and a cup of coffee, what do you think we want?" I do not know why, after a year of such rebuffs, I so completely failed to anticipate his answer, which was, of course, "We don't serve Negroes here." This reply failed to discompose me, at least for the moment. I made some sardonic comment about the name of the diner and we walked out into the streets.

This was the time of what was called the "brown-out," when the lights in all American cities were very dim. When we re-entered the streets something happened to me which had the force of an optical illusion, or a nightmare. The streets were very crowded and I was facing north. People were moving in every direction but it seemed to me, in that instant, that all of the people I could see, and many more than that, were moving toward me, against me, and that everyone was white. I remember how their faces gleamed. And I felt, like a physical sensation, a *click* at the nape of my neck as though some interior string connecting my head to my body had been cut. I began to walk. I heard my friend call after me, but I ignored him. Heaven only knows what was going on in his mind, but he had the good sense not to touch me—I don't know what would have happened if he had—and to keep me in sight. I don't know what was going on in my mind, either; I certainly had no conscious plan. I wanted to do something to crush these white faces, which were crushing me. I walked for perhaps a block or two until I came to an enormous, glittering, and fashionable restaurant in which I knew not even the intercession of the Virgin would cause me to be served. I pushed through the doors and took the first vacant seat I saw, at a table for two, and waited.

I do not know how long I waited and I rather wonder, until today, what I could possibly have looked like. Whatever I looked like, I frightened the waitress who shortly appeared, and the moment she appeared all of my fury flowed towards her. I hated her for her white face and for her great, astounded, frightened eyes. I felt that if she found a black man so frightening I would make her fright worth-while.

She did not ask me what I wanted, but repeated, as though she had learned it somewhere, "We don't serve Negroes here." She did not say it with the blunt, derisive hostility to which I had grown so accustomed, but, rather with a note of apology in her voice, and fear. This made me colder and more murderous than ever. I felt I had to do something with my hands. I wanted her to come close enough for me to get her neck between my hands.

So I pretended not to have understood her, hoping to draw her closer. And she did step a very short step closer, with her pencil poised incongruously over her pad, and repeated the formula: " . . . don't serve Negroes here."

Somehow, with the repetition of that phrase, which was already ringing in my head like a thousand bells of a nightmare, I realized that she would never come any closer and that I would have to strike from a distance. There was nothing on the table but an ordinary water-mug full of water, and I picked this up and hurled it with all my strength at her. She ducked and it missed her and shattered against the mirror behind the bar. And, with that sound, my frozen blood abruptly thawed, I returned from wherever I had been, I *saw* for the first time, the restaurant, the people with their mouths open, already, as it seemed to me, rising as one man, and I realized what I had done, and where I was, and I was frightened. I rose and began running for the door. A round, potbellied man grabbed me by the nape of the neck just as I reached the doors and began to beat me about the face. I kicked him and got loose and ran into the streets. My friend whispered, *"Run!"* and I ran.

My friend stayed outside the restaurant long enough to misdirect my pursuers and the police, who arrived, he told me, at once. I do not know what I said to him when he came to my room that night. I could not have said much. I felt, in the oddest, most awful way, that I had somehow betrayed him. I lived it over and over and over again, the way one relives an automobile accident after it has happened and one finds oneself alone and safe. I could not get over two facts, both equally difficult for the imagination to grasp, and one was that I could have been murdered. But the other was that I had been ready to commit murder. I saw nothing very clearly but I did see this: that my life, my *real* life, was in danger, and not from anything other people might do but from the hatred I carried in my own heart.

II

I had returned home around the second week in June—in great haste because it seemed that my father's death and my mother's confinement were both but a matter of hours. In the case of my mother, it soon became clear that she had simply made a miscalculation. This had always been her tendency and I don't believe that a single one of us arrived in the world, or has since arrived anywhere else, on time. But none of us dawdled so intolerably about the business of being born as did my baby sister. We sometimes amused ourselves, during those endless, stifling weeks, by picturing the baby sitting within in the safe, warm dark, bitterly regretting the necessity of becoming a part of our chaos and stubbornly putting it off as long as possible. I understood her perfectly and congratulated her on showing such good sense so soon. Death, however, sat as purposefully at my father's bedside as life stirred within my mother's womb and it was harder to understand why he so lingered in that long shadow. It seemed that he had bent, and for a long time, too, all of his energies towards dying. Now death was ready for him but my father held back.

All of Harlem, indeed, seemed to be infected by waiting. I had never before known it to be so violently still. Racial tensions throughout this country were exacerbated during the early years of the war, partly because the labor market brought together hundreds of thousands of ill-prepared people and partly because Negro soldiers, regardless of where they were born, received their military training in the south. What happened in defense plants and army camps had repercussions, naturally, in every Negro ghetto. The situation in Harlem had grown bad enough for clergymen, policemen, educators, politicians, and social workers to assert in one breath that there was no "crime wave" and to offer, in the very next breath, suggestions as to how to combat it. These suggestions always seemed to involve playgrounds, despite the fact that racial skirmishes were occurring in the playgrounds, too. Playground or not, crime wave or not, the Harlem police force had been augmented in March, and the unrest grew—perhaps, in fact, partly as a result of the ghetto's instinctive hatred of policemen. Perhaps the most revealing news item, out of the steady parade of reports of muggings, stabbings, shootings, assaults, gang wars, and accusations of police brutality, is the item concerning six Negro girls who set upon a white girl in the subway because, as they all too accurately put it, she was stepping on their toes. Indeed she was, all over the nation.

I had never before been so aware of policemen, on foot, on horseback, on corners, everywhere, always two by two. Nor had I ever been so aware of small knots of people. They were on stoops and on corners and in doorways, and what was striking about them, I think, was that they did not seem to be talking. Never, when I passed these groups, did the usual sound of a curse or a laugh ring out and neither did there seem to be any hum of gossip. There was certainly, on the other hand, occurring between them communication extraordinarily intense. Another thing that was striking was the unexpected diversity of the people who made up these groups. Usually, for example, one would see a group of sharpies standing on the street corner, jiving the passing chicks; or a group of older men, usually, for some reason, in the vicinity of a barber shop, discussing baseball scores, or the numbers, or making rather chilling observations about women they had known. Women, in a general way, tended to be seen less often together — unless they were church women, or very young girls, or prostitutes met together for an unprofessional instant. But that summer I saw the strangest combinations: large, respectable, churchly matrons standing on the stoops or the corners with their hair tied up, together with a girl in a sleazy satin whose face bore the marks of gin and the razor, or heavy-set, abrupt, no-nonsense older men, in company with the most disreputable and fanatical "race" men, or these same "race" men with the sharpies, or these sharpies with the churchly women. Seventh Day Adventists and Methodists and Spiritualists seemed to be hobnobbing with Holyrollers and they were all, alike, entangled with the most flagrant disbelievers; something heavy in their stance seemed to indicate that they had all, incredibly, seen a common vision, and on each face there seemed to be the same strange, bitter shadow.

The churchly women and the matter-of-fact, no-nonsense men had children in the Army. The sleazy girls they talked to had lovers there, the sharpies and the "race" men had friends and brothers there. It would have demanded an unquestioning patriotism, happily as uncommon in this country as it is undesirable, for these people not to have been disturbed by the bitter letters they received, by the newspaper stories they read, not to have been enraged by the posters, then to be found all over New York, which described the Japanese as "yellow-bellied Japs." It was only the "race" men, to be sure, who spoke ceaselessly of being revenged — how this vengeance was to be exacted was not clear — for the indignities and dangers suffered by Negro boys in uniform; but everybody felt a directionless, hopeless bitterness, as well as the panic which can scarcely be suppressed when one knows that a human being one loves is beyond one's reach, and in danger. This helplessness and this gnawing uneasiness does something, at length, to even the toughest mind. Perhaps the best way to sum all this up is to say that the people I knew felt, mainly, a peculiar kind of relief when they knew that their boys were being shipped out of the south, to do battle overseas. It was, perhaps, like feeling that the most dangerous part of a dangerous journey had been passed and that now, even if death should come, it would come with honor and without the complicity of their countrymen. Such a death would be, in short, a fact with which one could hope to live.

It was on the 28th of July, which I believe was a Wednesday, that I visited my father for the first time during his illness and for the last time in his life. The moment I saw him I knew why I had put off this visit so long. I had told my mother that I did not want to see him because I hated him. But this was not true. It was only that I *had* hated him and I wanted to hold on to this hatred. I did not want to look on him as a ruin: it was not a ruin I had hated. I imagine that one of the reasons people cling to their hates so stubbornly is because they sense, once hate is gone, that they will be forced to deal with pain.

We traveled out to him, his older sister and myself, to what seemed to be the very end of a very Long Island. It was hot and dusty and we wrangled, my aunt and I, all the way out, over the fact that I had recently begun to smoke and, as she said, to give myself airs. But I knew that she wrangled with me because she could not bear to face the fact of her brother's dying. Neither could I endure the reality of her despair, her unstated bafflement as to what had happened to her brother's life, and her own. So we wrangled and I smoked and from time to time she fell into a heavy reverie. Covertly, I watched her face, which was the face of an old woman; it had fallen in, the eyes were sunken and lightless; soon she would be dying, too.

In my childhood—it had not been so long ago—I had thought her beautiful. She had been quick-witted and quick-moving and very generous with all the children and each of her visits had been an event. At one time one of my brothers and myself had thought of running away to live with her. Now she could no longer produce out of her handbag some unexpected and yet familiar delight. She made me feel pity and revulsion and fear. It was awful to realize that she no longer caused me to feel affection. The closer we came to the hospital the more querulous she became and at the same time, naturally, grew more dependent on me. Between pity and guilt and fear I began to feel that there was another me trapped in my skull like a jack-in-the-box who might escape my control at any moment and fill the air with screaming.

She began to cry the moment we entered the room and she saw him lying there, all shriveled and still, like a little black monkey. The great, gleaming apparatus which fed him and would have compelled him to be still even if he had been able to move brought to mind, not beneficence, but torture; the tubes entering his arm made me think of pictures I had seen when a child, of Gulliver, tied down by the pygmies on that island. My aunt wept and wept, there was a whistling sound in my father's throat; nothing was said; he could not speak. I wanted to take his hand, to say something. But I do not know what I could have said, even if he could have heard me. He was not really in that room with us, he had at last really embarked on his journey; and though my aunt told me that he said he was going to meet Jesus, I did not hear anything except that whistling in his throat. The doctor came back and we left, into that unbearable train again, and home. In the morning came the telegram saying that he was dead. Then the house was suddenly full of relatives, friends, hysteria, and confusion and I quickly left my mother and the children to the care of those impressive women, who, in Negro communities at least, automatically appear at times of bereavement armed with potions, proverbs, and patience, and an ability to cook. I went downtown. By the time I returned, later the same day, my mother had been carried to the hospital and the baby had been born.

III

For my father's funeral I had nothing black to wear and this posed a nagging problem all day long. It was one of those problems, simple, or impossible of solution, to which the mind insanely clings in order to avoid the mind's real trouble. I spent most of that day at the downtown apartment of a girl I knew, celebrating my birthday with whiskey and wondering what to wear that night. When planning a birthday celebration one naturally does not expect that it will be up against competition from a funeral and this girl had anticipated taking me out that night, for a big dinner and a night club afterwards. Sometime during the course of that long day we decided that we would go out anyway, when my father's funeral service was over. I imagine *I* decided it, since, as the funeral hour approached, it became clearer and clearer to me that I would not know what to do with myself when it was over. The girl, stifling her very lively concern as to the possible effects of the whiskey on one of my father's chief mourners, concentrated on being conciliatory and practically helpful. She found a black shirt for me somewhere and ironed it and, dressed in the darkest pants and jacket I owned, and slightly drunk, I made my way to my father's funeral.

The chapel was full, but not packed, and very quiet. There were, mainly, my father's relatives, and his children, and here and there I saw faces I had not seen since childhood, the faces of my father's one-time friends. They were very dark and solemn now, seeming somehow to suggest that they had known all along that something like this would happen. Chief among the mourners was my aunt, who had quarreled with my father all his life; by which I do not mean to suggest that her mourning was insincere or that she had not loved him. I suppose that she was one of the few people in the world who had, and their incessant quarreling proved precisely the strength of the tie that bound them. The only other person in the world, as far as I knew, whose relationship to my father rivaled my aunt's in depth was my mother, who was not there.

It seemed to me, of course, that it was a very long funeral. But it was, if anything, a rather shorter funeral than most, nor, since there were no overwhelming, uncontrollable expressions of grief, could it be called — if I dare to use the word — successful. The minister who preached my father's funeral sermon was one of the few my father had still been seeing as he neared his end. He presented to us in his sermon a man whom none of us had ever seen — a man thoughtful, patient, and forbearing, a Christian inspiration to all who knew him, and a model for his children. And no doubt the children, in their disturbed and guilty state, were almost ready to believe this; he had been remote enough to be

anything and, anyway, the shock of the incontrovertible, that it was really our
father lying up there in that casket, prepared the mind for anything. His sister
moaned and this grief-stricken moaning was taken as corroboration. The other
faces held a dark, non-committal thoughtfulness. This was not the man they had
known, but they had scarcely expected to be confronted with *him;* this was, in
a sense deeper than questions of fact, the man they had not known, and the man
they had not known may have been the real one. The real man, whoever he had
been, had suffered and now he was dead: this was all that was sure and all that
mattered now. Every man in the chapel hoped that when his hour came he, too,
would be eulogized, which is to say forgiven, and that all of his lapses, greeds,
errors, and strayings from the truth would be invested with coherence and looked
upon with charity. This was perhaps the last thing human beings could give each
other and it was what they demanded, after all, of the Lord. Only the Lord saw
the midnight tears, only He was present when one of His children, moaning and
wringing hands, paced up and down the room. When one slapped one's child in
anger the recoil in the heart reverberated through heaven and became part of the
pain of the universe. And when the children were hungry and sullen and dis-
trustful and one watched them, daily, growing wilder, and further away, and
running headlong into danger, it was the Lord who knew what the charged heart
endured as the strap was laid to the backside; it was the Lord alone who knew
what one *would* have said if one had had, like the Lord, the gift of the living
word. It was the Lord who knew of the impossibility every parent in that room
faced: how to prepare the child for the day when the child would be despised and
how to *create* in the child — by what means? — a stronger antidote to this poison
than one had found for oneself. The avenues, side streets, bars, billiard halls, hospitals, police stations, and even the playgrounds of Harlem — not to mention the
houses of correction, the jails, and the morgue — testified to the potency of the
poison while remaining silent as to the efficacy of whatever antidote, irresistibly
raising the question of whether or not such an antidote existed; raising, which
was worse, the question of whether or not an antidote was desirable; perhaps
poison should be fought with poison. With these several schisms in the mind and
with more terrors in the heart than could be named, it was better not to judge
the man who had gone down under an impossible burden. It was better to remember: *Thou knowest this man's fall; but thou knowest not his wrassling.*

While the preacher talked and I watched the children — years of changing
their diapers, scrubbing them, slapping them, taking them to school, and scolding
them had had the perhaps inevitable result of making me love them, though I
am not sure I knew this then — my mind was busily breaking out with a rash of
disconnected impressions. Snatches of popular songs, indecent jokes, bits of books
I had read, movie sequences, faces, voices, political issues — I thought I was going
mad; all these impressions suspended, as it were, in the solution of the faint nausea produced in me by the heat and liquor. For a moment I had the impression
that my alcoholic breath, inefficiently disguised with chewing gum, filled the
entire chapel. Then someone began singing one of my father's favorite songs and,
abruptly, I was with him, sitting on his knee, in the hot, enormous, crowded

church which was the first church we attended. It was the Abyssinia Baptist Church on 138th Street. We had not gone there long. With this image, a host of others came. I had forgotten, in the rage of my growing up, how proud my father had been of me when I was little. Apparently, I had had a voice and my father had liked to show me off before the members of the church. I had forgotten what he had looked like when he was pleased but now I remembered that he had always been grinning with pleasure when my solos ended. I even remembered certain expressions on his face when he teased my mother—had he loved her? I would never know. And when had it all begun to change? For now it seemed that he had not always been cruel. I remembered being taken for a haircut and scraping my knee on the footrest of the barber's chair and I remembered my father's face as he soothed my crying and applied the stinging iodine. Then I remembered our fights, fights which had been of the worst possible kind because my technique had been silence.

I remembered the one time in all our life together when we had really spoken to each other.

It was on a Sunday and it must have been shortly before I left home. We were walking, just the two of us, in our usual silence, to or from church. I was in high school and had been doing a lot of writing and I was, at about this time, the editor of the high school magazine. But I had also been a Young Minister and had been preaching from the pulpit. Lately, I had been taking fewer engagements and preached as rarely as possible. It was said in the church, quite truthfully, that I was "cooling off."

My father asked me abruptly, "You'd rather write than preach, wouldn't you?"

I was astonished at his question—because it was a real question. I answered, "Yes."

That was all we said. It was awful to remember that that was all we had *ever* said.

The casket now was opened and the mourners were being led up the aisle to look for the last time on the deceased. The assumption was that the family was too overcome with grief to be allowed to make this journey alone and I watched while my aunt was led to the casket and, muffled in black, and shaking, led back to her seat. I disapproved of forcing the children to look on their dead father, considering that the shock of his death, or, more truthfully, the shock of death as a reality, was already a little more than a child could bear, but my judgment in this matter had been overruled and there they were, bewildered and frightened and very small, being led, one by one, to the casket. But there is also something very gallant about children at such moments. It has something to do with their silence and gravity and with the fact that one cannot help them. Their legs, somehow, seem *exposed*, so that it is at once incredible and terribly clear that their legs are all they have to hold them up.

I had not wanted to go to the casket myself and I certainly had not wished to be led there, but there was no way of avoiding either of these forms. One of the deacons led me up and I looked on my father's face. I cannot say that it looked like him at all. His blackness had been equivocated by powder and there was no suggestion in that casket of what his power had or could have been. He was simply an old man dead, and it was hard to believe that he had ever given anyone either joy or pain. Yet, his life filled that room. Further up the avenue his wife was holding his newborn child. Life and death so close together, and love and hatred, and right and wrong, said something to me which I did not want to hear concerning man, concerning the life of man.

After the funeral, while I was downtown desperately celebrating my birthday, a Negro soldier, in the lobby of the Hotel Braddock, got into a fight with a white policeman over a Negro girl. Negro girls, white policemen, in or out of uniform, and Negro males — in or out of uniform — were part of the furniture of the lobby of the Hotel Braddock and this was certainly not the first time such an incident had occurred. It was destined, however, to receive an unprecedented publicity, for the fight between the policeman and the soldier ended with the shooting of the soldier. Rumor, flowing immediately to the streets outside, stated that the soldier had been shot in the back, an instantaneous and revealing invention, and that the soldier had died protecting a Negro woman. The facts were somewhat different — for example, the soldier had not been shot in the back, and was not dead, and the girl seems to have been as dubious a symbol of womanhood as her white counterpart in Georgia usually is, but no one was interested in the facts. They preferred the invention because this invention expressed and corroborated their hates and fears so perfectly. It is just as well to remember that people are always doing this. Perhaps many of those legends, including Christianity, to which the world clings began their conquest of the world with just some such concerted surrender to distortion. The effect, in Harlem, of this particular legend was like the effect of a lit match in a tin of gasoline. The mob gathered before the doors of the Hotel Braddock simply began to swell and to spread in every direction, and Harlem exploded.

The mob did not cross the ghetto lines. It would have been easy, for example, to have gone over Morningside Park on the west side or to have crossed the Grand Central railroad tracks at 125th Street on the east side, to wreak havoc in white neighborhoods. The mob seems to have been mainly interested in something more potent and real than the white face, that is, in white power, and the principal damage done during the riot of the summer of 1943 was to white business establishments in Harlem. It might have been a far bloodier story, of course, if, at the hour the riot began, these establishments had still been open. From the Hotel Braddock the mob fanned out, east and west along 125th Street, and for the entire length of Lenox, Seventh, and Eighth avenues. Along each of these avenues, and along each major side street — 116th, 125th, 135th, and so on — bars, stores, pawnshops, restaurants, even little luncheonettes had been smashed open and entered and looted — looted, it might be added, with more haste than efficiency. The shelves really looked as though a bomb had struck them. Cans of beans and soup and dog food, along with toilet paper, corn flakes, sardines, and milk tumbled every which way, and abandoned cash registers and cases of beer leaned crazily out of the splintered windows and were strewn along the avenues.

Sheets, blankets, and clothing of every description formed a kind of path, as though people had dropped them while running. I truly had not realized that Harlem *had* so many stores until I saw them all smashed open; the first time the word *wealth* ever entered my mind in relation to Harlem was when I saw it scattered in the streets. But one's first, incongruous impression of plenty was countered immediately by an impression of waste. None of this was doing anybody any good. It would have been better to have left the plate glass as it had been and the goods lying in the stores.

It would have been better, but it would also have been intolerable, for Harlem had needed something to smash. To smash something is the ghetto's chronic need. Most of the time it is the members of the ghetto who smash each other, and themselves. But as long as the ghetto walls are standing there will always come a moment when these outlets do not work. That summer, for example, it was not enough to get into a fight on Lenox Avenue, or curse out one's cronies in the barber shops. If ever, indeed, the violence which fills Harlem's churches, pool halls, and bars erupts outward in a more direct fashion, Harlem and its citizens are likely to vanish in an apocalyptic flood. That this is not likely to happen is due to a great many reasons, most hidden and powerful among them the Negro's real relation to the white American. This relation prohibits, simply, anything as uncomplicated and satisfactory as pure hatred. In order really to hate white people, one has to blot so much out of the mind — and the heart — that this hatred itself becomes an exhausting and self-destructive pose. But this does not mean, on the other hand, that love comes easily: the white world is too powerful, too complacent, too ready with gratuitous humiliation, and, above all, too ignorant and too innocent for that. One is absolutely forced to make perpetual qualifications and one's own reactions are always canceling each other out. It is this, really, which has driven so many people mad, both white and black. One is always in the position of having to decide between amputation and gangrene. Amputation is swift but time may prove that the amputation was not necessary — or one may delay the amputation too long. Gangrene is slow, but it is impossible to be sure that one is reading one's symptoms right. The idea of going through life as a cripple is more than one can bear, and equally unbearable is the risk of swelling up slowly, in agony, with poison. And the trouble, finally, is that the risks are real even if the choices do not exist.

"But as for me and my house," my father had said, "we will serve the Lord." I wondered, as we drove him to his resting place, what this line had meant for him. I had heard him preach it many times. I had preached it once myself, proudly giving it an interpretation different from my father's. Now the whole thing came back to me, as though my father and I were on our way to Sunday school and I were memorizing the golden text: *And if it seem evil unto you to serve the Lord, choose you this day whom you will serve; whether the gods which your fathers served that were on the other side of the flood, or the gods of the Amorites, in whose land ye dwell: but as for me and my house, we will serve the Lord.* I suspected in these familiar lines a meaning which had never been there for me before. All of my father's texts and songs, which I had decided

were meaningless, were arranged before me at his death like empty bottles, waiting to hold the meaning which life would give them for me. This was his legacy:
nothing is ever escaped. That bleakly memorable morning I hated the unbelievable streets and the Negroes and whites who had, equally, made them that way.
But I knew that it was folly, as my father would have said, this bitterness was
folly. It was necessary to hold on to the things that mattered. The dead man
mattered, the new life mattered; blackness and whiteness did not matter; to
believe that they did was to acquiesce in one's own destruction. Hatred, which
could destroy so much, never failed to destroy the man who hated and this was
an immutable law.

It began to seem that one would have to hold in the mind forever two ideas
which seemed to be in opposition. The first idea was acceptance, the acceptance,
totally without rancor, of life as it is, and men as they are: in the light of this
idea, it goes without saying that injustice is a commonplace. But this did not mean
that one could be complacent, for the second idea was of equal power: that one
must never, in one's own life, accept these injustices as commonplace but must
fight them with all one's strength. This fight begins, however, in the heart and
it now had been laid to my charge to keep my own heart free of hatred and
despair. This intimation made my heart heavy and, now that my father was irre-
coverable, I wished that he had been beside me so that I could have searched his
face for the answers which only the future would give me now.